MARIA FITZHERBERT
The Secret Wife of George IV

MARIA FITZHERBERT
The Secret Wife of George IV

James Munson

CARROLL & GRAF PUBLISHERS
New York

Carroll & Graf Publishers
An imprint of Avalon Publishing Group, Inc.
161 William Street
16th Floor
New York
NY 10038-2607
www.carrollandgraf.com

First published in the UK by Constable,
an imprint of Constable Robinson Ltd 2001

First Carroll & Graf edition 2001

ISBN 0-7867-0904-9

Printed and bound in the EU

To

Richard Mullen

Pleniorem vitam concessit amicus amoenus
Caro amico vitae cessi donum lepidae

CONTENTS

———•—•——

Illustrations ix

Acknowledgements xi

Introduction 1

1 A Recusant Childhood 5

2 Twice Wed, Twice Widowed 21

3 The Most Accomplished Prince of His Age 55

4 Miladies Abroad 91

5 A Dangerous Greatness 123

6 The Buzz of the Day 153

7 Questions in the House 181

8 His Majesty's Disorder 211

9 Passions and Errors 237

10 The Late Princess Fitz 259

11 Like Brother and Sister 283

12 The Final Break 307

13 Mrs Fitzherbert Without a Title 329

Epilogue: Mrs Fitzherbert's Honour 367

Notes 373

Bibliography 391

Index 405

ILLUSTRATIONS

Between pages 114 and 115

Mrs Fitzherbert, engraved by Jean Conde, 1792 after Richard
Cosway. Private Collection/Bridgeman Art Library

Walter Smythe, Maria Fitzherbert's father

Lulworth Castle painted by Theodore de Bruyn 1781 (Courtesy of
the Lulworth Estate)

Maria Fitzherbert by Sir Joshua Reynolds (Courtesy of the Lulworth
Estate)

Swynnerton Hall, Staffordshire

No six, Tilney Street, near Park Lane

King George III

Queen Charlotte Sophia of Mecklenburg-Strelitz by Valentine
Green after Benjamin West 1776 (By courtesy of the National
Portrait Gallery, London)

George IV by John Raphael Smith after Thomas Gainsborough
1789 (By courtesy of the National Portrait Gallery, London)

Out of Fits, or The Recovery to the Satisfaction of All Parties, anonymous, published by S.W. Fores, 5 May 1786

The Padlock. To Be. Or Not To Be. A Queen! is the Question, anonymous, published by S.W. Fores, 3 April 1786

Between pages 290 and 291

Charles James Fox, an engraving by H. Robinson

Richard Brinsley Sheridan, Esq, an engraving by R. Hicks from an
original portrait by Sir Joshua Reynolds

Illustrations

Carlton House (Guildhall Library, Corporation of London)

The great staircase of Carlton House 1811 (Guildhall Library, Corporation of London)

Lady Jerningham, an engraving from an original drawing by Hopwood

Love's Last Shift, anonymous, published by S.W. Fores, 26 February 1787

The Royal Pavilion (Photograph reproduced with the kind permission of the Royal Pavilion, Libraries and Museums (Brighton and Hove) 2001)

Dido Forsaken. Sic transit gloriae Reginae, anonymous, but James Gillray (1757–1815), published by S.W. Fores, 21 May 1787

Bandelures, anonymous, but James Gillray (1757–1815), published by S.W. Fores, 28 February 1791

Mrs Fitzherbert from the painting by George Romney

The Guardian-Angel, James Gillray (1757–1815), published by H. Humphrey, 22 April 1805

Maria Fitzherbert from a painting in watercolours

ACKNOWLEDGEMENTS

———•◦•———

My first duty is to acknowledge the gracious permission of Her Majesty Queen Elizabeth II for allowing me to work in the Royal Archives, housed in Windsor's great Round Tower and to quote from material under Crown copyright. My second duty is to acknowledge the kind permission of the Earl of Crawford and Balcarres to examine the manuscripts of Lady Anne Barnard which are in his private possession. Without these, the story of Maria Fitzherbert's life would be incomplete. Lord Crawford embodies the finest traditions of the British aristocracy and without his kindness the author's work would have been far less enjoyable. Thirdly I would like to express my gratitude to two people at the Royal Pavilion, Brighton: Mr Andrew Barlow, Keeper of the Royal Pavilion and Fine Art and the ever-resourceful, Mrs Maureen Simmonds, Support Officer (Museums). She made available to me the Pavilion's collection of material relating to Maria Fitzherbert and gave me much wonderful assistance.

I am also grateful to the following: His Grace the Duke of Devonshire, for permission to examine and quote from material held in the Devonshire Collections, Chatsworth; Lord Portarlington, for his help with the Portarlington MS; Mr Nicholas Fitzherbert, for sharing his unrivalled knowledge of Fitzherbert family history; Mr Wilfrid Weld of Lulworth Castle, for answering my questions regarding Lulworth and Mr K.B. Smith, the Custodian of that same Castle which was Maria Fitzherbert's first married home; Lord and Lady Stafford, for their help and for allowing me to visit their beautiful home, Maria's second married home; and finally to Laurence

Acknowledgements

Pollinger Ltd for permission to examine the Lovelace-Byron Collection in the Bodleian Library. I would also like to put on record my indebtedness to Dr Christiane Thomas of Vienna's Haus-, Hof- und Staatsarchiv for her help. Before her untimely death she was a scholar, an Austrian patriot and a wonderful friend.

I am greatly indebted, as hitherto, to the staff of the Bodleian Library, Oxford (Duke Humfrey's Library, the less elegantly named but better lit, Room 132 and the Upper Reading Room), especially to Helen Rogers and Vera Ryhajlo. I am also indebted to the following institutions and individuals for permission to use and quote from material in their possession: the British Library; the National Library of Ireland, Mr Gerard Long and Dr Noel Kissane; the City of Leeds Archives Office; the National Library of Scotland and Mr Kenneth Dunn; the University of Nottingham Library; the Österreichisches Staatsarchiv und Kriegsarchiv and Herr Direktor Hofrat Dr Peter Broucek; the Österreichisches Haus-Hof- und Staatsarchiv and its Director, Dr Franz Dirnberger; Dr B. Woelderink of the Koninklijk Huisarchief, Amsterdam; Mrs H.F. Peeters, Department of Special Collections, Koninkliske Bibliotheek, Amsterdam; Annemarie Los of the Royal Netherlands Embassy; Mr H.G. Belsey, Curator, Gainsborough's House, Sudbury; the Whitworth Gallery, Manchester; the Richmond-upon-Thames Libraries; the Tong Archaeological Group and its Director, Mr Alan Wharton; the Huntington Library, San Marino, California; the Churchill Archives Centre at Churchill College, Cambridge; the Houghton Library, Harvard University; the Morgan Library, New York City; the John Rylands Library in the University of Manchester; the Bar Convent Trust and its Archivist, Sister M. Gregory, I.B.V.M; the William L. Clements Library in the University of Michigan; the Georgetown University Library; the Westminster Diocesan Archives; the William Salt Library and Mr David Farr; the Department of the Environment; English Heritage; the Sheffield Central Reference Library; Liverpool Record Office; the Environment Department, Shropshire County Council; the Shropshire County Council Local Studies Library; and Pauline

Acknowledgements

Parkhouse for her help with Fitzherbert family history.

Some of the greatest centres for research are this country's county record offices, which other nations look on with envy and we take for granted. Those which proved especially helpful in the writing of this book were: the Centre for Kentish Studies; the Northumberland Record Office; the East Kent Archives Centre; the Warwickshire Record Office; the Hampshire Record Office; the Staffordshire Record Office; the Shropshire Records and Research Centre; the Dorset Record Office; the Northamptonshire Record Office; the Gloucestershire Record Office; the Durham Record Office; and the Oxfordshire Archives.

I should also like to acknowledge the work done by Maria Fitzherbert's two previous biographers, W.H. Wilkins and Sir Shane Leslie, and by that great editor, Arthur Aspinall, whose editions of royal correspondence have made research a much less harrowing task.

Finally I must thank the following for their help: Lady de Bellaigue and Miss Pamela Clark (Royal Archives); Dr A.F. Kerr; Mrs Anselma Bruce; Monsignor Gerard McKay of the Roman Rota; Mr Leo Curran; the Very Rev. Robert Byrne and the Rev. Jerome Bertram, both of the Oxford Oratory; Mrs Cornelia Oddie; Hilde R. Jansen of the Royal Netherlands Embassy; Mr Richard Horrocks, Manager of the Liverpool Record Office; Mr Peter Day, Keeper of Collections, Chatsworth; Dr William Oddie; Mr A.L. Morris, Principal of Concord College; Sister Benedict Rowell; the Rev. Richard Barrett; Mr Eric Waters, of the YMCA, Brighton; Fr Vincent Cushing, OFM; Mrs David Bruce-Smythe; the Rev. David Foley; Mr Peter Simmonds (for a unique tour of the Royal Pavilion); Dr Anthony Harnden; and Miss S.G. Acton. I would also like to record my gratitude to my editor, Carol O'Brien, for her patience and understanding.

Mr greatest debt is to the scholar and writer to whom this book is dedicated.

James Munson
Horspath, Oxford

INTRODUCTION

The story of Maria Fitzherbert's marriage to the Prince of Wales, later King George IV, has fascinated people eversince rumours of their secret and illegal wedding were first whispered in December 1785. Their life together, far from being a secret, was always well known, at least in London. Their courtly romance, meetings, quarrels, separations and reconciliations were all played out as high drama against the backdrop of London society and high politics. But the central question remained unanswered: if Maria had refused to be his mistress and could not be regarded as his wife, what was she? The question has never ceased to fascinate.

Their marriage, if it was a marriage, was illegal because it violated the Royal Marriage Act and the Act of Succession. Had it been officially acknowledged the Prince's father, King George III, would undoubtedly have had it declared illegal. If he had not done so the Prince would never have become King. Either way, the monarchy would have been shaken to its foundations.

The story of the Catholic widow, born Mary Ann Smythe and her young Prince has usually been told by her biographers from a viewpoint she would have liked. Previous writers, beginning in 1856, all wrote from a partisan point of view, coloured by a desire to present Maria as a romantic heroine who was ill-used and whose pure love was won and then spurned by an unworthy Prince. While this biography does not set out to 'debunk' it does bring Maria Fitzherbert into focus by using material never before consulted and letters hitherto suppressed.

In the event, Maria was never a defenceless romantic heroine.

She had survived the untimely deaths of two husbands before she met the Prince and had learnt to be self-reliant. She was practical, strong-willed, highly emotional, and liked male company, although she remained a virtuous woman. She had a tremendous sense of the ridiculous and her humour was sometimes very earthy. She could be pompous but she could also be kind and considerate. She liked society and could more than hold her own in a world dominated by men.

Maria's exotic marriage was for almost thirty years part of British political life. If a secret, it was a secret known throughout the Establishment and was protected by that same Establishment against the laws of the land. The marriage coloured national politics and affected the various crises which divided Parliament and the nation. After her death the same forces that had protected her when alive did so with her memory.

Maria's marriage had placed her and her husband in a terrible dilemma. She wanted to be recognised as the Prince's wife and not as his mistress but she also wanted to protect her privacy and to escape the awful penalties of the law. The immature Prince, who thought much less of his marital vows, wanted a wife who would be no more demanding than an agreeable mistress. He wanted to prove that a member of the Royal Family could have a purely private life. Both the Prince and Maria failed.

This left Maria with two contradictory desires. The first was to protect her privacy and secrets. She agreed to burn her letters to and from the Prince and with various members of the Royal Family. She only insisted on keeping those papers which, in her eyes at least, proved she had been married. As an old man, George IV, and later his executors, were also anxious to cover up the story of the marriage and fires raged even after the King's death as the Duke of Wellington carried on the work of destruction.

Maria's second desire grew after her husband's death in 1830. This was for her great romance to be remembered as she wanted it remembered and she naturally worried about finding a suitable biographer. In the end she settled for conversations with Lord

Stourton, an adoring cousin who was determined to present her as a devout Catholic and an injured woman who, but for religious bigotry, would have been Queen of England. In the event, Maria's story, properly understood, does shed valuable light on the plight of Catholics in British history.

When the twenty-eighth Earl of Crawford, whose family has kept the papers of Maria's closest friend, Lady Anne Lindsay, began writing his own biography of his ancestor's famous friend, he noted that previous biographies were 'coloured by the Catholic point of view'. W.H. Wilkins in 1905 and Sir Shane Leslie in 1939 discovered a great deal in their biographies and did much valuable work but they followed where Lord Stourton had led. By trying to make Maria a saint Lord Stourton had robbed her of her nature as a woman. He had, for all his good intentions, skewed subsequent writing.

Luckily for succeeding generations, not everything was destroyed in the burning of letters. Maria had no idea how much her best friend, Lady Anne Lindsay, had written about her in her marvellous journal nor could she have known that Lady Anne's family had kept Maria's letters. Previous biographers knew nothing of these letters or of Lady Anne's journal. Also, the Duke of Wellington's work was not as thorough as he might have wished and letters did survive. Decades later Lord Esher found them and showed them to King George V and Queen Mary. The King then ordered Esher to burn the letters which, while extremely valuable, do not show the Prince and Maria at their best. Instead, Lord Esher probably took them home and they eventually ended up in the Royal Pavilion in Brighton, where they remain. Some were used by Sir Shane Leslie although less flattering ones were ignored.

In addition to these two major collections there are the surviving papers of Maria's adopted daughter, Minney Seymour (the Portarlington MS) and the papers of those families of which she was, at different stages in her long life, either a part or connected: the Smythes, the Welds, the Fitzherberts and the Seymours, all carefully kept in various county record offices.

Almost as helpful are the letters of friends such as Eleanor Creevey, in the Northumberland Record Office, and of MPs and cabinet ministers who observed her at first hand, especially those of James Bland Burges, MP, in the Bodleian Library, Oxford.

Therefore Maria's and George IV's plan to shape history by destroying the evidence failed, as it always does. What emerges is a woman whose story fascinates us today as much as it did over two hundred years ago when the twice widowed Catholic lady first attracted the attention of the most eligible bachelor of her day.

James Munson
Horspath, Oxford

Note
Eighteenth century letters and diaries abound in what are, to modern eyes, misspellings and unusual abbreviations: 'ye' for the, 'ym' for them, 'yt' for that and 'wt' for what or, sometimes, with. Numerous 'sics' would have cluttered the text and destroyed the period flavour. The author has therefore left original quotes as they were written and omitted all sics. The modern monetary equivalent for sums mentioned in the text is given after the original sum, usually within square brackets.

#2   10-29-2017 3:32PM
Item(s) checked out to p10831058.

TITLE: Autumn
BARCODE: 3365650124435
DUE DATE: 11-26-17

TITLE: Oprah [large print] : a biography
BARCODE: 3365604919119
DUE DATE: 11-26-17

TITLE: Full black : a thriller
BARCODE: 3365605574782
DUE DATE: 11-26-17

TITLE: Maria Fitzherbert : the secret wi
BARCODE: 3365602837265
DUE DATE: 11-26-17

1

---·•·---

A RECUSANT CHILDHOOD

The world into which Mary Ann Smythe was born on 26 July 1756 was a curious mixture of county society and high treason, of Georgian mansions and the executioner's block, a world of primogeniture, rent-rolls, manors, county routs, advantageous marriages and, above all, land, combined with the fear of betrayal and arrest. The Smythes of Shropshire were a distinguished, wealthy and well connected family who had property in several counties. They had played their part in English history and occupied a secure place in eighteenth-century English society. They could, and sometimes did, claim royal blood. Mary Ann's grandfather, Sir John Smythe, and then her uncle, Sir Edward Smythe, were not only Lords of the Manor of Acton Burnell but baronets. Their parish church contained family memorials. As their motto, *Rege Semper Fidelis*, proclaimed, the family had been loyal to the King and one ancestor, George Smythe, had his estates sequestered because of his religion and of his loyalty to Charles I.

Not all was what it seemed. The Smythes were Catholic recusants. In 1569 one of them was attainted because of his involvement in the Northern Rebellion against Elizabeth I and her reformed church. In Mary Ann's day Englishmen still believed that the Church of Rome yearned to exercise a civil and not just a religious authority in England, that the Pope had the power to release English Catholics from any oath – whether of loyalty to the Crown or of truthfulness in a court of law – and that the Catholic Church allowed its followers not to keep faith with 'heretics'. When Mary Ann was only fifteen the *London Chronicle* carried two articles in one issue about a 'Romish priest' who was plotting to burn Portsmouth's docks.[1] The average person believed that Catholics were neither thoroughly honest nor thoroughly British. Stories of Guy Fawkes, the Papist plot of 1678, and the excesses of the Inquisition were all part of the common fund of knowledge: they were the horrors Englishmen had escaped by being Protestant. Those in authority, if not the general public, also knew that before the Pope appointed Vicars General (de facto bishops) for England he first consulted the Old Pretender, 'James III'. The aim of anti-Catholic laws had been, at first, to rid England of Catholics at a stroke but when these failed, the laws were aimed at starving the Church to death. Its services were illegal and its clergy, including bishops, could and did find themselves in court on capital charges two hundred years after the Reformation. Its priests were arrested and, on occasion, executed. Popular fears and prejudices were revived in 1715 and again in 1745 when first the Old Pretender and then his son tried to regain the throne. Catholics were said to be always active in converting unthinking Protestants, according to the *Advice to Protestants of All Capacities, how to behave themselves when they are tampered with to change their Religion*.[2] This curious mixture of social status and outlawry, of mistrust and fear, of acceptance and suspicion would mark Mary Ann's life and help to form her character.

The seat of the Smythes was Acton Burnell Hall in the Shropshire village of the same name, some eight miles south of Shrewsbury and a few miles west of Wenlock Edge. The village dates from a Roman settlement and Watling Street runs through the parish. By the eighteenth century the village was devoted to farming, with a mill on the estate and a poor house at the village cross roads. The Smythes were originally a County Durham family from Ash Hall. The eighteenth century accepted a variety of spellings of the same word, spellings which could reflect pronunciation. Mary Ann's surname was usually spelt Smythe but both her first husband and the Prince of Wales spelt it Smith. This may imply that the pronunciation was 'smith' and not, as today, one that rhymes with 'writhe.' Despite being attainted under Elizabeth I and having their property sequestered by Parliament during the Civil War the family remained loyal. Mary Ann's great-grandfather, Edward Smythe, was created a baronet by a grateful Charles II in 1661. Edward married the co-heiress of Sir Richard Lee of Langley Hall in Shropshire, thereby making Mary Ann a very distant kinsman of the Lees of Virginia. For the second time in the family's history it enlarged its holding of property through marriage, their new property being Acton Burnell manor which annually produced £285.15s. in rents and had 240 heavily wooded acres which had once before played their part in English history.

In the grounds of Acton Burnell Hall stood the ruins of Acton Burnell 'Castle', or fortified manor house, built in the 1280s by an earlier lord of the manor, Robert Burnell, when Bishop of Bath and Wells and Lord Chancellor to Edward I. In 1283 Parliament met in Acton Burnell: the Lords were in the bishop's manor house, while the Commons were, so tradition holds, a hundred yards away in a tithe barn later known as 'Parliament Barn', the ruins of which can still be seen.

Sir Edward obviously liked his new Shropshire property and he was buried in its parish church in 1714. This is a small insight into the curious position held by Catholics: while Sir Edward did not communicate in the church he was yet buried and commemorated in what was still 'his' parish church. Before he died he set aside £1,000 – a considerable sum – as a trust to help poor members of the family. As we shall see, it is unlikely that Mary Ann's parents ever had to draw on it. The second baronet built a new stone hall with two bays, fashionable sash windows and a lantern. The house was solid but not grand. Bishop Burnell's Castle was now converted ignominiously into a barn.

The family took advantage of the agricultural prosperity that marked so much of the eighteenth century and enlarged their new hall in the 1750s. They landscaped the park and built a prospect tower, as well as a 'shell grotto', so beloved by the ladies as a place to take tea. By the time of Mary Ann's birth the baronet was her father's brother, Sir Edward Smythe, who cut a considerable figure in local society and visited London: as a child Dr Johnson's friend, Mrs Thrale, spent much time in the circle of a Catholic mantua-maker in London and was much favoured as a pet of Sir Edward Smythe and his wife. But Sir Edward and all his family were cut off from the full enjoyment of their position and wealth. They lived in a curious twilight world. While Catholic peers and landed families could be presented at Court and while Catholic poets like Pope could achieve fame, they still came under what were termed the Penal Laws. Catholics such as the Smythes could not exercise their rights as patrons of their parish church. As recusants they could not assume any of the offices of county society: JPs, lords lieutenant or sheriffs.

Catholics could not become officers in the county militia, important centres of local life. They could not act as guardians, executors or suitors in any court of law. They could not hold any office under the Crown. Technically they could not live in the Cities of London or Westminster, nor could Catholic peers be in the Sovereign's presence. (These laws were ignored by George III's reign.) Mary Ann's uncle could not become an MP, while her cousin, Lord Stourton, and another uncle, Lord Langdale, could not take their seats in the Lords. (One benefit of this exclusion meant that wealthy Catholic landed families were excused the sometimes crippling costs of parliamentary elections.) While Catholics could become barristers they had to practise 'below the bar', that is they could not plead in court. Not surprisingly, many specialised in that peculiarly English mystery of conveyancing. They could become apothecaries but they could never become

Fellows of the Royal College of Physicians because this required a degree from Oxford, Cambridge or Trinity College, Dublin. They could not become teachers, or officers in His Majesty's army or navy, although by the 1750s Catholics were being allowed into infantry regiments but not as officers. If a gentleman wanted to follow a military career he had to leave the United Kingdom.

Catholics could not attend either English university. They could not establish Catholic schools and in theory they needed a special licence to send their children abroad to be educated, usually in France. Foreign-born Catholics could not become British subjects. A Catholic could not possess arms or ammunition and if he owned a horse worth more than £5 he could suffer the same penalty as for holding arms. It was punishable by death for anyone to harbour a Catholic priest or bishop. Catholics were required to give the government details of all their property so that the Crown could levy special taxes. While today we are used to the government's knowing every intimate fact of our lives, in the eighteenth century this was regarded as intrusive. It does mean, however, that we have detailed information about holdings of wealthy Catholics like the Smythes.[3]

Most devastating of all, at least in theory, was the land tax of 1692. Catholics such as the Smythes were subject to double taxation on their holdings. In the beginning some families were ruined by the tax but as the eighteenth century wore on the tax became less onerous because it was a fixed rate based on the 1692 assessment. So as land value increased the burden became less. There would be new legislation enforcing the tax eight years after Mary Ann's birth but it was rarely invoked because respect for the rights of property outweighed any dislike of 'Popery' among the landed gentry who had to enforce the law. Catholics still bitterly resented this tax, as they did the requirement to pay a double contribution towards the militia but this only applied when the militia was called out. Under one act of William III, no Catholic over the age of eighteen could inherit property and no Catholic could purchase any manor or estate. This too was usually unenforced but, as we shall see, it did open the way to court actions by covetous Protestant relations.

Most of these laws had been passed as statements of national faith, to comfort fanatics in the House of Commons and to reassure people who looked on Papists as incipient traitors. Informed people knew that the large body of anti-Catholic laws could never be totally enforced. The ramshackle nature of local government, Englishmen's inherent tolerance and the reluctance of JPs to proceed against their Catholic neighbours, made many, but by no means all, the restrictions meaningless. But in Mary Ann's childhood she would have heard stories of Catholics who 'used to go in a cart at night to hear Mass; the priest dressed in a round frock to resemble a poor man.' Well into the 1780s Mass – which was still illegal to celebrate – was referred to as 'prayers' and High Mass as 'high prayers'. In 1747 Bishop Laurence York told Rome that he was 'compelled to fly from house to house, from city to city'. For a year and a half he had been 'more a fugitive from my ordinary residence'. Twenty years later, in 1767, Fr John Baptist Maloney was sentenced in Croydon to perpetual imprisonment 'for exercising the functions of a Roman priest'. The informant on whose evidence he was convicted got his £100 reward but after four years the priest's sentence was commuted to banishment.

Shropshire in Mary Ann's childhood was governed by a clique of Whig grandees whose philosophy, as well as natural prejudices, would have prevented them from harassing their Catholic neighbours. As the memory of 'Bloody Mary' Tudor, the Armada, the Popish Plot of 1678 and James II's disastrous reign faded, so too did the willingness to enforce the law. While the first Stuart attempt to regain the throne, that of 1715, revived fears and led to some new laws, the second attempt in 1745 failed dismally to attract the support of English Catholics or to attract new laws.

A final but unintended burden on Catholics arrived with Lord Hardwicke's Marriage Act in 1753. This act was passed to stop secret and irregular marriages, as all the law had previously required was a free exchange of vows. After 1753 all weddings still had to follow the publication of banns, but now had to be conducted in front of witnesses, in accordance with the Prayer Book and, normally, in an Anglican parish church. Only Jews and Quakers, but not Catholics, were exempted. Between 1753 and 1836 Catholics had either to be married twice (a private Catholic wedding and a public Anglican one) or once (in an Anglican church). Those found guilty of violating the law were subject to fourteen years transportation. Many Catholics argued that, since both weddings were valid (which in Catholic teaching they were), and that since they had to be married by the Anglican rite, they might as well forego the Catholic service.

Despite all this, a careful balance was being created by the 1750s through 'the power of common sense'. On the one hand there were the penal laws and the popular prejudice against Papists. England's security, prosperity and independence, as well as Englishmen's liberties, all depended on her 'glorious constitution in church and state'. An independent Church and a limited parliamentary monarchy were guaranteed by the 1701 Act of Settlement which stated that the Sovereign, any heir to the throne and his or her spouse must be Protestant and in communion with the Church of England. On the other hand, and despite the 1745 uprising, there was a growing reluctance of the governing class to enforce the laws against Catholics as long as Catholics accepted the status quo. However, as Mary Ann Smythe later found, actual tolerance was always at the mercy of popular prejudice.

The delicate balance was due to several other factors, factors that would also shape the young Mary Ann's life and influence how others saw her. In her childhood, most Catholics lived, as her family did, in the shires, especially in Staffordshire, Lancashire, Yorkshire, County Durham and Northumberland 'in the neighbourhood of the old families of that persuasion. They are the servants, or the children of servants, who have married from those families, and who chuse to remain round the old mansion, for the convenience of prayers, and because they hope to receive favour and affluence from their former masters.' This has often been

11

referred to as 'seigneurial Catholicism' and in many ways, Catholicism was 'a hereditary allegiance'.[4] There were some Catholics in London and larger cities such as Norwich, Manchester or Liverpool but most lived in the country as they had done for almost two hundred years. They lived quiet lives and married within their own circles. This way of life produced among old families a certain religious pride. Mary, Lady Blount 'used to say with honest pride that the Blounts had held their Worcestershire estates in lineal descent from the Conquest, and had in no instance been known to abandon their Religion or their King'.

While it was against the law to build a Catholic church, there were a few 'chapels' in towns such as Bath or Wolverhampton. Usually, however, what priests there were said Mass in the manor houses of the great families: the Smythes had had Benedictine monks staying at Acton Burnell from at least 1715. In 1706 ten Catholics were reported as living in the village and all were part of the Smythe household. By 1767 the number had grown to forty-nine, the majority of whom were still attached to the great house. In the whole of Shropshire there were probably well under five hundred Catholics at Mary Ann's birth. Like Quakers, who were not allowed to marry non-Quakers, Catholics had traditionally married Catholics, thereby encouraging the accumulation of wealth among landed families. This also made virtually all the Catholic gentry and aristocracy some form of kinsmen.

The increasing tolerance was helped by the view that English Catholicism was in decline. One contemporary observer, with admittedly somewhat eccentric views, bemoaned: 'The truth is, within the present century we have most rapidly decreased.' 'As the weight of oppression lightened, and the severity of penal prosecution ceased, the stern vigour of their [Catholics'] minds relaxed, and they every day lost something of that enthusiasm of soul . . . Men of family grew daily less zealous . . . and they insensibly reformed first their politics, and soon after often conformed to the established Church.' Some even argued that, had it not been for the 1745 rebellion, all anti-popery legislation would have been suspended. This impression was strengthened because the number of men becoming priests was declining and because some well known Catholics 'conformed' to the Established Church.

The exact number of Catholics cannot be known but at Mary Ann's birth there were probably between 60,000 and 80,000 in a population of about 6,300,000, but this number included foreign Catholics living in London. The number was relatively stable but the increase in population was not reflected among Catholics: between 1700 and 1750 the population of England and Wales had increased by about a million while the number of Catholics remained about the same as in 1650.

What eighteenth-century Catholics believed, and how they believed, is important for understanding the career of Mary Ann Smythe. We must not think Mary Ann's religious heritage the same as the more pugilistic Catholicism of Victorian converts. In the 1750s there had been no pronouncements on the Immaculate Conception, Papal Infallibility or rigid rules on inter-marriage with non-Catholics. The importance of the Papacy was much less stressed than it is today. As pronouncements such as bulls or encyclicals from Rome were inoperative in England and Wales, because English laws forbade their promulgation, English Catholics existed in something of a vacuum.

The most influential guide for Catholics in the eighteenth century, Bishop Challoner's *The Garden of the Soul*, was published in the year before Mary Ann's birth. It included in its Evening Devotions for Families a prayer for 'our chief bishop', not 'the Pope'. In 1749 one Catholic priest published a book to explain to Englishmen what Catholics really believed and almost seemed to boast that, regarding Papal Infallibility, 'No Catholick, as I know of, will allow the Pope any inherent Gift or Quality of Infallibility sticking to him like birdlime.' Not surprisingly the author got into trouble with Church authorities but his views were not all that untypical.[5]

While Catholics stood apart from their fellow Englishmen in one important sense, in most others they were virtually indistinguishable. Whereas in the seventeenth century recusants led their own almost separated lives in isolated pockets and in accordance with pre-Reformation customs and habits, by the middle of the eighteenth century this had all but vanished. (Two survivors were fasting and abstinence but they too were less stringently enforced. The same was happening in the Church of England as well as in continental Catholicism.) A Catholic writer boasted that recusants 'lived, peaceable and unoffending subjects, complying with the respective duties of civil life, and worshipping God in the very retired and secret manner, the lenity of government allowed'.[6] Priests did not wear distinctive dress and were addressed as 'Mister', while in 1772 the Grand Master of English Freemasons would be the leading Catholic peer, Lord Petre. We should also remember that, as far as women were concerned, anti-Catholic legislation, apart from that forbidding the setting up of schools, did not really affect them. As they could not vote, sit on juries, attend Oxford or Cambridge or enter the Commons, the restrictions against Catholics' doing so were irrelevant.

The two dominating facts were the absence of churches and the paucity of priests of whom there were under four hundred in the 1750s. For worship and for clergy Catholics were mainly dependent on the landed gentry like the Smythes, wealthy enough to pay for a priest and to have houses large enough to provide a chapel and a residence. For those Catholics not fortunate enough to live in or very near a 'great house' with a resident chaplain, Mass was an infrequent event. Its occurrence depended on the route of those priests' 'riding circuit'. Like Methodist preachers, priests rode round the countryside. When believers could not get to Mass they were encouraged either to improvise a service or to say their prayers privately. Bishop Challoner's *Garden of the Soul* had a service intended for those unable 'through distance of place, indisposition, or other unavoidable impediments' to get to Mass.

By the time Mary Ann received her religious training, Catholics in almost all cases accepted that the 1688 Settlement was here to stay. Indeed, increasingly as the century wore on, Catholics boasted of their patriotism and bitterly resented what they saw as slurs on it. One of the Catholic apologists quoted above insisted that 'The Religious Principles of Catholicks are not inconsistent with Civil Government of any Kind . . . the Supreme Magistrate is to be obey'd, not only for Fear, but for Conscience-sake.' Bishop Challoner's book contained a 'Litany in Behalf of Our Country' and in its order of service for Benediction there was a prayer that 'N. our king, who by thy mercy has undertaken the government of this realm, may also receive the increase of all virtues; with which being adorned, he may both avoid the monster of sins and being pleasing in thy sight, come at length to thee.'[7]

The facts regarding Mary Ann's father's life are scanty. Walter Smythe was the fourth child and second son of Sir John, the third baronet. He was probably born about 1721. Like most sons of wealthy Catholic families he was sent to France to be educated, in his case, to the Catholic College at Douai. Such schools for English Catholics were designed 'to educate, for the ecclesiastical state, a succession of youths, who might afterwards be sent on the English mission'. Not surprisingly, while religion and the classics were well taught, such schools 'were not calculated to qualify the scholars for business, the learned professions, or the higher scenes of life. Writing, arithmetic and geography were little regarded . . . modern history was scarcely mentioned, and little attention paid to manners.' Such schools were also cheap. 'The instruction, the dress, the board, the pocket-money, the ornamental accomplishments of music, dancing, and fencing, every thing, except physic, was defrayed by the moderate yearly sum of 30£.' Walter may well have followed this with a grand tour during which he saw 'objects of vast curiosity; he . . . kissed the Pope's slipper, and . . . visited Our Lady at Loretto'[8] after which, as a younger son, he had to make his own way in life.

One of the more popular paths open to such sons was to follow the example of the 'Wild Geese', those Irishmen who enlisted in the army of a Catholic sovereign in Europe: France and the Habsburg Empire were the two most favoured. Walter's father, Sir John, bought his son a commission in the Austrian army (possibly Waldeeks Dragoons) shortly before 1745.[9] In return Walter had an exciting few years in a foreign country and presumably saw action against the Turks and during the War of the Austrian Succession in the 1740s.

In 1751 Walter Smythe had a great piece of luck. Indeed, this may have been the reason for his leaving the Austrian army. His cousin, Clare Smythe, died unmarried and on 11 July he inherited the magnificent sum of £10,967.16s.7¾d. [£700,000]. Four years later, on 11 September 1755 in Walton, Lancashire, he married Mary Ann Errington, a member of one of the oldest and wealthiest Catholic families in the North of England which provided her with a suitable marriage settlement to add to Walter's new wealth.

We know that Mary Ann Smythe was born on 26 July 1756, although the location of her birth is the first of many mysteries that would surround her life. As Catholics were baptised by their own priests and not in the Anglican church, their names were not (normally) entered in church records. There were some Anglican priests who would enter the names, even though they had not baptised the child themselves, but this was not the case with Mary Ann. The received view is that Mary Ann was born in Tong Castle, near the Shropshire border, which her father appeared to have leased from the second Duke of Kingston. As the crow flies, Tong is some seventeen miles north-east of the family seat at Acton Burnell. The young baby was probably baptised at Acton Burnell by Dom Edward Ambrose Elliot. From her mother she got not only her name but her good looks. From her father she inherited her aquiline nose which would become one of her most famous – and most frequently caricatured – features.

Other children soon followed Mary Ann in an appallingly rapid succession. Fifteen months later, in October 1757, her brother, Walter, always known as Wat, was born. In 1758 John, known as Jack, was born. After that their mother had a break until the third son, Charles, was born in 1760. After Charles came Henry, who some sources show also being born in 1760, and after Henry, at least according to one record, there arrived a final son, Edward, who probably died young. A daughter, Frances, was born in 1762 and a final child, Barbara, in 1769. Of Mary Ann's childhood we know very little but a letter from 1811 confirms that she spent 'the earliest days of my youth . . . happy days' at her uncle's house at Acton Burnell. Perhaps while staying with her aunt and uncle she found a freedom she lacked in a home in which her parents were 'always so censorious'. There would have been the excitement of the local hunt's setting off, the glories of the park, still heavily wooded, the sham castle in which to play and the new octagonal shell grotto which the ladies of the family helped to build.[10]

Walter Smythe now had a fortune, a beautiful wife and, by 1762, a large family. He was later described as 'in every part of his life, an amiable, well-bred, pleasant man' who was, in his earlier years, 'a table companion, we mean after dinner, of the first class'. He therefore had all the qualifications to be a landed squire save one. He lacked a country house to call his own. Then, in 1763, good fortune struck again, this time through another cousin. The Welles of Hampshire had been a leading Catholic and Royalist family and owned several properties near Winchester. Their home was at Brambridge, just outside the village of Twyford and some six miles south of the cathedral city. By the 1760s all that was left of the family was one William Welles. In earlier days, probably in 1745, William, a Jacobite, gained notoriety for 'some unwarrantable expression' and thought it best to leave Hampshire. He sought refuge 'in the house of another Catholic family, of the name of Smythe, in Shropshire'. When the 'day of trouble had passed by, and the offence forgiven or passed over', he returned to Brambridge. He did not forget his cousins' friendship and in his will, left his estates to Mary Ann's father.[11]

The family moved into their new home when Mary Ann was six and soon made their mark on local life. Walter Smythe eventually bought more land, thereby increasing his rental income and his status as a gentleman of independent means. Like his father and brother he would now benefit from increasing agricultural prosperity. While the Smythes do not come across as a particularly pious family, Walter and his wife still allowed their fellow Catholics to come to Brambridge House to hear Mass. Later they set up a house in the village as a chapel which was a fairly bold act and shows how much tolerance there was in the district. They also gave the chapel a missal bound in red morocco with gilt back and sides. (By the early twentieth century the building had become a nurseryman's house while some traces of the chapel remained.)

In 1769 Maria's parents had what was probably their last child. Church records show that Barbara's godfather was Thomas Fitzherbert. The Fitzherberts of Staffordshire and the Smythes of Hampshire were obviously friends and in 1769 the baby's older sister, Mary Ann, now thirteen, might have met the twenty-three-year-old Thomas Fitzherbert. Nine years later he would become her second husband. On the other hand, the Thomas Fitzherbert mentioned as her sister's godfather might have been Mary Ann's future father-in-law: for many years the Fitzherberts had an infuriating habit of using Thomas as the heir's Christian name. In that same year Mary Ann's uncle, Henry Errington, married Maria, the dowager Lady Broughton, the widow of Sir Brian Broughton, Bt. and the sister of Lord Berwick. With Lady Broughton came Redrice House with its wooded park of about a hundred acres near the village of Upper Clatford, not far from Andover. This her first husband had bought for the enormous sum of £10,000 [£567,000] six years earlier. Money, as is its wont, had married money and Uncle Henry was now only a day's journey away from Brambridge.

Catholic controversialists such as Joseph Berington could lament that 'Nuns are ill-adapted to the business of education when this is supposed to consist of precepts and general instruction, with which they cannot be acquainted.' But wealthy Catholic families like the Smythes saw no reason not to send their eldest daughter to a convent to have her education finished. The parents of young girls normally chose English convents in France or Belgium and previous biographers have claimed that Mary Ann was educated at the convent of the 'Blew Nuns' in Paris. We now know she went instead to a convent school in Dunkirk, a town then best known in England as a place to buy tobacco and pipes and as a haven for criminals fleeing justice at home.

Undoubtedly the Smythes would have taken their daughter to the convent school and it was possibly on this visit that they first took Mary Ann to Paris where they went to watch King Louis XV dine in state at Versailles. It was this visit that saw her first notice from royalty. Like most Bourbons Louis had a healthy appetite. As she later told Lord Stourton, she watched the King in silence until 'seeing Louis the Fifteenth pull a chicken to pieces with his fingers, the novelty of the exhibition struck her fancy so forcibly, that, regardless of Royal etiquette, she burst into a fit of laughter, which attracted the Royal notice, and His Majesty sent her a dish of sugarplums by one of his courtiers.'[12] The dish was brought to the young Mary Ann by the Duc de Soubise and in later years he recalled the incident when talking to her.

We know little about Mary Ann's school days in the Dunkirk convent. But we can get some idea of her life in Dunkirk by looking at the records of the Blew Nuns' school in Paris because the regime in both would have been similar. In the Paris convent there were rarely more than eighteen 'choir nuns', three lay sisters and ten students. In addition there was a gardener, a sacristan and maids to look after the nuns and students. Those other than the nuns were something of an odd-lot and included girls as young as four and as old as fifteen. There was a mixture of French and English pupils, of young women 'trying' their vocation, of women on holiday, of Englishwomen who had become Catholics or of those who were thinking of doing so. There was no possibility that Maria could become a nun on a sudden adolescent impulse, as royal edicts had specified that the age for taking vows in France was eighteen. The average age of pupils was about twelve and they stayed about twelve months. Girls came and

19

went at irregular intervals and there does not seem to have been any terms kept.

In 1786, Lady Jerningham moaned that the cost of the Paris school was £200 and that she had to find money for extra lessons in geography, Italian, music and dancing. Dunkirk might well have been cheaper. If we assume that the course of studies followed in the 1760s was roughly the same as in the 1780s, we are probably right in regarding the convent as more of a finishing school than an academic hothouse. Even so, its curriculum was probably not less demanding than that followed by many female academies back in England and Mary Ann gained two advantages envied by many: she had learned French and she had gained a certain independence and polish which would mark her for life. She remembered her time there with fondness: 'They were so good to me that I can never forget it.' This was no mere conventional sentiment because later in life Maria would come to the aid of the nuns when their banker failed. She raised £150 – a considerable sum for a French provincial town – among English Catholics.

Mary Ann's early life in Shropshire and Hampshire had given her a certain rural earthiness which she never loss. Her upbringing and education had given her a sense of her place in English life and history, the knowledge that through the Smythes and Erringtons and all their many connections her heritage was a rich one. It was a heritage that had been established before the first Hanoverian had crossed the Channel. These lessons were not lost on the young lady who now returned home.

2

———•◆•———

TWICE WED, TWICE WIDOWED

By the mid-1770s Mary Ann, now back in England, was ready to enter the marriage market. The world of Catholic squires was a network of relationships between large families in which husbands and wives were found. One of the most desirable men was Edward Weld, the widowed master of Lulworth Castle in Dorset whom the Smythes already knew. Edward has had something of a bad press from Maria's previous biographers. Anxious to create a tragic aura round her life's story, they have portrayed her as an unfulfilled woman whose first two marriages were regarded merely as loveless preliminaries to her third. According to this scenario she only found true happiness when she met the Prince of Wales. W. H. Wilkins, her first biographer, described Edward Weld as 'twenty-six years older than herself and in delicate health' while Sir Shane Leslie, her second, wrote that 'There does not appear to have been any romance in the early life of Miss Smythe and it is easier to assign her acceptance of two older husbands to obedience than to love.'[1] There is absolutely no evidence for any of these assertions: Edward was far from being in 'delicate health' and when they married he was fifteen years older than his new wife, not twenty-six.

21

Edward Weld was a wealthy man: he owned over 12,000 acres in Dorset, Oxfordshire, Lancashire, Staffordshire and Derbyshire and had an annual income from his estates of £7,825 [£444,000]. A surviving portrait shows him as a handsome man with dark eyes, a small mouth, a somewhat long nose and a high forehead. Traditionally this is said to indicate great intelligence but it could as easily point to an early retreat of the hairline. At the time it put him in the centre of fashion. Women especially went to extraordinary lengths to have a high forehead. To raise the hairline they plucked hair, rubbed the forehead with walnut oil, applied bandages steeped in a solution of vinegar and cat's dung or applied plasters made of quick lime or ants' eggs. Edward Weld comes across as a man sure that his acres and his wealth gave him an unassailable position. Two aspects of the portrait show us he was a man of fashion: he wears no wig, thereby showing us he has brown hair, and he very prominently holds an open and elegant snuff box. Snuff boxes were accessories that made statements about their owners, as if in today's world he were to wear a Rolex watch or hold the keys to his Alfa Romeo. The overall impression is of an intelligent and proud man but then eighteenth century portrait painters seldom showed humble men. He was trim and was what today would be called athletic, although he was 'afflicted with fits' which may mean he was epileptic. He bemoaned in one diary entry for December 1773 that he had been 'keep within doors all day . . . N.B. Never did keep all day at home before but when prevented [?] by sickness.'[2]

Edward Weld had been well educated and had travelled extensively. Like most wealthy Catholics the boy had been sent abroad to finish his schooling. Two years before Maria's birth, he and his younger brother, John, entered the Jesuit college at St Omer in Artois, accompanied by a tutor, Father Angiers. The outbreak of war between England and France in May 1756 did not affect his studies. (Neither did the fact that Edward's uncle on his mother's side was an officer in the French army.) When the two boys left the school in 1759 their father had intended them to move on to the Jesuit University of Rheims to study philosophy for two years and then to travel, to acquire the accomplishments that befitted gentlemen. However, before they could set off, John died and in the autumn of 1759 Edward and his tutor went on by themselves. Edward took lessons on the harpsichord and learned to fence. He was also strong enough to withstand an operation during which the surgeon, without any anaesthetic, operated on the 'humours in Neddy's arm'. (It has been suggested that this related to a tubercular joint.)

Before setting off on his grand tour he had to give a 'publick defension before the rest of my Schoolfellows'. His main concern was for more money and he assured his father 'Dont imagine we shall make ducks and draks with it, you may depend on all the good oeconomy, Mr Angier is master of. We both continue in good health. Champagne agrees with most constitutions.'[3] Once in Paris he asked for yet more money and told his father that 'Silks are the only thing a man can appear in in France so you must not wonder if I get another light suit . . . You must not think I have a mind to turn fop.' In December 1761 Edward's father died and the twenty-year-old youth became master of Lulworth. His uncle, who was also his guardian, urged him to carry on to Naples, the usual climax of the grand tour. He did not return to Dorset until September 1762 not only with his silk suits from Paris but with refined tastes and an abiding love of music. In the following year Edward Weld married the Hon. Juliana Petre, the orphaned daughter of the ninth Baron Petre. Juliana's mother had been a daughter of the Lord Derwentwater who had been executed after the 1715 uprising. More to the point, Juliana brought with her a dowry of £10,000. It appears to have been a happy marriage though there were no children. Juliana died in 1772.

By 1773 Weld, now thirty-two, had been a widower for a year and seems to have settled into a pleasant routine. He spent little time in the isolated splendour of Lulworth but was mainly either in London or on his yacht or 'cutter'. His engagement book for that year shows that he was at sea for at least thirty days. In

September he sailed to Cherbourg from where he 'set off for Paris on horseback'. When sailing, he would come ashore to dine 'in ye. tent'. This was an unusual sport for a wealthy eighteenth-century squire and indicates he was an independently minded man. When at Lulworth he rode to hounds, shot hares and pheasants, visited neighbours such as the Framptons or gave what we would call dinner parties. (One wonders if he adhered to the traditional seating, whereby men sat on one side and women on the other, or followed the new fashion of having mixed seating.) A distant relation quizzed him about his bachelor's existence: 'How have you been amus'd by yr. own Ideas? Have they afforded, or do they promise an ample Fund of ye comforts and Happiness of Life?'[4]

When in London Edward must have been one of the most attractive unmarried men about Town. He went to concerts and visited the newly opened Pantheon in Oxford Street where he could enjoy the masquerades, *ridottos*, fêtes and concerts. Like everyone else, he gambled at cards and while he won eighteen guineas at loo and whist he also lost £125.9s.6d. By contemporary standards his losses were far from excessive for a single man with his enormous income. Even so, they were considerably more than the £17.12s.4d. he had been paying to his garden labourers each year. Edward's engagement book for 1773 shows that he also dined frequently with Juliana's family and with other recusant families such as the Shrewsburys, Arundells, Giffards, Stourtons and 'the Smiths' whom he met on at least four occasions.

Unfortunately, no engagement book for 1774 has survived in the Weld Papers but there are letters and these show that romance had entered Edward Weld's life. How he and Mary Ann met we do not know but by June a relation who lived in Brambridge wrote: 'I should be glad to know if you hold yr. Resolution of calling here soon.' By December his younger brother, Thomas, wrote from Oxfordshire with typical eighteenth-century forthrightness: 'Love, Love, Love is like a looseness [diarrhoea] – won't let a poor man go about his business.' Edward's sister, Mary, added a more restrained note: 'NB. <u>My compts</u> to Miss Smithe.' Two days later

Mary wrote on her own account to quiz him about his new love: 'How does <u>Miss Smith do</u>, will her charms detain you in Town longer than this week, or will you fly into the Country, to make your retreat, and then to return to town again for the 9th of next month, when you are in your Solitude, perhaps the bleeting of <u>some young Lamb</u> or other or the immaginary Cry of <u>ma ma</u> – will force you to a speedy return to Society.'[5]

Sometime in 1774 Edward Weld acquired rooms at what is now 158 Bond Street, one of London's most fashionable addresses, where the *beau monde* came to gaze and be gazed at. What was unusual was that Edward Weld chose to buy what he called his 'lodgings', a step indicating not only wealth but a certain seriousness of purpose: one assumes he had his forthcoming wedding in mind. Having said that, Mary Ann and Edward obviously were not rushing into marriage because in February 1775 a sailor in Weymouth wrote to Edward asking for a place on his cutter for the 'Tour I'm told you intend to make this season in your Yatch to Portugal or elsewhear'.[6]

Even if the couple had been in a hurry, time was needed for family lawyers to negotiate the dowry Maria would bring and to draw up the marriage settlement that would protect her rights. This was a long, legal agreement the drawing up of which was a tiresome process, however lucrative to lawyers. Because married women could not own property, it was important for Mary Ann and her parents to know exactly what she would have. (Her interests would have been looked after by trustees.) The settlement specified what money would be 'settled' on her by Edward in 'pin money' (£200 a year) and what she would receive should she be widowed: given Edward's age this was not unimportant. Sadly, Mary Ann's marriage settlement was lost by the Welds' London solicitors in 1827 but we know through surviving records that she was to receive £800 a year. This was to be paid quarterly, by standing order, on Lady Day (25 March), Midsummer, Michaelmas and Christmas. It is possible that her father also settled £500 a year on her.

Before the wedding Edward gave Mary Ann – she had yet to follow fashion and adopt the Latinised version of her Christian name, Maria – a diamond necklace and ear rings, a ring, a watch and 'other ornaments'. In addition, he converted a pearl necklace that his aunt had given him into a bracelet for his fiancée, a gift that would later plague her. In July 1775 the eighteen-year-old Mary Ann Smythe became Mrs Edward Weld. As so often happens in our story there appears to be some confusion about precise details. Most sources give the wedding date as 1 July 1775 but the Register of the Catholic chapel set up by Maria's parents reads 'Die 13 Julii 1775' as the date and this is confirmed by Edward's brother, Thomas. The confusion is most likely due to Lord Hardwicke's Marriage Act: the couple were probably married in an Anglican church on 1 July and celebrated their Catholic wedding in Brambridge later.

When Sir Bernard Burke, Ulster King of Arms, composed his *Reminiscences* he wrote that among the squires of England 'the Roman Catholic Gentry is, as a class, the most conspicuous for antiquity of descent, and, perhaps, for extent of territorial possessions.' Both these qualities marked the family into which the eighteen-year-old Mary Ann had now married. In several senses she was moving up. Within the recusant world the Welds were more important than the Smythes. They had played a larger role in English history. They were far wealthier, cut a larger figure in their county, owned a residence in Town and inhabited one of the most fascinating buildings in England.

Mary Ann's new Dorset home was in an even more isolated spot than Brambridge. Just over a mile away from the Castle, through Arish Mell Gap, was the Channel, while inland the Purbeck Hills rose in the distance. Nearby were the beauties of Lulworth Cove and the picturesque village of East Lulworth whose secluded location had allowed it to become something of a Catholic haven. We know that eight years before the marriage there were 114 Catholics in the village, including carpenters, thatchers, shoemakers, a tailor, a blacksmith, a maltster, a mason, labourers and 'the poor'. All these people looked to the Castle for protection, employment and religion. Like the Smythes, the Welds provided a chapel but whereas the Smythes had traditionally favoured Benedictines, the Welds preferred Jesuits as chaplains.

The nearest town was Wareham, a good six miles away. Weymouth, then a fashionable watering hole for the gentry with its assembly rooms, esplanade and bathing machines, was some sixteen miles distant. While isolated, Maria's new home was very beautiful. In 1782, Gainsborough would visit the Castle during his tour of the West Country. The Welds' steward invited him into the Castle and took him to one of the four turrets 'where the enraptured eye of Gainsborough feasted on a rich expanse of prospect'.[7] The view from the Castle was to inspire *The Market Cart* and *A Peasant Smoking at a Cottage Door*.

Lulworth Castle, of which the young Mary Ann was now mistress, had been built by Thomas Howard, the third Lord Bindon, between 1608 and 1610 with Portland stone taken from his previous house, Mount Poynings and from the ruins of nearby Bindon Abbey. It is an exact cube, eighty feet square and three stories high with a round tower at each corner. There were claims that it was designed by Inigo Jones.

The basement housed the kitchen, servants' hall, cellar, mill house, wet larder, bakehouse and wash house. The upper floors held the Castle's offices and the drawing-room, fifty feet by twenty-five with gilded chairs covered in silk, a library, saloon (with an organ), morning room, dining room (forty-four feet by twenty-two feet), the 'King's Room' with its state bed and furnishings in blue damask and various bedrooms. On the walls were paintings by Lely, Kneller, Holbein, Lorraine and Battoni and a *Last Supper* from the school of Rubens. On the outside there was a terrace round three sides and, while the Castle never had a moat, by the time Mary Ann first saw it the formal seventeenth-century gardens had been converted into wide lawns with those vistas so loved by romantic owners. In this case the vista included the Channel. The author of the *New Weymouth Guide* called Lulworth 'the most magnificent seat in this county.'

As for the Welds, Sir Humphrey Weld had purchased various estates in Dorset, including Lulworth, from James Howard, third Earl of Suffolk. Sir Humphrey had married a Catholic and had secretly joined her church. He stood well at Court and was appointed Cup-Bearer to Charles I's consort, Henrietta Maria, as well as Governor of the Isles and Castles of Portland and Sandsfoot. Within two years of acquiring Lulworth he had to garrison it for the King in his struggle with the rebellious Commons. In the following year, 1644, it was lost to the rebels, pillaged and stripped of its furniture, windows and even wain-scotting. To ensure the building could no longer be used, the roof, which consisted of five tons of lead, was taken down. Even when the ruined building was restored to the family, the Welds were forced to return to London: Parliament did not want Royalists so close to the Channel.

With the Restoration, Humphrey, like Charles II, came back into his own. He returned to Lulworth and set about restoring his home to its former glory. He was knighted and elected MP for Christchurch in 1661. (Catholics were not excluded from the Commons until twelve years later.) He seemed to be prospering and four years later he entertained the King, his illegitimate son, the Duke of Monmouth and the King's brother, the Duke of York. However when the Popish Plot of 1678 erupted, Weld, no longer an M.P., was one of those Catholics who suffered in its wake. He was accused of being 'a Papist or Popishly inclined'.[8] He lost his office, sold many of his goods and had to mortgage his estate. This did not save him and in 1684 he was outlawed for debt. The wretched man died the following year but was at least buried in Henry VII's Chapel in Westminster Abbey.

The religious problem remained and in some ways worsened. In the wake of the 1715 Jacobite uprising fifty-eight people in Dorset refused to subscribe the prescribed oath to the new King, George I. Another Humphrey Weld was among them. In 1722

Edward Weld, father of Mary Ann's future husband, succeeded Humphrey. He was noted for his peaceful nature and kindly regard for members of churches other than his own. In 1745, however, with the country once again anxious about another Stuart bid for the throne, there was talk of troops arriving from Flanders and 'a piece of a plot' in Dorsetshire and 'one Mr. Weld taken up'. This was Edward Weld who was arrested and taken to London when an unsigned letter was dropped between Poole and Lulworth. The letter, perhaps by someone with a grudge or more likely by *agents provocateurs*, accused him of involvement in a plan to land arms in Poole Harbour. The castle was searched but no incriminating evidence was found. Two days later he was released without charge.

If the Welds suffered from the Stuarts' efforts to regain the throne, as well as from the penal laws which affected all Catholics, inheritance multiplied their fortune. One Lancashire property alone brought in the enormous sum of some £6,000 a year. A seventeenth-century squire, if lucky, might have an income of £2,000 a year from his rents but £1,000 was the more usual income: the Welds were getting six times the average on just one of their several properties.

Much of the new work on Lulworth Castle had been undertaken by Mary Ann's husband. It was under his direction that the terrace was extended round three sides of the Castle and the formal gardens were modernised into more fashionable lawns and vistas. He removed the stables to a more suitable spot and enclosed the new garden with a wall four miles long. He must have had a green house large enough to grow pineapples, the greatest rarity in eighteenth-century cuisine, because his brother thanked him for sending 'pine apples' and wonders if he is sending 'more pines.' If so, Thomas asked, could Edward let him know because they might go missing on the stage from Dorset to Oxfordshire.[9]

Tradition claims that Mary Ann was the motivating force for yet more modernisation. Inside the house the couple wanted to get rid of the numerous staircases left over from the previous century. Even before their marriage Edward had brought in architects to design a grand central circular staircase approached by a columned hall. Their country home was now set to become a showplace of modern taste and design.

Mary Ann was of course expected to take her place in county society and to join her husband in visiting other landed families. Soon after their marriage, on 26 July 1775, her nineteenth birthday, Edward Weld and his young bride drove five miles to Moreton House, the home of his old friends, the Framptons. Mary Frampton recalled years later that the new bride 'was then very beautiful . . . perfectly unaffected and unassuming in her manners'. A second duty was to entertain: within a fortnight of visiting the Framptons, Mary Ann's brother-in-law, Thomas Weld, arrived with his wife from the family's Oxfordshire estate and stayed for a month. In the meantime Edward Weld moved quickly to register Mary Ann's place in Weld family history and, in a sense, to incorporate her into Lulworth Castle's history. He already owned a double portrait of himself and his first wife, who was placed to his right. He now had Maria's portrait inserted in some vacant space to his left. Sadly the location of that triple portrait is now unknown.

There was a tradition in the Weld family that Edward also arranged for an artist, whom Leslie later argued was Gainsborough, to paint his new bride. When sitting for the portrait Mary Ann wore her own hair. That is to say she did not powder it, wear a wig or add false hair, as was the fashion. But the artist decided that she should be shown *à la mode*. 'She was so indignant the first sitting at the artist's outline of her fuzzy head, filled in with grey impaste, that she jumped up saying. "Why, the man has given me a grey wig," and bounced out of the room, vowing that nothing would induce her to sit any more to him.' The painting has remained in private hands and has remained unfinished. It is a charming story but is hardly likely to be accurate. Gainsborough scholars say that the painting does not date from 1775 but from the mid-1780s and is not by Gainsborough. It may well be by

Reynolds. In addition, the hair style adopted by the painter was wrong for the mid-1770s and right for the mid-1780s.[10]

It would have been surprising if Edward and his new bride had not gone to London to stay in their new 'lodgings' in Bond Street. Given Edward's love of music Mary Ann might well have gone with him to the Pantheon or to hear one of J.C. Bach's concerts at the Hanover Square Concert Rooms. They could have visited the theatres or John Joseph Merlin's Museum of Mechanical Curiosities which included the new 'piano-forte'. There was the zoo at the Tower of London, the print shops with their latest caricatures, the daily promenading along Bond Street or visits to the mental hospital at Bedlam, where they could have taken tea with the inmates. They could have stopped in Oxford Street to see who was the latest culprit in the stocks and to watch the lower orders, mainly women, throwing rubbish and worse at the victim. At Westminster Abbey they could have debated the merits of the west towers, finally completed some ten years before by Hawksmoor. They could walk through the exclusive Kensington Park or the more mixed St James's Park where the classes mingled. There Mary Ann could have bought a glass of 'cillibub' from one of the milkmaids.

At night the lamp-lighters and link boys with their pitch torches to light the way could have guided the Weld coach to Vauxhall Gardens, across the Thames from the Palace of Westminster. Here they would have found 'pavilions, lodges, groves, grottoes, lawns, temples, and cascades'.[11] The same links could have taken them to the slightly more select Ranelagh and its famous rotunda. Here, for 2s.6d. each, they would have taken one of the boxes round the wall to listen to the orchestra and drink tea or wine. On Sundays they could have gone to one of the Catholic chapels attached to various embassies to hear a solemn High Mass. (Diplomatic immunity excused them from the Penal Laws.) They probably went to the Sardinian chapel in Lincoln's Inn Fields because there was a Weld family connexion: it was here in 1739 that Edward's father had had a Requiem Mass celebrated for his first wife. In these chapels where wealthy recusants could reserve pews, they largely avoided the laws against building Catholic churches.

Once back in Lulworth Mary Ann would have been expected fairly quickly to have settled into her new home and role. One of her principal duties was to supervise the domestic servants of whom there were twenty (twelve men and eight women), although she would not, of course, have been expected to supervise the coachmen, grooms, postilions, game keepers, huntsman, porters or gardeners. In the Castle there was a housekeeper, a butler (who doubled as Edward's valet de chambre), underbutlers, a lady's maid, footmen, housemaids, storeroom maids, kitchen maids, laundry maids, dairy maids and, last but by far not least, M. Jacques Gulien Lemouvons, the French cook who, at thirty guineas a year plus his 'demands' or expenses, was the most highly paid servant in the establishment.

Servants were supposed to be paid annually but often had to wait months and sometimes years for their wages. When they were given their money by Edward Weld they would write out a receipt in a small leather book, if they could write. If not, the housekeeper wrote out the receipt and they made their marks. Appropriately the butler (who earned £25 a year) had the grandest signature, complete with an appropriate flourish. After more than two hundred years these receipts still show the effort involved, the heavy amount of ink used by the quill pen and the rough feel of the sand used to dry the fresh signatures. Mary Ann was also expected to supervise menus and to interview new servants to replace those who left: sometimes the women left to marry or in some cases to become nuns. For his part Edward lived the life of a country squire with his sport, his cutter and his plans for improving his property. While he lived within his budget he was somewhat carefree in his methods and he was very generous.

Within three months of Mary Ann's marriage, tragedy struck. Early in October 1775 Edward was taken seriously ill and on the 16th his brother arrived from Oxfordshire. There is a story first recorded in 1905 by Wilkins who had heard it from Lady Constance Leslie who had heard it from her mother, Mrs Fitzherbert's adopted daughter, Minney Seymour, who had heard it from Mrs Fitzherbert, that Edward Weld suffered a riding accident. The story has all the trappings of a family legend that may well have grown in the telling. The point of the story was to substantiate that Mrs Fitzherbert 'had always been a most unlucky woman' and with Edward's death had lost a 'bounteous' income through an accident. According to the story, Edward had that October morning read over to Mary Ann his new will 'leaving her everything in his power'. He was about to call witnesses and sign when his wife intervened: 'Oh, do that later. It is such a lovely day, let us go for a ride.' It was during this ride that his horse stumbled and fell. He was brought back to the Castle and his brother was sent for. Ten days after the accident, on 26 October, Thomas Weld noted in his diary, 'My poor brother dyed.'

The difficulty with this story is that Edward survived for ten days after his brother's arrival and was conscious. Why did he not sign the will which supposedly would have been so generous to his new wife? Secondly, Thomas Weld was very careful in keeping records and the reference in his diary is not to 'my brother's accident' but reads: 'ye 16 Oct. I went Lullworth upon account of my poor Br's illness.' Finally, the story ignores two facts. There was a Marriage Settlement that set out what Mary Ann was to have and secondly, the Weld properties, like those of most landed families, were entailed. An entail was a provision originally inserted in a will which set restrictions on how property would be inherited. Its aim was usually to ensure that the property would continue to pass down through the eldest legitimate male and in effect made the present owner a tenant. Usually it applied to land, although it could apply to items of furniture, jewellery, works of art or even trees which were regarded as belonging to the estate rather than to the individual. Edward could only leave Mary Ann his personal property.

With her husband lying dead, Mary Ann's world, so full of

promise, security, wealth, position and travel, had vanished. Her husband was buried in the nearby Anglican parish church with considerable splendour: funeral expenses came to 200 guineas and this did not include the £170 spent to have prayers and Masses said in London and in monasteries abroad. The question now was what was Maria to do. The Framptons asked if she wanted to come to their house but in the short term she stayed at Lulworth, while her brother-in-law left for Oxfordshire on 2 November, not to return with his family until 4 July the following year. There was, of course, a possibility that Mary Ann might be carrying Edward's child and, if a boy, he would inherit all the entailed estates and possessions. Until this could be determined Thomas Weld, while the executor, was not necessarily the heir.

Relations between Mary Ann and Thomas do not seem to have been cordial. There was obviously some confusion as to what property was entailed, what obligations there were against the estate and what property had been Edward's to leave to his wife. Attached to Edward's will (the one he allegedly planned on superseding) there is a note from the lawyers: 'To perusing your deceased brother's will and finding that he had left his real property to you in fee.' A second refers 'to inspecting your deceased brother's marriage settlement with a view to finding his powers of disposal'. The question was a simple one: was Mary Ann, assuming she was not pregnant, entitled to anything other than the jointure of £800 a year? The answer seemed to be no. She now had to hand over what cash there was in the house and Thomas noted that he had received 'from Mrs Weld the remainder of what she had from Catton [presumably the estate's agent or man of business] £12.4s. 6d.' as well as the eleven guineas from 'my brother's purse'. On 17 November Thomas paid Mary Ann £200 which was either the first instalment of her jointure or the pin money owed her.

There were yet more complications. The first of these was the pearl bracelet that Edward had given his wife. In a story that reminds one of Trollope's novel, *The Eustace Diamonds*, Thomas claimed that it was not Edward's to give but a family heirloom and part of the entail. Mary Ann refused to return it and the argument dragged on for two years.

Eventually, Mary Ann was allowed to keep the pearls, if she agreed that her executors would return them within one month after her death. There is evidence of an ever bigger squabble concerning what property really belonged to Mary Ann. In the Weld Papers is what looks like the draft (not the copy) of a letter from Thomas Weld to Mary Ann which probably was never sent. The letter, which is not dated, begins 'My dear Sister, Little did I Expect my Good Nature would be so Excessively abused as I now find it is.' From Thomas's point of view it was not so much Mary Ann who was at fault but her 'friends', that is her trustees, who were probably her brother, her uncle or, at one stage, her father:

> Was it not out of meer good nature & affection for you that I offer'd you the house the Jewels horses & What return do I get for it; that yr. friends insist upon yr. having late sole possession of the house, so as to Exclude me & mine nay not only that but you may let it to whom you please now my Dr Sister Put yr. hand upon yr. Conscience & tell me Whether you think I meant to give it you in that manner . . . I meant it [the house in question] as a relief to you in yr. distress & till you was better provided . . . For my part I am amaized With the rest of the World to think that some of yr. friends . . . should Use me So Excessively ill.

The house in question may refer to Mary Ann's continued presence at Lulworth in the months when everyone wondered if there would be a posthumous child and before Thomas and his family took possession. It could have been the house in New Bond Street or a third property, perhaps a family holding in Staffordshire which may or may not have been in the entail.

Fortunately the squabbles did not permanently damage the young widow's relations with the Welds but they did leave a mark. No wonder she would lament in her old age that 'she had always been a most unlucky woman.' Whatever her later laments, Mary Ann, when she left Lulworth, did so as a widow with a guaranteed income for life of £800 per annum. She also may well have had an independent income settled on her by her father when she married. Unlike her brother-in-law, she had no liabilities. She also left with, or later acquired, four Weld family portraits. These included the Cornelius Janssen portrait of the Humphrey Weld who had bought the Castle which for such a short time had been her home.

Mary Ann's life over the following months is largely a blank. It may be that she stayed on at Lulworth until July 1776 when Thomas and his family moved in: by then it would have been obvious that there would be no posthumous heir. It may be that she took the house over which there was so much arguing or it may be that she moved into the 'lodgings' in Bond Street. It may also be that she lived in all three. Wherever she lived, as a widow she was expected to be in mourning for her husband for two years. Social custom demanded that a lady on her own, especially a widow as young as Mary Ann, needed some female companion to be with her if she lived an independent life. She could have returned, at least for a time, to her parents' home. It was about this time that her father, to whom she was devoted, is said to have suffered a stroke that left him paralysed. Her mother thus became solely responsible for two daughters and two sons, Charles and Henry, who had been sent to the Catholic Academy in Liège in the month before Mary Ann married.[12] This left her mother with Walter, eighteen, John, seventeen, Frances, who was thirteen and Barbara, just six. Wat's future was secure because he was now effectively in charge of the estate which he would in time inherit but the other boys would have to be found professions. Her sisters would need husbands. Maria's Uncle Errington now stepped in to help.

There was at one time a legend in Brambridge that Mary Ann had lived in a cottage in the neighbouring village of Colden

Common. This is probably based on the fact that an owner of the cottage in question had been given a shawl by Mary Ann. Of the choices open to her, living in a cottage was not one that she would have found very attractive. She could have found a companion and retired into private life in any town with a sizable Catholic presence, such as nearby Winchester. She could have retired to one of the Catholic convents in Europe, such as the Blew Nuns in Paris. Finally, while sincerely mourning her husband, she could slowly re-enter society.

This is the path Mary Ann, still under twenty and now independently comfortable, if not wealthy, chose and in due course she began accepting invitations to stay with various friends and relations in their country houses or London residences. Years later Frances, Lady Jerningham, the wife of a leading recusant landlord in Norfolk, wrote to her daughter and remembered Mary Ann when she was the 'widow Weld': 'She came to see me one morning in Charles Street and you found her face *too fat*.' Outside the recusant network there were friends such as Ralph Sneyd, of an important gentry family which was later friendly with the Prince of Wales (one Sneyd was his chaplain) and relations such as her uncle, the wealthy Liverpool landowner, Charles William Molyneux, the first Earl of Sefton. Lord Sefton, who was also a friend of Thomas Fitzherbert, had been born into a Lancashire Catholic family and had inherited the Irish title of Viscount Molyneux. In 1771 he was raised to an Irish Earldom by George III or as Lady Jerningham put it rather waspishly, 'He was hardly 20 when Lady Harrington got possession of Him, made Him Conform [leave the Catholic Church for the Church of England], and made Him Earl of Sefton.' The Earl was known for the hospitality of his table and was famous as a gourmand.

Isabella, Lady Sefton, would play an equally important role in Maria's life. She was a daughter of the Earl of Harrington and a leading light in society. She kept a box at the opera and became one of the seven mainly aristocratic ladies who determined membership of the fashionable Almack's Assembly Rooms in

King's Street, St James's, opened in 1765. Lady Sefton had what might be called an interesting youth. She 'had a very assiduous lover in Hugo Meynell, then one of the fashionable men of *bonnes fortunes*. When Lady Sefton was with child of the present Lord, Lord North said he supposed the child would be a *Hugo*not.' Georgiana, Duchess of Devonshire and an acquaintance, if not a friend, was another person who would later play a decisive role in Mary Ann's life. Georgiana described Lady Sefton as 'a compound of vanity, nonsense, folly, and good nature, she always contrives to put her faults in the clearest light. Of all women I ever knew she is the soonest affronted and the soonest appeased, and if she really likes any person she will fight through thick and thin for them.'[13] The Sefton link would prove crucial in Mary Ann's life and in large measure she would become part of the Seftons' circle in London.

Given these connections it should not come as a surprise to hear that some claimed Mary Ann was presented at Court where she would have curtsied to the same royal couple who would one day become her putative parents-in-law. She was the widow of a wealthy landed gentleman and, whatever the law said, in the event her religion was no bar. Both Lady Jerningham and Lady Sefton could have sponsored her at one of the Drawing Rooms held every Thursday during the season by Queen Charlotte during which the King usually joined her. In addition, after divine service in the Chapel Royal the King and Queen frequently held a reception in St James's when presentations could also be made. These were crowded, hot affairs, not helped by the current fashion for hooped skirts. Access to these Drawing Rooms and Sunday receptions was remarkably relaxed by our standards: all the person being presented needed was to be accompanied by someone with the *entrée*, that is, someone who had himself already been presented. In the event, people without the *entrée* but appropriately dressed in court attire could sometimes simply walk in. Hester Thrale, Boswell's great rival as confidante and biographer of Dr Johnson, is our only source for the story of Maria's presentation because

until 1785 no records were kept of presentations. In autobio-
graphical notes she wrote some time after the event she recalled
that: 'Mrs Fitzherbert was presented at Court – pretty Mrs Weld
a widow – when I was there with child of Susan Thrale.' However
Lady Anne Lindsay, Maria's best friend, later claimed that Maria
had never been presented.[14]

When the widowed Mrs Weld re-entered society in 1776 or 1777
it is not surprising that she would find a second husband within
the circle of landed English recusants with London houses. Thomas
Fitzherbert (who may or may not have been Barbara's godfather)
was in his early thirties, just under ten years older than Mary Ann
and, like Edward Weld, a great catch. He was the heir to a fortune
and to the headship of a famous Catholic family. It boasted on his
mother's side descent from Francis Throckmorton whose blood
had been shed in one of the frustrated attempts to place Mary,
Queen of Scots on the English throne. Thomas was curiously
described by a fellow recusant landowner as being 'an astonishing
pedestrian' but a man 'inclined to corpulence'. 'He endeavoured
to counteract that tendency by the most extraordinary bodily exer-
tions by which he was supposed greatly to have impaired his
constitution.' A wonderful story appeared in *The Times* on 24
January 1788 which claimed that Mary Ann had put her suitor's
'affections to the trial'. He was to walk from London to Bath and
back without any money. Thomas 'cheerfully undertook the
journey' and as he was 'well known on the road, the want of
money [proved] no inconviency'. Even if this anecdote was exaggerated, we can see it as a testimony to Thomas's love and
endurance. Whereas Edward Weld appears to have been a fairly
short man, Thomas Fitzherbert was 'tall and powerfully built'.
Mary Ann's friend, Lady Anne Lindsay, noted that Thomas was
'amicable & gentle tempered'. He was, unlike Edward Weld, interested in politics but like Weld he enjoyed music and may have
met his future bride at one of Lady Anne's musical evenings.

Despite the death of Thomas' brother, Edward, on 5 June, the couple were married nineteen days later, on 24 June 1778 in the splendid surroundings of St George's Church, Hanover Square. Thomas was still only the heir to the family home at Swynnerton and there were probably three brothers and five sisters living in the Hall with his parents. The young couple made their London home in Thomas's house in Park Street, near Hyde Park. A friend later recalled that he 'doated on' Mary Ann and that she was 'supposed to have been very much in love with him'.[15] Mary Ann's new husband was even more generous to her than Edward Weld had been. The marriage settlement stipulated that, should she be widowed, she would receive £400 a year 'during the term of her natural life'. Later this was increased to £1,000 with the stipulation that the income would carry on even if she remarried. Her trustees were her brother, Walter, her uncle, Charles, Earl of Sefton and Ralph Sneyd.

It was during this summer of 1778, when Mary Ann was beginning her new married life in London, once again as a lady of fashion, that momentous events were occurring in the world of English Catholics. Not for the last time Mary Ann's life would be shaped by events taking place round her. The spirit of toleration was gaining pace and in 1771 and 1774 the Irish Parliament had passed acts of toleration. By 1778 the uprising in the American colonies was causing London increasing worries. France was threatening to recognise American independence and war with the French seemed imminent. Britain needed more armed forces and Lord North, the Prime Minister, was anxious to recruit Catholic Highlanders. A secret mission to Scotland by a government representative to sound out Catholic opinion opened the way for concessions to English Catholics.

In April a committee of English Catholic laymen had been formed to campaign for new legislation to relieve Catholics and Thomas Fitzherbert supported its work. On 1 May, the day before George III and Queen Charlotte left to review the fleet at Portsmouth, the King received a 'most dutiful and loyal address from the Roman Catholic Peers and Commons of Great Britain'. The King supported the campaign and a private member's bill to repeal a 1699 act of William III quickly made its way through Parliament without divisions. On 27 May the Catholic Relief Bill received the Royal Assent. It was no longer a crime (punishable with life imprisonment) to be a Catholic bishop, priest, schoolmaster or a member of the Jesuit Order. The days of conviction on the word of informers (who were then rewarded) were over. The days of hiding in barns and of secretly conducted schools, like those at Brambridge, were over as well. Of great importance to land-holding families such as the Fitzherberts were two other clauses: the first recognised the right of Catholics to inherit land and abolished the right of a Protestant relative to claim the inheritance (as had happened in Maria's mother's family) while the second allowed Catholics openly and legally to buy land. A new oath of loyalty was required but it was one that did not give offence: Catholics had to renounce the Stuart claim and the supposed power of the Pope to depose sovereigns. For Catholics the summer of 1778 was heady with the sense of relief and while many disabilities and exclusions remained, the act 'shook the general prejudice . . . to its centre'. On 4 June, the King's forty-first birthday, 'a form of prayer for our most gracious Sovereign, George the Third, his royal consort Q. Charlotte, and all the Royal Family was read in all the Roman Catholic chapels throughout the Kingdom'.[16]

On 3 October Thomas' father died and Thomas the Younger was now Lord of the Manor of Swynnerton, a place he dearly loved while his twenty-two-year-old wife, Mary Ann, was once again mistress of a great house, albeit with a mother-in-law in residence. She was also now married to a man with considerable wealth at his disposal. Her new home was as impressive as Lulworth Castle. Swynnerton Hall had been built by the architect, Francis Smith of Warwick, in the 1720s. It was two and a half storeys tall with large Tuscan pilasters along the frontage. It was patterned after no less a building than Buckingham House (later

Palace) in London, although considerably smaller. The Staffordshire village of Swynnerton was like East Lulworth or Brambridge, a small recusant centre largely depending on the great house for its livelihood. At Swynnerton Hall itself there were seventeen servants and the footmen would have been dressed in the Fitzherbert livery, red turned up with green.

Swynnerton Hall remains as magnificent inside as it is impressive outside. The house is on a rise and from its windows one may still see, beyond the Park, Stafford Castle some twelve miles away and, in the distance, the Wrekin. The Fitzherberts had always been known within the recusant world as good hosts and an inventory in the year of Maria's marriage gives us an insight into life there. The great hall contained a billiard table and two large mahogany dining tables. The drawing-room had eleven mahogany easy chairs 'in canvas on castors with check fringed covers', a card table and eight family pictures, while the dining room had eighteen mahogany chairs. The inventory carried out at Thomas's father's death showed that the store room had three punch bowls, sixty-six octagon plates, thirty-six round plates, a tea kettle, a stand and lamp consisting of 120 ounces of silver worth £32, a coffee pot weighing twenty-seven ounces of silver and worth £7.11s.3d.

The cheeses in the 'cheese chamber' were worth £45; the green post chaise with its harness was valued at fifty guineas while the hogsheads of ale were valued at £15. The hogshead of sherry was worth £22 and in addition there were thirty-six bottles of brandy (worth £5 8s.) and sixty bottles of rum (worth £6 15s.) and, if this were not enough to drink, there were bottles of white port, claret, madeira, white wine and a pipe of red port. Even the 'dung in the field' was valued at £4.0s.0d. In addition to the Hall there was a dairy, laundry, brewhouse and bakehouse and in the fields, eighteen milch cows and twelve horses.[17]

When not visiting neighbours, or engaged in London's social whirl, the Fitzherberts continued to entertain and among the guests were Mary Ann's family. Her oldest brother, Walter, who turned twenty-one in the year of her marriage, was there and we assume Jack came as well. Jack, who would play a major role in his sister's life, was, a friend claimed, 'very like' Mary Ann and she herself would describe him as 'an amiable good soul'.[18] Her younger brothers, Charles and Henry, were now finished with their schooling in Liège and may well also have joined their sister. (Henry went on to follow his brother, Wat, into foreign service in Austria whereas Charles chose Sweden.) We know that Mary Ann's sister, Frances, six years her junior, came and during one visit fell in love with another guest, Carnaby Haggerston, a member of an old Northumberland recusant family and the heir to a baronetcy. They would marry in 1785. Frances' and Mary Ann's futures were to be intertwined and Frances was to lead what would be called an 'interesting' life. When not entertaining, Thomas Fitzherbert was busy with 'Capability' Brown whom he had employed to redesign the park at Swynnerton.

In Thomas Fitzherbert's own circle was Lady Anne Lindsay, a fascinating woman in her own right who was to become Mary Ann's closest female friend. Despite various ups and downs, their friendship survived until Lady Anne's death in 1825 and, as she is one of our chief sources of information about Mary Ann, she should herself be introduced. Lady Anne Lindsay, who was the eldest child of the fifth Earl of Balcarres, lived in London, in Manchester Square. Even though the square was still unfinished it did contain the Duke of Manchester's Hertford House (now housing the Wallace Museum) and this gave it a certain *éclat*. With her lived her younger sister, Lady Margaret Fordyce whose husband, a banker, had gone bankrupt and fled the country in 1774. Lady Anne was something of a blue-stocking and a gifted writer. Within selected circles, she was famous for her ballad, 'Auld Robin Gray', which had been published anonymously in 1771. She was a friend of Sir Walter Scott, David Hume, Dr Johnson and James Boswell. She was quick witted, cultured and charming. She loved society, the opera, the theatre and cards. She and her sister had good singing voices and also held musical evenings which

Thomas Fitzherbert attended. In the 1790s Lady Anne was described 'as the more bustling and active' of the two sisters. While she was 'quick and sensible, she has not the twentieth part of Lady Margaret's parts of judgment'. Her language was described as 'a frank, vulgar sort of half-Scotch. Lady Margaret is quiet, gentle, elegant . . . They are both extremely friendly.' Lady Anne strikes one as the sort of woman one would like to know.

When Mary Ann met Lady Anne she was engaged to the Hon. Thomas Noel, heir to Viscount Wentworth, but like many of her romances, this came to nothing. Lady Anne was also part of the Duke of Gloucester's circle and, not surprisingly, was presented to his nephew, the Prince of Wales. Because she was beautiful, gossips naturally assumed that she became more than just a friend to the young Prince. Whether true or not, by the 1780s she had been added to the Prince's growing number of honorary 'sisters'. Partly because of her 'set' she made enemies. The MP, Sylvester Douglas, later Lord Glenbervie, once noted that she did not appear 'in a dignified or respectable light in society'. Thomas Noel's sister, Judith, had no doubt that 'her Character <u>entre nous</u> being entirely gone & She is spoken of amongst Men as slightly as any Woman can'.[19] This fascinating Scotswoman would observe the curious life of her friend for many decades and would collect much information about her which was unknown to previous biographers. Often her journals and letters provide answers to questions about Mrs Fitzherbert's life that intrigued observers during her lifetime and have fascinated people ever since her death.

For over two hundred years there has been a debate about Mary Ann's ability to have children. The earliest book, as opposed to scurrilous tract, to mention her, Sir Thomas Clifford's 1817 history of Tixall, the neighbouring parish to Swynnerton, wrote that 'she had an only son, who lived but a few months.' As this was published in her lifetime and as it was written by someone who knew her, we may accept its reliability. Lady Anne recorded the birth but remembered that Mary Ann's son 'died as soon as born'.

Such losses, especially of the first child, were common occurrences in the eighteenth century and were more readily accepted than in our own day. It is obvious from letters that the little boy's death did not prostrate Mary Ann and in her surviving letters and conversations she never mentioned the baby.

Back in London the new Mistress of Swynnerton must have cut a dashing figure. Indeed it may have been about this time that she followed the eighteenth-century custom and Latinised her name to become Maria Fitzherbert, the name by which she is known to history. Henceforth in deference to her decision, she will be Maria. In her earliest extant letter, probably written in April 1780, she writes from London to her Aunt Frances, the wife of William Fermor. He was a friend of Horace Walpole and an antiquarian of some standing who would be present at the opening of Queen Katherine Parr's grave in 1782. His mother, Lady Browne, was Walpole's neighbour in Twickenham and impressed Walpole by always carrying a special purse of 'bad money' to give to high-waymen when they robbed her carriage.

Here we have the first surviving letter of the woman who was to play such a unique role in British history. In it Maria comes across as lively, witty and engaging. Like most Georgians, she paid little attention to spelling or capitalisation:

> I have been for this some time past in hourly expectation of your arrival in Town as yr sevt said she expected you every minute you are very cruel to keep us so long in suspense. If you dont come <u>very very</u> soon I shall quite despair. I darsay it is those <u>Idle good for nothing Monkis</u> [monkeys] that keep you where you are so long in short I shall be quite miserable if I dont see you as I have set my heart upon having many pleasant parties with you – it is much the pleasantest to be in Town at this time of the year.

Maria notes that Ranelagh pleasure garden was now open and she wants the Fermors to make up a party there. One of Thomas's brothers, Basil, an entertaining John Bull figure, was in London, as were other friends: 'My friend <u>Basil</u> is to be here tomorrow dont you envy my happiness he is rather more if possible attach'd to me than ever.' She passes on news of mutual friends and writes that her brother, Harry, has recently left London for Brussels to begin his military service in Austria. 'I am glad he is gone,' she adds, 'as I was fearfull staying long at home & having nothing to do might spoil him & make him like an acquaintance of ours.' Her grandmother, probably her Smythe grandmother, has been in London but has gone to visit a friend 'who at last has taken lady Blandford's House . . . at 320 pd a year pretty tolerable price for such a place.' (The price may have been 'tolerable' for people like the Fitzherberts but for most Englishmen it would have been inconceivable.) She humorously notes that 'Poor Lady Brown is so happy with Mr Fermor's goodness . . . she talks of nothing else & I have heard of it from every Creature with great encomiums of his goodness & generosity this displeases me very much for <u>I hate to have those I love spoke well off</u>.' Maria ends her gossipy letter, 'I think I shall tier you to death with reading all my Nonsense therefore must Intreat you & My Dr Mr F. to accept of my sincerest regard & attachment with wch I must beg to remain'.[20]

Although the Fitzherbert coachman, resplendent in livery, would drive the large family coach, Maria was allowed full use of one of Thomas's phaetons. These were a range of four-wheeled carriages which were becoming popular in the 1780s and were designed to be driven by people of fashion and wealth as a form of recreation. Maria's carriage was a pony phaeton because its design made it more acceptable for ladies in full skirts. Her husband let her use two of his fashionable Galloway ponies. Living as the Fitzherberts did so near to Hyde Park they would have made good use of her carriage. Not only were phaetons renowned for their speed, but their particularly high seat allowed spectators a good view of the 'person of quality' who was driving, much as Land Rovers do today.

Maria and Thomas, known in society as 'The Fitzes,' would also have seen the young Prince of Wales on his way for a ride in the Park. As an old woman half a century later she remembered just such an occasion in Park Lane when Thomas 'turned round and said "Look. There is the Prince."' A few days subsequently, when she was going with her husband to a Breakfast given by a Catholic friend they were once again in Park Lane when she perceived that the Prince had followed her, and had stopped to look at her.[21] She must have been told such an action was not that unusual on the Prince's part.

Like other ladies of fashion Maria would have long since abandoned her earlier natural look and followed the hair style set by the famous Georgiana, Duchess of Devonshire. This required ladies to use powder, pomatum and 'a large triangular thing called a cushion', that is, wire and false hair to build a mountain sometimes rearing up three feet. As Mary Frampton noted, 'the higher the pyramid of hair, gauze, feathers, and other ornaments was carried the more fashionable it was thought.' These could include bird cages, ornaments made of blown glass, feathers (which sometimes caught fire if taken too near a chandelier) or fresh flowers placed in small containers of water shaped to fit the head. Private houses and theatres had to provide 'powder rooms' (the euphemism for a ladies' lavatory still heard in America) to allow ladies and their maids a place to re-powder. Once a week the poor suffering female had to open up the structure to exterminate the accumulated vermin. Between sessions she could poke at them with a long rod. (Frequent washing of the hair and body was thought dangerous and was never easy to accomplish due to the lack of domestic plumbing.) At night women had to sleep in a sitting position with up to twenty-four pins holding the contraption together. During the day, they would have to sit on the floor of their carriage to have room for their towering hair. When worn to court these crazy structures were topped with the feathers required by etiquette. Eventually, when the head dress reached three feet nine inches Queen Charlotte banned them and then relented and ordered their height reduced. The problems for men of fashion could be almost as bad: in Paris men who had spent some two hours having their hair dressed would walk about with their hats under their arms so as not to disturb their dresser's creation.

If the Duchess of Devonshire set the fashion for hair, the Duchess of Rutland set that for waists: hers was said to be the size of an orange and a half. Corsets became a necessity as well as a torment and Maria was inclined to put on weight. If that were not enough, ladies also had to be sure that their skin was white. Just as today women risk skin cancer to get brown skin, so in the 1770s and 1780s they risked cancer by using white paints that sometimes contained arsenic or even mercury water to make their skins as white as possible. Maria would always be famous for her complexion and she might have been one of the few who did not have to resort to chemicals to achieve the desired result. She would undoubtedly have worn artificial patches whose position on the face would both show one's political loyalty and hide pimples and scars from chicken pox.

The year 1780 was to bring the London recusant society in which the Fitzherberts moved something more urgent to worry about than the latest fashion. As had been feared, the 1778 Relief Act had created something of a Protestant backlash. While John Wesley had demanded its repeal, the real agitation was led by the young Scottish MP, Lord George Gordon, who became one of the major leaders of outraged Presbyterianism in Scotland where rioting and protests kept a separate act from being passed. In London Lord George also became head of the Protestant Association which demanded the repeal of the act. The Association met at noon on 2 June in St George's Fields, Southwark (where, ironically, Southwark's Roman Catholic cathedral was later built) to march on Parliament with a petition. Soon the crowd became violent and Lord Mansfield (famous for his opposition to persecuting priests and bishops) barely escaped with his life.

That night and for six days London was under mob rule. The rioters, led by a small group, attacked and gutted the Catholic chapels attached to the Bavarian Embassy in Golden Square and the Sardinian Embassy in Lincoln's Inn Fields. A family connection of Maria, the brewer, Thomas Langdale, saw his house and warehouses in Holborn destroyed. The rioters broke into the casks of unrectified spirits and set them alight. Some drank the liquor and were suffocated or burned to death. The fires 'threw up into the air a pinnacle of flame resembling a Volcano'. Eyewitnesses wrote of seeing 'Newgate in flames, saw the Prisoners all make their escape and the whole of it burnt . . . Lord Mansfield's House Furniture Books . . . Manuscripts . . . we saw all committed to the Flames.' This witness, a young soldier, saw 'the whole of the Kings Bench Prison the new Brideswell The Fleet The Toll houses & gates on Black Friar Bridge all burnt to the ground'. The mob 'attacked the Queen's Palace [later Buckingham Palace] yesterday without affect . . . how it will End God Almighty knows not without a great deal of Blood shed . . . I believe all this for a Damned Mad Man Lord George G.' No one was certain as to the number of rioters and estimates varied from 15,000 to 70,000. As usually happens, there was an inner core, some said consisting of 'about 200 determined fellows' while the rest was made of the riff-raff that has always been part of London life. There was also talk of foreign involvement: 'Accounts are given of French and American gold being found on ye. rioters; of men under ye most Shabby appearance being discovered with white silk Stockings.'[22]

Catholics outside London genuinely feared for the worst as letters and messages were still able to leave the capital. The Weld Papers contain a letter from an unknown source, the same writer who wrote about French and American gold, showing that these fears were not groundless: 'Four of ye rioters went from London to Bath in a post coach and four. They wore ye insignia of ye mob, blue cockades. They stoped at Devises, enquired if there were any Cath: there: being told there was only one, and he a cobler, they said he was beneath their notice and drove on.' Once in Bath the discriminating trouble-makers were soon able to rouse a mob which attacked the Catholic chapel, then hidden away on the second floor of Bell Tree House and almost killed its Benedictine priest.

Some people began to panic and talked of asking Parliament to repeal the 1778 Act. In Dorset Maria's brother-in law, Thomas Weld, made plans to send his wife, once again pregnant, to stay with the Framptons in case Lulworth were attacked. One friend wrote about the cannons that were traditionally used to celebrate a young Weld's coming of age: 'Sir, I wish the Cannans may be had into the Castle to Pervent ther Falling into ye hands of ye mob, Stons to be throwen from ye Leads of ye Castle by ye woman may be usefull; may not ye Cannans be usefull if there muzels was Pointed to ye. Doors. from your Humbl. Sernt. William Hatchard.'

By 8 June the rioting was over, mainly due to the courage and determination of George III. Annoyed by the supine behaviour of his government and the magistrates, he proclaimed what amounted to martial law: 'George the Third, when attacked, prepared to defend his Throne, his Family, his Country, and the Constitution entrusted to his care. They were in fact saved by his decision.' Lord George Gordon was tried for treason but the jury refused to convict. He later became a Jew and submitted 'to one of the most painful ceremonies or acts enjoined by the Mosaic Law . . . he preserved with great care, the sanguinary proofs of his having undergone the amputation [circumcision].'[23] In other words, he travelled with his foreskin as a companion. In the future this bizarre man's paths would cross Maria's to cause her acute misery.

While the rioting was still at its height Thomas Fitzherbert had left the safety of his house to venture into the midst of the mob, possibly to check on property he may have owned in Queen Street, in the City of London where the mob did so much damage: 'and at the close of the day, being much fatigued and over-heated, he had the imprudence to throw himself into a cold bath, the consequences of which proved fatal.'[24] The trouble with this version of events is that cold baths do not normally kill. There is a second version, equally void of medical knowledge, which omits any reference to the riots and assigns the onset of Thomas's tuberculosis to his love of exercising: 'After one of his customary amazing pedestrian feats he was affected with pulmonary disease which became chronic.'[25]

The truth was that Thomas Fitzherbert, like so many Englishmen at the time, was tubercular, as his portrait in Swynnerton may well indicate. We must remember that in the eighteenth century consumption was a remarkably easy disease to pick up. After 'all types of physic' were tried the couple decided that the best thing they could do was to find a warm climate in which Thomas might regain his health and they chose Nice, which was highly recommended for those suffering from consumption and asthma. When Tobias Smollett, himself consumptive, lived in the town for eighteen months between 1763 and 1765, he had been enchanted: 'The small extent of country which I see, is all cultivated like a garden. Indeed, the plain presents nothing but gardens, full of green trees, loaded with oranges, lemons, citrons, and bergamots . . . and plats of roses, carnations, ranunculas, anemonies, and daffodils, blowing in full glory, with such beauty, vigour and perfume, as no flower in England ever exhibited.' Fitzherbert family tradition has it that as Thomas left Swynnerton for the last time he ordered the carriage to be stopped at the bottom of the park for one final look before setting out for the continent. Thomas and Maria were following fashion in choosing Nice which, since the 1730s, had grown in popularity among Englishmen: its main attraction, apart from its climate, was that it was virtually the furthest place south one could go without having to cross the Alps. The Fitzherberts were probably not aware of the one great tax advantage: because Nice was still part of the Kingdom of Savoy and not then in France, it was not subject to the *Droits d'Aubaine*, a French law that made the goods of any foreigner who died in France the property of the King of France.

The Fitzherberts would have found a well established but small English colony which by 1787 numbered 115 families out of a total population of some 12,000. Most Englishmen would have taken apartments or villas in the Saint-François-de-Paule area, known locally as 'le new borough'. Others had come to Nice for the climate, including one Frenchman, the Comte de Marin who befriended Maria and Thomas with carriage rides and gifts of luxurious food. Years later he would turn up again and attempt to make more of their friendship than Maria had intended. The Fitzherberts could also enjoy the views or walk along the Bay of Angels. They could have taken carriage rides up to the nearby town of Cimia (present day Cimiez), famous for its Roman ruins, or to Grasse, even then famous for its perfumes. Picnics were a favourite activity during the day, while at night there was the opera. Like Smollett, they might have visited the Sardinian galleys in the bay to see the slaves chained to their oars or, if this was considered too horrible a sight they could have rowed round the ships, listening to the slaves' chains as they rattled. (The ships were harboured at Nice to cope with raids by the Moors.) They could have visited the small city's ten monasteries and three convents or gone to a sung High Mass in the cathedral. Smollett, who disliked much of life in Nice, admitted that the air was dry 'and as for fogs, they are never seen'. 'Ever since my arrival at Nice, I have breathed more freely than I had done for some years.' [26]

Smollett's recovery was sadly not to be repeated in Thomas Fitzherbert's case. In April he made a minor change to his will regarding his estate in Staffordshire and on 7 May 1781 he died. For a second time, Maria, now in her twenty-fourth year, found herself a widow, this time in a foreign country and with only her brother, Jack, for support. A few days later the brother and sister erected a memorial to Thomas Fitzherbert in one of the chapels of the Dominican Friary in Nice:

Nobili Viro
Thomae Fitzherberto Anglo
Maria Smythe Conjugi B.M.
Joannes Fratri Opt.
Moerentes P.P.
III. Id. Maij MDCCLXXXI

Twice Wed, Twice Widowed

To the English Nobleman
Thomas Fitzherbert
Maria Smythe placed this
for her worthy spouse
John, for his best of brothers grieving
on the 3rd of the Ides of May 1781

By the middle of June Maria was in Paris where we know that she gave money to help poor English Catholic 'converts', perhaps as a gift in memory of her husband. (Later, when she had become a public figure, this was interpreted as a conspiracy with French Jesuits to promote Popery in England. In fact the Society of Jesus had been suppressed by the Pope eight years earlier.) While in Paris she wrote to the Fermors, to thank them for their letters of sympathy:

It gives me some comfort to find I have a few Friends left for such real friends as you have ever been to me are rare indeed to be found & at this Crisis the few friends I have are the only comfort I have in life & they are more necessary to me at this moment than I can describe the thoughts of which help to support the many severe trials with which I am over-power'd & without whom I should never be able to support myself but sink entierly under the heavy load of afflictions that opress me.

She had been 'very ill of a fever but it has now left me & I am rather better.' In a moving testimony to her dead husband she adds, 'If I had been worse I should have been happier as I might then have had some prospect of putting an End to a Miserble existence but I will not dwell any more upon this Melancholy Subject as I know you will feel my loss as well as myself.' She brings her letter to an end because she is already tired from having written a long letter to her mother and finishes, 'Do let me hear from you often as I shall certainly make some stay here I cannot get the better of myself to return to England.'

Back in September 1780 Thomas had made out a new will. He had increased Maria's jointure from £400 to £1,000 and disposed of those possessions not entailed. 'I give to my dear wife,' he wrote, 'all my plate whatever and wheresoever and all my household furniture, Pictures, Books, Linen, China, Wines and other Liquors, Coals and Candles which shall at the time of my decease be in or about my house in Park Street.' He gave her the house itself for the remainder of its lease and 'all my coaches, chaises, Phaetons'. Thomas recalled their fashionable life together in London and also left his wife 'the poneys or Galloways which she usually drives in my Phaetons'. With an income of at least £1,800 a year [£102,000] and a London home, it would be fair to say that she had now moved from being comfortable to being wealthy. This was of little comfort in 1781, in the heat of a Mediterranean summer or in the loneliness of Paris. Within six years she had lost two husbands, a baby son and two beautiful homes. Once again in mourning, she had little inclination to joke about 'hating to have those I love spoke well off'.

When many years later Maria's adopted daughter, Minney, was visiting Nice, Maria wrote to her and looked back on this period: 'How very kind of you, dearest, to think of me and all my sufferings at Nice' and added, in a second letter, 'I assure you I should be very sorry to have to pass my youthful days over again.' It would be just over a year before Maria could 'get the better' of herself and return to England. Thomas Fitzherbert had not just left her with an enhanced income but with a name that was soon to become famous in British history.

3

———⋅•⋅———

THE MOST ACCOMPLISHED
PRINCE OF HIS AGE

By the summer of 1782 Maria Fitzherbert had 'got the better' of herself and returned home. Where she lived is something of a mystery, as indeed is much of the period between her return and her meeting the Prince of Wales. Although she still had her house in Park Street she also took a summer house on Richmond Hill with its view over the Thames valley. Whom Maria chose as her companion we do not know but it may well have been her grandmother, the Hon. Maria Molyneux. There is no doubt that she would have had a companion. The accepted view in society was that for a lady to live on her own was 'an extraordinary and improper situation' and we know that her grandmother lived with her later. In addition, Maria had the patronage of another Molyneux relative, Lady Sefton.

In the eighteenth century people wealthy enough to live in London but not wealthy enough to own a house, took leases on houses and left Town for the country, the seaside or a spa once the season was over. Bath, Tunbridge Wells, Lymington, Weymouth and Scarborough remained popular but an increasing number of the *bon ton* took apartments or houses in Brighthelmstone, now more and more frequently being called Brighton. As a wealthy woman Maria was able to follow fashion. In later years she would visit Bath and other pleasure resorts and it is probable that she did so now but we know that by the summer of her return she was taking the air in Brighton thereby beginning a relationship with the seaside town that would always be associated with her name.

Within Maria's lifetime Brighton had been an impoverished fishermen's village of under a thousand inhabitants, known only because there was a weekly cross-Channel packet from Dieppe and because it was London's principal source of fish. Then in 1753 a doctor from nearby Lewes arrived and took up residence. In an age when physicians floundered about for cures, Dr Richard Russell hit on the idea of bathing in sea water, and even drinking the stuff, combined with a variety of other noxious medicines and the inevitable blood-letting. Brighton began to grow. Within two years of Maria's arrival the population reached 3,620. In 1765 the Duke of Gloucester, the King's brother, paid his first visit and the next year he was followed by an older brother, the Duke of York, although in his case the cure did little good and he died in 1767. In 1771 the King's third brother, the Duke of Cumberland, began coming on a regular basis and even took Dr Russell's house over-looking the sea front. His arrival may be said to symbolise the somewhat rakish air that has marked Brighton ever since. The Duke later introduced his nephew, the Prince of Wales, to Brighton where the annual race meetings, which started in 1783, and the presence of a certain Charlotte Fortescue, added to the attractions.

When Maria was settling into her Brighton lodgings a new *Guide for Ladies and Gentlemen* appeared. 'The salubrity of the air,' it begins, 'the excellent quality of the water, the pleasing, healthful, and convenient situation of the town, its moderate distance from the metropolis, the unrivalled beauty of the circumjacent country . . . give Brighthelmstone a superiority to the other watering-places.' There was a theatre in North Street and during the season, from late June to late September, there were performances four nights a week. 'If perfection is not reached, mediocrity is

surpassed.' Civic health was also well above mediocre: 'The inhabitants are remarkable for a strength of constitution and they are
naturally of alert, active, and sprightly dispositions.' There were
frequent 'card assemblies' and balls including 'Undress Balls' at
which the ladies did not have to dress as elaborately as in Town.

In the 1780s the Steyne still formed not only a large parade that
swept down to the sea, but 'a serpentine course of many miles
among the hills' which was perfect for those with carriages. Here
Maria could have taken out her phaeton and Galloway ponies. On
the Steyne's west side was the Castle Tavern, built by a neighbour
of Maria from Park Street. Its four assembly rooms and large coffee
room 'united simplicity with grandeur, and elegance with
propriety'. There was also a tea room, a card room and a ball room,
with balls every Monday. Finally, there were two subscription
libraries which were vital for the socially aware: when one arrived
in town one of the first things to do was to register at one of the
libraries. Journalists would then call in to see who the latest users
were and publish their names in the local paper.

Most important of all was the sea bathing. In a letter, probably
written in 1783, Maria described her routine to her uncle: 'I live
very quiet & very retired I am now laying in a Stock of Health for
the next Campagne I get up (wonderful to tell) at eight O Clock
every Morning & Bath every day in the Sea. Dine at half past four
& go to bed regularly at Eleven. I am certain this style of life will
prolong my life at least ten years.' Her bathing would have been
a complicated manoeuvre: 'By means of a hook-ladder the bather
ascends the machine, which is formed of wood, and raised on high
wheels; he is drawn to a proper distance from the shore, and then
plunges into the sea, the guides attending on each side to assist
him in recovering the machine, which having accomplished, he is
drawn back to shore. The guides are strong, active, and careful,
and in every respect adapted to their employment.' Ladies such
as Maria naturally had women guides.[1]

When not in Brighton, Richmond or Park Street, Maria, like
most unattached ladies of her rank, made the circuit of spas and

of friends and relations who would, in their turn, come to her in due course. September 1783, for example, found her in Lymington Spa. She told Lady Anne Lindsay, whose friendship she had renewed on her return from Europe, that she was worried about her father: 'My poor Father has been exceedingly ill with his old companion the gout and we have at last prevailed on him to go to Bath.' Maria also told Lady Anne that she was 'never so tired of any place in my life' as Lymington which was 'without exception the most melancholy place I ever was at'. Relief was at hand because a few days after writing she would leave to visit Uncle Henry's wife, still called, incorrectly, Lady Broughton, at Redrice and then travel on to London where she was 'obliged to go upon business'. October would find her once again in Brighton where she hoped to see her friend.

Maria Fitzherbert was used to a life of comfort, style and wealth. She was a woman capable of deep feelings and possessed of a lively, frequently earthy, sense of humour as regards the world round her. A few years after this a friend remarked on 'her very warm & accute feelings & disposition . . . her heart is an excellent one.'[2] She was a woman in her mid-twenties, very much in control of herself and her immediate environment, equally at home in London or Paris. She had a secure sense of her own worth and dignity. She was proud, although her enemies would later call her arrogant. An education in a French convent, the loss of two husbands and the months spent travelling in Italy and France had formed Maria's mature character. In addition she possessed a strong self-reliance, born out of necessity. She had many friends, all of whom were wealthy and most of whom were Catholic.

Maria was attractive, although inclined to put on weight. The portrait which the Weld family thought had been painted in the 1770s, dates from about this time and is probably by Reynolds. It shows her as a lady of fashion, a woman of spirit and intelligence as well as someone who has the beginnings of a double-chin. Although Maria had lost two husbands there was no reason why she should not, like her grandmother, marry a third time. Religion was no bar: her Church's rules on mixed marriages were far more relaxed than in later years and such marriages were increasingly common. Likewise, she had no wish to force her religious views onto others. An undated 'fragment' in Lady Anne Lindsay's papers records a conversation about Platonic relationships between men and women. Lady Anne noted that 'La Belle' – one of her nick-names for Maria – 'has been twice married & who means to do so again.' Not surprisingly, Maria had her fair share of interested admirers and in one of her most humorous letters to William Fermor she described her dismissal of one young man which probably occurred during the Brighton and Lewes races in 1783:

> I am sure you will be glad to hear that my poor <u>little Man</u> & I settled our affairs <u>in the DARK</u> perfectly to my <u>Satisfaction</u> dark I took care it should be & I believe he will remember it for some time for in going out of the Room he had like to have put an end of himself by tumbling over one of the chairs, & altho I was not dispos'd to laugh yr Verses & Nonsense came immediately to my assistance & I thought I should have expir'd upon the spot. I was not able to Speak for Laughing.

Carrying on in the same tone she asked Fermor to 'burn my letter otherwise the History of my little Man & me may perhaps become quite Scandalous & those that only know <u>that we have met</u> & that in <u>the Dark</u> I must own appearances would be much against me pray take care of my Reputation & indulge me.' If he couldn't bring himself to burn the letter he could hide it in the same place 'where I once found <u>Candide</u>'.

As Maria told Lady Anne, she was 'ashamed almost of being happy again'. But her natural spirits overruled her fears and Lady Anne, along with her sister, Lady Margaret, Maria's Uncle Errington and her aunt, Lady Sefton, now gave Maria her *entrée* back into the whirlwind of London society which by 1784 was centred not on the dull Court of George III and Queen Charlotte but on the King's brothers, the Dukes of Cumberland and

Gloucester and increasingly on the youthful Prince of Wales. It was, as the Prayer Book used to say, a 'naughty world'. Horace Walpole, who was now too old to be tempted, moaned that 'Dissipating is at high-water mark . . . Lateness of hours is the principal feature of the times . . . Every fashionable place is still crowded . . . gaming is yet general.'[3] This was the world Sheridan had laughed at in *The School for Scandal*, one filled by Lady Teazle, the careless wife, Charles Surface, the spendthrift and Sir Benjamin Backbite, the rumour-monger.

Adultery and illegitimacy were the talk of the town and it was said that every fifth child in London was illegitimate, compared to every sixth in Paris and every ninth in Dublin. Illegitimacy seemed to be an especially prominent feature of Whig society by the 1780s. As Lady Campbell later observed to her friend, Emily Eden, 'Does it not strike you that vices are wonderfully prolific among the Whigs? There are such countless illegitimates among them, such a tribe of Children of the Mist.' The children she had in mind belonged to the famous *ménage à trois* of the beautiful Duchess of Devonshire, her husband and her friend, Lady Elizabeth Foster. Among them they had four illegitimate children, while Georgiana's sister, the Countess of Bessborough, had two misty children herself. The Royal Family was not immune: Lord Wentworth told his sister that the Duchess of Gloucester's Lady of the Bedchamber, Lady Almeria Carpenter, had 'produced', that is, given birth to a child whose father was the Duke. Lady Anne's long engagement to Lord Wentworth had become 'common chit chat' but eventually collapsed, in part, because he would not give up his mistress and illegitimate children. When Lady Anne did marry her choice would be a younger man who probably had already had one illegitimate child and would go on to have two more. At the other end of the political and social scale, the radical pamphleteer who would make Maria's life a misery, Horne Tooke, had three illegitimate children, probably by two different women while another foe, John Walter, the founder of *The Times*, did not allow his having an illegitimate child to interfere with his denunciations of others who did the same.[4] The King's *bête noire*, John Wilkes, had been married, was estranged from his wife, kept a mistress, had a second family and used his illegitimate daughter as his housekeeper. Even Jane Austen felt able to permit Mrs Jennings in *Sense and Sensibility* to refer to a character's 'natural daughter' – albeit 'lowering her voice a little'.

Primitive forms of birth control combined with natural urges accounted for an amazing number of 'natural children', as they were known, and rumour produced many more. Lord Egremont, the owner of Petworth, patron of Turner, and friend of the Prince of Wales and later of Maria, recalled that in the 1780s 'there was hardly a young married lady of fashion, who did not think it almost a stain upon her reputation if she was not known as having cuckolded her husband; and the only doubt was, who was to assist her in the operation.' The Earl knew what he was talking about because he was credited with having left seventy-two illegitimate children at his death. It was rumoured that 'the Egremont nose could be traced all over Sussex.' Horace Walpole's father, the famous and long-lasting Prime Minister, had given his son an illegitimate sister, while yet another Prime Minister, Lord Melbourne, whose own paternity was sometimes questioned, would ask, 'Who the Devil knows who one's father is, anyway?'

Virtue was 'a phantom, a chimera, an ignis fatuus that bewilders the old, the decrepid, and deformed, but is never observed by the young, the gay, the spirited, and in a word, the *ton*.' As for the *ton*, it was 'never to be met with on the eastern side of Temple bar, where the tar of Thames-street, and the tallow of Blow-bladder-street contaminate the air, and give such an offensive smell to an alderman, or a common councilman's lady, as all the eau de luce in Warren or Bailey's shop cannot eradicate.' A 'complete gentleman' was defined as one 'who studies nothing but dress, address, and the graces and who devotes his whole time to cards; who detests musty authors, and still more their musty rules. A perfect connoisseur in cosmetics and perfumes, and a complete master of the ceremonies at toilettes and ruelles.'[5]

Gambling was as available as sex, particularly the fashionable card game of Faro based on 'faro banks' often located in the houses of aristocratic ladies and in one instance, of a royal lady, the Duchess of Cumberland, in Pall Mall. Indeed Pall Mall at one time had at least six faro banks. Sometimes the ladies received up to fifty guineas a night from the proprietor of the table and they used this, plus any earnings from the table, to pay their own gambling debts. These houses were not confined to the *bon ton*. The Prince of Wales's friend, George Hanger, remembered that 'if a gentleman in these days has but a few guineas in his purse, and will walk directly up to the Faro-table, he will be the most welcome guest in the house: it is not necessary for him to speak, or even bow, to a single lady in the room, unless some unfortunate woman at the gaming-table ask him politely for the loan of a few guineas: then his answer need be but short – "No, Dolly, no; can't."' Even worldly journals like *The Bon Ton Magazine* attacked these houses which existed 'to swindle the unsuspecting young men of fortune who are entrapped into these whirlpools of destruction' usually after they had been given too much wine. One of the most famous ladies who kept a 'faro table' was Lady Archer, 'a woman steeped to the crown of her head in infamy and vice'. Among Lady Archer's admirers was none other than Maria's Uncle Errington.

Another frequenter of these establishments was the man Maria would later describe as 'the most accomplished Prince of his age'. But he was much more than this. Charles Augustus Frederick, Prince of Wales and Duke of Cornwall, had been born on 12 August 1762 when Maria was a girl of six. He was the eldest of fifteen children born to George III and his consort, Queen Charlotte. Of these, thirteen survived childhood. The Prince became one of the most extraordinary combinations of vice and virtue ever to inherit the Crown. He grew up buffeted by the King's high moral code, the Queen's rigidity and the flattery of those round him. He was largely isolated from his parents and his childhood was tedious. He was clever and widely, if not deeply, educated. While he had a genuine interest in literature and learning, he was not inclined to hard work or perseverance of study. When writting to a close friend he admitted that 'I find my dear Hugh I have written to you upon a half sheet of Paper instead of a whole one, I hope you will excuse the great incivility, but I am really to <u>Georgelike</u>, alias lazy to write it over again.' His first biographer described his education as 'well calculated to render him a respectable scholar and an accomplished gentleman; but . . . it was ill calculated to make him either a prudent prince or a great monarch.'[6]

In 1774, when the Prince was twelve, his Governor, Lord Holderness wrote to him about the current gossip that Pope Clement XIV had been poisoned. The Prince became worried that he might suffer the same fate and Holderness told him he had no one to fear but himself: 'I know of but one person of whom the Prince should be diffident upon that account; I mean <u>George, Prince of Wales</u>, who, by giving a loose to his appetite, may be his own enemy and hurt an excellent constitution by <u>slow poison</u>.' Whereas his father was plodding and gauche, the Prince was quick and from an early age possessed a capacity for elegance and what would now be called a winning personality. He could be witty and was a great mimic. He genuinely loved art and music and had a good tenor voice. When he turned eighteen, one courtier, Charlotte Papendiek, wrote: 'His countenance was of a sweetness and intelligence quite irresistible. He had an elegant person, engaging and distinguished manners, added to an affectionate disposition and the cheerfulness of youth . . . He began his career with varied resources of amusement, rational in themselves, and usefull or agreeable to others. He was fond of music, sang well, and accompanied the piano on the violocello with taste and precision.' One MP wisely observed that if the King had 'possessed the grace of the Prince of Wales, [he] would have impressed all who approached him with a conviction of his capacity.' The father had the capacity while the son had the ability to convince others that he possessed what he did not.

The previous year, the Prince had described himself with

surprising honesty as well as accuracy. The Prince, he wrote in the third person:[7]

> is rather above the common size, his limbs well-proportioned, and upon the whole well made, though rather too great a penchant to grow fat. The features of his countenance carry with them too much of an air of hauteur, his forehead well shaped, his eyes though none of the best, and though grey, are yet passable, tolerable good eyebrows and eyelashes, <u>un petit nez retroussé cependant assez aimé</u> [a little turned up nose which is still rather attractive], a good mouth though rather large, with fine teeth, a tolerable good chin, but the whole of the countenance is too round. I forgot to add my uggly ears. As hair is generally looked upon as a beauty, he has more hair than usually falls to everyone's share . . . His sentiments and thoughts are open and generous, above doing anything that is mean (too susceptible, even to believing people his friends, and placing too much confidence in them, from not yet having a sufficient knowledge of the world . . .), grateful and friendly to excess when he finds a <u>real friend</u>. His heart is good and tender if it is allowed to show its notions . . . He has a <u>strict notion of honour</u>, rather too familiar to his inferiors . . .

The Prince then turned to his 'vices, or rather let us call them weaknesses – too subject to give loose or vent to his passions of every kind, too subject to be in a passion, but he never bears malice or rancour in his heart . . . he is rather too fond of wine and women.' Here again he was remarkably honest about himself or perhaps he was showing the capacity to detach himself from the realities of his own personality and of the world about him which was to mark his whole life. This comes out in a letter to the father of a close friend: 'I can not consider my self as call'd upon to explain any thing to the World at large.' As he would later say, 'I am a different Animal, a different Being from any other in the whole Creation.'[8]

The Court of George III and his consort was not one to provide much amusement to such a young man. It had all the dull formality of a petty German principality. One lady remembered the contrast between parents and son: 'The manners of the King would have almost choked a man who attempted a joke before he could get it out. Tommy Onslow once risked a joke of the mildest kind, and was disgraced. He had lost ten shillings to her Majesty at cassino; when he handed her half a guinea, saying, "There, please your Majesty, and sixpence for drink."' He did not appear at Court again. When George III and Queen Charlotte visited the Catholic peer, Lord Petre, the King found waiting for him 'his usual diet', that is bread pudding and potatoes while the Queen found in her dressing room her usual water gruel and barley water.

It is not surprising that the Prince sought his pleasures elsewhere. His parents and their Household, such as Charlotte Papendiek, lamented 'that some of those about the young Princes swerved from principle, and introduced improper company when their Majesties supposed them to be at rest; and after the divines had closed their day with prayer.' Years later the King would note, 'Almost all our young men of fashion have been spoiled by the same thing: by having a parcel of dirty toad eaters about them, who poison their minds.' By his sixteenth birthday it is accepted that George had not so much lost as thrown away his virginity, and he is supposed to have seduced Harriet Vernon, a Maid of Honour to the Queen and another woman known to history as Mrs M——, whose husband was in the Royal Household. Horace Walpole observed, 'truly, heirs apparent that grow up too fast, are a little inconvenient.'[9] When eighteen, the Prince had his first infatuation, with Mary Hamilton, who was seven years older than he. She had the wisdom to keep him at bay. He went into what his age called 'a pet' – the sort of behaviour his contemporaries would come to expect of this petulant young man – and wrote fulsome love letters. Then he dropped Mary to move onto his next great love but, it is worth noting, he kept Mary as a friend and confidante.

In December 1779 the Prince went to see *The Winter's Tale* at

Drury Lane and became infatuated with the actress, Mary Robinson, who was playing Perdita and who was four years older than he. To succeeding generations she has been known as Perdita and, as one of the definitions of this Latin adjective is 'immoderate,' it is not an unfitting name. She claimed to be the natural daughter of Lord Northington (she was not) and was at the time the mistress of Lord Malden, a friend of the Prince. (Lord Malden was also a friend of one of Maria's brothers, probably Jack, and in 1782 would urge his father to employ the young man as his steward.) Once again the enthusiastic lover besieged his chosen one with letters and this time they did the trick. She agreed to meet in private, although she refused to follow his wish that she sneak into Buckingham House disguised as a boy.

The Prince, ignoring Mary Hamilton's warning about Perdita's character, became her 'Florizel' and promised her a staggering £20,000 – over a million pounds in today's currency – when he came of age and he foolishly confirmed his offer in writing. He ordered a miniature of Perdita for himself and, probably, one of himself for her, from the society painter, Richard Cosway. Less flattering cartoons caricaturing 'Perdita' and 'Florizel' were soon appearing in London's shop windows and engravings were made of the Perdita miniature so that others could enjoy her beauty. After a few months the Prince grew tired of her or perhaps discovered that she had already served the needs of Lord Malden and others. He dropped her to seek his pleasures elsewhere. Perdita's dreams of a title were shattered. She wrote to her Florizel:

> I call Heaven to witness I am at this instant ignorant of the cause of your abandoning a woman whose life and soul should have been sacrificed to your peace and welfare. Your injustice surpasses your inconstancy . . . I once adored thee Florizel beyond human comprehension . . . I had every reason from your solem and sacred vows, to believe that when you obtained your liberty your Maria would be, the chosen friend of your bosom.

Perdita was also anxious about her financial future and, remembering the letters, added: 'I am no stranger to every thing that passes at Windsor. I have some friends nearer your Person than you imagine. A time will yet arrive when you will repent the steps you now take.' In the midst of all this the Prince had celebrated his eighteenth birthday and had been given his own 'establishment' or household but not his independence. This meant he had to ask the King – who asked his Prime Minister – to pay her £5,000 and an annuity of £500, half of which would on her death go to her daughter for her life.

In 1783 the MP for Liverpool, Colonel Banastre Tarleton, would win a £1,000 bet by obtaining Perdita's services as his mistress. She suffered a miscarriage that same year which resulted in a paralysing stroke. In 1798 Tarleton transferred his affections from Perdita to her daughter. By then the Prince was once again befriending 'his Perdita' and she eventually became a writer for the *Morning Post*, settled in Brighton and died, aged forty, in 1800.[10]

Having dropped Perdita, the Prince turned for companionship to Mrs Armistead, of whose early life his later biographer, Robert Huish, wrote, 'it becomes us not to speak.' She had already befriended Lord George Cavendish and would be passed on to Charles James Fox. There was also Mrs Billington, the celebrated singer who was known for 'the coarseness of her manners' as much as for her voice and Mrs Grace Dalrymple Elliott, the divorced wife of a wealthy doctor who, when not with the heir to the throne, was dispensing comfort to George Selwyn, William Windham and Lord Cholmondeley. (Any of these, or the Prince, may have fathered her illegitimate daughter, Georgiana.) When he tired of Mrs Elliott he turned to Lady Augusta Campbell, Lady Melbourne (mother of Queen Victoria's first Prime Minister), Elizabeth Billington, and the Countess of Salisbury.

Another of his loves was the Countess von Hardenburg, wife of the Hanoverian Count, Karl von Hardenburg. She was described by Charlotte Papendiek as 'a fine woman – rather of suspicious material from her inelegant manner, her repugnance to restraint and her want of real respect to royalty'. The countess at first rejected his overtures and the Prince fell ill. As he told his brother, Prince Frederick, 'I grew more & more fond of her, & to so violent a degree did I doat upon her, yt. it impaired my health & constitution very much . . . I have spit blood & am so much emaciated you would hardly know me again.' This was not his first collapse and it would not be the last but it was probably the first which resulted in his getting the woman he wanted.

Events now unfolded in a sequence worthy of a Viennese operetta. The *Morning Herald* reported that von Hardenburg had taken a house in Cork Street next door to, of all people, Perdita and that the Prince's carriage was reported as being constantly in front of the house. In truth, von Hardenburg's neighbour was not Perdita but a Polish countess named Mme Raouska and the carriage was not the Prince's but his uncle's, the Duke of Gloucester. When Count von Hardenburg heard of the affair he wrote to the Prince who panicked and asked the King for permission to flee abroad. This was not the last time the Prince would seek to rush away to Europe. The King naturally refused and reminded his heir that the country was at war. Then the German countess called the Prince's bluff and suggested they elope. This caused an even greater panic and the Prince ran to his mother, confessed everything and fainted. The Queen cried and told the King who acted in his usual straightforward way: he banished both the von Hardenburgs to Hanover. No wonder that society talked of 'the wild behaviour of a certain young person'.[11]

There was also talk that the Prince of Wales had approached the two daughters of Lord Spencer, Henrietta, married to the third Earl of Bessborough and Georgiana, wife of the fifth Duke of Devonshire, who would later become his close friend. Georgiana, 'the beautiful Duchess of Devonshire', was five years older than the Prince, ran up enormous gambling debts (and operated her own faro bank), spent fortunes on her fashionable clothes and jewels and would have an illegitimate child. She was active in opposition politics and was already playing an influential role in the Prince's future. The Prince's first biographer noted with Victorian verbosity, but with accuracy, of the twenty-year-old man: 'One of the greatest faults of the Prince of Wales, at this time, was his unbounded propensity for gallantry.'

Several things are worth remembering in this catalogue of affairs: the women with whom the Prince was seriously, if briefly, involved were older than he; fierce and passionate avowals of love were dispatched in lengthy letters; threats of suicide were flung about and copious tears were shed; and illnesses – real or feigned – arose when his demands were not met. As Maria would later observe after many years of close observation, the Prince 'always liked to make himself out worse than he was to excite compassion, and that he always wished everyone to think him dangerously ill, when little was the matter with him'. As the Duke of Wellington put it more bluntly. 'He loved a scene.' Gifts were showered; portraits, especially miniatures, then all the rage, were exchanged; and sex was usually demanded and frequently given. Then, like a summer's storm, the passion ended and the affair was wound up. Success was normal. The Prince 'had but one general aim, and if that aim were attained, he did not seem to trouble himself about the propriety or morality of the means which were employed for the purpose.'[12]

Part of the Prince's problem was that he had nothing to do. Without a career in the army or navy he had no obligations or duties to perform. The diarist, Douglas Sylvester, noted later a story from about this time: 'When the Prince first came out in life, it seems the King reproached him, one day, with his indolence in laying in bed very late in the morning. "I find, Sir," said he, "however late I rise, that the day is long enough for doing nothing."' He also had no close friends to whom he could turn. The Duchess of Devonshire described his life in 1782: 'As he only went out in secret, or with the King and Queen, he form'd very few connections with any other woman than women of the town. He rode constantly in the Park of a morning, where from the ladies in their carriages and on horse back he was considerably ogled.'

Maria later admitted that she was one of the ladies 'ogling' him. The Prince 'appear'd sometimes at the opera and the play where the same manège was continued from the boxes, and where much speculation was occasion'd by the bent of his R.H.'s lorgnette.' The King remained aloof and, to the Prince, censorious. The Queen, while more sympathetic, would not act without the King's direction. Prince Frederick, the brother who had been educated with the Prince and who had been his closest friend, had been sent to Hanover in 1780, partly to complete his military education and partly to get him away from his brother's influence. In the same year Lt. Colonel Gerard Lake, his first equerry, left to fight in the American war. Lake, a middle-aged man, had given the Prince sound advice and a listening ear and his removal was something of a disaster.

It was at Brookes Club in St James's Street that the heir to the throne associated with men who opposed his father's Court and the power of the Crown: the Duke of Devonshire, Lord Egremont (he who would eventually father the seventy-two natural children in Sussex), Lord Carlisle, Mr Fawkener and the rising star of the more radical section of the Whig party, Charles James Fox who remains one of the most extraordinary men in British political history. He was elected to the Commons when he was still only nineteen. He was 'rather a prodigy as a party man than eminent or sagacious as a statesman'. His supporters, who were 'dazzled by the splendour of his abilities were blind to his vices & worshipped his authority'.[13] By 1782 Fox was Foreign Secretary in Lord Rockingham's administration and had emerged as one of the closest and one of the most influential of the young Prince's friends. In large part the friendship was another means by which the Prince could carry on his war with his father. For years Fox had been disliked by the King as much for his immorality as for his political views. He had attacked the Royal Marriage Act, advocated letting reporters into the Commons, wanted a weakening of the Crown's influence (but not of the growing power of the Commons), supported the American colonists and wanted full political rights for Dissenters and Catholics. He had fought a duel and had had several mistresses (two of whom were discards from the Prince).

Fox was clever, arrogant, educated, dissolute, dirty and, when need arose, possessed of the most amazing energy. He was always in debt and sometimes his creditors seized his effects and books from his lodgings which were, appropriately, near Brookes Club in St James's Street. His style, however, was never hampered by his chaotic private life. While his political judgment was not always sound, he remained a most formidable force in national politics. Walpole, writing in 1781, described his behaviour: 'Mr Fox is the first figure in all the places I have mentioned – the hero in parliament, at the gaming-table, at Newmarket. Last week he passed four-and-twenty hours without interruption at all three, or on the road from one to the other – and ill the whole time, for he has a bad constitution.' Fox saw the young Prince's friendship and, on occasion, adoration, as invaluable for himself and his Parliamentary allies. But Fox was also a loyal friend who would give the Prince detached advice in the years to come. To some degree he was a replacement for the missing Lake.

Two other great influences on the young Prince were his father's brothers, the Dukes of Gloucester and Cumberland. In 1781 Horace Walpole described the situation, showing how the Prince's private life had already become inseparable from politics: 'The youngest uncle [Cumberland] has got possession of the eldest nephew, and sets the father at defiance. A moppet [the Marquis of Rockingham] in Grosvenor Square has conceived hopes from this rising storm, which are about as well founded as any of his pretensions have ever been.' Both Cumberland and Gloucester had married against the wishes of their brother. Cumberland had married a somewhat shady widow, while Gloucester had been banished from the Court for his marriage to the dowager Countess Waldegrave, an illegitimate niece of George II's Prime Minister, Sir Robert Walpole and a cousin of Horace.

It was Cumberland who had the greater influence over his

71

nephew, even if his familiarity and love of boxing offended the Prince. Not only had the Duke married a woman deemed to be vulgar by the Court but he allowed his London home to become a gambling house and he dabbled in Opposition politics against the King. When Walpole wrote his memoirs in the following decade he described Cumberland as 'weak and debauched', a view echoed by Wraxall who called him 'a very weak man'. The Duchess, continued Wraxall, 'by no means wanted talents, but they were more specious than solid, better calculated for show than for use, for captivating admiration than for exciting esteem'. Cumberland House in Pall Mall quickly became the major alternative to the Court, 'the central point of elegant amusement in the metropolis' in which 'a crowd of distinguished persons male and female filled the apartments once every week'.

Part of the dilemma faced by the Prince was the network of laws and Hanoverian customs that limited his choice of a bride. In 1783 his dilemma had been spelt out during a dinner party given for the Prince by Lord Lewisham and recounted by Horace Walpole:

> The foreign *Altesse* [the Prince of Wales] said he envied the Dukes of Devon and Rutland, who though high and mighty princes too, had been at liberty to wed two charming women whom they liked – but for his part he should be forced to marry some ugly German B—— – I forget the other letters of the word – and then turning to the Irish Master of the Rolls [Richard Rigby], asked what *he* would advise him to do? – 'Faith, sir,' said the Master, 'I am not drunk enough to give advice to a Prince of —— – about marrying.'

Walpole added that 'it is one of the best answers I have ever heard. How many fools will drink themselves sober enough to advise his Altesse on whatever he consults them!' There would be fools a plenty to do just that in the years to come.

Since he had turned twenty-one the Prince had more money

than ever: £62,000 [over £3.5m]. In addition there was a grant from the King of £30,000 [£1.7m] to set up his own establishment and a further £30,000 to settle his debts. More importantly, the King gave him Carlton House which had been the home of the King's mother. It stood on the site of Carlton House Terrace and had gardens running all the way down to Marlborough House. By November he could tell Prince Frederick, 'I am hard at work upon my mansion at Carlton House . . . I am adding & building considerable to it.' It was a task that would not be completed for thirty years. When Horace Walpole finally saw the Prince's 'new palace in Pall Mall' he was charmed: 'It will be the most perfect in Europe. There is an august simplicity that astonished me. You cannot call it magnificent; it is the taste and propriety that strike . . . but whence the money is to come, I cannot conceive . . . all the tin-mines in Cornwall would not pay a quarter.' Carlton House would soon overtake his uncle's Cumberland House as the anti-Court watering hole for the *bon ton*.

It was not long before public criticism began to be heard. In the summer of 1784 one pamphleteer, 'Neptune', referred to the Prince's 'irregularities' and 'juvenile indiscretions', to his 'imprudent choice of friends' and to the 'meanest and most dangerous debaucheries' and added that 'The public, Sir, are under no obligation to discharge those debts which your profussion has created.' Taking on the mantle of the prophet, Neptune warned: 'He is no longer juvenile, and he will do well to remember, that what are follies at TWENTY are vices at FORTY.'

In November 1783 the Prince took his seat in the Lords and the following month promised his father not to oppose His Majesty's government. He did not long keep his promise. That winter was one of the coldest in recorded history and on 30 January Londoners gathered to watch a man walk across the frozen Thames from Rotherhithe to Wapping New Stairs. Far more thrilling was the cut and thrust of Westminster, dominated by the question of who was to govern India. The coalition, of which Fox was a member, wanted a board of commissioners to replace the East India

Company. This was not for the good of India but to give the government and not the King the control over patronage and hence over the Commons itself. They were defeated in the Lords (urged on by the King) and not for the last time the Upper House protected the nation from the schemes of the lower. George III now took his chance to get rid of the Fox-North Coalition and installed the youthful Pitt at the head of a minority government. Fox's hatred of the King grew to even greater heights and when Parliament reassembled on 12 January 1784 the Prince attended the Lords as a measure of support for Fox. This gesture 'was not much relished by some of the members. It gave rise to an idle notion of a fourth estate to be added by way of tinkering of the constitution.'[14]

The King felt he had little choice but to dissolve Parliament on 25 March to give Pitt a working majority through a general election. This became one of the bitterest elections of the reign, a contest largely between the Crown and Fox. Fox's campaign in the enormous constituency of Westminster became the focus of attention. As Lord Wentworth told his sister, 'There is very little news going forward, save Electioneering . . . Politics . . . now leave no time for scandal'. Whig ladies, led by the Duchess of Devonshire, campaigned for Fox and wore fox tails in their hats. The Tory papers noted that 'the D—— of D—— grants *favours* to those who promise their votes and interest to Mr Fox.' Politics even invaded the Opera House when one evening the Tory Duchess of Rutland cried out, 'D—— Fox' before the entire house. The Whig, Lady Maria Waldegrave, replied, 'D—— Pitt' and the witty Lady Sefton added, 'This was a great <u>Aria</u> in the history of England.'[15]

When Fox was narrowly declared one of the two victors, his supporters carried him in a chair draped with laurel and when the mob passed Devonshire House the Prince stood on the garden wall with the Duchess of Devonshire on one side and the Duchess of Portland, whose husband led the Whig party, on the other. The Prince was dressed in Fox's colours, buff and blue, which also were the colours worn by the American rebels who had been waging war against his father. Afterwards came the parties and balls, some at Carlton House. At one the Prince drank so much that he collapsed on the ball room floor and, when being helped to his feet, was sick.[16]

These then were exciting times to be young, wealthy and in rebellion against one's parents. What was needed was another romantic adventure. The time and the woman were about to meet for we know that Maria was in London early in March. Her uncle, whom she normally referred to simply as 'Errington' urged her to accept her cousin, Lord Sefton's invitation to make up a party in the Seftons' box at the opera. As an old woman she recalled that she had agreed only 'on Lord Sefton consenting to her going in a Cap and Bonnet and a veil. She left the Opera leaning on Henry Errington's arm . . . and when at the door, with her veil down waiting for her carriage, the Prince came up to him and said, "Who the Devil is that pretty girl you have on your arm, Henry?" the latter told the Prince who she was and then introduced him to Mrs Fitzherbert.'

The Prince who met Maria in 1784 was described by his friend, the Duchess of Devonshire:

The Prince of Wales is rather tall and has a figure which tho' striking is not perfect. He is inclined to be too fat and looks too much like a woman in men's cloaths, but the graceful-ness of his manner and his height certainly make him a pleasing figure. His face is very handsome and he is fond of dress even to a tawdry degree . . . His person, his dress and the admiration he has met, and thinks still more that he meets, from women take up his thoughts chiefly. He is good natur'd and rather extravagant. From the usual turn of his character, and some shabby traits to his mistresses one should imagine he was more inclin'd to extravagance than generosity, tho' at the same time two or three very generous things to his friends in distress do him the highest honour . . . But he certainly does not want for understanding, and his jokes sometimes

have an appearance of wit. He appears to have an inclination to meddle with politics, he loves being of consequence
. . . He is suppos'd to be capricious in his tastes and inclina-
tions, but this more so than he really is.

There has always been some debate as to the date of meeting.
The Prince himself once dated it to 1781 and once to 1782 but these
might refer to his first knowing of or first seeing Maria. He was
not possessed of an aptitude for chronological exactitude. Her
recollection, given over half a century after the event, is confirmed
as early as 1789 when a pamphlet attacking Maria recalled that
'The first time the Prince saw Mrs F—— was in Lady Sefton's box,
at the Opera, and the novelty of her face more than the brilliancy
of her charms, had the usual effect of enamouring the Prince. There
may also have been a certain <u>triste</u> aspect which attracted the
Prince.' As Lady Anne Lindsay put it, 'Her fame was a spotless
one, but her heart seemed defended by the past.' As always with
Maria there is some confusion. Lady Anne claimed that it was in
her box at the opera that the Prince came up and asked 'Who is
that Angel . . . in a white hood?' One suspects this is an enhanced
version of the same incident. On her income Lady Anne could not
have afforded a box which in this case was probably Lady Sefton's.
Lady Anne may well have been one of the party.
Within days the young Prince launched another of his
campaigns to win the heart of yet another woman he desired and
society began talking. Lady Anne's long-standing fiancé told his
sister early in March that 'the Ball last night was most brilliant, &
well conducted. The only fault was that which is common to all
those things in this country . . . that it was too crouded. His
Highness is making fierce love to ye Widow FitzHerbert, & I think
will succeed.' Others had their doubts. Georgiana Devonshire had
seen many other such campaigns, and had once been a besieged
fortress herself. She noted that same month that 'Mrs. Fitzherbert
is at present his favourite, but she seems, I think rather to cut him
than otherwise.' Soon the *bon ton* was taking notice of Mrs

Fitzherbert. The Whig *Morning Herald* noted that 'Mrs. *Fitzherbert* is arrived in London for the season.'[17] Knowing readers would have smiled at that seemingly bald statement.

Decades later, when talking with Lord Stourton, Maria would refer with admirable understatement and some little dissimulation to the prospect which now opened up before her: 'She was very reluctant to enter into engagements fraught with so many embarrassments, and, when viewed in their fairest light, exposing their object to great sacrifices and difficulties. It is not, therefore, surprising that she resisted, with the utmost anxiety and firmness, the flattering assiduities of the most accomplished Prince of his age. She was well aware of the gulf that yawned beneath those flattering demonstrations of royal adulation.' A hostile biographer of the Prince would later say that Maria was not 'likely to surrender upon common terms'. She was looking to a 'more brilliant prospect'.[18]

This new romantic crusade had therefore something of the forbidden fruit about it. By refusing to become his mistress, was Maria inviting her latest suitor to offer marriage? Her later behaviour shows that she understood what was at stake because of her religion and any offer of marriage was probably the Prince's idea more than her demand. In other ways she fitted into the pattern already established: she was older (by six years); she was more widely travelled; she had seen more of life and of the world than he; and she was buxom. She was attractive, if not, like Perdita, stunningly beautiful. She had style, and she was sure of herself to a degree that some described as hauteur. She demanded respect. By so doing she met a need the younger man had felt for many years. In the midst of his passion for Mary Hamilton he had the insight to write: 'After the impetuous ardor of youth, and the violent impulse of passion is passed, then it is that one wishes to find a companion for life.'

Many years later Lady Charlotte Bury recorded a conversation that helps to explain the Prince's fascination with Maria:

I dined with Sir ——. In speaking of Mrs. F ——, he told me
that she had a stronger hold over the Regent than any of the
other objects of his admiration, and that he always paid her
the respect which her conduct commanded. 'She was,' said
Sir ——, 'the most faultless and honourable mistress that ever
a prince had the good fortune to be attached to; and certainly
his [later] behaviour to her is one of the most unamiable traits
of his character. I remember, in the early days of their
courtship, when I used to meet them every night at Sir ——'s
at supper. The Prince never forgot to go through the form of
saying to Mrs F. with a most respectful bow, 'Madam, may I
be allowed the honour of seeing you home in my carriage.'

The unnamed observer added 'that it was impossible to be in his
Royal Highness's society, and not be captivated by the extreme
fascination of his manners, which he inherits from his mother, the
Queen; for his father has every virtue which can adorn a private
character, as well as make a king respectable, but he does not excel
in courtly grace or refinement.'[19] The recollection of this unnamed
source not only rings true but accords with observations made by
others at the time. Maria had the ability to hold her own and part
of the appeal, therefore, lay in the elaborate and courtly mating
game which both parties enjoyed performing in public.

Another of Maria's appeals – as of other women whom the
Prince courted – was her matronly bosom. George Hanger, one of
the Prince's shadier retainers, recorded an exchange between the
Prince and Sheridan in which the Prince 'talked of the beauty of
the female bosom' and said he had read in Dr Erasmus Darwin
that man's fascination with this was because of 'our first suste-
nance'. 'Indeed,' said Sheridan, with a smile, 'then why do we not
feel the same delight at the contemplation of a <u>wooden spoon</u>?'
'Excellent!' exclaimed the Prince, 'excellent – in future I shall never
see a beautiful bosom but I shall think of Sheridan's wooden spoon
– nevertheless, you must allow that contemplation is one thing,
enjoyment another.'[20]

The Prince's relationship with Maria may also be seen, and probably was, part of his warfare with his father. It was part and parcel not just of his helter-skelter life, nor of the enthusiasms created by the current political upheavals but a hearkening back to the time when the naughty little boy had been banished the King's room only to thrust his head round the doorway and scream, 'Wilkes and Liberty!' It is an interesting comment on George III's family history that those sons who would marry illegally all married older and more experienced women, as had the King's two brothers.

The Prince now laid siege to Maria Fitzherbert with the 'flattering assiduities' to which she later referred. He undoubtedly showered her with jewels and presents and in May commissioned Gainsborough to paint his new love. The painting shows her in the height of fashion, her head resting on her right arm and with her distinctive nose and a somewhat pensive air as she stares into the middle distance, away from the viewer. There was in addition, a torrent of over-long love letters which were later destroyed. He told his absent brother, Frederick, in May that 'I have some very extraordinary business wh. I cd. wish to see you in order to talk over with you.' With uncharacteristic prudence, he added that it was 'impossible for me ever to trust it to paper.'

Maria's reaction to all this was a mixed one: feelings of enjoyment at her new social pre-eminence, whatever her reservations as an old woman, and panic at the legal consequences. First was the enjoyment. The *Morning Herald* reported that 'A new Constellation has lately made an appearance in the fashionable hemisphere . . . The Widow of the late Mr Fitzherbert has in her train half our young nobility. As the Lady has not, as yet, discovered a partiality for any of her admirers, they are all animated with hopes of success.' In her old age she remembered fondly James Hook's ballad, 'The Lass of Richmond Hill'. The song's opening line 'On Richmond Hill there lives a lass' seemed appropriate since Maria had taken a country residence in Richmond – but more to the point was the refrain:

> This lass so neat with smiles so sweet
> Has won my right good will;
> I'd crowns resign to call thee mine,
> Sweet lass of Richmond Hill.

Unfortunately, the elderly Maria's memory was conflating events. James Hook's song, which was not written until about 1787, was probably not sung at Vauxhall until the next year. Londoners would not have known, or cared, that the lass in question was most likely a Yorkshire girl but they would by then have seen how apt the song was to Maria.

The Prince decided to bring up his reserves. He approached the Duchess of Devonshire, told her of 'his passion for Mrs F. and his design to marry her'. We see here the impact Maria had had: never before had the Prince talked of marriage but only of possession. Any remonstrance from Georgiana was 'as always follow'd by threats of killing himself &c.' At last he got the Duchess to call on Maria. The Duchess later recalled that Maria 'agreed with me in the impossibility of his ideas; and her good sense & resolution seem'd so strong that I own I felt secure of her never giving way, and what I had occasion to observe of her conduct unfortunately prepossess'd me in this idea.' For her part, Lady Anne reminded Maria of the provisions of the Act of Succession and the Royal Marriage Act. In the midst of the enjoyment came the panic at the dilemma Maria faced. If she would not become the Prince's mistress and would not drop him, then she could only demand marriage but this he could not offer. 'I remember,' she told Lady Anne, 'my Mother always recommended . . . to throw cold water on my lovers if I did not like them.' The Prince's parents, who were well aware of his latest romance and its potential dangers, appreciated Maria's cold water policy and she later claimed that they sent her a friendly message praising her self-control. The difficulty for Maria was that she increasingly found this man both attractive and lovable.

* * *

Any marriage between the Prince and a Catholic could destroy the dynasty. The very basis of the constitution presumed this would never happen but, to be sure, Parliament had passed various acts to make it impossible. The most important was the Act of Settlement of 1701. The act was passed after the death of Princess Anne's heir, the young Duke of Gloucester in 1700. Its aim was to secure a Protestant succession to the Crown. Parliament excluded the Catholic Stuarts and defined England as a Protestant nation: 'Whereas it hath been found by experience, that it is inconsistent with the safety and welfare of this protestant kingdom, to be governed by a popish prince, or by any king or queen marrying a papist'. Parliament provided that anyone who 'is, are, or shall be reconciled to, or shall hold communion with, the see or church of Rome, or shall profess the popish religion, or *shall marry a papist*, shall be excluded and be for ever incapable to inherit, possess or enjoy the crown and government of this realm and Ireland, and the dominions thereunto belonging'. Such a person would be considered dead and the succession would pass on to 'such person or persons, being protestants'. The Hanoverian George III and not the Stuart 'Charles III' ruled because of this act.

The second constitutional block to the marriage was the Royal Marriage Act of 1772 which stated 'That no descendant of the body of his late majesty king George the Second, Male or Female . . . shall be capable of contracting Matrimony, without the previous Consent of His Majesty, His Heirs or successors, signified under the Great Seal, and declared in Council'. Any marriage contracted without the King's consent was 'void'. The punishment was *praemunire* under which those convicted would forfeit their possessions to the King and be subject to imprisonment 'at His Majesty's pleasure'. If a member of the Royal Family violated the Act, the King would then apply to the ecclesiastical court to annul the marriage. In the event, as Lord Eldon, a renowned Lord Chancellor, once remarked, it would actually be impossible to prosecute under the Royal Marriage Act because no one 'could prove the marriage except a person who had been present . . . [and] nobody present could be compelled to be a witness' because one cannot be forced to incriminate oneself in a British court. Even if one could prove an illegal marriage under the act this might well then have excused Maria from prosecution under the Act of Settlement. A clever barrister could have argued that if the Prince were not free to marry her, then there could have been no marriage, and if no marriage, then no violation of the Act of Settlement. This argument was put about in Maria's lifetime but two years after her death it was rejected by Lord Brougham, a former Lord Chancellor.

However, if a descendant of George II, having been told he could not marry, still wished to do so once he had passed his twenty-fifth birthday, he could notify the Privy Council of his desire. He would then have to wait twelve months and if, in that time, both Houses of Parliament did not declare their opposition to the match, he could get married. Within a few months of the bill's passing into law the King was shocked to learn that his favourite brother, the Duke of Gloucester, had been married for six years to Maria Waldegrave, the illegitimate daughter of one of the Walpoles. The stable door had not been shut in time. Critics also pointed out that because the Sovereign could still control both Houses of Parliament, he could alter the succession by having Parliament reject the marriage of one son in order to allow another to marry and carry on the line.

The third barrier was the 1753 Marriage Act (Lord Hardwicke's Act), which required vows be taken before a clergyman inside an Anglican church, unless permission were given for the marriage to take place elsewhere. The Book of Common Prayer had to be used and as always banns had to be read in the parish churches of both parties. Only Jews and Quakers were excepted. Dispensations or 'licences' to be married without banns and not in a church could only be granted by the Church of England. Obviously the Prince could hardly ask for banns to be read in Maria's parish church, St George's, Hanover Square.

The marriage would also have been illegal under an Act of 1714 which outlawed anyone's doing anything to prevent the heir from succeeding to the Crown. This could have been used against Maria and the punishment would be fearsome: being drawn to Tyburn where she would be hanged. Also, of course, until 1791 it was technically illegal for a Papist to reside in the City of Westminster, as Maria did. Finally, under the Royal Marriage Act it was illegal not just for a clergyman to solemnise a marriage forbidden by the act but for anyone to 'assist' or be present at such a marriage.

Therefore we have to ask, as did people at the time, could any such marriage be a real marriage? Yes and no are the answers. In English law, whatever the deluded Prince convinced himself, the answer was no because of the Royal Marriage Act, the Act of Settlement and Lord Hardwicke's Act. The marriage, if there were witnesses and a validly ordained priest of the Church of England to perform it, would, in the eyes of the Church of England, be a 'valid' marriage because the three basic stipulations had been met: the man and woman were capable of being husband and wife, that is, not already married or under-age (fourteen for men and twelve for women); each party had the 'will' to marry, that is, was not mentally incapable and was not being forced to act against his will; thirdly, there was an actual contract which really meant an exchange of vows.

To Maria's fellow Catholics it was also a valid marriage. As the decrees of the Council of Trent were not allowed into England, English Catholics were still governed by the pre-Reformation rules. These stipulated that a free exchange of vows between people who had no impediments constituted a valid, albeit in Maria's case, a clandestine, marriage. A Catholic priest did not have to be present. Of course, if either the Church of England or the Catholic Church argued that being 'free' to marry included being free of legal restraints, then the Prince was not free because of the Royal Marriage Act and the marriage could not be a valid marriage under canon law of either Church. There is one final point in this legal jungle: German usage meant that Maria could not become Electress of Hanover because she was not a member of a royal family.

We know that both Maria and the Prince understood at least the major provisions of the Royal Marriage Act and the Act of Settlement because the Prince told some of his friends that he would repeal the Royal Marriage Act when he succeeded to the throne. The Prince's confused thinking would suggest his understanding was somewhat shallow and the same was probably true for Maria who frequently asked Lady Anne to explain things to her. Maria's education in a French convent would hardly have included much English history, let alone constitutional law. Maria trusted the Prince who trusted his ability to 'get away' with things which would be, somehow or other, 'sorted out'. After all, English Catholics were used to having draconian laws ignored in their particular cases.

Matters came to a head in the same month in which Gainsborough began to paint his pensive portrait of Maria. They centred on her natural desire to escape, as she told Lady Anne: 'What shall I do my dear soul. I can't get rid of him somehow and it keeps me quite in a fever.' Lady Anne recommended Maria visit her parents who were then in Bath where her father was taking the waters for his gout. If a trip to Bath were not the answer, perhaps the continent would be far enough away. This time her friend's suggestion would do the trick. Lady Anne Lindsay had recently had a stroke of good luck. An elderly admirer informed her that he intended to leave a considerable sum of money to her and her sister, Margaret, and that he wanted to give them an advance on their expected inheritance. Lady Anne had never been wealthy. Now she had enough money to indulge in a luxury. She bought her own carriage, albeit a second-hand one, and knew that she could afford the £300 a year it cost to maintain it. Outside, her 'almost new' post-chaise was painted a dark chocolate while inside the seats were covered with a becoming shade of rose taffeta. (She replaced the former owner's widow's cipher with her and her sister's ciphers.) Lady Anne, now armed with carriage, ciphers and enough funds looked about for a companion for a leisurely continental jaunt. She had decided that for the first time in their lives she and her sister would be separated for a while. Anne saw herself as an ideal traveller: 'I am young enough to be gay, old enough to be discreet; great enough to be well received every where, and small enough to be anyone's equal.' Yet neither of the ladies she first asked to join her had the time or money for such a tour. When on 1 May Maria called at her house, Lady Anne confided her desire for a trip. For Maria this was just the solution she desperately desired. They agreed to meet in Dover.

At this stage in Maria's life Lady Anne Lindsay begins to play a major role. 'Sister Anne', as the Prince called her, was already in the confidence of the two lovers. The surviving letters in her papers and the journal she kept of their travels are the best – indeed the only – account of how Maria would spend the most crucial period of her life. Lady Anne's journal gives us the most perceptive, full and balanced portrayal of Maria Fitzherbert, while keeping an account of a friend who was now the talk of London society caused her to remember other aspects of Maria's life since they had first met in 1778.

Any biographer must approach his sources with due care and attention. Lady Anne was already aware that Maria's relations with the Prince were taking on historical importance and she was attracted by the unfolding drama in which she would soon play a role. She was aware that Maria had already had some message from the King and Queen approving her rejection of their son's demands. She also knew the Prince's disparaging comments about his own parents. Maria, he said, was as good as 'any twopence-halfpenny Princess from Mecklenburg' which was, of course, where the Queen had been born. As for 'old squaretoes', that is the King, (so dubbed for his unfashionable footware) the Prince did not think his father's abandonment of his early love for Lady Sarah Lennox (Fox's aunt) in order to marry a Princess of Mecklenburg should form a precedent for his successors.

Lady Anne was a superb writer and knew a good story when

she heard it. She had a strong romantic streak and liked, with a dram of literary license, to regard Maria as fleeing a call to be Queen of England. She also knew that she could increase her income through writing. There is evidence that she was considering writing another of the travel books that were so popular in the eighteenth century. One has only to think of Smollett's *Travels in France and Italy* and Sterne's *A Sentimental Journey through France and Italy*. When Boswell's *Journal of a Tour to the Hebrides* was published on 1 October 1785 it confirmed the new genre: travel books about the journeys of famous people. Lady Anne noted down conversations in her journal just as her friend and fellow Scot, Boswell, had done when travelling with Dr Johnson. But she was careful not to let Maria know that she was keeping a journal as her friend 'would have been annoyed at the idea of being recorded for anything'. Even so, Maria understood that no one knew her better than Lady Anne. In later years, when Maria was ill, she proposed leaving her papers to Lady Anne so that she could write her biography. Anne refused on the simple ground that she was five years older than Maria and in the event she would die twelve years before her friend. She also added the difficulty faced by all biographers: what she would write would not have been what Maria would have wanted. Even with these caveats we are left with a marvellous account, hitherto unused by Maria's biographers. Lady Anne's occasional exaggerations or insertions never detract from her journal's value.

The two women's plan to leave London quickly was soon in disarray. Lady Anne came down with a sore throat. For some reason the trip was put aside, probably because of the pleadings of the Prince. By early July Maria was really becoming anxious. On 5 July the Duchess of Devonshire told her mother that 'The Prince of Wales has been like a madman. He was ill last Wednesday and took three pints of Brandy which killed him. He was confined three days to his bed – I fancy he has made himself worse than he was in hopes to prevent the departure for Spa of a certain lady

who goes in spite of all on Wednesday.' The Prince confirmed
some of this when he wrote to Frederick on Sunday, 6 July that
within the next six weeks he hoped himself to leave for Europe
and to visit his brother, then in Vienna. In part he was, once again,
trying to run away from a problem, the 'enormous expence' of
rebuilding Carlton House. In part it was 'ye. wish of travelling for
ye. sake of dissipation & partly <u>ye. very very unpleasant situation
I am in at home</u>.' 'Luckily,' he added, the King 'cannot prevent
me.' He hoped to winter abroad, either in Vienna or Paris, 'I am
not sure which.' The Prince had intended to send his henchman,
George Hanger, to tell Frederick all about 'ye. secret' but had
changed his mind. Now, however, 'I think it safest to preserve it
in petto till I have ye. happiness, my dearest brother, of once more
seeing you.' He added that 'a very violent & nasty fever' had kept
him at home for a week. With his usual exaggeration he added,
'I am grown so thin, yt. I think you cd. not possibly know me.'[21]

In her old age, Maria remembered these months as ones in which
she felt like a besieged castle. Her admiring relative, Lord Stourton,
described her recollections: 'For some time her resistance had been
availing, but she was about to meet with a species of attack so
unprecedented and alarming, as to shake her resolution, and to
force her to take that first step which afterwards led by slow (but
on the part of the Prince successful) advances, to that union which
he so ardently desired, and to obtain which he was ready to risk
such personal sacrifices.' The 'unprecedented and alarming'
storming of the castle took place on the evening of 8 July 1784,
the night before she and Lady Anne had finally agreed to leave
for Spa. Four men – Thomas Keate, the Prince's physician, Lord
Onslow, a member of the Prince's circle and a great practical joker,
the Hon. Edward Bouverie, another member of the Prince's
Household and, most important of all, Lord Southampton, head
of his Household – arrived at Park Street 'in the utmost consternation.'

The frantic men told Maria that the Prince 'was in imminent
danger – that he had stabbed himself – and that only *her* immediate

presence would save him.' He was, in gambling terms, raising the stakes: if illness could win love, then a hint of death might bring about a marriage. (It is possible that he had just discussed his passion with Fox who had, once again, poured cold water on it.) Maria, who by now had got the measure of her passionate lover, replied that 'nothing would induce her to enter Carlton House'. While she moved in the great world and associated with people such as Henry Errington and the Seftons, she retained her virtue and dignity: these she would leave at the door were she to enter Carlton House. Eventually she was 'brought to share in the alarm' but even then she did not lose her self-control. She was perfectly aware of the antics associated with the Prince and feared 'some stratagem derogatory to her reputation'. She therefore insisted 'upon some lady of high character accompanying her, as an indispensable condition; the Duchess of Devonshire was selected.'

When the party got to Devonshire House they found the Duchess entertaining friends to supper and cards. She was probably not playing herself: given her current gambling debts of £2,200 [£125,000] she was wise in her abstention. She later told her mother what happened: 'They told me P. had run himself through the body and missed his heart by the breadth of a nail and that to prevent his tearing off his bandages Mrs F. was to send him some flattering message such as a kind of promise of marriage.' The Duchess wanted this confirmed by Keate and he 'swore that he had barely missed his heart and they said Lord Southampton was sent for as there was an idea of informing the King for if P. had died they might all have been tried for their lives.' In a later memorandum the Duchess remembered that the Prince had demanded Maria's presence. The Duchess was told that 'she was waiting without and would and indeed cd not go unless I wd accompany her.' The Duchess went out to find Maria in her carriage. The reinforced group set out for Carlton House.[22]

Once Maria was brought into the Prince's bedroom she found him bandaged and lying in bed, 'pale and covered with blood'. He foamed at the mouth, tossed about in agony, had blood stains on his shirt and struck his head against the wall. The sight 'so overpowered her faculties, that she was deprived almost of all consciousness'. She was not so overwhelmed, however, that she did not notice some brandy and water beside the bed. The Prince told her that the only thing that would 'induce him to live' was her promise to become his wife. A ring, now in the Royal Archives, Windsor, was produced, probably one belonging to the Duchess, and the bizarre occasion ended as the Prince put it on her finger, thereby regaining some composure. The melodramatic tantrum was over. To the Prince it constituted a marriage. To Maria, if it meant anything, it was a promise to marry after she returned from Europe. The question everyone asked and still asks was put to Maria by Lord Stourton. Did she 'not believe that some trick had been practised, and that it was not really the blood of His Royal Highness.' Some suggested the Prince had torn off the bandage placed on the wound caused when Keate had recently bled him. She answered 'in the negative' and added that 'she had frequently seen the scar'.

Maria and the Duchess now fled back to Devonshire House but not before they had talked to Lord Southampton. The poor man was, quite naturally, 'very much frighten'd'. On their way back the two women discussed what had happened. Maria now said she regarded her promise to marry the Prince as 'null' because it had been extorted under duress. (She could have added that he was probably drunk and she may well have believed he had been play-acting. After all, she did not see the 'wound' until months after this event.) Once inside, the two women drew up a document which they both signed. Because it had gone midnight the two ladies dated the document as of 9 July:

On Tuesday the 8th of July 1784 Mr Bouverie and Mr Onslow came to me & told me the Prince of Wales had run himself thro' the body, & declar'd he wd tear open his bandages unless I wd accompany Mrs Fitzherbert to him.

We went there & she promis'd to marry him at her return,

but she conceives as well as myself that promises obtain'd in such a manner are entirely void.

The Duchess and Maria signed the statement and others of the party who had come back with them affixed their seals. The poor Duchess was so frightened that she wrote to Lord Southampton 'an account of all I knew – marriage and all', which implies he had not been in the bedroom. Southampton wrote back that 'he should not tell the King and that he looked upon it as a boyish act'.[23]

The following day Maria set out for Dover. Her departure meant that Gainsborough was unable to finish his portrait and it was delivered unfinished by 'His Highness's orders'. While travelling Maria wrote to Lord Southampton 'protesting against what had taken place, as not being then a free agent'. As she set out for France the Prince went to Lord Southampton's country estate 'for change of air'. If Maria thought her absence would put an end to this affair she would be proved wrong. It was only the beginning of a relationship that would last, on and off, for twenty-seven years, one that would give her a unique place in British history.

4

MILADIES ABROAD

When Lady Anne arrived in Dover she had some difficulty in finding Maria, who had moved on to a more suitable hotel and they had little time to accomplish their first task – selecting a way to cross the Channel. For Maria this was always difficult as throughout her long life, with its frequent travels, she never ceased to hate the sea. Lady Anne was quite content to take a place in the ordinary Dover packet boat at half a guinea per person. 'Fitz' – as Anne often calls her – did not like 'the common packet! to her who was running away from being Queen of England'. Maria's servants, who took their cue from their mistress, included her lady's maid and her butler. They were aghast at the thought of their 'lady . . . going in a boat with all sorts of creatures'. So a packet was hired at six guineas plus two guineas for each of their two carriages. For her part Lady Anne was accompanied by her own maid and footman.[1] A final member of their party was a gentleman anxious to leave England whom they had allowed to join them disguised as one of Maria's servants. (One suspects he was fleeing imprisonment for debt.) Both Maria and Lady Anne later noted that they 'boldly crossed the ocean' – a phrase that obviously had become a joke between them – and had a terrible crossing.

Once in Calais the party made for the Hotel d'Angleterre, whose innkeeper, Dessein or Dessin, had been made famous in Sterne's *Sentimental Journey*. Sterne's book made Dessin's fortune as well and the innkeeper, whose real name was Pierre Quillac, soon became one of the wealthiest tradesmen in Calais. For virtually every British visitor to the continent, Calais (or any other port of entry) allowed the first thrilling glimpse of the forbidden fruit of Catholicism. Of course, for Maria the outward signs of a Catholic country, be they crucifixes, monks, nuns, or statues, had less of the mysterious. It was different for Lady Anne who was delighted when a Capuchin friar came to her room asking for alms. Maria's reaction was the opposite; like many European Catholics she thought such practices should be stopped.

After recovering at Calais the two ladies and their retainers set out with Maria driving her own fashionable phaeton with her own horses, probably the Galloways Thomas Fitzherbert had left her. This meant she could not enjoy the speed of having a relay of post horses, but she was able to display both the quality of her own horses and her skills as a coachwoman. Lady Anne's post chaise, though less elegant, had room for the servants and what one assumes was a mountain of luggage. Their vehicles attracted attention, as English-made carriages had the same reputation for quality and wealth that a Rolls-Royce would command in a later age. In addition to their own servants, the ladies would have had a courier, who would have galloped ahead to arrange a team of horses for Lady Anne, and a postilion in gigantic boots. The courier would also have announced the approach of two great English ladies to innkeepers who would be glad to receive them. Of course, all this cost a large amount of money. Lady Anne's income, with its recent addition, was now £900 a year, while Maria had at least £1,800 and perhaps, £2,300: even without any money from the Prince, it was twice the income of an Earl's daughter. They would need their money because English 'milords' expected to be cheated by fawning Europeans. For English 'miladies' it was even worse: 'All women are cheated and all postilions will cheat,' concluded Lady Anne.

It seems that neither lady had given too much thought to her itinerary. The fashionable watering place at Spa was their first goal. After Spa they thought they would winter in Paris where they would join up with Lady Margaret. As their carriages bounced along Maria confided to her friend that they were less than twenty miles from 'the Benedictine convent at Dunkirk, where I was educated'. Lady Anne insisted, after some feeble protests from her friend, on visiting the convent. Maria recalled that 'the Nuns are the sweetest, best, old creatures in the world, all women of family in England, but old as the Deluge.' When they arrived at the convent Maria played a trick on the nun-porteress. She told her that her name was 'Roberts' but the porteress recognised her as did the other nuns who cried out, 'It is our dear child.' To Maria it was as if she were a teenager all over again. The two ladies sought permission from the local bishop for a feast and then went into the town to purchase various luxuries for the sisters who seemed to have fallen on hard times. As a special treat the nuns were permitted to have coffee after the meal.

The long evenings in a variety of inns allowed the two women time for many intimate talks and Maria revealed her warring feelings regarding the Prince. Lady Anne did not write everything down in her journal, but did record enough for us to see the terrible dilemma Maria faced. She would complain one day that the Prince had not written and then moan the next when she received one of his lengthy and impassioned missives. Sometimes Maria's claims that she had no ambition can be rather amusing. In Ghent she told Lady Anne (who, we recall, had £900 p.a.) that she would be satisfied to live in the quiet countryside on £5,000 or £6,000 a year. Lady Anne, who well knew her friend's love of London society and its round of pleasures, suggested that if that were the case she could surely find 'some mild old gentleman in Devonshire'. This prospect did not appeal to Maria who replied most emphatically no, because she 'did like a sweet clean handsome young fellow' which was in many ways a description of the Prince if by clean she meant someone not averse to bathing as opposed to 'clean-living'. Her friend asked if she meant a 'sweet, handsome young squire' to receive an equally frank reply: 'No, a man should be something more, to raise his wife a little out of the mud.'

It is almost certain that Maria believed herself when she announced she had 'no ambition' and could follow this with a confession that all she wanted was a handsome young man of aristocratic station with an income in the top one per cent of the country. Perhaps one of the attractions between Maria and the Prince was that they both could define words as they wanted and then be absolutely convinced of their own rectitude in acting in a way contrary to usual expectations. Yet Maria also possessed another trait that the Prince conspicuously lacked: caution. Though confiding in Lady Anne, she was aware that friendships, especially in the fashionable world, could quickly sour and added, 'Remember, be we friends, be we foes, in future you must never betray me.'

On at least two occasions Maria nearly came in contact with one of the Prince of Wales' discarded mistresses, a Mrs Clare, who seems to have been some distant relation of Maria. When Maria and Lady Anne arrived at some inn in the Low Countries, the innkeeper said that Mrs Clare would soon be arriving and he assumed all the English ladies would want to be close to one another. Maria was so furious that she ordered her carriage and left, while the innkeeper puzzled at yet another example of eccentric English behaviour. The two ladies later encountered the Hon. Edward Bouverie, one of the four men who had arrived at Maria's home to tell her that the Prince had tried to kill himself. Bouverie, second son of Viscount Folkestone and later MP for Northampton, had acquired the Prince's cast-off mistress and it seems his travels were connected in some way with Mrs Clare's as well as with his duty to report back on Maria. Indeed, when Maria again met Bouverie in Brussels she would pointedly tell him that both he and the Prince had lived too much with a relation whom Maria hated. This must have been Mrs Clare.

However much Maria wished to keep away from the Mrs Clares

of this world she was no prude. Lady Anne noted a conversation between Bouverie and her friend when he informed her that Mrs Clare had told the Prince that Maria 'had thick legs'. 'Impossible,' replied Maria. Bouverie continued in a playful spirit: 'How could you disprove such an abominable calumny. Were you not obliged,' said he lowering his voice, 'to show him a little bit . . . Hey?' Here we get a rare flavour of Maria's conversational tone: 'Pooh, you foolish fellow!' she said, laughing. Yet the ever alert Lady Anne adds, 'I suspected from her manner that there must have been an ankle at least produced in confutation.'

Back in England the Prince had made a rapid recovery from his botched 'suicide' by taking a holiday in Brighton. Stories of his quixotic behaviour abounded: in one, noted by Mary Hamilton, he rode from Brighton to London at four in the morning, attended only by Colonel Lake and two grooms, then walked eight miles, after which he rode back in the afternoon. Some said he came to see Fox at Mrs Armistead's, others were sure he had come up to buy a fan 'for a lady', while yet others knew for a fact that he had come up to invite the Duc de Chartres to Brighton. He was, however, still surrounded by problems. The first of these was his friend, Georgiana Devonshire, who wrote to him within hours of the 'wedding', 'terrify'd out of my sences'. In a somewhat disjointed letter she felt 'I must tell you & Mrs F. too that I never thought this wd take place & therefore acquiesced, but it is indeed indeed madness in both.' She would hold off writing to Maria 'if you will delay it & consult Charles Fox – for God's sake do, je tremble, je vois des suites affreuses.' Her letter seems to imply that the Prince planned another, proper, marriage ceremony because she continues: 'I cannot be present for it is not a marriage, & I cannot be by at what I do not think one. It is not shabbyness or fear for myself, but what I fear for her and you. I always shall certainly shall shew her ev'ry mark of regard, but I cannot be by at what I do not think a marriage. Indeed it is not . . . I have been quite wild with the horror of it ever since. I never thought it cd come to this . . .'

Georgiana wrote to Onslow on 18 July, urging him to get the Prince to see a surgeon to establish whether or not he had been genuine in his suicide attempt. The Prince reacted with fury. He doubted her friendship, protested his 'innocence' and 'irreproachable integrity' and accused her of being 'unkind and ungenerous' in using Onslow as a middle-man. He insisted that his behaviour to Maria had always been 'perfectly honorable'. She was 'this most amiable of women', 'the dearest to me thro' life, whose character to all who know her must be most unblemished and respectable . . . <u>my ever beloved Maria wh. I am not only not ashamed of but must ever glory in</u>'. He refused to see Georgiana again until she recognised the reality of his attempted suicide. He longed for death, bemoaned the lack of true friends and apologised for writing such a long letter.

Maria and Lady Anne probably reached Spa about three weeks after landing at Calais. What they found was one of the most famous meeting places for European royalty and aristocracy: as Emperor Joseph II said, it was the 'café de l'Europe'. It was not without reason the town had given its name to all the watering-places of Britain. Beside the baths which established its fame, it now boasted Europe's first casino. It was also one of the few places at which the British aristocracy mingled socially with their European counterparts. A footman, who stayed there some years before, decided that Spa's amusements were much like Bath's, except that there was company from 'all countries in Europe'. Lady Anne noted that the Bishop of Liége licensed the gambling places and wondered whether the good cleric also derived a revenue from licensing the two hundred women who provided other types of entertainment. The bishop certainly had his own 'favourite', although the precise nature of that lady's functions are, perhaps mercifully, unrecorded.

The round of pleasures put a demand on travellers, especially ladies. When not taking the waters at the Pouhon spring, there were walks, concerts, balls, gambling, plays, assemblies and dinners. Before breakfast, visitors went to the spring for water and then drove up to the Geronstere which was at the top of a mountain some two miles from Spa. They walked between sipping glasses of water and then returned home for breakfast between nine and ten. In addition to the bathing and riding there was the constant dressing, a frequent and complicated procedure. As Judith Milbanke, Lady Anne's great foe, wrote from Spa, there were 'Baths, Breakfasts, dinners and suppers <u>never ending</u>' while the 'company here is changing every day'.

The evenings were passed in three of Maria's favourite amusements: dancing, music and gambling. Lady Anne wrote to her sister that 'the French Society is very limited, one family of various branches, all rich & agreeable, but in the Finance, being the whole of it – the Fitz tires, looks at me & yawns – she says she hates to be translated [moved about] I coax her and tell her so long as she acts like Alexander the Great – she may yawn as much as she pleases & be as little of the Hero as ever she likes before me her Valet de Chambre.' Having expressed her annoyance, Lady Anne went on to analyse Maria's situation: 'There is nothing so right as stroaking yr. overdrove virtue on the back to encourage it is to secure its continuance, frighten it & it fails – hers wont but it is the better for kind words I see <u>Relations have baited it</u> sadly or rather [be]<u>rated</u> it.'

As much as she enjoyed her time in Spa, Maria never forgot why she was travelling. Letters from the Prince did not allow her to do so. One day she walked about with a missive of nineteen pages before showing parts of it to Anne. Although the letter was later burned by the Duke of Wellington, Maria's executor made an abstract before committing it to the flames: the Prince insisted that he had broken off all relations with Lady Melbourne and that he would (this time successfully) kill himself if they could not live as husband and wife. He sent her a gift of bracelets 'not as a Lover to his Mistress, but such as a husband has a right to send and a right to expect his wife will receive'. He also reminded his 'wife' that gifts were now in order: 'You know I never presumed to make you any offer with a view of purchasing your Virtue. I know you too well.'[2] According to Lady Anne, the Prince also said he was prepared to abandon the throne and all prospects of riches. No doubt his claim that he could live in genteel poverty, if it did not strain her credulity, would have threatened the £6,000 per annum he was prepared to give her. When Edward Bouverie turned up, he advised Maria that she should seek refuge in a convent, convinced that the Prince would not follow her there. Whether this was another joke we shall never know.

According to Lady Anne, messengers arrived frequently with more letters. When Maria's executor went through her papers he counted twenty-three from the Prince, 'principally written in 1784'. They were 'mostly rhapsodys . . . urging his suit'. While there may have been more, it is unlikely that Maria would not have saved all she received. If so, and remembering that the vast majority were written in 1784, then the Prince wrote on average once a week. Sometimes the couriers came nominally from Georgiana Devonshire to avoid discovery. In addition, the Prince had arranged couriers with the help of his friend, the Duc de Chartres, who was in London. Maria later recalled that 'the speed of the couriers exciting the suspicion of the French Government, three of them were at different times put into prison.'[3] The French government probably became suspicious not so much because of the couriers' speed but because of their connection with the disreputable and conspiratorial Duc de Chartres who was already causing much annoyance to his cousin, the King of France. One can only pity the benighted French official who tried to interpret the sprawled outpourings from the Prince's pen.

Spa was full of gossip about Maria and the Prince. She attracted attention, said her companion, by the 'lustre of her beauty' and by the splendour of the sable great-coat she wore. One assumes that she was prepared to sacrifice a great deal to fashion if she wore a fur coat in the Spa summer. Whispers were heard as she passed through the rooms and soon all Spa was convinced that the Prince of Wales was on his way. It must have been quite a disappointment when only one of his aides, a Colonel Slaughter, arrived. Then another visitor appeared, Maria's brother-in-law, Basil Fitzherbert. Lady Anne liked him, although he was 'an honest country squire, who talked of dogs, horses, wheels and economy'. One wonders if he had come not only to take the waters but to see what he could do for his sister-in-law and to protect the family name of which she already was the most celebrated bearer. He may also have hoped to see his sister, a nun in a Parisian convent.

Another feature of Spa life was flirtation which flowed from the elaborate rituals of courtly compliments beloved of the age and which also grew out of the town's reputation as a marriage-mart. Later an English pamphleteer would denounce Maria for having had an affair in Spa, but there is not a hint of this in contemporary records. As well as many continental aristocrats, there were many fashionable Englishmen there. Maria and Anne became quite friendly with the future Duke of Bedford, as well as with two sons of aristocratic families who would eventually play crucial roles in Maria's life, Orlando Bridgeman and Captain the Hon. Hugh Conway. That same summer Captain Conway had come to Europe with his brother, a Suffolk rector who was suffering from 'a disorder of the lungs'. Lady Anne saw that Captain Conway, a sailor, admired and perhaps loved Maria. It was impossible, particularly for men, to do otherwise, 'each being made a confidant, each being treated as a brother'. As we shall see, Maria's enjoyment of flirting would help feed a lie that would persecute her in later years.

All this travel was exhausting and all her life Maria would be a constant complainer about the discomforts involved. When Lady Anne and she were in Ghent she had berated the innkeeper so much about the faults of his establishment that he finally burst forth: 'The Emperor has been here Madam, and made no reflections.' (Had Maria known, she could have pointed out that the Emperor had remarkably simple tastes. His travelling breakfast service, on display recently in Vienna, consisted only of a white glazed coffee pot, cup and saucer and a brown milk jug.) On their various journeys, the two ladies followed that frequent habit of eighteenth-century travellers of inviting some people they met to accompany them or to meet them at the next spot on what was a more or less established route. An elderly Dutch baron accompanied them part of the way and his manner and sayings became another shared joke between the two ladies. Basil Fitzherbert seems to have been with them almost all the time from Spa until they finally reached Paris.

Some time in September the ladies moved on to the Netherlands. At this time it was not a country in the modern sense but a curious form of republic, the United Provinces, of which Holland was the largest part. They were governed by 'Their High Mightinesses the Estates General' in an uneasy alliance with the Stadholder, a Prince of the House of Orange who enjoyed certain hereditary rights. The Provinces were in considerable turmoil, divided between partisans of the reigning Stadholder, Willem V, who was backed by Britain, and the so called 'patriots' who were middle-class 'reformers' backed by France.

The connections between the Provinces and Britain were very extensive in the eighteenth century. The Dutch held almost half the huge British National Debt while the Orange family and the British royal family had many links. Willem V's mother was a daughter of George II and Willem's three immediate predecessors had all married British princesses. Many people in both countries saw the young Princess Louise, who was only fourteen, as an ideal potential candidate for the hand of the Prince of Wales in a few years times. Leading circles in Amsterdam were well aware of the Prince's obsession with Maria and there was naturally great interest in seeing the woman who might just be able to upset the Stadholder's plans. According to Lady Anne, many letters had arrived from English ladies to their Dutch friends full of gossip. Some even went as far as to claim that Maria was notorious for granting favours to virtually every man in London, and was only denying the Prince what he yearned for until he would marry her.

Of course it could still suit Dutch interests for Maria to distract the Prince for a few years and thereby to keep him away from any German princess until their own princess was old enough to marry him. Maria's Catholicism made things even better because her religion ruled out any chance of a marriage.

Soon an invitation arrived from Willem V for Maria to visit him at his semi-regal court. When an elderly Maria looked back on her time in Holland she painted a rosy picture: 'In Holland, she met with the greatest civilities from the Stadtholder and his family, lived upon terms of intimacy with them, and was received into the friendship of the Princess of Orange . . . Frequent inquiries were made about the Prince and the English Court in confidential communications between her and the Princess, it being wholly unknown to the Princess that she was her most dangerous rival.'

If the fourteen-year-old Princess did not know about the real situation she was probably the only person in the Hague without that knowledge. At the time, however, Maria was not all that concerned with the invitation from semi-royalty; she was far more upset when days passed without a letter from her own fully royal admirer. Lady Anne attempted to pacify her by saying that the Prince, no doubt, would soon be in pursuit of her. Maria, however, already had a frank understanding of his character, and burst forth: 'Following me! I dare say he is following some new woman at Brighton.' She then burst into alternate bouts of tears and fury. Eventually she calmed down when she heard that George III had forbidden his son to leave the Kingdom.

It was probably during Maria's stay in the Hague that the Prince proposed the 'Holland Plan', which may have been occasioned by the appointment of his friend, James Harris, as the new British envoy. The Prince certainly had correspondence with someone in Holland who answered various questions. By piecing together a letter in 1785 from Maria to Lady Anne with references in a letter from the Prince to Maria in November 1785 we can get some idea of what the Prince was proposing. Maria was told not to tell anyone: 'It was not want of Confidence in you,' she later told Lady

Anne, 'but the being tied up in the Strictest manner possible in Secresy.'

The idea seems to have been that once Maria returned to England, and once the Prince turned twenty-five, they would both go to Holland to be married. The Prince forgot that British law would still apply and that the King's government would have little trouble in having the marriage declared illegal. He also overlooked the diplomatic ramifications. In what position would such a Dutch marriage place the anglophile Stadholder vis à vis his cousin, George III? Would the Dutch Government accept something that might cost them their British support? Maria's view seems to have been that, while she saw some attraction in the plan, she had her qualms, as she told Lady Anne: 'I dont in the least understand wt. change Holland can make I wish my dr. Soul you would explain it in a little I am very glad he is convinced it cannot be in England.' It was not until November 1785 that the Prince finally accepted that 'your situation would be just the same here or there as if married in England.'

While Maria pondered the Holland Plan she may have got news of the problems facing her lover back home. When the Prince was not writing to Maria he was driving his friends mad with his misery. Fox's mistress, Mrs Armistead, remembered how he 'cried by the hour, that he testified the sincerity and violence of his passion and his despair by the most extravagant expressions and actions, rolling on the floor, striking his forehead, tearing his hair, falling into hystericks, and swearing that he would abandon the country, forego the crown, sell his jewels and plate, and scrape together a competence to fly with the object of his affections to America'.[4] (One wonders how he would have been received.) The Prince also bombarded his brother, Frederick, with letters describing how he would fly to Europe to bring Maria back.

The Prince was not only anxious to have Maria but to get away from his debts. In the eighteenth century tradesmen over-charged aristocratic customers and grossly over-charged royal customers, because they knew it could be months if not years before they were paid. As one pamphleteer put it: 'A tradesman who resides within the circle of fashionable life, must know that business cannot be done among the Nobility without giving long credit.'[5] Customers, for their part, had to live on credit largely because their own income, usually from land, came in so infrequently. When the Prince wrote to his father from Brighton that he needed to go abroad due to 'the peculiar and very embarrassed situation of my affairs, arising from the necessary expenses I incurred during the course of last year' he was, for once, not exaggerating.

The King in reply only referred to the Prince's 'reprehensible conduct, which has grown worse every year' and cited the expenses over Carlton House and coupled them with the Prince's support for Fox. In August the King held out an olive branch: if only his heir would pay his debts and not incur fresh ones, he would 'see whether I can contribute towards getting it [financial relief] sooner effected'. A crisis was reached a few days later in September when the King was told that the Prince really was going to leave England. An order arrived from 'his father and his Sovereign strictly to charge and command him by this paper not to leave the realm without having obtained my particular leave'. The King demanded accounts from his heir, only to be horrified when he discovered that the amount owed came to, at least, £147,293 [just under £8 million].

The exchange of letters in which the Prince still insisted he must leave England and the King still commanded him to remain, would continue well into the new year. Early in September Mary Hamilton heard that on one of Lord Southampton's visits to the King 'he was so long closetted with their Majesties from 2 till 6 (and dinner waiting from 4) that it occassioned much speculation in ye house particularly too as ye King and Queen seem'd much agitated. Very long letters have also lately come from ye Prince to ye King.' In fact the Prince had a case: George III was stingy with money. The King, for example, amused society by refusing to take a box at the opera. When the Prince went he had to pay for his own box. George had also withheld income due his son from the Duchy of Cornwall. The Prince did not receive an income really large enough to support the style expected of a Prince of Wales and his income would go further in Europe. In defence of the King one should add that he knew, through Lord Southampton and others, that the real problem was not so much money as Maria.

Meanwhile, at the Hague, the two visiting ladies spent many happy evenings with various members of the Orange family. The Stadholder himself was a stolid figure, well aware of his own limitations. Only a few years earlier he had admitted, according to Sir Joshua Reynolds, that 'I feel I have no ability to be at the head of so many affairs.' As Maria later remembered, she became a friend of the young Princess Louise with whom she would correspond for many years and whom she would see in London. When a visiting German prince, Heinrich Reuss XIII, Prince of Reuss-Greiz, began to take too strong a romantic interest, not in the Princess but in Maria, Lady Anne and she decided to flee southward to Brussels. Maria remembered that the Stadholder allowed them the use of the royal barge to begin their journey.[6]

After this Dutch interlude, Maria and Lady Anne made their way south to what was then known as the Austrian Netherlands. The court at Brussels, presided over by Archduchess Maria Christine, sister of Emperor Joseph II, was well known for its high culture. One of Brussels' main attractions for Englishmen was the splendour of its churches' liturgies. The inspiration came from the music-loving Habsburg Regents who maintained a full musical establishment in their chapel. Lady Anne was anxious to experience the brilliance of a sung High Mass, but when she suggested to Maria that they go, the Catholic lady, showing the not unfamiliar attitude of many 'cradle Catholics', said she felt too unwell.

By this point the two friends had been travelling for several months – Lady Anne's journal never pays too much attention to dates – and they were anxious to get to Paris where they planned to pass the winter and where they would meet up with Lady Anne's sister. Basil Fitzherbert was still with them as they entered France and he emerges as the stereotypical English squire who had little use for 'all that fal-lal' that surrounded the lives of French royalty and aristocracy. When the two ladies pointed out the splendid display of a marquis in a carriage drawn by six horses, he replied, 'They [the horses] are brutes, d'ye see, that go here and there and never together.' As for French women, or at least the upper-class ones, Fitzherbert, still a bachelor, had an even lower opinion than of French horses: there were not any who were 'innocent'. It might have reassured public opinion back home that Basil Fitzherbert's Catholic faith did not make him any more sophisticated or 'European' than his Protestant neighbours back in Staffordshire. Lady Anne nevertheless liked him and thought he would be glad to flirt with her more if she had not been a 'heretic'. The choice of word was hers, not his.

Back in England Lord Wentworth's sister, who thoroughly hated Lady Anne, wanted to know what was going on as rumours were flying round. She asked her aunt, 'Pray have you heard whether Ldy Anne is returned from her foreign Tour? Her companion Mrs Fitzherbert has taken a house in Normandy & means to settle there, which is a very prudent measure for which she deserves commendation.' In the new year Miss Milbanke read in the newspapers 'that Ladies Anne & Margaret are still at Paris. I wish they may be too strongly charmed with that Metropolis to leave it speedily, but should they return, pray let me hear some account of them, their dress and manners, which must be quite compleat now they have received a Parisian Polish.'

Maria and Lady Anne, now joined by Lady Margaret, would be in Paris from January to June 1785. They stayed in the Hotel de Danemarck and nearby was a stationer's shop where Lady Anne bought two beautifully bound duodecimo volumes, now in the National Library of Scotland. Here she wrote up their various visits and her accounts bear all the hallmarks of episodes that might have appeared in a travel book.[7] In typical eighteenth-century fashion the three ladies went about in their travelling clothes – riding habits, including hats with feathers – and would visit places which later generations would have been forbidden to enter. They went to see the Bastille where the Governor confided to Lady Anne that he was 'vexed' that 'the ladies in England should intertain an Idea of this place so foreign to the truth – criminals are not punished – this is one of those common errors people fall into from having received false information.' Lady Anne does not record seeing the Bastille's most famous prisoner, the Marquis de Sade, nor could she know that the poor Governor would be the first victim of the revolutionary mob four years later.

On another occasion the three women visited the 'Hotel Dieu' or hospital. Maria, who was 'frightened to death', came anyway and all three 'pour'd plenty of lavendar water on our handkerchiefs and braved the dangers of infection'. They found that the hospital, which usually had 5,000 patients, provided beds which accommodated two, four or six people each. They decided not to see the room with women in labour or the mortuary but did visit those devoted to amputations and the mentally ill, where patients begged for snuff. Despite all the horrors there was still room for romance, as Lady Anne records: 'While I was moralising behind', a young surgeon 'was making love to Mrs F: asking his ten thousand questions, and taking her (as I supposed for something not very difficult of attainment) was begging to know when he might wait on her.' Lady Anne suggested her friend 'tell him that she should be happy to see him at C——n House!!' When they were visiting an orphanage the young surgeon turned up again and 'was continuing his love to Mrs F: I saw she had made an insersion into his heart.' Lady Anne was amused at the general tendency of Frenchmen, even shopkeepers, to 'make love' to women and she learned to put this to good purpose: a little joke or *bon mot* could save her ten *sous* a yard on cloth.

At Choisy-le-Roi, some seven miles south of Paris, Maria, Lady Anne and Lady Margaret visited the chateau built by Louis XV for his recreational activities. The chateau's naughty history appealed to Lady Anne who decided to try out the King's bed. 'Altho I cannot boast that I have slept <u>with</u> Louis quinze yet as I was resolved to have the power of bragging that I had couched under the same canopy.' She went up the bed's ladder, stretched out full length but then discovered that the King seldom slept there: he spent most of his time in Madame de Pompadour's bed. The party was also intrigued by the famous round dining room table with a centre that dropped down to the kitchen beneath to rise again with another course.

There was a visit to Bicêtre, the gaol for 6,000 criminals where the ladies saw the area devoted to the criminally insane who were chained to their beds. Lady Anne was fascinated by an English prisoner who had been there for twenty-seven years and, although no longer unwell, preferred to stay where he was. More memorable was the time spent with the monks at St Denis, then a Benedictine abbey about four miles outside Paris. There the two ladies were given a *'meagre* dinner' of soup, vegetables, eggs and fish 'which being half-stinking from the great distance it is carried' had little appeal. The wine was 'flat' but at least it was 'unadulterated'. Before arriving, Lady Anne had thought 'that *monks* lived far better'. Good roast beef, she wrote, might be an occasion for sin: rotten fish was safer. At least, and at last, there was champagne for the ladies but not for the monks. 'After we got up from table,' she continued:

> they all got round us, to insist that we should go into the ajoining room; *giving the exact reason why* by its *name* – we of course blushed, stammerd, pouted & would not – the Fathers continued their intreatys, at last we were forced to give up the point and entering their closet . . . [sic] but I will not allow my pen to make an illusion which may be thought too free, even altho' we have no such *terme* in our

107

creed as that which I was thinking of, when about to mention some vases which demanded, what could not be called 'Holy water.'

After the visit to the monks' lavatory the ladies saw the French crown jewels, the death masks of various French kings and the coronation robes of Louis XVI. They were amazed to see that the coffin of Louis XV, who had died in 1774, had not been buried. It still lay in state under a black pall and was surrounded by lamps. The visitors were told that the body of the last King must remain unburied until his successor died. Every day masses were said for the dead Sovereign's soul, which in Louis XV's case was probably very helpful.

The three ladies also went to see the profession of a nun at the convent of a very poor order in which most of the sisters were English. One nun was Thomas Fitzherbert's sister, Mary, and through her influence they got places in the 'inner church'. The Protestant Lady Anne was uncomfortable at what awaited the 'young victim of Holy prejudice'. Even so, she and Maria had both sent their diamonds before the service so that the new nun could enter the chapel in worldly finery which was then dramatically discarded. When the novice's voice grew weak Lady Anne turned to Maria: '"Good God," said I to Mrs F: "she is repenting what she is about – is it not yet time for her to stop – poor child!"' Maria explained that it was not the novice who was chanting but her sister who stood behind her as the girl did not have a good singing voice.

Another day saw Maria and Lady Anne visiting Les Invalides and next door, L'École Militaire, where they toured the school and stables. Maria must have been rather bored with the pensioners and wanted to see the students (whose regime was rather relaxed) but, Lady Anne tells us, 'it seems 'tis against the rules for women to be admitted into this place unless when the young men are employ'd.' The 'three Venuses departed, mounting their heavenly cars drawn by doves since the fates had decreed that the sons of

Mars à la Francois were not to be visible.' Had Maria had her wish to see the young men she might have been attracted to a young Corsican student named Napoléon Buonaparte.

French royalty, with all its gaudy and seemingly invulnerable splendour, fascinated almost all eighteenth-century English visitors, who avidly visited places connected with current or recently deceased Bourbons. Given the role of Louis XVI's troublesome cousin, the Duc de Chartres as the Prince's postman, and his friendship with the Prince himself, it is hardly surprising that the ladies visited his family's Paris home, the Palais Royal. (He was to succeed his father as Duc d'Orléans this same year.) The Palais Royal housed one of the world's best art collections. While walking round, Lady Anne spotted one picture that was less than edifying and immediately called over Maria and her sister. 'Neither would believe me till lurking behind a book case I made them observe it in the great Gallery.' The three tourists also went round the rooms of the young sons of the Duc de Chartres where they saw the influence of the Duc's mistress, the Comtesse de Genlis, famous as an educational reformer. The rooms contained tools and material to teach the Princes brickmaking, chemistry, surgery, carpentry, armaments and everything they would need if, like Robinson Crusoe, they were 'thrown upon a desert Island'. The visitors were fascinated to know if the Comtesse practised what she preached, only to be told by the guide, who like most guides was a fount of all wisdom, that 'while nobody talked & spoke better than Madam Genlis, no body acted more like the rest of the world, for that her conduct had been as free as any womans in Paris.'

When writing up these visits, Lady Anne carefully noted how things they saw or people they met bore on Maria's extraordinary situation. Undoubtedly she had 'polished' her accounts and undoubtedly, like most people, she had enhanced her own role compared with an apprehensive woman who simply did not know what to do. While in the Palais Royal she added, regarding the gossip surrounding Madame Genlis, that 'in Paris there is always a party for and against every thing & person who is noted.' The Comtesse's 'public systems for virtue' may have created enemies who 'may, to pull her down, suppose private wandering from her own path which (except in one Instance the duc de Chartres) have never existed.' The moral would not have been wasted on Maria.

Another occasion for one of Lady Anne's homilies was the group's visit to the Carmelite convent in the Rue Saint Jacques, the strictest convent in Paris. This was famous as the final home of Louise de la Vallière, the mistress of Louis XIV, who was ousted by Madame de Montespan. Like so many of his mistresses, she then took the veil as Sister Louise de la Miséricorde in 1674. Her story appealed to Lady Anne's romantic streak. As the nuns chanted in the background the trio visited a side chapel which held a portrait of the convent's most famous nun. It showed La Vallière as a penitent tearing off her velvets and jewels in renunciation of a 'life spent in impurity and wantonness'. Lady Anne assumed she had sat for the portrait as an act of penance and 'to shew to others the agonys which sin gives, sooner or later to that mind which is conscious of having err'd, tho in favour of a King.' She then went on: 'I desired one of our party to look at this picture as it contained a charming lesson to all those who are made love to by Princes & the sons of kings.' Maria hardly needed any homily to bring home the message: do not put your trust in kings, much less in king's sons.

Lady Anne's final homily was delivered towards the end of their time in Paris when 'we three ladies' drove out to Marly where they dined with a Mon. S——, the lover of Madame du Barry after the death of Louis XV. Like many wealthy Frenchmen he had a fashionable *jardin anglais* through which they walked to see the famous water works that powered the fountains at Versailles. They were then shown the Pavilion which Louis XV had built for Madame du Barry at Louveciennes. As they walked round the building Lady Anne wondered belatedly about the propriety of their visit, but the ladies were reassured with words that would in time apply to Maria: 'She is no longer courted, to be sure, no longer a queen whose smiles are studied. Even the King's brothers from time to time see her.'

The visitors would have loved to have seen Madame du Barry in person when suddenly the dead King's mistress appeared. Lady Anne, and probably Maria as well, had expected 'a tall thin noble looking French figure with much rouge & a great deal of countenance.' Instead they saw a 'middle sized fat fair comfortable looking woman such as one might find in most country societys – no rouge an open, hearty countenance . . . something commanding & superior too in her air.' The next sentence, for those who remember Madame du Barry's fate during the Revolution has a deadly ring: 'Her neck seemed to pride itself in shewing her face to the English ladys. Her face seemed to say, pray neck, carry me nobly.' (Du Barry's last lover, the Duc de Brissac, was butchered by the mob that descended on Versailles and his head was flung into the sitting room of this same Pavilion while Madame du Barry herself would be dragged screaming to the guillotine.)

However much Maria and the Ladies Anne and Margaret enjoyed Marly, St Denis, Les Invalides and the Palais Royal they knew their tour would be incomplete without a visit to Versailles. There were difficulties however. Maria had an important enemy in France, the British Ambassador. The Duke of Dorset was a 'King's friend' and despised the Cumberlands, Gloucesters, the Prince of Wales and all who associated with him, including Maria. The Duke had the ear of Queen Marie Antoinette who, according to Lady Anne, resented the fact that the Prince of Wales had not written her flattering letters. The French Queen and various of the Bourbon princes had heard the gossip sweeping round London from the Duc de Chartres and no doubt the Queen had heard about Maria from her sister, the Archduchess-Regent in Brussels. In London, newspapers were already reporting that the Bourbon princes wanted to see Maria and it seems that the Queen wanted to have a look as well. The Duke of Dorset however exerted all the pressure he could to frustrate the royal family's desire.

At last a way was found. The new Archbishop of Narbonne was to be installed at Versailles. For Anne and Margaret it would be another splendid Catholic ceremony and a chance to see Versailles. For Maria it would almost be a family occasion as the Archbishop, a descendant of the recusant Dillon family, was connected to various friends and relations of Maria. Indeed he had all sorts of qualifications to be an Archbishop except religious faith. Fortunately, he was converted on his deathbed. It is not clear whether the three ladies actually went to Versailles on that occasion or on another day but when there they stayed with a French duke who had a residence in the town.

The usual custom was for the first rank of the British aristocracy to be presented to the King and his family. Because Lord Balcarres's daughters and Maria were not in this rank they had to be content with an arrangement that would allow the French royal family to look at Maria while the three visitors looked at them. Once the plans had been made the Queen arranged for her personal hairdresser to come to Maria, an honour which must have particularly delighted her. The Queen had her own reasons. She knew her hairdresser was a great gossip and when next dressing her hair would entertain her with all the latest news he had picked up about the goings-on in London from Maria.

It was ten years since Louis XV had been succeeded by his grandson, Louis XVI, a much maligned King who was well read and well intentioned but who had a fatal lack of resolution. The rigid routine of court etiquette went on, even though more and more of the nobility regarded it as outdated and absurd. Among these ceremonies few were more ridiculous than the way the Bourbons dined in public twice a week. Although one English traveller said 'all people without exception' were allowed to see this, privileged guests were allowed to stand close by for a better view of the spectacle. When Maria swept into the room to watch the *Grand Couvert* she was accompanied by Lady Anne and apparently by her brother-in-law, Basil, who, with his squire's contempt for anything French, must have sneered at this pinnacle of French tomfoolery.

Seated at the horse-shoe shaped table were the King, his even more rotund brother, 'Monsieur', the Comte de Provence, the dandified youngest Bourbon brother, the handsome Comte d'Artois, and their saintly sister, Madame Elizabeth. Each of the Bourbon princes was accompanied by his wife and, like Cinderella, Marie Antoinette must have outshone the two drab and ugly sisters-in-law, both Princesses from Piedmont. Standing behind the Queen was none other than the Duke of Dorset who whispered in her ear throughout the meal. One assumes that the Queen, who never ate much in public and drank only water, was more interested in this gossip than in the menu. However the King, a noted trencherman, consumed nine plates of food. Lady Anne, like a good reporter, had some paper hidden in her muff and jotted down all the French names of the dishes. The shortsighted King had no sooner seated himself than he took up his eye glass to stare at Maria, an example followed by his two royal brothers, by the Queen, as well as by the three Princesses. It must have been a formidable thing to be openly stared at by the King and Queen of France and by five other royal personages. After Marie Antoinette lowered her glass she stared at Maria through her fan. Maria whispered to her friend that she 'was ready to die of it' yet Lady Anne noted: 'I saw she was gratified.' Maria Fitzherbert was not someone who could easily be put down, not even by the King and Queen of France.

By the time of Maria's visit there were storm clouds gathering over the French monarchy. The previous year *The Marriage of Figaro*, Beaumarchais's comedy ridiculing the social order, was finally allowed to be performed at the Comédie Française. The Queen, already unpopular with most Frenchmen, was suffering because of the 'affair of the necklace'. Two criminals used her name to trick Cardinal de Rohan into standing security for a vastly expensive necklace which they said the Queen wanted and which they then stole. Most people believed Marie Antoinette was involved. (This bizarre incident would two years later cause unexpected problems for Maria.) Meanwhile the Salon at the Louvre was remarkable for paintings obsessed with blood and death. Even so, no one watching the royal family at table could have guessed that of these seven royal personages three would perish at the hands of political murderers, while the other four would be lucky to escape France with their lives.

According to Lady Anne the 'lustre' of Maria's beauty did not attract the attention in Paris that it had done in Spa, the Netherlands or London. Her friend believed that her looks were not those to please the French. This was not an example of Frenchmen's haughtiness for by the 1780s there was a mania for things English, be they country parks or, in a few years, new constitutions. Difficult as it is to believe, imitation of things English even extended to fashion. An old acquaintance of Maria, although an increasingly hostile one, Hester Thrale, now Mrs Piozzi, was in Paris at the same time and noted that 'Hats <u>a la Anglais</u> seem the mark of distinction for Women of Fashion & elegant manners.'

As the spring of 1785 turned into summer new pleasures opened up for the visitors. There was the new park at the Palais Royal which the Duc de Chartres had established to earn some much needed money. There Maria would have found fountains and paths where 'you walk & chat, & drink Lemonade'. There were shops under the elegant colonnade and 'pavilions full of People who come for this Conversazione al Fresco'. There were the races at Sablon (where most of the jockeys were English) and the Tuileries' gardens which were 'resorted to by the most fashionable people in Paris; and about the months of May, June, and July . . . look like an earthly Paradise'.

In the midst of all these diversions, Maria was suddenly threatened with scandal by meeting a friend from her past. If the English press had picked up a hint of this it could have seriously damaged her relations with the Prince. When Maria was in Nice four years

114

The 1792 engraving of Richard Cosway's romanticised portrait of
Maria Fitzherbert. Round her neck is the miniature of the Prince
which she wore in public after her marriage.

Walter Smythe, Maria
Fitzherbert's father,
an 'amiable, well-bred man,'
in the uniform of an officer
in the Austrian army.

Lulworth Castle, Dorset, Maria Fitzherbert's first married home,
painted by Theodore de Bruyn. The chapel to the right was added
after her time there.

Maria Fitzherbert as she appeared in the late 1780s in all her glory as the Prince's 'secret' wife. The painting is by Sir Joshua Reynolds.

Swynnerton Hall, Staffordshire, the home of Thomas Fitzherbert,
Maria's second husband.

No. six, Tilney Street, near
Park Lane, Maria's London
home for the second half c
her life.

King George III whom his son found aloof and censorious.
The King was a better sovereign than a father.

Queen Charlotte, the Prince's mother, with whom he and Maria had
a stormy relationship.

The Prince of Wales in Gainsborough's 1782 portrait, about the
time that Maria fell in love with him.

OUT OF FITS,
OR *THE RECOVERY* TO THE SATISFACTION OF *ALL PARTIES*.
Published 5th May 1786, by S. W. Forex at the Caricature Warehouse, No. 3, Piccadilly.

Above, caricature published on 5 May 1786, shows Maria and the Prince exhausted after love-making. *Below,* another published on 3 April 1786, shows a dominating Maria leading the Prince to the altar.

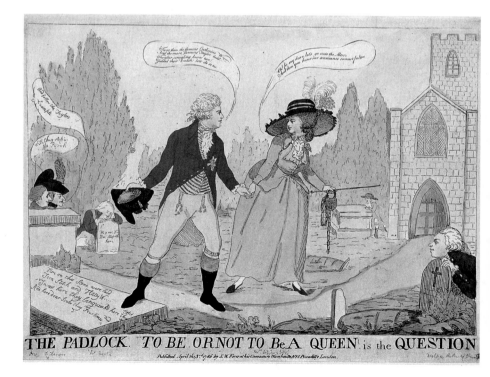

THE PADLOCK. *TO BE OR NOT TO Be A QUEEN* is the QUESTION

Published April the 3rd 1786 by S. W. Forex at his Caricature Warehouse No 3 Piccadilly London.

earlier caring for her dying husband, Thomas Fitzherbert, a hand-some young Comte de Marin became attached to them. He had entertained her with carriage rides and had sent various luxurious foods during those sad days. After Thomas's death, Marin had attempted to continue his friendship motivated, one strongly suspects, by the prospect of marrying a wealthy widow, but Maria had settled back into London life. She came across Marin, perhaps in Paris but more likely while at Versailles, either late in 1784 or in 1785. (Marin may well have heard that she was there and sought her out.) When they met, Maria gave him the cold shoulder and, one gathers, when Maria gave any man a cold shoulder he quickly realised he was suffering from frost-bite.

Marin now demanded £70 as a repayment for all the money he had spent on her in Nice. Maria indignantly rejected his demand. Undoubtedly Marin was a rogue but there is a hint in Lady Anne's account that he may have had some letters from Maria that could have proved embarrassing. Maria sought Lady Anne's advice who told her to pay the money, but when Maria refused, her friend suggested they both ask Lady Margaret, who endorsed her sister's view and Maria reluctantly gave him the money.

That should have been the end of the Comte de Marin but, sadly for Maria, it was not. As her fame increased in the 1780s stories began appearing of her time in Europe. A pamphleteer calling himself 'Nemesis', in reality a disreputable clergyman named Philip Withers, implied she had 'contracted an intimacy' with a French marquis in Plombiers, and he had a letter to prove it. 'The consequence of this intercourse was a necessity of retiring to Paris.' Withers, like Gibbon, confined his salacious bits to his footnotes and asked in one note: 'Does the author [of the alleged 'letter'] design to insinuate that Plombiers was unable to furnish a midwife and the other accommodations necessary for a lady obedient to the divine command – increase and multiply?' Nemesis went on to allege that in 1788 the marquis came to England to recover £2,000 he had loaned Maria who, he claimed, would only pay if he gave her the love letters she had written. Maria's agents were able to get the sum reduced to £200 but the marquis kept the letters which Nemesis threatened to publish. There are enough resemblances to argue that Withers' invention was an exaggerated corruption of the Marin episode.[8]

While Withers' libel would be a problem for the future, Maria had a problem that was very much of the present. One reason for her worry over Marin's threat was that she now had in her travelling writing desk another letter from the Prince. Although it was later burned, she confided its main points to Lady Anne. The Prince was now offering her two choices. The first was for her to return to England, to convert to the Church of England and then to wait till he reached twenty-five on 12 August 1787. He would then (under the Royal Marriage Act) declare before the Privy Council his intention to marry her. (He assumed the government would not use their Parliamentary majority to reject this.) The second choice was for Maria to return and to marry him at once but privately. She would keep her own name and live in her own house. She would also be given a 'proper sphere' for herself and any possible children when the Prince became King.

The Marin episode had brought home how much she needed a man to protect her. The proposals also showed her how difficult it would be for her to be with the man she loved. Either way she faced heart-breaking decisions with no guarantee that her sacrifices would bring what she wanted. She consulted Lady Anne and, taking her advice, rejected both plans. Lady Anne believed – incorrectly – that there was a plot by some in the Opposition, notably Fox, Sheridan and the Duchess of Devonshire, to bring about a marriage as they hoped 'to manage [the Prince] thro' Mrs. Fitzherbert'. We may assume this is what she told Maria.

This may also be the best place to look at the role of the Duchess of Devonshire. At some stage during her long absence Maria received a letter from Georgiana Devonshire. The Duchess, whose relationship with Maria fluctuated over the years, later recalled that the Prince was 'always persecuting me to write to her to persuade her to marry him, but the most I ever did was urging her to come to some determination . . . and indeed, however weary'd I was by his importunitys, I yet should never have consented to write so much had I not felt secure of her resolution.' Whilst Georgiana's letter has disappeared, we have Maria's reply and can assume that the Duchess repeated once again what may be called the Fox-Devonshire view: Maria should decide whether to do what the Prince wanted or tell him to leave her alone.

Maria's reply, written in stilted language, referred to 'the very unpleasant and cruel situation I feel myself in'. Her feelings had not changed and would not change: by implication, marriage was out of the question and 'I believe that no one can say but that my reasons are just & painted in their true colors.' As regards returning to England, Maria rejected the Duchess's view that this would help. Her return would be interpreted as giving in to the Prince's plans. Obviously the Duchess had cited Fox's view that Maria should return, go through with a marriage even though both Fox and the Duchess 'know in their own breasts they cannot approve off, and I am confident there is not one of them that will take it upon themselves to say it is a legal proceeding'. Whatever happens, she pointed out, it will not be the Prince or his friends who will suffer but Maria. Before Georgiana fainted at the criticism of Fox, Maria added, 'I don't speake with any want of regard or respect for his [the Prince's] friends, but they are certainly not my Freinds and it is very natural for them to say <u>such & such are the proposals, it is not our affair, & she is of an age to take care of herself.</u>' She ends her letter by 'imploring your Interest with <u>him</u> as no one is so likely to succeed as yr.self'.

In England, as the spring wore on, the crisis over the Prince's debts once again came to the boil and he renewed his threat to leave England. He was undaunted by his father's threats and in March sent yet another servant abroad, this time to Paris. He got ready to leave immediately his servant returned. The King was kept informed of all this through Lord Southampton who got his information from Fox who considered his young friend's plan the 'worse of all possible things'. Southampton and Fox met at Brookes Club and the MP denounced the suggested trip as 'bad for himself, bad as it was offensive to the K——, bad as it cd. not be the means of extricating H.R.H. from his present difficultys, & might involve him in greater'. He had pointedly 'warned H.R.H. from going to Paris'. For once Fox and the King were in agreement: the real problem was not Maria but the debts. Lord Southampton discussed the recent letters between father and son and Fox admitted that he had not seen all the King's letters. He added incisively that 'H.R.H. was very apt in his statements to keep back parts of a case that did not exactly make for the opinion he wished to receive.'

Fox told Southampton that he had warned the Prince 'of the powers of the Family Marriage Act, & of the clauses in the Act of Settlement', just as Lady Anne had warned Maria. The Prince was unimpressed and Fox added that it was 'too foolish to suppose even a man of sense to know what he meant'. So convinced was Fox that this latest threat to decamp to Europe was serious that he set out the next day for Newmarket to persuade the Prince to give up his plan, at least till he had a reply from the King to his last letter. The King immediately renewed his warning not 'to run away from his situation, in direct defiance of the solemn injunction I have laid upon him' and added that not only the Prince but those who 'bear a part in it' would have to answer to him. If only the Prince would economise and reorganise his Household, then the King might help him with a loan of £150,000.[9]

The Prince still carried on with his wild scheme and early in April insisted that his proposed tour 'has not been formed with views of gratifying any desire I might have of seeing foreign countries, but simply & honourably to clear myself from the confin'd embarrassing & truly improper situation I at present feel myself in'. In truth, it was to allow him to win over Maria by the charm, if not the logic, of his arguments. Those who read newspapers were kept informed of the latest developments: the day after this letter to the King *The Daily Universal Register* reported talk about a private trip to Europe. Five days later the King took advantage of the *cul de sac* into which his son had rushed: if the real reason for the trip were debts, the Prince need only reform his finances with help from his father, after which there was no need for a trip. Matters were complicated because the Prince refused to give the source of his loans. The gossip was that with Sheridan's help he had 'gone to the Jews' and borrowed £10,000 from Moses Aaron of Crutched Friars on a *post obit*, a devise by which an heir promised repayment of a loan after his father's death gave him the means to do so. The Prince actually only received £7,500 and the balance in jewels including, rather oddly, a diamond cross and rosary. (This device meant that the transaction was not a loan but a sale.)

This same month, and within days of yet another warning against fleeing the country, the Prince asked Sir James Harris, H. M. Minister at the Hague, to call on him. He was regarded by the Prince as a medium through which he could talk to the government without talking to the King. Harris noted in his diary that the Prince wanted to travel to the Hague privately as the 'Earl of Chester'. Would he 'distress me or not if he was to come . . . in a private character?' Rather inconsistently, the Prince asked if Harris 'could present him [to the Stadholder] as such'. Harris pointed out that he could not be part of any tour that the King forbade and that the Prince must always travel 'with all the splendour attached to his rank'. A private trip, even if allowed, would not work. The Prince burst out, 'But what can I do, my dear Harris? The King hates me . . . he always did, from seven years old . . . We are too wide asunder ever to meet. The King has deceived me . . . I cannot trust him, and he will never believe me.' Poor Harris denied this and added that travel would solve nothing. He then tried to bridge the ever widening chasm between father and son and between government and Prince. He got some 'vague assurances' from the Foreign Secretary that the government would 'not be adverse to increase HRH's income' if he would begin paying his debts, renounce going abroad and be reconciled to his father. Harris also consulted the Whig leaders, the Duke of Portland and Fox, who supported this plan.

The Prince had other problems to face. There was talk that the Hereditary Prince of Prussia, heir to Frederick the Great, wanted his eldest daughter, Frederica, to marry the Prince. Eventually the Princess would be allocated to Prince Frederick, the Prince's younger brother and would become a thorn in Maria's flesh. In addition to talk, there were now more printed attacks on the Prince from the pen of William Combe, later editor of *The Times* and famous as the author of the *Tours of Doctor Syntax*. *The Royal Dream: or the P—— in a Panic . . .* was a wholehearted attack, mainly in verse, on the Prince and his associates and a defence of the King. There was mention of a foreign trip to sample 'Parisian charms', and a warning against the continued friendship with Fox:

In his base heart the secret wishes crave
To soil the crown and make the prince a slave.

Then early in May the newspapers commented on the secret correspondence with Maria and noted that the 'love letter' style of the Prince's letters was approved by their recipient. James Harris bumped into the Prince at Mrs Sturt's faro bank in St James's Square and was invited to call at Carlton House. With his proposals in hand, he saw the Prince in his dressing room on 23 May to be told that he had given up the idea of travelling to Europe, at least for the time being. Encouraged by this, Harris said he would ask Pitt to increase the Prince's income to £100,000 a year on two conditions. He must allocate £50,000 per annum for debts and second, he must 'cease to be a man of party, and reconcile yourself to the King'. The Prince poured cold water on all this: Pitt would not do what he promised and, if he did, both Parliament and the King would not co-operate. The Prince would never 'abandon Charles and my friends' even though Harris pointed out that Fox agreed 'that a Prince of Wales ought to be of no party'. When Harris urged how pleased the King and Queen would be with a reconciliation the Prince retorted: 'What, my dear Harris, will you force me to repeat to you that the <u>King hates me</u>? He will never be reconciled to me.' Harris's original manuscript shows the degree of the Prince's virtual paranoia: 'He wishes me dead – ruin'd – that I should appear contemptible in the eyes of the world.'[10]

The Prince now took out the correspondence with the King dating from 1784. He gave the letters to Harris and the diplomat found them 'harsh and severe . . . void of every expression of parental kindness or affection'. If there were no point in Harris's approaching the King, might he not try the Queen and the princesses? This too was knocked down. The diplomat then suggested marriage as a way to win over the King. At this the Prince exploded: 'I never will marry! My resolution is taken on that subject. I have settled it with Frederick. No, I never will marry!' When Harris remonstrated he added, 'I owe nothing to the King. Frederick will marry, and the crown will descend to his children; and as for myself, I do not see how it affects me.'

Here we have an expansion of his second proposal to Maria. To be fair to the Prince in his confused (and confusing) ideas about marriage he may have had in mind the marriage of his ancestor, Georg Wilhelm, Duke of Brunswick-Zell who had married morganatically. His grandson eventually became George I of England, showing that in British, Irish and Hanoverian law a morganatic marriage did not affect the succession. Harris was shocked and pointed out that without children 'you have no solid hold on the affections of the people'. If the Prince came to the throne unmarried while the Duke of York were married with sons, 'your situation, when King, will be more painful than it is at the moment. Our own history furnishes strong examples of the truth of what I say.' The Prince was angry at this and walked round the room but he was not angry with Harris but frustrated with himself and his situation.

Poor Harris. He saw unfolding before him a scandal in which the Prince of Wales somehow thought he could be both King and married to a Catholic who could conveniently not provide him with heirs so that his Protestant brother and his children could inherit. Ahead lay a constitutional crisis with unforeseen consequences for a dynasty that had only possessed the Crown for seventy-one years. It was also a dynasty that only five years before had seen London under mob rule in the name of anti-Popery. The year before, in Brighton, officials had seized a parcel from Rouen addressed to the writer, Hannah More, and found a 'popish prayer-book'. The whole parcel was ordered to be burnt in accordance with an Act of James I. Harris might also have remembered that English life still had a vicious streak in it: the previous year, Mary Bayley was ordered by the court to be burned at the stake in Winchester for murdering her husband. What would be Maria's fate should she be convicted of the crimes involved in marrying the Prince? What would the London mob think of the spendthrift heir to the throne's secretly taking a Catholic wife?

5

---•·•·•---

A DANGEROUS GREATNESS

Early in June 1785 the situation suddenly changed for Maria, the Prince and Lady Anne. The Lindsay sisters received news that Lady Anne's aged friend, the city magnate and MP, Richard Atkinson, had died and had left the sisters a fortune. (Some claimed it was £35,000 [just under £2,000,000] while others placed it at £14,000 [about £750,000.] Lord Wentworth's sister, and Lady Anne's putative sister-in-law, Judith Milbanke, 'was much surprized at the immense Legacy Atkinson has left Lady Anne – the Connection between her, Mr Atkinson & my Brother formed the most mysterious Trio I ever heard of & I have ideas concerning it I do not chuse to commit to paper.' 'Mysterious' or not, Lady Anne and her sister had little choice but to return to London because there was a chance that Atkinson's family was 'determined to plague her' over the inheritance. For the Prince, Lady Anne's return meant he could find out exactly what was going on. For Maria, it was a blow because it left her alone in Paris, not knowing what to do, even though her family urged her to stay in Europe for at least a few more months. The plan for the party to set off for Switzerland lay in disarray. She therefore sent for her brother, Jack, to join her in Paris and lamented her fate to Anne:

'I do realy think I am doom'd to be unhappy in some way or other.' For those interested in Maria's history Lady Anne's departure means that her marvellous account of the tour comes to an end. Luckily Lady Anne saved Maria's letters so that we have a good substitute for the journal.

It says much for both Maria and Lady Anne that they were able to travel together for almost a year, without having an argument big enough to cause a parting of the ways. Close friendships often burst apart under the strains of travel, but theirs held, although one suspects they had a few stormy scenes. This was to be expected when Maria was receiving letters that both excited her and then depressed her. How does Maria Fitzherbert emerge from Lady Anne's pen in what is the most extended and most balanced portrait of her in the days before she became the Prince's wife? She comes across very much as an upper-class lady of her time, devoted to the pursuit of pleasure and prepared to put up with all sorts of annoyances to attain it. She had a great capacity for attracting friends, particularly men, whether they be English squires such as Basil Fitzherbert, young aristocrats such as Captain the Hon. Hugh Conway, Parisian physicians, German princes or even rogues such as Marin. There is absolutely no hint in this journal of any affair and, had there been, Lady Anne, who was no prude, would have at least implied its existence. What we do see is that Maria, like so many ladies of her time, enjoyed flirtation and slightly risqué conversation, yet when things took a more dangerous turn, as with Prince Heinrich Reuss XIII, she fled. Maria, like Lady Anne, was no prude but she was also not a woman to sell herself cheaply.

Previous biographers have portrayed Maria Fitzherbert as an honorary Victorian or almost as a saint; as the twenty-seventh Earl of Crawford, who did so much to preserve her memory, put it, books about her were a bit too 'coloured by the Catholic point of view'. She was neither a Victorian nor a saint. Even before her marriage to the Prince of Wales she was a woman of considerable pride who demanded both deference and as much luxury and comfort as possible. (These traits obviously amused Lady Anne with the acute observation that having less money gives.) We also get some small insight into Maria's attitude towards religion. Her surviving letters, the notes of her conversations and first-hand observations never portray her as a 'religious' person in the modern sense. Twenty years after her marriage Maria expressed 'her particular abhorrence of [word blacked out] (of Berkeley Sq) because he makes a fuss about going to Church & won't go to Bed without saying his Prayers & making his Wife say hers too'.[1]

In Maria's old age, there is no question but that she was very devout but this was not the case in her youth. On this trip she showed, at least according to Lady Anne's journal, no interest in the splendours of European Catholic liturgy. She was annoyed with the begging friar in Calais and she refused to join Lady Anne at High Mass in Brussels. The Prince, who already knew her fairly well, could at least suggest that she give up her Church and Lady Anne, who knew her even better, could not decide if she would do so or not, which means that this was, at the least, an open question. Lady Anne would observe years later that 'she is a rare instance of a Catholic having religion enough for herself individually without endeavouring to influence any other person.' Maria's friend put her conclusion very neatly in a description that applies to most of us: 'I thought La Belle had an undefined sort of principle, spliced by pride.'

During her travels Maria kept a small Commonplace Book into which she would transcribe 'little things of a poetical sort as pleased her fancy . . . they were all Lovesick.' The following are some of the aphorisms, poetry and reflections she entered:

Advice is like a jest which every fool is offering another and yet won't take himself.

I find myself, as Dryden expresses himself, in so many ways oblig'd and so little able to return favours that, like those who owe too much, I can only live by getting further in your debt.

I ask no kind return in love
No tempting charm to please:
Far from the Heart such gifts remove
That sighs for peace and ease.

Nor cure nor peace that heart can know
That like the needle true
Turns at the touch of Joy or Woe
But turning trembles too.

No Law is made for Love,
Love is not in our choice but in our Fate.

What's Royalty but power to please oneself?
How wretchedly he rules
That's served by cowards and advised by fools.

Marriage, thou curse of love and snare of life,
That first debased a mistress to a wife!

To two selections she gave titles. The first she called 'Fortune':

I can enjoy her whilst she's kind
But when she dances in the wind
And shakes her wings and will not stay,
I puff the Prostitute away.
The little or the much she gave is quickly resigned
Content with poverty, my soul I arm;
And Virtue, though in rags, will keep me warm.

The second she entitled 'Woman's Honor':

Woman, Sense, and Nature's easy fool
If poor weak woman swerve from Virtue's side,
Ruin ensues, contempt, and endless shame

And one false step entirely damns her name.
In vain, with tears the loss she may deplore
In vain, look back to what she was before
She falls like Stars that set to rise no more.

Two things stand out from this selection. The first is the absence of religious quotations either from the Bible or from Catholic writers. The second is the importance of virtue and the rewards of behaving correctly in retaining one's self-respect.

At the end of the day Maria did not change churches. It is not fair to assume that this was only a matter of 'pride', although that was certainly an element. Undoubtedly there was a conviction on her part that she was in the right Church for herself: she could, after all, have become a proud Anglican. One never finds in her surviving letters or comments any of those bitter jibes at other churches sadly present in the writings and speech of some Catholics. She had the quiet and comely conviction that the religion to which her forefathers had adhered for century after century was the one for her.

Lady Anne's observations also give us some insight into Maria's general intellectual outlook, or perhaps one should say her non-intellectual outlook. She had a good head for business affairs and a common-sense approach to life but never in Lady Anne's journal and very rarely in any surviving letters or reminiscences do we find her expressing any general view on art, religion, books, history, politics or serious issues of the day. She often turned to Lady Anne to explain things or at least to help her think through a problem and she seems to have become somewhat flustered when faced with the task of writing an important letter, usually to the Prince. She would then turn to Lady Anne for help. Lady Anne's task was often to tone down some of her more outspoken language which reflected her strongly felt emotions, fierce temper and direct speech. Lady Anne's somewhat sour comment is: 'Her letters contained more of sound than sense' which may be interpreted: her letters reflected her emotions rather than her gift for intellectual analysis or clever turn of phrase.

Lady Anne Lindsay is not without her own feelings. Yet her limitations and prejudices are quite obvious and easily spotted. Maria's great gift was in the art of putting people at their ease and she seemed to excel particularly with men younger than she, men whose company and youth she found attractive. In 1800 Lady Anne would be at the Cape of Good Hope as the wife of Andrew Barnard, secretary to the Governor. She had much time to reflect on her friendship with someone who was now one of the most famous women in England, a friendship that was almost twenty years old. She concluded her analysis of Mrs Fitzherbert's character thus: 'In spite of much nonsense, some haughtiness, some duplicity, I like her. She is . . . lovely and lovable amidst her circle of foibles and follies . . . whose inconsistencies will deserve a long chapter from some historian who will attempt to draw her character and will make no real likeness because she has no fixed character but a medley of inconsistent and inconsequent particulars.'

When Lady Anne returned to London she went to live in Maria's house in Park Street. Within weeks a letter arrived from her friend who was in a sad way. While Jack Smythe had finally arrived, Maria was down with another of her 'swell'd faces', probably due to tension. (Yet another letter from the Prince had arrived.) She was worried about the beds in Park Street: she had written to the servants to have them 'well scour'd' but apparently this had not been done and she had heard there were bugs. Far worse was a developing rift due to a talk Lady Anne had had with Maria's mother who apparently told her about the Holland Plan, what Maria calls 'a certain affair in Holland etc.' In replying to her mother Maria had 'sent the old answer for no other can I or will I give'. In this letter, quoted earlier, she implied that in theory she could see some attraction in a Dutch wedding but added that she could not see how such a marriage would make any difference. 'I am very glad,' she added, that 'he is convinced it cannot be in England.'

Maria also hoped that time and weather would be on her side: 'By the time I come there [England] the weather will be bad for any sailing parties at least I am sure Nothing shall make me Sail there or any Where else.' Maria felt that Lady Anne believed her friend would change her mind once she was back in England. 'If I suspected that I should much as I dislike staying on this side would I remain till some fortunate event had made him change his Mind.' The fortunate event was, of course, a royal marriage either with the Dutch or the Prussian princess. 'Oh my drst. wt. a Cruel Situation mine is!' Maria's plan was to travel to Geneva and then on to Lausanne or some other Swiss town where she would 'fix myself for the summer'.

Before Maria and Jack set off she had to go to the British Embassy to apply to the Ambassador's secretary for her passports. After he had checked with the French police to see if Maria had any outstanding debts or criminal charges against her, he could issue her with passports for Switzerland, signed in the King's name. It was no doubt wise that she had paid the roguish Comte de Marin or he could have caused severe embarrassment to her. No doubt the Ambassador, the Duke of Dorset, would have been pleased. He may, of course, have paid less attention because by this time His Grace was preoccupied with another lady of the Opposition. Lady Elizabeth Foster, the third part of the *ménage à trois* at Devonshire House, was stopping in Paris on her way to Italy where she was to give birth to the Duke of Devonshire's child. Dorset was rather enamoured of Lady Elizabeth, perhaps unaware of the full extent of the curious situation back in London. At least he would have some consolation the following year when the Duchess of Devonshire herself was in Paris and he was able to find a substitute in her for Lady Elizabeth.

In London the Prince was, of course, delighted to hear a first-hand account of his beloved. He asked to have a look at Lady Anne's portrait of the young Dutch Princess which she had brought with her, perhaps as a preconcerted ploy agreed with Maria. When he handed it back he told 'Sister Anne' that he 'admired the artist more than I did the subject'. Lady Anne also noted a conversation with another semi-detached member of the Royal Family, indeed the lady who had occasioned the Royal Marriage Act, the Duchess of Cumberland. She was highly favourable to Maria and to any potential marriage but she doubted that any clergyman could be found who was 'daring enough' to marry the Prince and Maria.

Despite the Prince's desperate letters to Maria and his oft professed love, he had not been living a life devoid of amusement. There were the pleasure gardens at Ranelagh and balls, suppers and routs, many at Devonshire House. He was in Brighton on at least five occasions between Maria's departure and her eventual return in December 1785 and in May the papers had reported that a house was to be fitted up as his Brighton residence. In July, on arrival from Tunbridge Wells and accompanied by the ubiquitous George Hanger, 'he amused himself with shooting pigeons . . . so close to the window of a young married lady that she proceeded to hysterics'. The Prince 'graciously enquired after her the next day'.[2] There were also race meetings to attend and there were always female companions. In July the Prince was at Salisbury for the races and came to the race ball with 'his present Déesse Lady Bamfylde', wife of Sir Charles Bampfylde. 'Ly Bamfield is the only woman in the House & the Prince open'd the Ball with her . . . & drove her all the time the next day on the course in Mr Bouverie's Phaeton. She is grown fat, old & ugly but his R.H. is not famous for his taste in females.' This same source also reported that the Prince did not get up till almost noon, 'very shabby & a little 'tosicated. He came from London in a Coach with five of his attendants himself Bodkin [squeezed between others], driving through Salisbury as fast as the horses could go, laughing ready to kill himself all the way. His people neglected to take horses at Andover, so one died as they came on the Course & another that night. However the folks here all think him huge good Company & are quite delighted.'[3]

Lady Bampfylde was not the Prince's only companion. There

was also Elizabeth, Lady Melbourne, whom he had already promised Maria back in July 1784 that he would drop. As one diarist noted, she was 'no longer in her first youth when she became the object of his admiration' but she had a 'commanding figure, exceeding the middle height, full of grace and dignity, an animated countenance, intelligent features, captivating manners and conversation'. She was beautiful, well read, intelligent and, most important for the Prince, she was a good listener. Lord Byron, later her daughter-in-law's lover, paid tribute to 'the magical influence . . . that you possess not only over me but anyone on whom you please to exert it'.[4] Gossip naturally made the Prince and Lady Melbourne lovers whereas they may only have been friends.

When society was not gossiping about the Prince's love affairs it could engage in the mania for hot-air ballooning or for Sir John Wodehouse's 'learned pig' which had been taught 'to spell any word from an alphabet laid on the floor in a semi-circle, to tell the hour of the day, the day of the month &c.'[5] Then there was the old Duke of Norfolk who, rumour had it, 'is going to be married to a blowzy black Miss Eld you must have seen about town. It is said she has a pretty fortune but has refused several good match[es] on the strength of belief in a Fortune-teller who in her youth fortold she would be one of the first Ladies in England – a good reason for marrying an old Sot who is carried up to bed dead drunk by eight o'clock every night – yet it is told as a truth that it is to be a match.' In the event the Duke did not marry the 'blowzy black' and died the following year.

By early July Maria was in Geneva where she was 'quite charm'd' with the beauty of Switzerland. She had gone to various people's homes and to assemblies and had visited the Duke and Duchess of Gloucester who were in Switzerland as part of their European tour. She found the Duchess 'so gracious' and was also looking out for watches for Lady Anne. Within a few weeks Maria and Jack were in Lausanne and she had received 'another express' and her letter to Lady Anne reads like an emotional roller-coaster. As regards the letter she admits that:

> there is nothing essentially new, yet it has cast me down and made me so low-spirited and unhappy that I feel ready to hang myself . . . Alas! my dear friends, why was I born, or why do I exist to be a burthen to myself & a torment to my friends? Do you think him sincere? Surely he cannot [be] if he will persist in tormenting me to consent to what must be so much to our mutual disadvantage. I do assure you I feel so worn out . . . that at moments I am determin'd to run all risks A moment's reflection convinces me I am wrong; the length of time it has gone on, & the continual prey it has been on my spirits makes me sometimes think that nothing can happen to make me more thoroughly wretched than I am.

Maria described the little villa she had taken beside Lake Constance, noted how 'I hate that little devil Miss M—— she is a spiteful ill-natur'd little animal' and then came to the Gloucesters. 'You have no idea what good friends the duke & I are.' 'He is quite without any degree of <u>royalty</u>' and his visits to her have 'caus'd some talk as you may imagine in a place like this'. She then returns to his nephew, the Prince. Whereas earlier in the letter she seemed to be wavering in her determination to reject his proposal, she now described how the Duke 'speaks with great affection for a friend of mine, I dont dislike him the worse for that, for that person merits <u>everything</u> from me, but what in justice to myself & him I cannot grant him.' By deciding to carry on with the tour Maria also missed the wedding of her sister, Frances, to Sir Carnaby Haggerston. 'This makes my banishment more irksome.'

By August the English papers were openly referring to the Prince's affair with Maria and by September she was back in Geneva. There she again met the Gloucesters and the Duke, if not his Duchess, became a friend. He wrote to his nephew in a delightfully clear hand and used that favourite eighteenth-century adjective to describe Maria: 'I have had the pleasure of seeing a great deal of Mrs Fitzherbert whom I find a most amiable Woman. I am rejoiced at having had it in my power to shew her any attention.' When looking back on this period the Duke told his nephew, with a reference that may be to his disagreeable Duchess, 'I felt myself particularly called on some Unfortunate Occasions, to give her [Maria] every Publick mark of Attention, also trying to make her long Exil, as bearable as I could.' From the Duke's next comment we see how Maria could enter a fairly restricted society and make an impression with her naturally engaging personality: 'I cannot Express how much she made our little society, comfortable, by her friendly and constant good humoured behaviour.' For her part Maria wrote to Lady Anne, who was 'far from well either in health or spirits, & says if not better must go either to Spa or Tunbridge', that the Gloucesters are 'a great resource particularly the Male part of them who is really one of the best & most amiable men I ever saw.' As for the Duchess, 'her character is pretty well known' but she was kind to Maria '& that is all I want or expect from her'. There were balls and fêtes constantly and Maria had been able to locate the watches Lady Anne wanted at four guineas each.

Life seemed idyllic but Maria was homesick. When she got a letter from Lady Anne she 'retires to a quiet corner & reads every line at least a dozen times over'. 'My affairs go on as usual,' she writes, 'god [sic] knows wt. will become of me I had letters yesterday & sent of my answer this morning.' In addition to letters from her lover there were letters from her family urging her to stay in Europe. 'That,' she insists, 'I certainly shall not do I have not exactly fix'd my return but you will see me ere long.' Then, contradicting herself, she admits that another winter in Europe would be a better choice 'but what is life worth if one is to drag on ones existence in the way I have done for this some time past.' She sometimes thought she would 'loose my senses' which may be a good thing because then she would be excused by the world.[6]

* * *

October 1785 was the month in which Maria Fitzherbert's future was finally settled. Jack's and her return to Paris meant that she would either have to carry on to England or to accept another autumn and winter in the French capital which would take her into 1786. The time for a decision was getting closer. While she was back in the Hotel de Danemarck the Prince was on another visit to Brighton where he met Hugh Elliott who was, like James Harris, a career diplomat. Elliott was in Brighton for a holiday but his new friend saw him, like Harris, as a possible conduit to Pitt and on to the King. Once again the Prince convinced someone of his desperate plight. When Elliott wrote to Pitt he referred to 'the imminent danger to wh. H.R.H. is exposed from a manner of life that can be thoroughly understood but by those who are eye-witnesses of it . . . in my opinion H.R.H. risks being lost to himself, his family & his country if a total & sudden change does not take place.' Once again the Prince wanted permission to travel privately to Europe and once again, although Elliot's letter was 'shewn to the King', nothing came of it.

The Prince was frequently seeing Lady Anne, her sister and the Cumberlands '& we have by yt. means had constant opportunities of talking ye. subject over with each other'. According to the Prince, when he asked 'Sister Anne' what Maria should do Lady Anne replied:

> Do, says she, she has nothing else to do but to act exactly as you have desir'd her. Were she not absolutely compel'd by the urgency of both your situations & biass'd by her affection wh. she [Lady Anne] said she really beleiv'd to be very sincere as well as what had previously passed eighteen months before between us as the consent you had so lately given, she said yt. gratitude alone . . . to a man who had made every sacrifice upon earth for you & wd. if there had been as many more have made them all to you, wd. make you in ye. manner I wish'd.

Given Lady Anne's opposition to the marriage, this sounds more like what the Prince wanted her to say than what she actually said.

Lady Anne also acted as a conduit for information about Maria. When she was unwell the Prince wrote to thank Anne for sending on reassuring news: 'You have relieved me excessively, I hope & trust she will be better soon.' According to the Prince, Anne had also been advising him about proceeding, for he wrote back: 'I think you are perfectly right respecting yr. ideas of writing to her Relatives; it was ye best way of hinting her situation to you [them] without alarming you [them] too much . . . I shall be totally guided in this by yr. prudence & judgment, & I only hope yt. as soon as it is in your power you will see me either at yr. own House or some third place: you really know not what I have suffer'd.' It may be that Lady Anne was only trying to help the Smythes cope with this extraordinary situation by clarifying matters. Yet it appears that she was advising the Prince to write to Maria's parents, knowing that he would urge them to support his plans for their daughter.

The best way to approach Maria's parents was through her Uncle Errington whom the Prince knew from his gambling activities. Better than a letter was a personal meeting and he set out for Redrice but, as he later told Maria, he met her uncle 'half way upon ye. road between Red Rice and London'. The Prince showed Errington 'the papers from Holland' which related to the Holland Plan. Errington apparently agreed the Prince's view that the Plan was worthless and 'yt. there was but one thing for us now to do, & yt. was to be married as soon as possible & yt. can only be done by yr. immediate return to this country'. Errington also agreed that the marriage should take place immediately on Maria's return, without reference to her family or to anyone else 'as you will then be received by ym. all with open arms. This was yr. uncle's advice to me as man to man.' Errington was told by the Prince to bring Maria's mother up to date. Whether she had by now yielded we do not know but Errington's advice that the ceremony should take place without reference to Maria's family meant that they might avoid trouble if the King were to take action to have the marriage declared illegal.

All this supports the view that by the autumn Maria had come to a partial decision and confirms a statement she later made that her first promise to the Prince was that 'she would never marry any other person'. Put another way, she had agreed in principle to marry him. A day came, most likely toward the end of October, when she finally yielded altogether. She wrote to explain her decision to Lady Anne who, Maria knew, would be hostile. This letter has never been quoted in full before yet it gives us the key to Maria's entrance into British history. After referring to her 'deplorable' situation she went on:

> Ah Lady Anne dont think I am insensible of all the obligations I am under to —— [the Prince] I feel it strongly & think he merits every thing from me I have told him I will be his I know I injure him & perhaps destroy forever my own tranquility but I have nothing to reproach myself wt. upon that head as you must well know every thing I have done to make him give up a persuit that in the end must Infalible make us both Unhappy could I banish from my idea the fatal consequences that may attend such a connexion I then might be happy in attaching myself for life to the man that has gone thro' so much for my sake & to whom I feel myself very sincerely attach'd to, but alas whenever I look upon it in a favourable light that Idea vanishes . . . & leaves such an oppression upon my mind that I scarce know how to support myself.

She then added a rather conventional promise for an unconventional marriage: 'All I can say is that since it is to be I shall make it the Study of my life to to make him happy.'

In trying to understand why Maria Fitzherbert took the decision she did, we must look at the remainder of this letter. 'Wt will become of me my dr. friend[?] I have nothing to trust but his

Honor.' She went on: 'It is certain it is in his power by having a proper conduct in the beginning to establish my reputation in the Eyes of the World & wch if he does not do I must Sink under it.' In other words, once they were married it was the Prince's public behaviour which would establish her as his secret wife and not as his mistress, which was a somewhat odd view, given the secrecy and illegality of the marriage. Obviously all the Prince's talk about the Holland Plan and constitutional rearrangements had not got very far because Maria wrote: 'He does not seem to have form'd any plan for me.' Maria's pride now came to the front: 'I dont doubt but he will do every thing he can I am neither ambitious or Interested but it is natural that I should wish that it should be understood upon what footing we are together this I am sure you will agree wt me is but Just.'

Maria accepted that the marriage 'according to law in England is not valid yet a Marriage it certainly is according to every other law both human & divine. I shall mention this to him & I wish you wd prove to him how necessary it is for we live in a Malicious World.' Finally she added that she felt sorry for 'our poor little friend at the Hague' especially as 'it' – a marriage with the Dutch Princess – would have done well. 'This again hurt me to death that I shd. be the cause of a thing so much to his advantage not taking place.' Lady Anne should tell the Prince that she was coming and if replying, write to Calais. On 2 November, the Prince, Lady Anne and her sister were at the Cumberlands for another of their strategy meetings. The Prince grabbed 'Sister Anne's' hand and exclaimed, 'She is coming, she is coming . . . I have had letters from her . . . she will be here in a week . . . all preaching is in vain. One glance at those black eyes . . .' at which the heir to the throne broke off and walked away singing merrily in his much admired voice. As he explained to Lady Anne on a later occasion, 'Maria as a pretty woman . . . would be a pretty woman only, but as my wife she will be the comfort of my heart . . . and friend.'

The following day the Prince sat down to write what must be one of the longest and most prolix love letters in the English language from which we have quoted above. The Prince's sprawling handwriting covered forty-three quarto pages with prolific underscoring. The fact that Maria kept it when she agreed to burn her correspondence is a sign of its importance to her as something of a 'prenuptial agreement'.[7] The Prince, who began, 'I hardly know, <u>my dearest & only belov'd Maria</u> how I am to begin . . .' wanted to bring Maria up to date and immediately referred to a 'train of extraordinary & wonderful events' that was developing. Given that Maria had accepted his proposal, trusting that he would arrange something, he now set out the various options available. He referred to the Holland Plan and said his conversations with Elliott had come to nothing. He added that Pitt did suggest to the King that he should travel, only to have the King say, in the Prince's words, that he 'only wish'd to go abroad in order to marry an English lady whose name my father did not then recollect'. So the plan proposed to Harris and Elliott had finally been shot down. Instead the King wanted his heir to marry the Stadholder's daughter: this act would bring with it a settlement of his debts. The Prince had then told Elliott to tell Pitt to tell the King that he would never marry 'unless it was the woman I cd. prefer to all the world'.

The Prince now got to those arguments that really hit home. He had asked Elliott if the King were really angry at his proposed marriage. According to the Prince, Elliott said 'no, yt. he had said that what was decreed in Heaven cd. not be subverted on earth; in short, yt. ye. only way for my father now to act was entirely to connive at it, wh. he [Elliott] believ'd was his intention.' The Prince told Maria that if he married any woman but a German and had children by this marriage, these children 'wd. not after my decease succeed to the German dominions'. Where he got this idea is anyone's guess. What the King now apparently wanted was for Frederick to marry the Hereditary Prince's daughter, thereby securing the Hanoverian succession. The Prince of Wales was therefore free to marry Maria. On his father's death, he would resign his rights to Frederick who would then become Elector of Hanover.

Frederick, whom the Prince refers to as 'king' would then be willing 'to do anything I chuse respecting you, such as either acknowledging you as my wife or anything else I may please . . . & shd. yt. be ye. case I shall instantly subscribe to those terms respecting you, for there is no sacrifice, <u>my beloved wife</u>, yt. I will not make for thee.'

We can only assume in all this muddled thinking that the Prince presumed that Frederick would also become King of Great Britain and Ireland. The Prince's letters were very much like his speech and a conversation between him and a member of the government was later described by William Fawkener: 'They both talked much nonsense, but the Prince most. He said he never heard worse reasoning in better language.' The Prince had also 'supp'd last night with your friend Lady Anne with whom I had already talk'd a great deal respecting you'. Not surprisingly, given their own marital history, the Cumberlands supported the Prince and would delay their departure for Europe 'to give a sanction by their presence to our happy tho' secret union'. The only other witnesses would be the Duke and Duchess of Devonshire. 'In short, everything is settled.'

Once Maria sent information regarding her arrival, George Hanger would await her in Dover and bring her to London. The Prince 'shall either meet you in a hackney chaise by myself between Rochester and London, or wait till I hear of yr. arrival in Park Street, to wh. place I shall fly upon ye. wings of love ye. moment I know you are come.' He added in a somewhat less romantic note, that she must not arrive in London 'till it is dark' and that 'I think I had better come into the house ye. back way thro' the stables & ye. garden, you know what I mean.' As yet he had no place in which to be married: Maria should decide. However they must be married as soon as she arrived, before the news of her return leaked out.

The Prince now tried a little moral blackmail: Maria must not 'deceive' him by not returning. If she doesn't return she will 'stamp me with the epithets of a liar & a scoundrel' because he has told everyone she is returning. By implication this would probably lead to yet another suicide attempt. The Prince referred to his extraordinary letter as 'tedious' which it is. It is also confused and long-winded. He ended: 'Come then, oh! come, dearest of wives, best & most adored of women, come & for ever crown with bliss him who will thro' life endeavour to convince you by this love & attention of his wishes to be ye. best of husbands & who will ever remain unto ye. latest moments of his existence, <u>unalterably thine</u>.'

In a P.S. he added that he was enclosing a parcel and a letter from Lady Anne and 'at ye. same time an eye, if you have not totally forgotten ye. whole countenance, I think ye. likeness will strike you.' The 'eye' in question was a miniature of his eye, part of a set painted for him by his favourite miniaturist, Richard Cosway. Hers he kept for himself. The eyes, painted in watercolour on ivory, were set in gold lockets. Cosway, who only charged five guineas per eye, was much in favour just then because he was helping the Prince to decorate Carlton House and to build up his art collection. For his part, Horace Walpole decried this latest fashion for 'eye' portraits, as he told Lady Ossory: 'Do you know, Madam, that the fashion now, is not to have portraits but of an eye? They say, "Lord! don't you know it?"' Walpole may have seen these as 'French folly' but the Prince would soon be wearing the miniature round his neck. Walpole would have been even more annoyed to know that there was also a fashion for miniature mouths. On Maria's return the Prince would arrange for Cosway to paint their portraits in miniature.

In trying to understand this extraordinary course of events we should remember that most people's behaviour, whether royal or not, usually conforms to their age and class. The Prince, in his indebtedness and sexual carryings-on, was really little different from other sons of wealthy men, and aristocratic circles in the eighteenth century took a fairly relaxed view of sexual morality. Contemporary literature abounded with seducers such as Lovelace in Richardson's *Clarissa*, and dubious marriages, as when the Vicar of Wakefield's daughter was secretly married by a 'popish priest'.

Her father was relieved only to discover that the villainous husband 'has been married already by the same priest to six or eight wives more'.

The Prince was in his own way sincere and honourable. When the fifth Duke of Marlborough's heir wanted to gain access to a girl whose parents demanded marriage, he arranged for his brother to impersonate a priest. While this did not occur until 1817 the Prince could easily have done the same in 1785. As Lady Anne once wrote, the problem with the Prince was not that he had no honour but that he had 'too much Honor! an Honor which might one day prove the source of calamity to this country'.[8]

By the beginning of December the Prince was growing frantic as Maria waited to cross the Channel. He had to rely on Lady Anne for news. On the 1st he asked her to come to Carlton House: 'I suffer more for this poor Woman than I can possibly express, being the unfortunate & I may almost say the innocent cause of her Distress.' On the 3rd he wrote that he had been at Windsor because of a sister's illness and that he was 'not a little anxious concerning her situation . . . not a word from Dover as yet.' A couple of days later he wrote about the lack of news: 'In short I am perfectly distracted.'

At some stage in all this – perhaps late in November – Lady Anne travelled to the Hague. Why we do not know but it was an odd time of the year to cross the Channel and experience Dutch weather, especially as a wedding was looming. Given the attention she had devoted to Maria's tortuous romance it is unlikely that Anne would have wanted to be away when it was nearing its climax, even if her opposition was stronger than ever. She privately believed the Prince should marry the Dutch Princess, and she was 'grieved that affections so generous and tender as his seemed to be' should be bestowed on the 'lovely, but inconsequent and violent' Maria. Did she want to make one final effort to help in the proposed Dutch marriage? In November the newspapers were filled with stories about it, although by the end of the month they were announcing that the idea had been given up. At some stage, whether before her departure or after her return, Lady Anne did explain that Maria was being held back due to one of her 'swelled faces'. Obviously Lady Anne had had some sport with the Prince's carrying-on for he wrote: 'You laugh at me about my nerves' but he had really been 'excessively ill'. He insisted, in a sentence that should have been carved on his tomb, 'Believe me what ever you please to think <u>men have nerves as well as women</u>.' Lady Anne must have mentioned, presumably with tongue in cheek, the idea of Maria's retreating to a convent, which suggestion received a dismissal that sounded as if it had come from his father: 'As to Nunnery that is all flummery.'

We know that Maria was finally back in London by Friday, 9 December and there is some evidence that she might have arrived by 30 November. One of her earliest acts was to dash off a note for a servant to take round to Lady Anne's: 'For god sake my dr Friends call upon me if it is but a moment. I must see you——.' The Prince was ecstatic when he wrote to 'Sister Anne': 'Wedn night or rather Thursday morng four o'Clock I have just left my Maria who desires you will call upon her as early Tomorrow Morning as you can. I am happy than words can express excuse my not adding another Word but I have almost lost my Senses.' Perhaps in response to this, Lady Anne wrote to Maria to tell her that she had heard of her arrival but that Maria must not come to her house. The Prince would explain everything. A visit by Maria would only increase the gossip swirling round London.

Maria and the Prince had a lot to discuss and the couple walked round the garden having what must have been a heated discussion. Using language that showed her own frank attitude she described the Prince and herself as 'bellowing like pigs'. The first problem was obvious: should they get married? Here the attitude of Charles James Fox who the Prince probably still expected to support him and who, Maria already knew, preferred her to become a kept woman, like his Mrs Armistead, came into play. On 10 December Fox wrote to the Prince to protest against the 'very desperate step (pardon the expression) of marrying her'. Fox then set out clearly the constitutional objections. A marriage with a 'Catholick throws the Prince contracting such marriage out of the succession'. If Mrs Fitzherbert should later become a member of the Church of England it would not avail because she would have been married as a Catholic. 'Sir,' he wrote, 'this is not a matter to be trifled with.' The country was still 'full of its old prejudices against Catholicks, and justly dreading all disputes about succession'.

If Frederick became the heir, Fox argued, could not a party of more radical Whigs form round the Prince and Maria's children and argue that the constitution should be changed for their sake? Fox argued that the marriage could not be 'a real one'. Talk of it would divide the country and keep 'men's minds in perpetual agitation'. There would be demands either to annul the marriage or to legitimise any children. When he turned twenty-five could the Prince really apply to Parliament to accept a secret marriage of several years' existence? Could a woman who had lived with him as a secret wife ever become Queen? This can only be a 'mock marriage'. The Prince replied the following day with a whopping lie: 'Make yourself easy, my dear friend. Believe me, the world will now soon be convinced that there not only is, but never was any grounds for these reports, which of late have been so malevolently circulated.'

Another problem was the difficulty the Duchess of Cumberland had foreseen: finding a clergyman prepared to risk not only his career but possibly his life. The Prince sent his private secretary, Colonel Gardner, to find a priest. The colonel first approached the Rev. Philip Rosenhagen, who was a military chaplain. He had spent some ten years in Europe to avoid gambling debts but in 1781 was appointed Rector of Little Easton. He was also a hack writer and a radical in politics. Gardner bombarded Rosenhagen with at least six letters in which he promised, on the Prince's behalf, future preferment. Rosenhagen would not co-operate, partly because he was made no specific offer of preferment, partly because he genuinely feared a constitutional upheaval and partly because he was terrified of the legal consequences. Eventually he was sent to Ceylon as Archdeacon of Colombo and died in 1798.

Next the Prince thought of the Rev. Johnes Knight who was Rector of Welwyn in Hertfordshire and also of a City church and who 'had known George the Fourth since the latter was a child in frocks'. When Knight discussed matters with Colonel Lake, now back in England, he replied that 'I shall not dream of such a thing!' However he agreed to go to the Prince who 'described in the most impassioned language the incurable devotion which he felt for the lady'. He showed the priest his wound and added that if he could not marry Maria he would succeed in his next suicide attempt. The Prince said that if Knight would not help him he 'must find out another clergyman who will'. This made Knight fear the Prince would get some disreputable man who would 'betray the Prince's secret to Mr Pitt' and he agreed. Plans were made: at this stage the Prince still said that the Duke and Duchess of Devonshire would be the witnesses. But when Knight got home he thought better of the matter and wrote asking to be relieved of his promise which the Prince did.

It will be helpful to mention here three statements made by the Prince to Knight which help us to understand Maria's surrender and the Prince's understanding of the crisis he was provoking. Knight later told Sir William Fraser: 'You have no idea what were his powers of persuasion: he could when he chose be the most delightful of men; indeed irresistible.' Secondly, the Prince told Knight that he would 'repeal the Royal Marriage Act the instant he came to the Throne'. Finally, when Knight told the Prince to his face that he could not oblige him, the Prince shook his hand and, referring to his letter releasing Knight from his promise, replied, 'If he had not let me off, I must inevitably have fled from England.' The clergyman added, 'To this royal logic I joyfully assented, though for the life of me I never could make out how banishment must necessarily follow my resolution to conform to the law.'[9]

Eventually the Prince found a priest who was prepared to break the law. The Rev. Robert Burt was one of the Prince's Chaplains in Ordinary. This poor man has had a hard time at the hands of Maria's previous biographers who wrote that the payment of £500 by the Prince was to get him out of the Fleet Prison for debtors. In truth, Burt came from what is usually called a 'good', that is well-off, family whose wealth came from the West Indies. There is no proof that he was given £500 but a promise of help must have been made because six years later he wrote to ask for the Prince's help in getting a prebend's stall in Rochester Cathedral. In the event he did not get the desired appointment, even with the Prince's help, and died a few months later.[10]

There was also the problem of the Smythes. Jack, who returned with Maria, could be counted on to support her. But what of her other brothers and sister? Maria explained to Lady Anne that her father and mother had arrived from Bath and with Uncle Errington had talked with the Prince: 'after long reservations' her family were won over. Years later, when writing to Maria's mother, the Prince said he confided 'in that known goodness of heart which I have ever experienced from You upon all occasions'. To what degree the Prince's promise of £10,000 [£540,000] a year for Maria played a part in the family's change of mind we shall never know. In the eighteenth century such consideration was not so much 'mercenary' as a sign that a woman's parents were sensibly concerned about their daughter's future. The few surviving comments indicate that Maria's mother had far more influence over her than her increasingly ill father. It may be that Maria's later insistence on this sum as that due her was in part because it was the amount promised her parents. Her brother, Walter, opposed the marriage and this did nothing to bring them any closer. By their subsequent behaviour we are safe in assuming her sister and her other brothers, Charles and Henry, approved, connived or at least accepted what was happening.

It is hardly surprising that all the activity at Carlton House and Park Street and all the scurrying of servants in royal or Fitzherbert livery with messages for the Prince, Maria or Lady Anne set off a fusillade of rumours. Society was enthralled at the drama unfolding in its midst. On 12 December Lady Anne told Maria, 'You know all London is talking of what it is believ'd will soon take place.' The previous night a great dinner had been given whose guests included the Archbishop of Canterbury and the Lord Chief Justice, Lord Mansfield. Lady Anne was later told by Lord Mansfield, her friend, that she had been named as the promoter of the marriage and as the person who provided a meeting place for the lovers. This annoyed and frightened her and she wrote to Lord Mansfield: 'Had my advice been taken his conduct woud have been different to what it is likely to be.' She sent Maria a copy of her letter for the Prince and her to read and added that it was 'more than probable that the King and Queen may see my letter'. In her reply to the Lord Chief Justice, Lady Anne denied any match-fixing and said that she had not seen the Prince since Maria's return and had only called on Maria. The proposed marriage was 'improper' and to help it was to betray her King, her country, the Prince and Maria. While she had been with Maria she had been firm against the Prince, which was true, but she also claimed she had 'stimulated' Maria to leave England which was an exaggeration. On her return in the summer she had advised the Prince and 'I think the Royal ears have been poisn'd' against her. When Lord Mansfield replied to Lady Anne he said that 'I did not believe there was the least Ground' for accusing his friend but urged her to be careful.

In winding up her letter to Maria and the Prince, Lady Anne wrote in obvious distress: 'Dear Souls! I dare not even put up a prayer to God for you <u>mutually</u>, for <u>this Act of Parliament</u>, but if you <u>are</u> married (which it is my Duty to wish you may never be) I'll make it up.' The Prince and Maria replied to Lady Anne in a joint note, probably written the following day. The Prince thanked her for the letter: 'All I can say is that I had sooner perish than recede from what has past.' Maria added, 'My affairs rest the same as when I saw you; a day or two at farthest will finish everything.' She also asked if she could borrow Lady Anne's carriage: with her parents in town she may have needed an extra carriage or she may have wanted not to use her own which could be recognised.

The stage was now set for one of the most extraordinary royal weddings in British history. On the evening of 15 December the Prince, accompanied by Orlando Bridgeman, the twenty-three year old MP for Wigan, arrived in Park Street. Bridgeman was a friend of the Smythes and one of the Prince's party. He, however, waited outside the drawing room. Inside were Mr Burt, Maria, the Prince and the two witnesses, her brother, Jack, and Uncle Errington. The original plan for the Duke and Duchess of Devonshire to attend had fallen through. (Lady Anne heard that the Duke had forbidden his wife to attend.) We can only imagine what thoughts crossed Maria's mind as she heard, for the third time in her life, the words of the Prayer Book service. It is ironic that in her and her new husband's case, the three causes 'for which Matrimony was ordained' would not apply. Marriage was ordained 'for the procreation of children' and there is no evidence that there ever were any children. Secondly, marriage was ordained 'for a remedy against sin, and to avoid fornication'. In the Prince's case the remedy proved a complete failure. Thirdly, marriage was ordained 'for the mutual society, help, and comfort'. While in future years the marriage did bring her help in monetary terms and in acquiring an unequalled place in Society, it only periodically brought either much comfort.

Immediately the service was over the Prince wrote out a marriage certificate on a plain sheet of quarto paper: 'We, the undersigned, do witness yt George Augustus Frederick, Prince of Wales, was married unto Maria Fitzherbert, this 15th of December 1785.' It was then signed: George P., Maria Fitzherbert, Henry Errington and John Smythe. The certificate or marriage lines was then given to Maria and now is in the Royal Archives where the hurried scrawl still indicates how nervous the Prince must have been. The only eye-witness to record the event was Maria herself and her recollection was expressed in words Lord Stourton preferred: 'She was then hurried to England, anticipating too clearly and justly, that she was about to plunge into inextricable difficulties; but having insisted upon conditions, such as would satisfy her conscience and justify her in the eyes of her own Church, she abandoned herself to her fate.' The 'passive' tone he adopted does not accord with her behaviour at the time and the religious language is probably as much Stourton's as Maria's: she certainly did not use such language in 1785.[11]

Where the couple went for their honeymoon, if indeed they had one, we do not know. Previous biographers wrote that they went to Maria's own rural villa at Richmond – or to Ormeley Lodge on Ham Common. The carriage was said to have broken down at Hammersmith – or Twickenham – where the couple may have had supper in an inn while the damage was made good. There may or may not have been deep snow on the roads. It is a touching tale but there is no evidence and this, like so much in Maria's life, must remain a mystery. There is even a possibility that the couple separated and instead of going on a honeymoon Maria actually went to Bath with her parents.

For over two hundred years people have asked why Maria changed her mind and decided to marry the heir to the throne secretly and illegally. As in all our actions there was a variety of motives, each of which shaded into the others. The most obvious is that she genuinely loved this extraordinary young man. Her Catholic faith, which would have insisted on a wedding, does not appear to have been a factor. People have assumed that because she was 'religious' in her later years she must have been religious throughout her life. This was not the case.

Another factor was what could be called Maria's sense of her own self-importance: to observers this was pride bordering on arrogance. One of the earliest pamphlets to attack her referred to her as 'an experienced dame, who had been twice a widow'. Such a woman 'was not likely to surrender upon common terms. She looked forward towards a more brilliant prospect which her ambition might artfully suggest, founded upon the feeble character of an amorous young Prince. She adopted the stale artifice of absenting herself for some months.' Robert Huish had no doubt about this aspect of her personality when he wrote in 1831 that Maria's marriage to Thomas Fitzherbert had 'continued her in that state of habitual importance which would effectually preserve her from being tempted into any degradation of her character . . . it became the public opinion, that the relation in which she stood with the Prince of Wales could only be justified *to herself* by the solemnity of some engagement, or the sanction of some ceremony . . .' She was also caught: she had refused to become a mistress and demanded something else. Now that the Prince had offered marriage, thereby risking his right to the throne, how could she refuse?

While Maria fully understood that her wedding was illegal she also knew that other marriages such as Cumberland's or Gloucester's were ultimately tolerated, if not accepted. Might not this be her case? While she would never become Queen, or even Electress of Hanover, she might still be recognised as the legitimate wife of a King. We know she understood the basic provisions of the Royal Marriage Act but she also probably knew how unpopular it was. Acts of Parliament can always be repealed. Who knows what the Prince might do once he were King? We should also mention here an unsigned paper, written in 1785 and entitled 'Thoughts on the Kingdom of Ireland . . .' which was found among the Prince's papers. While it contains no reference to legal restrictions on the King of Ireland it did argue that the heir to the throne should be installed as Irish King: 'Ireland has hitherto been a royal farm, unimproved because unoccupied.'[12] The very fact that the Prince had the paper shows how his mind was working.

Twelve years later the Prince returned to this idea and proposed a 'mission to Ireland' based on a 'request signed by . . . the leaders of the Irish Opposition'. He 'sent this letter to Mr. Pitt, desiring him to lay it before the King. Of course, the proposal was negatived.' When the Prince did have ideas with some merit they were usually knocked down by the King, his government or both.

Fox's nephew, Lord Holland, gave in his *Memoirs of the Whig Party*, published in 1854, another, more cynical interpretation of Maria's motives. Lord Holland wrote that he was told by 'a friend of mine, a man of strict veracity' who had in turn been told by Maria herself, that 'it was at the Prince's own earnest and repeated solicitations, not at Mrs. Fitzherbert's request, that any ceremony was resorted to. She knew it to be invalid in law; she thought it nonsense, and told the Prince so.' To support this Maria supposedly told Lord Holland's unnamed friend that if she had believed it to be a real marriage she would have had religious scruples which only could have been allayed by having a Catholic priest perform the marriage. Maria is supposed to have told this same person 'that she had given herself to him, exacted no conditions, trusted to his honour, and set no value on the ceremony which he insisted on having solemnized.' As evidence of Maria's intentions none of this would stand up in court because it is all hearsay evidence in which an unnamed person repeated a conversation with Maria to a third party who later published it.

There are however some elements in this story that ring true. We now know that when Maria returned she did so knowing that the Prince had no definite plan for her future and that she had to trust him. We know that the Prince was fully aware that both Maria and the Duchess of Devonshire considered the July 1784 'ceremony' a farce. We know that it was the Prince who sought out a clergyman to marry them, not Maria. There are, however, difficulties. Maria fully understood the law that marriages had to take place in the Church of England. She may well also have understood that in English Catholic teaching an Anglican marriage was perfectly valid. She knew that she was breaking at least two laws and laying herself open to severe penalties. Why do this if she thought it all a farce? Why not simply become the Prince's mistress and have done with it? The perks would have been the same. If she had not really wanted a marriage herself, why did she spend almost a year and a half in Europe to avoid the Prince, only to return to become – in her eyes – his mistress? Her self-possession had demanded a secure position which only marriage could give her: Perdita, after all, had never married the Prince and where was she now? On balance it is reasonable to reject this argument but questions do remain.

What is certain is that far from being swept off her feet, Maria Fitzherbert knew exactly where she stood. When Maria was compiling her Commonplace Book, Lady Anne had called the entries 'all Lovesick' but then added, 'but tho' at that time the Hue of her mind might be so it is not its general character'. Lady Anne had gone on: 'Poor F——! I wish she had eschew'd dangerous Greatness, to have fed her chickens & enjoy'd a life of a country Happiness, which She was better suited to.' Lady Anne was wrong here. Maria had no desire to live among chickens and squires but to shine in London society as the wife – not the latest mistress – of the Prince of Wales, even if she could not be a Princess, let alone a Queen. Lady Anne was correct in one thing: it would prove a 'dangerous Greatness'. Maria was now beginning one of the grandest, and most passionate, as well as most public, of the world's great love affairs.

6

---·•·---

THE BUZZ OF THE DAY

The wedding set off a new wave of speculation. Within days one
Whig MP, Sir Gilbert Elliot, wrote to his wife during 'a half-hour's
sitting at Lady Palmerston's toilet . . . She says the report is that
Mrs Fitzherbert is or is to be, at Carlton House; that she was
married by a Roman Catholic priest; is to have 6000£ a year, and
is to be created a Duchess.' Others, such as Robert Hobart, an MP
in the Irish parliament and an aide-de-camp to the Lord
Lieutenant, the Duke of Rutland, wrote to Dublin from London
on Christmas eve: 'The lie of the day is that the Prince of Wales
is to marry Mrs. Fitzherbert, but I believe, totally without foundation.'

Three days later Hobart wrote again, this time taking the
marriage for granted. His letter shows how quickly things were
changing. 'The Town,' he writes, 'still talk of the Prince of Wales's
marriage.' The Prince, he reported prematurely, has taken a box
for Maria at the opera and 'constantly passes the greater part of
the night with her'. He referred to the new importance that had
overtaken the Smythe family and mentioned 'Prince Carnaby',
Maria's recently acquired brother-in-law, Sir Carnaby Haggerston.
Walter Smythe 'appears already much elated with the honour that

is intended, or rather the dishonour which has already attended, his family'. Traditional anti-popery feelings come out in Hobart's comment on the Prince's 'new establishment' for, he wrote, 'no doubt' the Marchioness of Buckingham, who had recently become a Catholic, 'will be first lady of the bedchamber', while her aunt, the Italian-born dowager Countess of Westmeath, could become Maria's 'necessary woman' [emptier of chamber pots]. 'If pride, arrogance, and self-sufficiency be qualities for a Popish Minister,' Hobart continued, 'the noble Marquis himself, by embracing that religion which he appeared to encourage in his wife, may be at the head of the Papistical court.'

In the meantime the Prince set about telling his siblings. He wrote to his second brother, Prince William, then in the Royal Navy, to tell him and to warn him to keep it secret. William replied: 'My best compliments to M and tell her she may rely in my secrecy.' There was really little need for Prince William to be secretive because the news was spreading so quickly already. As to the King and Queen, we are not sure when they found out but find out they did. Sadly, the Queen's diary has not survived for 1785–6 and in her letters to her brother, Karl, she does not mention any ceremony: she was far more concerned with the death of her other brother, Georg and then with the death of Karl's wife. The newly-weds received support from Maria's sister, from Uncle Errington and his wife and, not surprisingly, from the Prince's two uncles, Cumberland and Gloucester. The Duke of Gloucester, now in Milan, had been hearing 'various reports' of a marriage from newspapers and British travellers. He waxed enthusiastic: 'I have seen so much of her that I think I can with truth say she has few like her; I am convinced she loves you far beyond herself . . . I only allow myself to rejoice that the two People I have every reason to love the most seem to be so happy in Each other. It must last because there is so much Good Temper, and good Judgement.' His disagreeable Duchess did not share his enthusiasm. She 'burst out and repeat'd with violence some late reports'. The Duke then 'took up a very serious <u>Ton</u> and said from the Near Relationship between <u>Us</u>, it became <u>her</u> little to talk upon that subject . . . I plainly saw that Your Attachment was most serious, and Respectable that I order'd <u>her</u> and my children to avoid talking of what they could not understand, but to alter <u>her</u> style of speaking of your Amiable Friend, for that I should resent it and she would Repent it.' The Duke, whose Duchess had led him into the arms of Lady Almeria Carpenter, reported that his mistress 'loves and is most sincerely devoted to . . . The Amiable and Estimable Lady you are probably now Embracing.'[1]

In Maria's own circle, somewhat unexpectedly, Lady Sefton was not keen on the marriage, although she later changed her mind, while Lord and Lady Clermont, great leaders in society, and the Marchioness of Salisbury, all Maria's friends before the wedding, stood by her. For the Duchess of Devonshire things were difficult. Her mother, the ever prudent Lady Spencer, asked, 'What will you do about going to the opera with Mrs Fitzherbert? I wish it could be avoided, for it is certainly very plain that both he and she mean to shew they are not upon the same footing they were. She cannot be his wife, what then is she?' Should her daughter 'countenance and support such a marriage'? Better for Georgiana to stay out of London until 'some respectable people, if any such will do it, have set you an example'. She could plead the need to nurse her baby daughter. (Had she done so the most fashionable Duchess would have been doing a most unfashionable thing.) Lady Spencer heard that the Duchess of Portland, whose husband headed the Whig party, was told by her Duke not to call on Maria. While Lady Beauchamp and Maria's aunt, Lady Broughton, did call, Lady Spencer felt 'these cannot be examples to follow'. If the Prince or Maria asked the Duchess to support them, she should ask 'what you are to say to me and to the world and on that score to beg they will excuse your taking any part'.

The Duchess replied that same day to describe her growing hostility to Maria:

As to Mrs. F. I never will go to the Opera with her, I never did and never will, and she knows it. What I mean to do is this: I know that her intentions once were perfectly honourable and prudent; seeing another turn had taken place, I strongly dissuaded him from his ideas, and I declare I do not know that anything has taken place. She encourages him, you say, in public and she receives his visits. I search into nothing and only wish to keep entirely out of it. I shall leave my name with her, and if I have a large assembly, ask her, because I have done so before and because Mrs. F., an unmarried woman suffering the visits of an unmarried man, is no reason for not being civil to her. But this is all I will do, and I will avoid the assembly if you like it, and indeed from my own choice I shall not have one.

On 18 February the *Morning Post*, whose editor made his money from blackmailing famous people, reported: 'It is confidently reported, that a certain marriage has been solemnized by a *Romish Priest*, who immediately quitted the Kingdom.' The editor presumably got his money and there was no sequel. It was hardly surprising that rumours were becoming more widespread. As Lady Anne noted about Park Street, there was 'a veil of mystery which pervaded everything in the house'. Horace Walpole told Lady Ossory:

Oh! but the hubbub you are to hear, and to talk of, and except which, you are to hear and talk of nothing else, for they tell me the passengers in the streets of all ranks talk of it, is a subject to which I suppose your letters have already attuned you, and on which I alone, for certain reasons will say nothing . . . I do not know a tittle from any good authority; and though a mass of circumstances are cited and put together, they command no credit: whoever believes, must believe upon trust. The rest must be the work – or the explosion, of time – though secrecy does not seem to be the measure most effected.

The 'certain reasons' Walpole mentioned were the circumstances surrounding the marriage of his illegitimate niece to the Duke of Gloucester: irregular royal marriages were a sore point with Walpole.

Three days later Walpole wrote to his friend, Sir Horace Mann, the British Minister at the Grand Duke of Tuscany's Court in Florence. One of Mann's tasks was to keep an eye on the Young Pretender who lived there and he had written how Cardinal York had recently given various Stuart jewels to Madame Albany, the wife of the Young Pretender. Walpole, clearly becoming rather sensitive about the 'rise of the Smythes', had his own bit of gossip about demi-royalty: 'I am obliged to you for your accounts of the House of <u>Albany</u>; but that extinguishing family can make no sensation here when we have other-guess matters to talk of in a higher and more flourishing race . . . I know nothing but the buzz of the day . . . I hope it is essentially void of truth, and that appearances rise from a much more common cause.' He hoped, in other words, that Maria was now the Prince's mistress, not his wife.

On 10 February newspapers reported the shocking news that Maria had taken a box at the Theatre Royal in the Haymarket, the home of the Italian Opera company. In London, as in Paris, Vienna, St Petersburg or Florence, the opera house was the gathering point for the ruling elite to see and be seen. *The Daily Universal Register* noted a rival paper's 'illiberal insinuation' regarding the new box. It also noted that a correspondent, wishing to defend Mrs Fitzherbert, asked 'whether a lady of eighteen hundred a year cannot afford that sum, without being obliged to an *increase* of *connections*?' Taking the box was, in effect, a first public announcement from Maria that she had arrived on the social scene. 'Every lady possessing an opera box,' Lord Mount Edgcumbe remembered, 'considered it as much her <u>home</u> as her house, and was as sure to be found there, few missing any of the performances.' There were, after all, only thirty-six boxes, so having one was a considerable achievement. A box, which was considerably larger than today, was filled 'exclusively with the highest classes of

Society, all, without exception, in the full dress then universally worn'. Audiences presented 'a finer spectacle than any other theatre in Europe, and absolutely astonished the foreign performers to whom such a sight was entirely new'. This is why Georgiana Devonshire and her mother were so exercised about appearing at the opera with Maria. After performances, or 'representations', the audience retired to the coffee-room, 'the best assembly in London . . . and all the first society was regularly to be seen there.' Theatre-lovers, seated in the pit below, sometimes took a different view as they went 'to enjoy good Poetry, and good acting; unannoy'd by chattering Quality' above. In 1791 Horace Walpole recalled that 'the Prince went to her publicly at all hours, appeared at her windows in a morning, [and] had Mr Smith her brother with him when he received others in a morning.' Even more, Walpole noted that 'a whole [box] was taken in her name at the opera, where he sat openly with her.' The audience would have known which was her box because fans sold in the theatre printed the plan of boxes.

In the letter which Countess Spencer wrote to her daughter about her appearing at the opera with Maria, she tackled the vexed question straight on: 'Why does a private gentlewoman take every subscription in her box at the opera to herself, why does she change from a very prudent behaviour about him to a very imprudent one, suffering him to sit and talk to her all the Opera, to carry her picture (or her eye), which is the same thing, about and shew it to people, letting his carriage be constantly seen at her door, especially in a morning to carry him home?'

When Lady Jerningham heard of the marriage in March she too noted with some outrage and perhaps a little jealousy that her fellow Catholic 'has taken a Box to herself at the Opera, a thing which no Lady but the Dutchess of Cumberland ever did – a hundred guineas a year!' (One hundred guineas or £105 equalled almost £5,700 in current terms.)

Society was fascinated with the secret that was becoming known to everyone in the Establishment. Maria herself would later refer to her marriage as 'the *One Truth which all the world knows'*. Henry Swinburne, another recusant, wrote to his brother about 'the magnificent concert at Mrs Conway's house. The Prince and Maria were there and 'Mrs Fitzherbert wears his picture in full view round her neck: therefore I suppose matters are settled between them.'[2] Slowly the news was filtering out through the provinces and Ireland as we can see in the letter books of the sixth Earl of Denbigh who lived at Newnham Paddox, near Rugby. Early in the month the Earl wrote to a friend in Town: 'Surely there cannot be any truth in the Report of the Prince being married to a Catholic Widdow. Is it believed or not? If true the consequences of it may be dreadful to our Posterity.' That same day Lord Wentworth (Lady Anne's old beau) wrote to Lord Denbigh: 'As to the R——l Marriage, that is so old a subject that it is scarce talked of. But I believe it is very plain. She thinks she is married.' Three days after this Lord Denbigh's friend again wrote to the Earl: 'Horrid as it is, I fear it to be the General Opinion that there has been a Kind of Marriage. At Lord Peter's [Petre's] supper on his son's Wedding he [the Prince] waited behind her chair and took no notice of any other person. Consequences most dreadful to think of.' (As Lord Petre was the most politically active of the Catholic peers, the Prince's behaviour would have caused even more alarm.) The same day the Earl wrote to Hugh Carleton, the Solicitor General of Ireland: 'As to a certain Great Marriage many people on this side of the water are of opinion that the Lady thinks herself so. At this distance I can form no real opinion about it, therefore shall only say, God forbid.'[3]

By March news of the wedding was also spreading round Europe. On the 10th Mann told Walpole that it had reached Florence. At first Sir Horace treated the news 'with contempt' but added that 'it seems to be too universally spread not to require an investigation.' On 24 February the *Leyden Gazette*, which in the past had been given money by the opposition in London, published the following: *'Le bruit général'* was that *'le Prince de Galles a fait des démarches sérieuses pour se lier par le noeud du marriage,*

159

et l'on dit, qu'ill a jeté ses vices sur une veuve de deux maris, agée d'environ 35 ans [she was 29], *appelé Madame Fitzherbert, de la réligion Catholique.'* There was also an item in the *Berlin Gazette* referring to the marriage. By 21 March Lord Pembroke, writing from Florence, told his son that 'All the foreign Gazettes assure the P. of W. is married to Mrs Fitzherbert. A word of it, I beg, in your next.' Interestingly Lord Pembroke was tolerant but frightened: 'The <u>unlawfully</u> is the only danger; it may create a breed of Pretenders; was it <u>lawfull</u>, Mrs. F. would do as well as any Princess whatsoever.'

While European newsheets were spreading the story, Maria and her Prince were enjoying themselves. In the spring the Duke and Duchess of Cumberland returned from Europe and they reopened Cumberland House in Pall Mall, next door to Carlton House. In March London newspapers reported that 'Mrs Broadhurst is shortly to receive *masks* – the Prince – Mrs Fitzherbert, and all the fashionable *world* are to be of the party – Dominoes are to be rejected – consequently many of the ton for *that night* only mean to figure [dance] away in *excellent characters!' The Daily Universal Register* went on to give a short biography of Maria which had moments of truth unusual in papers of the day. It had her parentage and two marriages, more or less right, her childlessness and her foreign travel until 'pressing solicitations brought her back to England'. Her Catholicism was not mentioned.

Having, as it were, introduced Maria to those who felt they should know what was going on, the paper became bolder ten days later. 'The Prince's musical talents are of the first rate. His *voice* is pleasing. He is *attached* to, and peculiarly happy in *humming* old *pieces*. His Highness has lately *set* the *'Dainty Widow'* much *higher* in order to suit his *pipe.'* Even without a detailed knowledge of eighteenth-century sexual slang the underlying message is pretty obvious. In a more elevated tone the paper went on in a report of Dublin news: 'The report in this metropolis respecting Mrs F——h——t is, that her marriage has actually taken place; and that in conformity to the etiquette of such a connection, she did not return visits. That she was pregnant, and owing to that circumstance her spouse had publicly avowed his marriage. It is probable, that to the various families of the *Fitzes*, we shall shortly have the new name added of *Fitz George*.'

On 17 March Lord Wentworth wrote that the marriage was 'an alarming subject, especially as pregnancy is said to be already visible'. That same day another Londoner wrote that the Prince 'goes by my door every day at the same hour and seems very constant to her at present. It is said she is with child. After a while she will be a most unhappy woman.' Whether this was a prediction or a wish we do not know.[4]

The Prince enjoyed teasing his audience as to the nature of their relationship. When Horace Walpole and Lord Hertford dined with him at Carlton House he never mentioned Maria. Lord Lothian also dined with the Prince and reported to the Duke of Rutland: 'I believe when he has been spoke to about it he has always been violent and I cannot find out that he has denied it [the marriage] preemptorily. He has said to one of the most intimate in his family when asked upon the subject, that he might answer, if asked the question, in the negative.' He added, 'You know the general topic of his conversation about women,' and 'he never mentioned her to me amongst others. I am very sorry for it, as it does him infinite mischief, particularly amongst the trading and lower class of people and if true must ruin him in every light.'

Not to mention Maria was one thing but to deny the marriage outright was another. What would Maria's reaction have been had she read the letter from Thomas Orde to the Duke of Rutland in May that 'The Prince denies the thing, but has at the same time dropped hints of *her* belief in the connection, and has wished, therefore, that their happiness may not be interrupted by conjectures and rumours.' There were other occasions, as when the Prince acted as best man for the first time. John Wilkes told his daughter that a 'most respectable lady' asked, 'Was your R.H. never before at a marriage?' to which he replied, 'laying his right hand with eagerness upon his breast, "Never, on my honour."' Assuming these reported conversations to be relatively accurate they show the confusing and confused state of the Prince's mind. He both believed that Maria had been his wife since July 1784 and that this was a private arrangement which he could deny in public.

In March Henry Swinburne was at Almack's Assembly Rooms in St James's where he saw the other side of Maria's husband, the side he had shown at Lord Petre's son's wedding supper. 'The Prince of Wales,' he wrote, 'never moved from Mrs Fitzherbert's side, and supped <u>en petit comité</u> with her, Lady Beauchamp, Lady Horatio Waldegrave, and Mrs Musters, who all paid her the deference they would to a Princess of Wales.' About two in the morning Maria 'yawned, and his Royal Highness, pulling out his watch, showed her the hour. Up she rose, he called her chair, and off she went, he following directly.' The Prince's public attentions to Maria were noted. They were as much an example of his genteel manners, for which he was famous (and which decades afterwards Dickens would mock), as a game being played to perplex onlookers.

For some of Maria's older friends, such as Lady Anne, coping with the new situation could be difficult. Lady Anne knew that the Prince dined almost every day in Park Street and this carried on well into 1787. (When the Duke of Gloucester finally returned in November 1787 he wrote from Dover that he wanted to pay his respects to the Prince 'either at Carlton House or <u>Park Street</u>'. Lady Anne knew, also, that there were certain hours when the pair wished to be alone and during these hours – probably in the late afternoon, after dinner – one did not call. Even still, there could be difficulties and some time in 1786 she wrote to Maria to invite both her and the Prince, 'yet we dare not ask you both for fear that certain folks woud think we shew'd too much Bravery in inviting you thus to shew you off at present.' Which one, therefore, should she invite? This was meant to be humorous although the humour had a bit of a sting in its tail. Maria, however, was not amused and replied in a semi-regal letter:[5] 'Dr. Lady Anne, I could not answer your note before I had seen the P. to deliver your message to him he desires me to say that he cannot any more than

162

myself wait upon you tomorrow. Believe me my dr Lady Anne I am the last person in the world that would willingly act in the most trifling manner to cause you the least Uneasiness & for that reason alone neither the P. nor myself can avail ourselves of yr Invitation.' The next letter in Lady Anne's papers would not be until January 1788.

However annoyed Maria was by her friend's ill-timed humour, she did not let it halt her move up the social ladder. When Lady Anne had visited Park Street before the contretemps she noted that the mantel was covered with invitation cards from more duchesses and countesses 'than I thought the peerage contained'. This display owed much to Maria's snobbish butler with whom Lady Anne had had to contend while touring Europe. Maria now made a second public announcement of her new status when on 18 March the papers noted that she had rented Lord Uxbridge's house in St James's Square. (It appears she kept the Park Street house until at least 1792.) What is beyond doubt is that this was a large step. In February, probably during a visit to Brighton, she wrote to William Fermor: 'You know of old what a terible Scribe I am & how much I detest the very Idea of taking up my pen indeed I grow worse & worse every day & realy Believe in a short time I shall not be able to write atall.' Since arriving in Brighton she had only written five letters '& those to my Mother an ATTENTION I should never have been forgiven if omitted'. (This was a trait she shared with the Duchess of Devonshire, although Her Grace would not have liked the comparison.) She would like to visit the Fermors but 'you know my Circumstances & how I am tied by the Leg'. Maria was 'going up to Town the day after tomorrow to bid adieu to my House in Park St wch I own I feel sorry to quit. I hope to be able to get into my new House wh I leave this place which will be the end of next Month.' The Petres, one of the leading recusant families, had been visiting her and, once she was in London, Uncle Errington '& My Lady' must come.

In Maria's letter she had noted in a postscript that 'Bell is Standing by me & desires her kind Love to you.' This is our first introduction to a woman who would play an important part in Maria's life. Bell was Miss Isabella Pigot who became Maria's 'companion', thereby guaranteeing respectability and a *de facto* lady-in-waiting. Bell, like Maria, came from a military family, although in her case her relations were able to take commissions in the King's services. While Bell came from a 'good family' we may assume she had little money. This woman would be loyal to Maria and the Prince over many years and would frequently be 'a piggy in the middle', a role she rather enjoyed playing. To the old Duke of Cumberland she was 'little *Belly*' while her surviving letters show her to be rather excitable in a school-girlish sort of way. One acquaintance, Lady Forester, remembered her as 'a most singular person', a frequent visitor to the great houses in Staffordshire and Shropshire who 'remained in each House long enough to pay all her expenses. Everyone was delighted to have her' and to hear her royal gossip. She was obviously a woman of some *esprit* and a fitting companion for the high-spirited Maria. Once, when too late for the coach she boarded a hearse. On another occasion she fell asleep while sitting near the fire. She was so close that her 'head-dress took fire and was all in a blaze'. When someone quickly pulled it off her head and probably thereby saved her life 'she fumed at him instead of being grateful.'

Maria now had an imposing new address, a heady round of social entertainments and a lady-in-waiting who understood her place in the scheme of things. Maria discovered, however, that her new demi-royal status was not without drawbacks. Shortly after the marriage someone chalked the ominous words, 'No Popery,' on her front door. Maria, whose mind must have turned back to the Gordon Riots ordered her name plate removed from the door. The evidence of what could happen was all round: she had only to be driven past the Bavarian Embassy chapel to see the burnt out shell left by the Gordon rioters. In the preceding November newspapers deplored the increasing boldness of Catholics and, a fortnight later noted that a man had been arrested for attempting to convert a young girl to Catholicism. While Lady Jerningham, who believed in the marriage's existence, felt, 'it is a very hazardous undertaking, as there are two acts of Parlement against the validity of such an Alliance . . . God knows how it will turn out – it may be to the Glory of our Belief, or it may be to the Great dismay and destruction of it!' When Lord Lothian wrote to the Duke of Rutland he said he was 'amazed that some member of Parliament has not mentioned it [the marriage]' so that the rumour could be contradicted. What would he have said to have learnt that the Earl of Denbigh had asked his contact in London to send him the text of the ninth clause of the Bill of Rights regarding the marriage of Papists into the Royal Family?

While chalk could be washed away and rumours contradicted or upstaged by newer ones, newspapers and political caricatures were harder to control. Newspapers at this time were scarcely more than scandal-sheets, under the control either of the government or the Opposition: of the fourteen London papers in 1790, nine were controlled by the Treasury and five by the Opposition. Editors accepted subsidies, or sometimes guaranteed annuities, for their support and chopped and changed to get more money. Papers were small and had few readers: circulation ranged from about 800 to perhaps 3,000. Stories, called 'paragraphs', were small and in most cases also there for a purpose. Papers sold 'puffs' in which individuals paid to have themselves noted: a survey in 1797 would report that forty-two people who regularly 'apply to have themselves puffed in the Newspapers' included the Prince of Wales, Maria, Perdita Robinson, Prince Frederick, the Prime Minister and John Wilkes. When papers were not being paid to 'puff' they were paid not to mention a subject: this was a 'suppression fee'. Sometimes papers published a 'paragraph' in order to frighten someone into paying them a 'contradiction fee'. The fees charged were multiples of the advertising rate but as no advertising duty was paid, the papers made more money. Maria, while sometimes benefiting from the press's attention, more often suffered and her sufferings would cost the Prince a lot of money.

In all the public debates over the marriage Maria did have supporters. *The Daily Universal Register*, the forerunner of *The Times*, could sometimes be one. It had defended her taking a box at the opera and in April wrote that 'The report which increases Mrs Fitzherbert's age to thirty and upwards, springs from the malicious minds of antiquated virgins and stale widows.' (Of course the 'paragraph' could well have been paid for by Maria or the Prince.) The paper also gave its readers a biographical sketch which, as so often is the case, was misleading in most points: it claimed, for example, that Maria had been under sixteen at her first marriage. To reassure its readers it added that her grandmother 'resides with her'. Bell Pigot was not mentioned.

The second source of public information was caricatures. The first to include Maria Fitzherbert appeared in 1786 and the last, thirty years later, in 1816.[6] Caricatures, which used exaggeration, distortion, vulgarity and sexual motifs to ridicule the great, the powerful and the famous, were published in London as prints. By the 1780s they had entered something of a golden era. They could be bought by the better-off in the Strand at William Humphrey's, in Bond Street at Hannah Humphrey's, in Drury Lane at William Holland's and in Piccadilly at Samuel Fores'. The leading caricaturist was, of course, James Gillray, 'the foremost living artist in his genre, not only amongst Englishmen, but amongst all European nations'. Gillray was a fanatical Protestant. His caricatures, which eventually numbered some 1,500, were usually available at Hannah Humphrey's shop and when a new one was posted in her window it was 'besieged by the public'. In addition, caricatures were extremely 'democratic' and appealed to those of 'high and low birth alike' because they could be understood by almost everyone. In some cases caricatures were published in magazines while some were also reproduced abroad, in the German magazine, *London und Paris*.

Those who did not appreciate all the references would still appreciate the bawdy humour. The cost of the prints, usually a shilling, combined with the smallness of the print-run – probably

500 to 1,500 – meant that most people could never own one. Therefore foreign visitors should not have been amazed at the crowds which gathered outside the print shops to have a free look. However those who looked in at the widows could also describe what they saw to their friends who could repeat endlessly what they had heard. Some shops even staged exhibitions where for a shilling, visitors could inspect hundreds of prints. Customers could also hire a folio of caricatures for an evening's entertainment, much as people today hire videos. Sometimes people outside London could get hold of caricatures: 'newsmen' could take them on their rural rounds and one newsman from Bath sold Parson Woodforde in Norfolk two prints for a shilling each. Likewise distributors in London offered a mail order service. In addition, large numbers of prints were exported, mainly to America and Europe: in 1780s America the caricatures' anti-government and anti-royal humour was much appreciated, while in Europe their freedom of expression was envied.[7]

The Prince also spent money to suppress caricatures in the 1780s, as well as in his later years. The Royal Archives have lists of 'suppressed caricatures' for 1819–1822 which show that some £2,204. 10s.0d [about £84,000] was spent to suppress caricatures, songs and poems. Payments ranged from the £7 paid for 'Mr. Cruickshank's expenses from Brighton and back to negotiate with King £2 and presented him £5 for his trouble', to £100. In return the Prince got a receipt which read, as in one case, 'Received of [left blank] the sum of Eighty Pounds for the copyright of Two Plates . . . and I hereby pledge myself not to Engrave or Publish any other upon the same subject.' It was then signed and a 2s.6d. stamp affixed.

Some people were amazed that 'the public prints, at least all those which I have seen, so licentious at all other times, upon this [the marriage], as well as every other subject, are at present totally silent'. This correspondent wondered if the caricatures had been 'bought off or whether they have been terrified by the late prosecution against them'.[8] In the event this writer was premature in thinking that Maria had escaped notice. On the day before, 13 March, what is probably the first caricature had appeared: 'The Follies of a Day or the Marriage of Figaro'. The anonymous artist used Beaumarchais's play, performed at Covent Garden in December 1784, as his basis. We see the Prince and Maria holding hands in a sitting room. Maria is not very well done because the artist probably had little idea what she looked like. George Hanger is shown giving her away and the officiating clergyman is Louis Weltje, the Prince's Comptroller and Clerk of the Kitchen and Cellars. The forty-one year old Weltje had been born in Brunswick in 1745 and is said to have had a pastry shop at some stage. With his brother he established a club at 63, St James's Street about 1779 which had then come under royal patronage. He joined the Prince's establishment in 1783, became his master's principal man of business and was widely disliked. Instead of holding a Prayer Book, Weltje holds a book entitled *Matrimony* and *Hoyle's Games* which was a reference to Edmund Hoyle's books on whist. A corkscrew hangs from Weltje's pocket to remind viewers of the Prince's notorious drinking habits but its shape resembles a cross and rosary to remind us of Maria's religion. Coming out of Weltje's pocket is a paper on which we can read 'Weltje's Natu Bill' which implies either that Maria is pregnant or that she has already given birth at which Weltje acted as a man-midwife. In her hair Maria is wearing a form of court dress which for ladies included feathers. Here she is sporting three feathers and a gold band on which we read 'Ich Dien.' Both the three feathers and the motto – 'I serve' – belong of course to the Prince of Wales. On the wall are a portrait of Maria and, for sexual titillation, a painting entitled 'Leda and the Swan'.

Seven days later there appeared a caricature that was to become famous. Some of the Whigs were annoyed with Maria because the Prince was spending too much time with her and not enough on politics. 'The Royal Toast. Fat, Fair and Forty' was the first print which presented Maria as obese and considerably older than she was and may well be the first appearance of this phrase in print. Again we have the three feathers and the 'Ich Dien' motto. Lady

Anne insisted that 'round, lovely and twenty-nine' was more accurate.

By the standards of the time the cartoon was relatively mild as was another published a fortnight later and drawn by Gillray who signs it 'Carlo Khan,' the nickname given Fox during the 1783 debate over the India Reform Bill. 'Wife & no Wife – or – a trip to the Continent'. Here we have what is meant to be a European Catholic church with Edmund Burke, the Irish born Whig MP and writer, performing the ceremony. Burke was popularly though wrongly supposed to be a secret Catholic. Fox is giving Maria away while behind him lurks George Hanger once again. Looking on is a man with wine bottles in his pockets, probably Weltje. To the left of the picture the coachman, Lord North (obvious because of the blue ribband of the Garter) is fast asleep. The caricature confirms the popular view: if there were a marriage, it had to be a Catholic one and disreputable.

By the end of March at least nine prints had been published: no wonder Lord Wentworth wrote, 'A most wonderful quantity of prints have appeared about a reported marriage, some of them have humour & many very bad & very blackguard.' In her lifetime Maria would be shown in at least 127 caricatures, of which thirty-nine appeared in 1786. The earliest ones obviously concentrated on the wedding and on personal attacks on her. She was shown not only as fat and old but as inordinately proud of her bosom. In 'The Introduction of F—— to St James's' the Prince carries Maria astride his shoulders in a provocatively vulgar position with one breast exposed and her left arm pointing to the palace. Here again we have what we may call the *Maria Dominatrix* motif. In 'The Pot Calling the Kettle Black . . .' Maria confronts Prince William's mistress, the actress, Mrs Jordan: 'Get out you strumpet . . . I'm an honest woman' while Prince William says to his brother, 'why you know George we leaped the Broom [set up house] as well as you. If tho' you palaver'd a good deal to quit the lady's consience, why I did it with less gammon.'[9]

* * *

By taking a public role without making sure people knew she was married Maria had accepted that her reputation was in the Prince's hands. As she said: 'He does not seem to have form'd any plan for me.' How was he to do this if he could not publicly admit the marriage and thereby admit that he had broken a host of laws? Maria was to some degree asking for the moon. Innuendo and gossip were the best she could get. In trying to understand her motives we should remember that however much she loved the Prince she also loved society. The legal and constitutional problems simply had to be put aside until a better day would sort them out. She could have married a country squire and retired into a private life, something Lady Anne came to think she should have done. She chose instead to live in the very centre of the *bon ton*.

With Maria at his side the Prince could make Carlton House a rival for the Cumberlands' as the alternate Court to prim Windsor. Maria now acted as hostess to glittering social occasions to which came not only Fox but Sheridan and Sir Philip Francis, the wealthy Whig MP said to have been the author of the *Junius Letters*. Other frequent guests included: William Windham, another Whig MP and a replacement for Lady Anne Lindsay's lost love, Lord Wentworth; Thomas Erskine, Whig MP, the Prince's Attorney General and the barrister who had got Lord George Gordon off the judicial hook five years earlier; and Edmund Burke, the great philosopher and Whig MP for Beaconsfield. The group would soon be joined by Charles Grey (later second Earl Grey and also, in time, father of the Duchess of Devonshire's daughter, Eliza). For a brief while the Prince's famous friend, 'Beau' Brummel, was part of the set but he and Maria did not get on. His wit was a bit too sharp and after he called for '*Mistress* Fitzherbert's carriage' he was not invited back. One final and rather odd frequenter was Lord North, formerly the King's first minister and now in opposition to Pitt. His visits were rare because his eyesight was failing and his health was poor. Others in the Prince's set included Lord Moira,[10] later Lord Southampton and John Willett Payne, a naval officer who had fought in the colonial war. Whilst still an active officer and MP for Huntingdon, he was also the Prince's private secretary and confidant.

There were other, less reputable, men who were part of the Prince's gambling and whoring worlds. The dissolute Duc de Chartres, now the Duc d'Orléans, when in England was a drinking partner but more important was the Prince's equerry, George Hanger, who 'supervises his hours of relaxation, and less important concerns'. He was the third son of Lord Coleraine, and later succeeded to the title. He was handsome, impetuous and a spendthrift. He too was a veteran of the American war in which his judgement had often been faulty and during which he had become a friend of Banastre Tarleton (the current lover of Perdita). As Hanger wrote in his memoirs: 'Human nature is in general frail, and mine I confess has been wonderfully so: I could not stand the temptations of that age of extravagance, elegance and pleasure.' With only £840 a year it is not surprising that Hanger was constantly in debt. He was kept afloat by the Prince, who sometimes paid his gambling duns. One such debt resulted from a bet as to which could run faster, turkeys or geese. Twenty turkeys were set against twenty geese. The Prince backed the turkeys and the race started at 4 p.m. Unfortunately, as evening came on the turkeys began roosting in trees. The Prince tried to get them out with a stick with a red flag tied on the end but Hanger's geese won. One magazine wrote of Hanger that 'some men affect wisdom, who are extremely ignorant; but it seldom happens that a person excessively foolish, still affects folly . . . With an affection of indifference, he is an egregious coxcomb.'[11]

As the spring of 1786 turned into summer the position of the Prince and Maria appeared outwardly more secure with each passing day. The parliamentary diarist, Nathaniel Wraxall, summed it up as follows: 'Mrs. Fitzherbert, commonly regarded, if not as the heir apparent's wife, yet as united to him by a ceremony substituted in place of a legal marriage, received in all companies the consideration and respect which the sanctity of such a supposed connection was calculated to inspire.' There were dinners, balls, routs, visits to the growing number of West End faro tables and trips to Ranelagh to take tea. There were still the sittings for Sir Joshua's portraits and there was the excitement of the latest society fad, magnetism (later to be called mesmerism). Here practitioners 'magnetised' their subject who then went into a 'crisis' or trance during which he could hear but not speak or move. The result was similar, it was said, to 'the effects of laudanum'.

The Prince's financial crisis into which Maria had unwittingly stumbled, to which she had contributed and from which she benefited was still unresolved. He could give her an allowance of £3,000 a year to offset the costs of her new position, even though the stalemate about his debts reached the previous year had continued and the indebtedness had grown worse. Back in April, Fox and Sheridan discussed the Prince's finances during a debate on the Civil List in the Commons. Fox pointed out that the 'dignity of the Crown, and even the national advantage, require that the Heir-Apparent should be enabled to live, not merely in ease, but in splendour'. He pointed out that the last Prince of Wales, the King's father, Prince Frederick, had had £100,000 per annum, double the money received by the present Prince. The House ignored Fox's pleas. The King, of course, knew everything: the debts, 'the house fitted up for Mrs. Fitzherbert [and] of the hunting seat purchased in Hants', where, as one courtier remembered, 'the Prince had a seraglio, the brother of the females being raised from groom to the head of the stud stables.' In June the Prince wrote to the King 'to throw myself upon your Majesty's benevolence, hoping for your gracious assistance'. His debts were now just under £270,000 [about £14.5 million] of which, it was said, some £54,000 [£2.9 million] had been spent on setting up Maria in St James's Square. The King demanded fuller explanations and an agreement to a schedule for repayment. There were rumours the Prince might disband his Household and declare himself bankrupt.[12]

Captain Conway's son later wrote that the Prince told his father,

Hugh, that he, and presumably Maria, would close up shop and, accompanied only by Jack Payne, go to Europe where they could live on the 'footing' to which he was born: '*Je suis né pour être le premier*' he supposedly told Hugh. Captain Conway then went to see Pitt who, like Fox, Sheridan, Portland and Burke, was himself greatly in debt. Pitt was 'disposed to undertake the payment of his debt, provided the rest of the money he asks might be appropriated to some specific purposes; but the Prince would not consent to that.' The Prince, having refused Pitt's offer, told Lord Southampton on 7 July that he would close down Carlton House (while Maria would close down her new house in St James's Square), stop the work, sell his horses and most of his carriages, dismiss his Household, except for four men, devote the bulk of his income to paying off his debts and retire to Brighton. The announcement loses some of its drama when we remember that the season ended in July and that most of society was leaving for their country homes. Also it was not unusual for wealthy families to face what we now call a cash flow crisis which involved closing down a London house and retiring to the country or Europe. When writing to Hugh Conway the Prince referred to 'ye. scheme I was reduced to take.' 'To speak fairly,' he asked, 'how can I, situated as I am at the present moment, go into the world [inserted above: go into society] without a family [household] without Attendants in short without any one Single thing wh. my Rank & Situation in life entitle me to, as a private Man I may travel, but I never can remain with any sort of propriety as an individual in the Country . . .' In a postscript he adds, 'My dearest Mrs. Fitz. desires her best Love to Lady Mary & you.'

On 10 July the papers got wind of the scandal and carried stories of a loan which rumour said Maria had offered the Prince. Lord Wentworth told the Earl of Denbigh, 'The late break up at Carlton House is the chief topic of conversation.' As always, politics were involved and the Prince's critics, who saw the move as 'a sticking measure', felt that if it were also an attempt 'to throw reflexion on the King and to raise the credit of the Prince . . . it has not answered'. If the Prince thought 'that his Majesty will be induced by any motives to pay his debts . . . he is mistaken'. Maria's Parisian enemy, the Duke of Dorset, was in London, in part to campaign for a Garter ribband. He heard that the Prince 'means to go into Germany next winter; his discarded household looks quite in the dumps and well they may, *cars il n'ont pas de quoi manger.*'[13]

Needless to say the caricaturists had a field day, especially with the news that the Prince travelled to Brighton in a hired post chaise. One cartoon showed Maria and him in their hired coach as she reads *The Principles of Economy*. Atop the coach is a medley of food stuffs, homemade wine, furniture and a cradle. Inside is a box marked 'Child bed Linnen'. The Prince's factotum, Weltje, is the coachman. The implication is that the real reason for the trip is for Maria to have her baby away from London. Another cartoon took its cue from Sheridan's play, *School for Scandal*, in which the Prince, standing in for Charles Surface, sells the family portraits including 'Farmer George and his Wife' which sold for a crown (five shillings or twenty-five pence). The second lot is a portrait of Maria.

By the end of July the pair were in Brighton where Weltje had leased a farmhouse and had already begun to re-design it as a 'Marine Villa'. A separate house nearby was now taken for Maria. Initially onlookers were impressed by the couple's new way of life. Lord Mornington told the Duke of Rutland that there was much talk of the Prince's 'reform'. Others, such as Pitt's niece, Lady Hester Stanhope, recalled that Maria 'had a great deal of tact in concealing the Prince's faults. She would say, "Don't send your letter to such a person – he is careless, and will lose it" or, when he was talking foolish things, she would tell him, "You are drunk to-night; do hold your tongue."'

Gossips, taking their cue from cartoons and rumour-mongers who knew that the mystery of the marriage would be enhanced by a child, talked of Maria's pregnancy. A randy young prince and an attractive woman must surely have a baby to round out the picture.

What was still only a potential constitutional crisis would become a real one once a baby were born. Gossips, like cartoonists, needed a baby and for the past two hundred odd years there has been much talk about whether or not Maria Fitzherbert had a child by the Prince. One supposed child was a James Ord,[14] allegedly born in the autumn of 1786 and eventually taken to America. He possibly travelled on the same ship as Bishop John Carroll who had been secretly ordained in the chapel of Lulworth Castle as America's first Catholic bishop. Bishop Carroll had been a friend of the Weld family.

Ord eventually entered the Jesuit College at Georgetown, now Georgetown University. He left the Jesuits when his vocation was not proved and in time came to believe that his parents were Maria Fitzherbert and the Prince. Indeed, he claimed to have written to her about his background. He learned of his alleged parents through family members. The problem with the story is that there is no evidence other than allegations, claims and a predisposition to believe what one sets out to prove credible.

There is a second candidate, one Henry Augustus Frederick Hervey, born on 1 December 1786 whose family 'believed' he was Maria's son. His father was an Irish bishop's son, Andrew Barnard, who in 1793 would become Lady Anne Lindsay's husband and who would in time father two more illegitimate children. It has also been claimed that Hervey was not the child of Andrew Barnard and his mistress but of Lady Anne and the Prince of Wales. Lady Anne altered her will to leave money to Hervey's children after he was drowned, while the Prince later left £30,000 to a 'natural son' who was, like Hervey, an officer in the East Indies. Whether the Prince's son and Lady Anne's supposed son were the same man is not proved: there were many men serving in the East Indies beside Hervey. Lady Anne could have left money to Hervey's children because she knew their father was her husband's son: she was very kind to his other illegitimate children.[15]

A third candidate was a Mrs Sophia Elizabeth Guelph Sims, the wife of a baker, who asked the Lord Mayor of London for help in

1839. She claimed she was a child of the Prince and Maria, though, she admitted, Maria was unaware of her existence. When the Lord Mayor asked for an explanation she replied that Maria was told that she had been still-born. This was the first in a succession of spurious claims and Mrs Guelph Sims was sent packing. Supporters of Ord's and Hervey's claims recall that when Lord Stourton suggested that Maria write a statement on the back of her wedding certificate – 'No issue from this Marriage. Witness my hand, Maria Fitzherbert' – . . . she 'smilingly objected, on the score of delicacy'. Lord Stourton referred to an 'impostor' who had written to the Duke of Wellington. Whether this was Ord or Hervey or someone else we do not know. Claiming money or social standing, on the grounds of being the illegitimate child of a famous parent was a fairly regular occurrence at the time. The difficulty with all this is that coincidences usually are just that. One cannot prove a positive fact by refusal to sign a negative statement any more than one can prove the fact's non-existence by a statement claiming it exists. Even if Maria had signed the statement she could have lied to protect her reputation, the Royal Family and the then King, William IV, who was a friend. Signing or not signing proved nothing.

While there was gossip in 1786 that Maria was pregnant this soon died away, yet her ability to conceive did not end nine months after her wedding. A careful reading of the surviving manuscript letters and diaries, as well as the numerous published diaries and letters reveals not one comment about an actual birth. Given the public nature of the Prince's and Maria's lives, such a thing could not have been kept secret by having Maria go on another foreign trip, as the Duchess of Devonshire would do with Grey's child in 1791 or her friend, Lady Elizabeth Foster, had done with hers in 1785. (In both cases the truth still got out.) There is no evidence that Maria disappeared for any length of time.

It is worth remembering that the Prince's first biographer, Robert Huish, collected not only facts but gossip in order to blacken his subject's reputation. His book, published within months of the

King's death, was clear about any possible children: 'It has been mentioned as rather a remarkable circumstance that no issue was ever known to emanate from any of the amours of either the Prince of Wales or the late Duke of York: we have it, however, in our power to contradict that statement.' The child he mentioned was a boy baptised George Howard who was reputedly born to one of the Prince's mistresses, Lucy Howard. He died in his second year and was reportedly buried in the churchyard of Brighton's parish church. Had there been a child by Maria, or rumours of a child, Huish would have noted it. Likewise, when in 1832 Lady Anne Hamilton published anonymously her scandalous book, *The Authentic Records of the Court of England, for the Last Seventy Years* (later editions had the more alluring title, *The Secret History of the Court*) she accused the Royal Family of an impressive list of sins – mostly invented – but she made no reference to any child by Maria and the Prince.

Much more important is the witness of Lady Anne Lindsay, who knew Maria better than anyone other than the Prince. Like others she wondered about the birth of a child. In two fragments from letters probably written in 1786 and probably to her sister, Margaret, Lady Anne referred to the rumours of pregnancy: 'You say you do not think either of them much wishes for one – she from the fear of its making a sad bustle, she knows not how . . .' In the second undated fragment Lady Anne wrote: 'God forbid she should [have a child], there is no saying what turn he [the Prince] might take if she had a lovely child or two. You may say that you do not think either of them much wishes for one.' Yet Lady Anne, who was as frank about these matters as most people of her generation, never referred to a child's being born. We must remember that her relationship with Maria was one which included not a little jealousy and occasional anger. Lady Anne must have opposed the marriage in part because she feared a child might be born. It would have been impossible for her not to have mentioned a birth either in her letters or in her journal.

As an older woman Maria would 'adopt' two young girls and

when she thought she would lose one, she fought like a tigress to keep her. In her will she would be most generous to both girls. Yet in that same will, which she knew her executors would implement without publicity, she left nothing to any other child. Again, to pack a child off to America with no provision was not in keeping with her character or indeed with the Prince's. When the Prince, by now King, was confiding his life story to his last secretary, Sir William Knighton, he made no reference to any children by Maria. Indeed, in a memorandum on George IV, Knighton, who despised Maria, quoted the King as saying: 'and had there been children such children could only rank among the bastardy of the country.' Finally we must remember that there were many means of birth control available at the time and there is no reason why these could not have been used.

The Prince and Maria spent the summer and autumn of 1786 in semi-retirement. A sign of the estrangement within the Royal Family occurred on 2 August when a madwoman tried to stab the King. (When Maria's erstwhile friend, Hester Thrale Piozzi, read about this in Italy she imagined that Maria was behind the assassination.) As the King could not be bothered to send a messenger to the Prince with the news that he was unharmed, his son heard it in the normal way. When he did he rushed to Windsor to join in the family's joy at the King's survival: the King did not ask to see him and the Prince did not ask to see his father. He could only gain entrance to his mother's room after which he left the Castle, had his supper in the White Hart and rode back to Brighton. The King's behaviour, combined with his refusal to give the Prince any real work to do, shows that it takes two to make an estrangement.

When not in Brighton the couple visited various country homes that their owners had put at their disposal: Gloucester's house at Bagshot, Lord North's at Bushey, and Wynnstay, the Welsh estate of Sir Watkins Williams Wynn which they visited in late August. Maria's family also continued to enjoy their new found status. As was his wont, Horace Walpole dipped his pen in venom as he described a party at the house of Lady Clifford, Maria's first cousin. Guests included various 'pinchbeck royalties', Lady Molyneux, Maria's father and her aunt, Lady Langdale. The occasion reminded Walpole of a meeting that once took place in Windsor Castle during the early years of George I's reign. Present were Lady Dorchester, the mistress of James II, the Duchess of Portsmouth, mistress of Charles II, and Lady Orkney, the only English mistress of William III. Lady Dorchester reportedly cried out, 'God! who would have thought that we three royal whores should meet here!'

By the end of October Maria and the Prince were back in London as Maria still had her houses in St James's Square and Park Street and the Prince could use Carlton House. Money remained tight: some minor bills were settled and a nine per cent dividend was paid on larger debts. There were visits to Newmarket (some said they were paid for by Maria) and a round of society gatherings. Despite the talk of retrenchment there were also new expenses involved in fixing up the Marine Villa and in December Maria would begin sitting for a new full-length portrait by Sir Joshua Reynolds. Sir Joshua was also painting the Prince and both portraits would be praised by the papers as 'perfectly like [the sitters]'. Maria's portrait 'promises to equal any thing ever produced from the pencil of that great master'. The painting '*generalised* all those ideas of beauty . . . and at the same time presented a faithful *individuality*'. The Prince's was condemned because of the '*extravagance* of *curl* which is annexed to the head' which makes for 'too feminine an appearance'.

As with the earlier portrait by Gainsborough, Reynolds' remained unfinished and it was later cut down to a half-length portrait. Here we see a triumphant Maria, her fair frizzed in the fashion of the day, with curls gentling resting on her shoulder. She looks out at the viewer against a range of fiery red swirls behind which is a black background. Her face shows a powerful woman with dark eyes and fixed lips. Her famous bosom is quite prominent. It confirms a quip from Horace Walpole that 'fine ladies . . . do not exhibit a profussion of naked bubbies down to their shoe-buckles, yet they protrude a prominence of gauze.' Her place in the firmament earned her an inclusion in Thomas Carnan's Almanack for 1787. The almanack was in fact a one page calendar and at the top there were portraits of four of the best known celebrities of the day: the Prince of Wales, the recently deceased Dr Johnson, Hester Thrale Piozzi and Maria Fitzherbert. (A copy of the Almanack survives in the John Rylands Library in Manchester.)

April 1787 began badly when the Prince attended a party given by Lady Hopetoun. When he arrived at midnight he was 'pale as ashes, with glazed eyes set in his head, and, in short, almost stupefied'. The Duchess of Cumberland, made him sit down but when the guests went into supper he consumed one and a half bottles of champagne. He 'posted himself in the doorway', flung his arms round the Duchess of Ancaster and 'kissed her with a great *smack*', threatened to pull Lord Galloway's wig off and knock out his false teeth, after which his friends got him to his carriage.[16] It was not a promising start to a year that would bring Maria's marriage to the centre of the political stage.

7

---·•·---

QUESTIONS IN THE HOUSE

The problem of debt still loomed. When the Prince approached his father in April 1787 the King refused to help unless he had a complete break-down of what was owed and to whom and a promise to change his way of life. The official Opposition also refused to take up the matter, in part because Portland and the Prince were no longer on speaking terms and partially because Fox feared adverse publicity. Burke, whose fame was in part based on his constant call for royal retrenchment, could hardly propose increased spending. So the Prince and the young bloods among his parliamentary 'friends', headed by Sheridan, decided on raising the question of his debts in the Commons to force the King and his government to act. They knew that they had a great deal of public support, at least among the governing classes who expected young men to run into debt, who accepted that parents had a moral duty to 'provide adequately' for their children and who believed that the King was stingy. While most of the 1787 session was devoted to drawing up charges against Warren Hastings there was still time for MPs to act.

On 20 April Nathaniel Newnham, one of the City of London's MPs, put a question to William Pitt:

Whether it was the design of the Ministers to bring forward any proposition to rescue the Prince of Wales from his present very embarrassed condition? For though he thought that His Royal Highness's conduct, during his difficulties, had reflected greater honour and glory on his character than the most splendid diadem in Europe had upon the wearer of it, yet it must be very disagreeable to His Royal Highness to be deprived of those comforts and enjoyments which so properly belonged to his high rank.

Pitt replied that 'it was not his duty to bring forward a subject of such a nature . . . except at the command of his Majesty,' and he had received no such command. Newnham then gave notice he would bring forward a motion on 4 May.

The Prince and his friends were playing with fire: did they really think the Commons would discuss his debts without discussing his marriage? Did they think all MPs not pledged to Pitt and the King would support them? As Sir Gilbert Elliot wrote to his wife: 'There seems a considerable division of opinion even amongst those who might most naturally have been expected to take a decided part for the Prince.' More ominously 'several <u>of our country gentlemen</u> are against him, and I doubt [not that] the extremely delicate subject of his connection with Mrs Fitzherbert, and the constitutional dangers . . . belonging to this most equivocal condition of things, will force itself into the discussion, though not very pertinent to it.' Sir Gilbert found the Prince's conduct 'a most heavy offence against duties and interest too sacred and too important . . . to be excused even by the levity or the <u>passions</u> of youth.'

Four days after Newnham asked his question Elliot's predictions came true. Pitt rose to put a question to Newnham: did he intend to persevere with his motion and what would be its 'scope and tendency'? The motion would deal with 'a subject of the highest importance in itself and of the greatest novelty'. Newnham now hedged somewhat: *he* had not forced the issue and he hoped the government would take up the question. As to the exact form of the motion about the Prince's 'situation', he was still unsure. Fox now rose to score a point against Pitt. He got perilously close to the truth when he referred to the Prince's situation as being 'of peculiar novelty, but so were the circumstances that gave rise to it, and it was also of equal delicacy'. Given that, did the House really want to have 'an investigation of the causes from which these circumstances originated'? It would be, he warned, 'a painful work'. In short, Fox was trying to blackmail MPs into granting the Prince his money in order not to bring the rumours of Maria's marriage into the chamber. Pitt would not be moved. He agreed that 'the principal delicacy of the question would lie in the necessity for inquiring into the causes of the circumstances' and he preferred to 'avoid discussion'. But if Newnham persisted he would 'discharge his duty to the public, and enter fully into the subject'.

A pamphlet war now began and by the end of April the most notorious radical pamphleteers were openly discussing Maria's marriage. John Horne Tooke brought out a seventy-five-page pamphlet, *A Letter to a Friend, on the Reported Marriage of His Royal Highness the Prince of Wales*. Tooke, a Cambridge graduate and an ordained clergyman, had forsaken his orders to become a radical pamphleteer back in the 1760s. Even his friends accepted that he 'was more a sophist than a philosopher . . . he was a sort of intellectual juggler.'[1] Tooke hated Fox and saw Maria's marriage as a way to get at him. He had also supported Pitt's attempt to broaden the county franchise, an attempt which the Whigs had defeated. This was another reason to attack Fox. In addition, Tooke hated the Royal Marriage Act because it condemned the King's children 'to a life of forced celibacy until – (or rather UNLESS himself, like the pope) shall be pleased to grant a dispensation'. It was 'something worse than castration', a plight from which the princesses were, we assume, excused. The law was also an example of George III's lust for arbitrary power as it gave him the power to alter the succession. If he refused his heir the right to marry until he was twenty-five and, after that, if he ordered the Commons also to refuse (which he could still do) but did give permission for another son to marry, he could then ensure that the succession would pass over once his offending heir had died.

On the third page of the pamphlet Tooke openly referred to Maria as 'this most amiable and justly valued female character, whom I conclude to be in all respects, both *legally*, really, worthily and *happily for this country*, her royal highness the Princess of Wales'. Her marriage was an 'honourable union . . . in conscience . . . [and] in law, as firm as formal and as solid, as any other civil contract that can possibly be effected between men'. He accepted that the marriage of a Catholic did give 'well-founded alarm for the safety of *Church* and *State*' but insisted that the Act of Settlement, 'a scarecrow for the spiritless', touched only the succession, not the marriage. Then he went on to claim for Maria that *'her royal highness* is NOT a papist.' Maria 'has not performed any one act of any kind whatever' which shows her to be a Catholic. She was, indeed, 'both ready and willing at any time to give proof of her conformity to the established religion of the land.' The marriage was not only valid but legal. Whether Tooke believed all this or was just stirring up trouble we do not know. What is clear is that with friends like this, Maria needed no enemies. Not surprisingly, the Prince had copies bought up in both London and Dublin.

Three days later, on 27 April, Newnham returned to his proposed motion. He regretted that his attempt to force the government to take up the Prince's debts had failed and he now moved that a humble address be presented to the King 'to grant him [the Prince] such relief as his royal wisdom should think fit, and that the House would make good the same'. At this moment the fat fell into the parliamentary fire as one of the MPs for Devon, John Rolle, stood up. Rolle was one of that group know as 'country MPs' or 'the King's friends'. Briefly put, these men almost always supported the man chosen by the King to be his first minister. Rolle was a 'completely independent country gentleman, strong-minded, original and unpredictable'. (So unpredictable was he that three days after this he introduced a bill regarding a national friendly society, in other words, a nucleus for state pensions. He got nowhere.) He was also somewhat gauche: Wraxall remembered that 'Nature had denied him all pretension to grace or elegance . . . [he] reminded me always of a Devonshire rustic, but he possessed plain common sense, a manly mind and the faculty of stating his ideas in a few strong words.' Such men are always difficult for Parliament to absorb. Rolle had been the butt of humour in 1784 when, after Pitt's victory, a collection of clever political satires appeared in various Whig newspapers under the title *Criticisms on the Rolliad*. This was meant to be a mediaeval epic centred on the exploits of a Norman duke, Rollo, whom Rolle claimed as an ancestor. It was ludicrous to the Prince's supporters that such a man, so far outside the *bon ton*, should intervene.

Rolle told the House that 'he had nothing to expect from his present Majesty, nor from his successors', although there had been talk in 1785 that he would get a peerage,[2] and he then stated that: 'If ever there was a question which called particularly upon the attention of that class of persons, the country gentlemen, it would be the question which the honourable Alderman [Newnham] had declared his determination to agitate, because it was a question which went immediately to affect our Constitution in Church and State.'

Because Fox was not in the chamber, Sheridan now stood up. Everyone knew that his star was rising in the Carlton House firmament, to the annoyance of Fox. The Irishman denied that there was any danger to 'the existence of Church and State'. He wasn't even quite sure what the words meant and believed that Newnham's proposed motion 'originated only in a consciousness of the unparalleled difficulties under which the heir to the Crown was so long suffered to labour'. If the Commons were to insist on discussing the Prince's private life he was sure the Prince would give 'an unequivocal and complete reply' in the House of Lords. 'How far such a discussion might be proper he left to the feeling of the gentleman to whom he alluded [Rolle] to decide.' In other words, gentlemen should not discuss other gentlemen's marital habits, regular or irregular.

Rolle was not put off by all this and said that if Newnham insisted on his motion, which Rolle 'thought highly improper to be proposed' he would 'do his duty' as 'an independent country gentleman'. Members must not avoid doing 'their duty' to 'Church and State'.[3] Pitt now intervened. If Newnham persevered he would vote against the motion which meant that the Government opposed the whole idea. But if Newnham insisted on his motion, Pitt stated that during any debate he 'should be driven, though with infinite reluctance, to the disclosure of circumstances which he should otherwise think it his duty to conceal'. Pitt had now increased the stakes. The House was convulsed at this and many urged Newnham to withdraw his proposed motion but he stayed seated. He would not be put off by Pitt's threat. Sheridan now rose to say that he could not see why the 'country party' should be alarmed. The only question at present was that of the debts. Given what Pitt had just said, Newnham could not now withdraw his proposed motion without allowing a slur to stick to the Prince. If the Prince did try to make Newnham drop his motion 'it would then seem to the country, to all Europe, that the Prince had yielded to terror what he had denied to argument. What could the world think of such conduct, but that he fled from inquiry and dared not face his accusers?' This was, of course, all a smoke screen to appeal to MPs' sense of honour in defiance of their sense of truth.

Pitt, having consulted with others, returned to answer Sheridan that same evening. He wanted to avoid any 'misinterpretation', as Sheridan had said that 'the insinuations which had been thrown out made it impossible for the friends of the Prince . . . to withdraw their motion'. Pitt climbed down rapidly to avoid embarrassing the King and unsettling the country by letting Parliament debate the truth: 'The particulars to which he alluded, and which he should think it necessary to state more fully to the House, related only to the pecuniary embarrassments of the Prince' and there was 'no reference to any extraneous circumstances'. Sheridan put the knife in: he was glad Pitt had made his position clear for otherwise Members would have misconstrued what he had really meant. But even Sheridan could not avoid mentioning 'the subject' and added, 'As to that matter [the marriage], any sort of allusion to it would have been in the extremest degree indelicate and disrespectful.' The Commons must not debate the true situation but only refer to it by innuendo and implication.

Sheridan duly reported to the Prince what had happened. The next day, Saturday, 28 April, Pitt repeated his recantation to Lord Southampton for the Prince's ears. The Prince snubbed Pitt by telling Southampton to tell him that 'he never received verbal messages except from the King'. But the Prince knew now that Pitt was on his side. Observers noted that for a minister as young as Pitt, 'to be on bad terms with the heir-apparent, was awkward.' The price for Pitt's support was simple: neither the Crown nor the government must be embarrassed by any reference to an illegal marriage. As one parliamentary observer noted: 'From this time he [the Prince] was eager to declare that he was not married, and Mrs. FitzHerbert insisted that she should not be considered.'[4] Maria, therefore, appears to have been fully in the Prince's counsels and to have accepted that the secret marriage must remain a secret, even if it meant lying to the Commons.

During this weekend Fox called on the Prince and they agreed that the orator would have to make the main speech in defence of his friend. Fox left the duplicitous Prince still believing what he had been told in writing in December 1785 and what his friend now repeated. Years later the Prince, now King George IV, remembered that when Fox referred to the rumours of a marriage, 'I contradicted the supposition at once, with "pooh", "nonsense", "ridiculous", &c., upon which Fox, in the heat of debate, and piqued by Rolle, was induced, not merely to contradict the report, which was right enough, but to go a little further and to use some slighting expressions.' Fox was a complicated man, gifted in many ways but remarkably child-like in others. The second Earl of Minto summed him up well in his unpublished biography, now in the

National Library of Scotland: Fox was marked by a 'kind simplicity of his heart'. 'His disposition was singularly kind & amiable, frank confiding & warm hearted; & he was no less indulgent to himself than to others.' In other words, he believed what he was told.[5]

Sheridan meanwhile called on Maria to warn her that 'some explanation would probably be required' regarding her marriage. Just as in 1785 she was at the mercy of those about her and told Sheridan that 'they knew she was like a dog with a log round its neck, and they must protect her', presumably from the rigours of the law as well as from a Commons' discussion of her private life. On Monday, 30 April, things got even worse. The House was discussing the poor laws and Rolle spoke about the 'vast increase of bastard children' due, he said, to 'the luxury of the times'. The Commons then moved directly onto the Prince's affairs. (The reports of the debates then were not verbatim and MPs probably often used stronger words than the somewhat brief and bland accounts imply.) Newnham stood up to discuss his motion and demanded that Rolle explain what he had meant by 'use of the expressions relative to Church and State'. Two years later *The Times* published a story that 'On a certain day, when a certain CHARLEY was going to the House of Commons, a certain young Gentleman called out to him . . . in those remarkable words of Othello – "Be sure you prove my love a whore."' The story, in which 'Charley' refers not just to Fox but to fools and constables in general and 'gentleman' to the Prince, may be apocryphal but it contains a truth.

Fox, surrounded by Sheridan and the new MP, Charles Grey, now stood up in a hushed chamber. It was a moment of high drama with 'silence pervading the House, which as well as the gallery, was crowded to the utmost degree'.[6] Fox now made a startling statement regarding 'that miserable calumny, that low malicious falsehood, which had been propagated without doors [outside Parliament] and made the wanton sport of the vulgar'. Now all this was bad enough but it was beneath the attention of gentlemen and MPs. However: 'when it appeared that an invention so monstrous, a report of a fact which had not the smallest degree of foundation, a report of a fact actually impossible to have happened . . . Had there existed in the kingdom such a faction as an anti-Brunswick [Hanover] faction, to that faction he should have certainly imputed the invention of so malicious a falsehood . . . a tale in every particular so unfounded, and for which there was not the shadow of anything like reality.' Fox went on to say that the Prince would willingly appear in the House of Lords 'to submit to any, the most pointed questions, which could be put to him respecting it [the marriage].' The marriage 'never had, and common sense must see, never could have happened.'

After Pitt tried to wind up the debate Rolle rose to his feet. He wanted to make Fox's denial absolute: 'They all knew that there were certain laws and Acts of Parliament which forbade it; but though it could not be done under the formal sanction of the law, there were ways in which it might have taken place, and those laws in the minds of some persons' – a reference to anti-Catholic legislation – 'might have been satisfactorily evaded, and yet the fact might be equally productive of the most alarming consequences. It ought therefore to be cleared up.' Fox, probably rattled by Rolle's questioning, immediately replied that 'he did not deny the calumny in question merely with regard to the effect of certain existing laws, but he denied it *in toto*, in point of fact as well as law. The fact not only never could have happened legally, but never did happen in any way whatsoever, and had from the beginning been a base and malicious falsehood.'

Rolle then asked if Fox could 'contradict the report [rumour] in question from authority' to which Fox, remembering his conversations with the Prince, replied, 'I have it from the most direct authority.' When Sheridan asked Rolle if he was not satisfied, the MP only answered that 'the right hon. gentleman had certainly answered him, and the House would judge for themselves of the propriety of the answer.' Sheridan tried again to isolate Rolle but in vain and Pitt then tried to silence Sheridan for harassing Rolle. Sheridan replied that Rolle's attitude was not 'honourable and

manly, fair or candid' and that he should not refer to 'such trai-
torous insinuations and reports'.[7] All Rolle would reply was that
'the honourable gentleman had not heard him say that he was not
satisfied.' Grey then joined in to attack Rolle, after which Pitt
wound up the debate by deprecating 'discussion of a question of
so delicate a nature, and asked every gentleman, to whom the
harmony and happiness of the kingdom was dear, to join with
him in so deprecating'.

However much Maria now hated Fox – and this hatred may
well have begun with his December 1785 suggestion that she
should become the Prince's mistress – he had saved her from public
scandal and the frightening consequences of the law. As Wraxall
later noted, she had been the prime object in these debates and
she was lucky not to have been 'brought to the bar [of the House]
and personally interrogated', as the Duke of York's mistress, Mary
Anne Clarke, would be in 1809 for far less serious charges. Had
this happened, it would have been a disaster for the Prince and
the monarchy and it could have resulted in her facing criminal
charges.

As Sir Gilbert Elliot wrote the following day: 'I think yesterday
was a very good day for the Prince, as the story of Mrs Fitzherbert
was what staggered great numbers, and he offers such unreserved
satisfaction on every point which has been stated against him, that
the natural desire of every man to relieve him from so unbecoming
a situation seems now to have nothing to contradict or restrain it.'
In a later letter Elliot mentioned two things that the Prince would
not have liked to hear. The first was that it was right for Parliament
to 'relieve' the Prince from 'the natural consequences of his age
and situation' but, by implication, not a second time. The other
thing was that whilst walking down Fleet Street Elliot had followed
a crowd into the Mitre Tavern. Once inside he saw a large group
of men and women 'assembled to <u>debate</u> on the payment of the
Prince of Wales' debts. I heard eight speeches by no means so bad
. . . as three-fourths of those I hear in Parliament.'

Sir Gilbert had admitted that all this 'leaves Mrs. Fitzherbert in an awkward way', although he preferred her as a mistress. This was a common attitude as seen in an anonymous caricature dated the same day as his letter, 1 May, and entitled 'An Extravaganza of Young Solomon besieging Fitzhubub.' As well as laughing over the latest caricature the crowd inside the Mitre may well have been reading a new edition of Horne Tooke's pamphlet which had been rushed into print after Fox's speech. With tongue firmly in cheek Tooke refused to believe Fox would ever sacrifice 'a defenceless woman's character (with whom, I suppose, at least there was friendship) for so mean a consideration as a paltry sum of money! No. I will never believe it.'[8] Tooke needed a marriage to attack the Royal Marriage Act.

Once the debate was over, Sheridan and Grey walked over to Carlton House. The Prince, who had been kept informed by messengers running between Carlton House and the Commons, then wrote to Fox to ask him to come to Carlton House the following day. 'When I see you,' he wrote, 'I will relate to you what has passed between my Friend [Maria] and me relative to ye seeing you', which again implies that Maria was involved in at least some of the proceedings which led up to Fox's statement. The Prince said he felt 'more comfortable by Sheridan and Grey's account of what has passed to-day. I have had a distant insinuation that some sort of message, or terms, are to be proposed to me to-morrow.' The letter was signed 'ever affectionately yours, George P.' So it would seem that the ploy had payed off and that the government were going to cave in.

A story has survived that after the debate Fox met Orlando Bridgeman at Brooks's Club. Bridgeman, who had stood guard outside Maria's sitting room during the wedding, approached the MP: 'Mr. Fox, I hear that you have denied in the House the Prince's marriage to Mrs Fitzherbert. You have been misinformed; I was at the marriage.' We all love dramatic confrontations in history and this is suitably dramatic but there are difficulties. Some sources say it was Bridgeman and others, that it was Uncle Errington who confronted Fox. The story was popularised in the nineteenth century by W.M. Massey in his *History of England* and he got it from Lord John Russell's *Memorials and Correspondence of Charles James Fox*. Fox probably found out the truth from either Grey or Sheridan and then realised that he had been misled or rather, lied to by the Prince: he could not admit the lie by breaking with the Prince, an act that would also be political folly.

Throughout this whole episode friends observing Maria were amazed that 'her behaviour has been perfectly amiable throughout'. This supports the argument that she knew perfectly well what was going on and was party to the Prince's plans. Her friends, even Sheridan's wife, who knew nothing of her involvement, rallied to her: 'I am glad for the honour of the fine world that they have shewn more good nature and attention to her than perhaps the outrageously virtuous would approve. Everybody has been to visit her since the Debate.' When, however, Maria read the account of Fox's speech she was beside herself and her temper, which was furious when outraged, erupted, not at Fox's denial but at the extent of that denial. It was one thing for her to know that she was married and for the public to wonder, but another for the public to be told she was not married. Fox's comments, in effect, had declared her to be a mistress. Her avoiding Mrs Clare, the Prince's discarded mistress, in the Netherlands had now come to haunt her with a vengeance.

That same morning the Prince called and later remembered that he had 'found her in an agony of tears'. He was also afraid that 'the great power she had over me would be turned to make a breach between me and Fox, against whom she was exasperated'. Lord Stourton, in his *Memoir of Mrs. Fitzherbert*, quoted Maria's cousin, Mrs Butler, in whose house Maria was then staying. This cousin remembered that the Prince played a more duplicitous role. On entering the room he took hold of Maria's hand, caressed it and said, '"Only conceive, Maria, what Fox did yesterday. He went down to the House and denied that you and I were man and wife! Did you ever hear of such a thing?!" Mrs Fitzherbert made no reply, but changed countenance and turned pale.'

Throughout that day friends continued calling to offer support: as Maria said later, 'the knocker of her door was never still during the whole day.' Among them was Lady Anne to whom she told a different story: true, she had 'burst into tears, said that she had indeed been shamefully used' but then went on to say 'that the Prince had been "like a mad thing" at the liberty Fox had taken in exceeding his commission, that as to herself she did not care three straws about the matter'. This comes nearest to what Maria probably thought. As an old woman she told Lord Stourton she believed her husband when he said Fox had gone too far. She gave yet another version to Sir Philip Francis and in a great passion said that Fox had 'rolled her in the kennel like a street walker; that he knew every word was a lie, and so on, in a torrent of virulence'. Poor Sir Philip found all this too much and got away 'as well and as fast' as possible. He also noted that Maria 'abhorred Fox, and never would be reconciled to him, notwithstanding many advances on his part, of which at his request I was more than once a bearer'.

Two series of events were now unfolding. On the good side, even though Newnham had still not introduced his Motion, the government were beginning to move. Pitt called on the Prince and 'after a conference of an hour . . . went to his Majesty and returned to the Prince between three and four'. That same day, after seeing the King, Pitt wrote to the Prince 'that the King was ready to afford him the relief he desired'. As the letter was vague the Prince sent Sheridan to get the details which were that the King would settle his debts and increase his income. Eventually a settlement was agreed: the King asked his faithful Commons to pay the Prince's debts of £161,000 [about £8,700,000] and to give him £20,000 [about £1,080,000] for Carlton House. For his part the King would increase the Prince's allowance by £10,000 a year [nearly £540,000]. There was a sting in the tail because the King assured the Commons he was only asking for the money on the 'well-grounded expectation that the Prince will avoid contracting any new debts in future'.[9] One wonders if the King really believed this or, for that matter, if anyone did. In return the Prince would rein in Newnham and avoid a showdown.

On 4 May the motion was withdrawn by Newnham and on the same day the Prince invited all those who had supported Newnham, Sheridan and Fox to Carlton House for a reception, during which he thanked the 180 MPs who turned up for their support. The Prince and Maria had won their dangerous game. The meeting showed that 'his side of the question, which was at first only sanguine enough to imagine that he would have a good handsome minority, now thinks he will have a decided majority.'[10]

Diarists and historians differ as to what happened next. The version usually accepted is that of Fox's nephew, Lord Holland: the Prince sent for Grey on 2 May and, after 'pacing in a hurried manner about the room', said that '"Charles [Fox] certainly went too far last night. You, my dear Grey, shall explain it"; and then in distinct terms (as Grey has <u>since the Prince's death</u> assured me), though with prodigious agitation, owned that a ceremony had taken place.' The year before this version appeared Lord John Russell had published another note from Grey stating that the Prince 'confessed it [the marriage] to me in the interview I have mentioned'. Grey, anxious not to have his new parliamentary career ruined by getting caught up in the Prince's affairs, pointed out that Fox must have assumed he had 'authority' for everything he said. The Prince should talk to Fox and explain everything. He then pointed out the obvious: 'No other person can be employed without questioning Mr Fox's veracity, which nobody I presume is prepared to do.' The Prince was obviously 'chagrined' at this and threw himself onto a sofa saying, 'Well, then, Sheridan must say something.'[11] This recollection was confirmed by the first biography of Sheridan, published in 1825.

The Prince would have agreed George Hanger's analysis of their playwright-friend: 'Sheridan has a constitution that will bear anything.' On 4 May, after Newnham had withdrawn his proposed motion, Sheridan addressed the Commons and wound up a rambling speech by 'paying a delicate and judicious compliment to the lady to whom it was supposed some late parliamentary allusions had been pointed, affirming that ignorance and vulgar folly alone could have persevered in an attempt to detract from a character, upon which truth could fix no just reproach and which was in reality entitled to the truest and most general respect.'

Sheridan's first biographer referred to 'those few dexterously unmeaning compliments' which meant everything and nothing: everything to Maria's *amour propre* and nothing to all who presumed she was a mistress whatever she said. Lord Holland later dismissed it as 'some unintelligible sentimental trash about female delicacy, which implied the displeasure of the Prince and still more of Mrs Fitzherbert at what had passed in Parliament' but which fell short of saying that Fox had lied. Sheridan also repeated, in words the Prince would later regret, that the Prince would be prepared to have his financial affairs examined, even though this would be 'painful' to 'her, whose injured name must be involved'.[12]

Some MPs, such as Daniel Pulteney, felt that 'Sheridan attempted, very foolishly, to repair the statement respecting the marriage by saying today . . . her situation was "truly respectable," at which everyone smiled.' Lady Louisa Stuart told a friend on 6 May, 'We hear of nothing but the Prince of Wales . . . the Prince's friends have taken the trouble very fairly to declare Mrs. Fitzherbert <u>something</u> in the . . . Commons. I do think that poor woman has been cruelly used on the whole, and I pity her, for she seems modest, unaffected, and unpretending, but not very wise, as her conduct has shown.' In the event Maria had played her cards very well: the Prince had got his money and she had kept the Prince.

While there was some chance that Rolle could still cause trouble or that the King might reject the Prince's accounts, which he submitted on 14 May, neither happened. In truth the Commons were tired of the affair and wanted to move on. On 21 May Pitt formally told the House of the King's decision and that same day Gillray published another savage cartoon entitled *Dido foresaken*.

Sic transit gloriae Reginae. Maria as Queen Dido, her right breast exposed, sits astride a pyre made of money bags from which smoke already rises. A girdle inscribed with the word 'Chastity' surrounds her waist and is broken. A wind, blown by Pitt and his supporter, Dundas, carries off her coronet, complete with Prince of Wales feathers, along with a crown, sceptre and orb. Maria would now never become Queen. In her right hand is a gold crucifix and on the shore are a Rosary and various instruments of torture and the words, 'For the conversion of heretics.' A rowing boat, inscribed 'Honour', pulls away from the shore and in it sits the Prince, whose 'bubble' reads, 'I never saw her in my life.' Also in the boat are Fox, whose 'bubble' reads, 'No, never in his Life, Damme' and Burke. In the distance is Windsor Castle to which they are headed.

Gillray was correct in one aspect. Three days after his cartoon was published the principal members of the Prince's Household were received at a Drawing Room by the King: 'The Prince's household all kissed hands . . . The Queen and Princesses seemed delighted, and the King very cheerful.' On the following day the Prince had a three-hour audience of the King and the first payment, of £10,000, was authorised on 17 August. It was not until 29 May 1789 that the total was finally paid. As agreed, Parliament advanced £161,000 towards the Prince's debts and £55,200 towards furnishing Carlton House.

Gillray was, however, wrong in another, major aspect: Maria had not been deserted and the couple were not estranged. Some writers have assumed that there had been a break followed, after many pleas from the Prince, by a reconciliation. There is no proof of this other than Maria's reminiscences as an old lady and these are not accurate. Often events are pushed together and a certain dramatic intensity is introduced. Her fury was not at the Prince but at the excesses of Fox's oratory. Once these had been redressed, her fury, abated and her pride, restored, things could get back to normal. Indeed, on the day following Sheridan's statement the couple made as public a statement of their relationship as possible by attending a performance of Paesiello's *Gli Schiavi per Amore* at the opera. As the Prince sat with Maria in her box he was said to look 'so cheerful'.[13]

There was, however, a political price to pay. The Prince, who appreciated Pitt's decision to help him, felt less close to Fox who in turn was annoyed at his ill-use by the Prince. The lessening in their friendship was also due in part to Maria's fury at Fox. The Archbishop of Canterbury noted that 'Mrs Fitzherbert's connections are abusing Fox, I hear, loudly, for having said more in the Commons than he had authority for.' The Prince's secretary noted the next year that his 'coolness to Fox was much increased by Mrs FitzHerbert, who never would forgive his public declaration . . . and had taken every opportunity of alienating the Prince's mind from him'. However Fox needed the Prince even more than the Prince needed, or thought he needed, him and the two men continued to meet but in secret. The Duke of Portland, who had opposed the Prince's plan all along, was furious and would not speak to the Prince until political necessity made him do so. Finally, Fox came to believe Burke's warning that Sheridan was trying to worm his way into the Prince's inner circle.

What papers called 'the Royal Circus' was once again on the road. Observers such as the Shakespearean scholar and literary figure, Edmund Malone were amazed: 'I do not know what rules the ladies govern themselves by. She is courted and queens it as much as ever.' For his part His Grace of Canterbury put it as succinctly: Maria was 'more received than ever she was, and stands more forward'. His letter also shows that the quote from *Othello* about proving my love 'a whore' was now doing the rounds. On 25 May Lord Ailesbury met the Prince as he went past Buckingham House in his phaeton 'in which I understood he took Mrs Fitzherbert to Epsom races, and on his return . . . he was at the Duchess of Gordon's ball . . . Mrs. Fitzherbert danced a good deal.' That same day Maria and the Prince went to supper at Sir Sampson Gideon, Bt., the son of the famous Jewish financier who had done so much to help earlier governments raise money. Another guest described it as 'the most magnificent ball and supper I have seen in this country'. 'The Prince sat at table with Mrs. Fitzherbert, and all her particular friends near him; his attention to her has been more marked lately than usual.'[14]

The restoration of normal relations was caught in a painting probably by Matthew William Peters who had painted the ceilings of Carlton House and was also a member of the same Masonic Lodge as the Prince. The painting, which is really not all that good, shows a large party standing and sitting rather precariously in a boat. The Prince leans against Maria as he stares adoringly into her face. She looks away, over her right shoulder, perhaps toward Sheridan who sits beside her. There are other figures in the boat, including Sheridan's wife, and above is a celestial scene in which angels flit about. One points its hand towards Maria's hat while another holds its torch aloft in what one assumes is a sign of triumph. The painting now hangs in Wimpole Hall.

The parliamentary crisis over the debts did not, of course, take place in a vacuum and Maria's frantic life went on regardless. Three days after the Duchess of Gordon's ball the Prince became ill with a fever that was real, not psychosomatic. Maria nursed him until he recovered and for her trouble came down with the illness herself. By 16 June she was recovered and the Prince was once again visiting her daily. The greatest difficulty now was not medical but legal. So far we have been concentrating on the parliamentary debates but in the midst of these Lord George Gordon re-emerged from his riotous past. In January 1787 he had been charged with two libels and by the end of April he was talking about bringing forward 'a witness' who would help his case. Opinion amongst lawyers was that he was referring to Maria and there were stories that the madman had called in Park Street to warn her that a subpoena would be forthcoming. On 3 May *The Daily Universal Register*, our best source for Gordon's activities, reported that he said that 'nothing shall prevent' a subpoena and, as the paper put it, once he gets 'THE LADY into the COURT OF KING'S BENCH he will *examine* her himself'. Four days later the paper warned Maria: 'A *certain* Lady has been made unfortunately public since her enigmatic elevation. During the whole of last spring, she was the sport of every print-shop. But matters are now changing . . . The sketch of a caricature engraver might be passed off with a laugh – But a parliamentary debate, or a public conversation with Lord George Gordon, in a Court of Justice, are *serious things.*'

On the day following this warning, 8 May, Maria's brother, Walter, accompanied by a friend, went to Lord George's house and, as Gordon later wrote to Pitt, said 'that he would call me to an account if I went to Mrs Fitzherbert's house again, or wrote to her, or to him, or took liberties with their names in public, as Mrs. Fitzherbert was very much alarmed when my name was mentioned'. Gordon repeated that he would not be threatened and would apply to Maria or to her brother-in-law, Sir Carnaby Haggerston, until he had a written answer as to her *'proper title'*. Lord George now rushed off to the King's Bench to get a restraining order and the court agreed to bind Walter to keep the peace. Gordon also wrote his letter to Pitt who ignored it. On 4 June Gordon returned to Park Street to serve his subpoena on Maria to appear as a witness in his defence. He was later described as a 'very grotesque figure' because, after his recent conversion to Judaism, he wore the wide, round hat and sported the beard which were the hallmarks of Jews in the eighteenth century. He served the subpoena and handed the required shilling (or 'conduct money') to the servants. Then, as he later told the court, he was 'turned out of doors'.

The titled madman was standing trial for having criminally libelled Queen Marie Antoinette and the French Ambassador. He had accused the Queen of being 'the leader of a faction', which charge was, in eighteenth-century eyes, almost a treasonable offence. In court he said that 'the French Queen was as great a —— [whore] as the Empress of Russia'. When the Attorney General asked to know 'to what parts of his defence the evidence of Mrs. Fitzherbert would be applicable', Lord George said that he had

had a conversation with Maria when in Paris 'with the relation of which he intermingled so many allusions to the situation of that lady, either too indelicate, or too absurd for repetition, that Judge Buller was compelled to interpose'. Gordon's libel had been tied up with 'the affair of the Necklace', the scandal then rocking the precarious French throne, but why he wanted Maria no one could understand. Just possibly he wanted her to confirm that what he had written was the talk of the town and that he was not libelling the Queen. More likely he wanted to widen his net from necklaces and French factions to his traditional anti-popery. In the event the court refused to accept the need for Maria to appear. Gordon escaped to Amsterdam where he tried to stir up trouble and was expelled. Once back in England he hid amongst Birmingham's Jewish community until arrested in December 1787. He was eventually sentenced on 28 January 1788 to five years imprisonment and would die in Newgate.

Late in June Maria's aunt, Frances Fermor, died and Maria wrote her uncle a touching letter of condolence: 'If the first of all Characters & the best & most religious of all human beings can secure happiness in another World there is no one has so just a Claim to it as our much-lov'd Friend.' Referring to the loss of two husbands she continued: 'But I know from fatal experience that Greif such as yours must have time to conquer it . . . All I have to implore of you is to be persuaded that no one person living can be more interested in every thing that regards you than I am or more sincerely & truly attach'd to you.'[15]

Early in that same month the Prince and Maria went to Brighton for the summer. The town was already taking on its somewhat rakish air and when the crotchety diarist, John Byng, visited it the following summer he was not pleased. Although the assembly room was 'magnificent' and there were numerous bookshops, 'Brighton appear'd in a fashionable, unhappy bustle, with such a harpy set of painted harlots, as to appear to me as bad as Bond St in the spring, at 3 o'clock, p.m.' 'We did not leave Brighton till past seven o'clock; where is plenty of bad company, for elegant and modest people will not abide such a place!' The Prince and Maria liked it for the same reasons that Byng disliked it. They also wanted to check the progress of the Prince's new Marine Pavilion being built in the classical style by Henry Holland, paid for by Weltje and rented from him by the Prince. Once in Brighton they resumed the relaxed life they had spent there the previous summer and indeed remained there for most of the year. Maria had her own residence and the Prince was spending a fortune in giving her jewellery, plate and furniture. In July the *Morning Herald* noted that the Prince had not been 'in better health or more buoyant spirits', while a few weeks later the *Morning Post* noted that he was 'certainly more sober', while Maria 'looks more elegant than ever. One could hardly help exclaiming with the army of Mahomet II, when he shewed them his Irene, Such a woman is worth a Kingdom!'

The Prince played cricket and went to the races at Lewes, while the couple took evening walks on the fashionable Steine, went to the theatre and bathed in the sea where Maria's bathing-woman, Martha Gunn, and the other women always referred to her as 'Mrs. Prince'. There were balls and dances and a visiting Irishman watched Maria as she danced a minuet with the Irish MP, Isaac Corry. 'After dancing down, she sat down with her partner and in a few minutes the Prince and Duke of Cumberland came and sat beside her. The Prince expressed affection in his looks and the Duke esteem. She discovers strong sensibility and considerable dignity in her countenance and deportment.' Someone who, as a boy, saw Maria later wrote that while 'nobody ventured to call her "Princess," every one . . . enthroned her as a queen . . . to be invited to meet her at the palatial Pavilion was acknowledged to be a covetable distinction.'[16] The couple entertained guests including not only the Cumberlands but the Duchess of Rutland (whose husband, the Lord Lieutenant of Ireland, had asked her not to associate with Maria) and the Princess de Lamballe, a close friend of Marie Antoinette.

When news reached the Prince in August that his favourite

brother, Frederick, now Duke of York and Albany, had at last been allowed to return to England, he raced off to London for a tearful reunion. While there were celebrations when the Duke visited Brighton, the real festivities occurred in Town. The Prince, however, never forgot his father's preference for his second son and after one drinking bout, when it was Frederick and not he who was lying on the floor in a stupor, his brother observed, 'Aye, aye, Gentlemen. There (as my father says) lie *all* the *hopes* of the family.'[17] Six days after Frederick's return, on 9 August, the Prince, dressed in royal purple and wearing his Garter star, appeared at a Drawing Room, his first visit since his illness in May. Family feelings had obviously improved because on the Prince's twenty-sixth birthday the event was observed at Windsor, the first time in five years. There was a concert and a supper at 11 p.m. in St George's Hall. In London there were widespread illuminations: 'No description can convey an adequate idea, let it suffice to say, that a more beautiful display of artificial light has not been exhibited in the metropolis . . . for many years.' What had not improved was the Prince's ability to handle money. When the Duke of Portland heard that he was negotiating a personal loan from the Duc d'Orléans he contacted Sheridan and stopped it. In the new year there would be more gossip about other loans. Some said that the Prince had taken out a 'post obit' with his brothers, Frederick and William, for £10,000 with a promise to pay £30,000 within six months of any one of them succeeding to the throne. If the money were not paid within six months the sum rose to £60,000. Others claimed that the Prince and the Duke of York had jointly raised a loan of 3,600,000 guilders in Holland at six per cent.

The new year 1788 would be as crucial for Maria and her Prince as 1787 had been and it began badly. Early in January Maria wrote to Lady Anne to berate her friend for not seeing her: 'What have I done to be so severely punish'd by yr absence. I am sure I am not conscious of anything.' She hadn't left the house for a fortnight and was 'wretched about my poor Father who has been dying'. She had left her sick bed to go to Bath 'to pay him the last sad offices of filial affection'. Walter Smythe died on 14 January *'omnibus Sacramentis munitus'* [fortified by all the sacraments]. Among the books preserved in the Presbytery Library in Winchester are several belonging to him, including a missal bound in red morocco. On its fly-leaf is written 'Walter Smythe's Anniversary to be kept on Janry. 14 and four Masses annually to be said by the incumbent of this Chapel for the Repose of his soul and that of Mary his Wife and the rest of his family . . .' Back in London Maria was treated to the story in *The Times* about Thomas Fitzherbert's walking to Bath and back to prove his love. The paper claimed that this walk led to his illness and eventual death. The implication was obvious: Maria had caused her second husband's death by her excessive demands.

In February the event for which society had been waiting finally got under way. On the 13th the trial of Warren Hastings began in Westminster Hall on charges which the Commons had been debating. Hastings had been the first Governor-General of India but was impeached for various crimes in a bipartisan effort led by Whigs such as Burke and Fox. This was tolerated by Pitt and the King who could not stop it. The diplomat, Anthony Storer, quipped that 'the town is to be amused with the grand spectacle of Mr Hastings' trial. This excites our expectation as much as the boxing matches have engaged our attention.' He also noted that 'Lady Almeria Carpenter is as much affichée with the Duke of Gloucester as Mrs Fitzherbert is with the Prince' and that the King walks up to twelve miles when travelling from Windsor to London, 'which is more than the Prince of Wales can do *à l'heure qu'il est.*'[18]

This famous trial, which the Lord Chancellor thought would 'be over in six weeks' would drag on for 145 sittings and cost Hastings £70,000 [about £3,780,000] for even in the eighteenth century justice was expensive. He would finally be acquitted in 1795. When the trial first opened the hall was filled with the

Commons before whom processed High Court judges, peers, arch-bishops, bishops, royal princes, the Duke of Norfolk as Earl Marshall and the Lord Chancellor. There was a throne to which all uncovered and bowed and boxes for the Queen and princesses, for the princes and for ladies. It resembled nothing so much as an elaborate performance of *Iolanthe*. The 'managers', or those MPs in charge of the case, wore court dress while the peers wore their robes. Sir Gilbert Elliot, who was one of the managers, told his wife: 'It is difficult to conceive anything more grand or imposing than this scene . . . Everything that England possesses of great-ness or ability is there assembled, in the utmost splendour and solemnity.' The opening speech against Hastings, given three days later, was by Britain's (and Ireland's) greatest orator, Edmund Burke. During the speech it was said that the famous actress, Mrs Siddons, broke into tears while Sheridan's wife fainted away. The Duke of Newcastle had his own gallery in which the Queen and princesses sat on that opening day and in the corridor leading to it his guests could partake of a 'handsome cold collation'. (This service continued for at least a year or two.) However all eyes were turned not to Queen Charlotte but to find out where Mrs Fitzherbert was sitting.

Attendance at the great spectacle was 'the object of every one's desire . . . for the first few years'. Those ladies such as Maria who were lucky enough to get tickets faced an ordeal almost as trying as Warren Hastings'. They had to get up at six to dress, breakfast and be at Westminster Hall by nine o'clock where they had to stand round 'shivering, without either fires or beaux to warm them, till eleven, when the managers made their appearance'. The day's session did not usually begin much before noon and lasted until it was too dark for the MPs to read. When the trial was adjourned on 3 March, Sir Gilbert Elliot celebrated by going to the opera after which he 'got squeezed in the coffee-room against Mrs. Fitzherbert, in such a way that it was impossible to make my escape from her for ten minutes, though neither of us knew whether to take notice of the other or not'. Elliot was one of those who thoroughly disliked Maria, whom he called 'this sham queen' and he wondered 'what it was that could make her triumph over all the youth and beauty of England. I could not, however, discover the cause of so much power, although I think she looks much handsomer this year than I ever remember her.' Elliot escaped when the arrival of the Prince and the Duke of York cleared a space.

However much Hastings' popularity might decline, the Prince's was continuing. As *The Times* wrote, perhaps with financial encouragement: 'We esteem, we love and cheerfully obey the Prince . . . no Prince ever merited the affections and confidence of a free, generous and discerning nation' as much as he did. The *Morning Post*, whose editor's subsidy had been stopped by the Prince, took a different view: his drinking and gambling had become notorious. When the Prince then refused to renew the subsidy the criticisms continued, including comments on his 'dissipations' and marriage.

By April Maria had sufficiently come out of mourning for her father to give 'a grand dinner to a select part of the nobility' in the house she was then renting in Park Place. Not long after this she was 'among the winning Ladies at Newmarket'. There were balls to attend and the Prince's four new 'cropt greys', purchased at a cost of 400 guineas, to pull his phaeton in even greater style. These phaetons could be dangerous vehicles and one evening in June, as the couple were 'taking an airing', the Prince's overturned in Kensington Gore and Maria was thrown on to the street. She was confined to her house and the public was kept informed of her condition. *The Times*, with tongue in cheek, reassured readers that she was only suffering from a '*swelling above the knee*'. The next day the paper warmed to its subject: 'That Mrs F—— should *fall* in the Prince's sight, was no *small weight*: But that they should *tumble together* is not at all surprising; for when the royal reins were *loosed* the *uncurbed steed* became *unmanageable*.' A caricature, 'The Careless Driver', appeared in the August issue of *Rambler's Magazine* and soon a new fashion arose in the 'West End of Town' and many ladies began contemplating similar accidents to get attention from their husbands.

There were also happier interludes for Maria and her Prince. In addition to the usual round of London pleasures, there were private theatricals and dinner parties at which they could appear as husband and wife. There were also 'assemblies', what we would call receptions, and one given by the Society hostess, Lady Vanneck, produced a royal prank. Her ladyship was a person of large proportions and the Prince 'measured the breadth of Mrs. V. behind with his Handkerchief, and shew'd the measurement to most of the company'. Sometimes the Prince's sense of humour displayed a cruel streak. At another assembly he asked for the elderly Duchess of Bedford to cross a large room 'and when she had taken the trouble of crossing the Room, he very abruptly told her he had nothing to say to her'. These stories, and the ones which follow, were recorded by Robert Conway who either witnessed them or heard of them from his brother, Hugh, now the Prince's Keeper of the Privy Purse and Master of the Robes.

On another occasion, sometime in the spring of 1788, the Prince called not on Lady Vanneck but on her eldest daughter, Miss Vanneck, with two of his equerries so that the visit would not produce a scandal. On entering the room he said, 'I must do it; I must do it.' When Miss Vanneck asked to what 'it' referred the Prince 'winked at St Leger and the other accomplice, who lay'd Miss V. on the Floor, and the P. positively whipped her'. This was to win a bet 'wch. I suppose he made in one of his mad Fits'. According to another source the Prince told Miss Vanneck what he wanted and 'by immediately, in the presence of the whole company, putting his hand up her petticoats, with which before she would rescue herself, he gave her several loud slaps. These are the amusements of an heir Apparent 26 years old.'[19] The next day he wrote Miss Vanneck 'a penitential Letter, and she now receives him on the same footing as ever'.

Sometimes the victims of the royal pranks were not so obliging. On one occasion this year, when the Prince was visiting

Newmarket with the Duc d'Orléans and his natural brother, L'Abbé de la Fai, they found themselves on a bridge. Looking down into the river the Abbé said it was possible to charm a fish out of water. This led to a dispute which led to the inevitable bet. Before the Abbé bent over to tickle a fish with a little switch he said 'he hoped the P. wd. not use him unfairly by throwing him into the water. The P. answer'd him that he wd. not upon his Honor'. No sooner did the Abbé lean over the bridge than of course the Prince 'took hold of his Heels and threw him into the Water, which was rather deep'. The Frenchman was furious and once out of the river he grabbed a horsewhip and began chasing the Prince 'saying he thought very meanly of a P. who cou'd not keep his word. The P. flew fr. him, and getting to the Inn locked himself in one of the Rooms'.

Usually these adventures occurred when Maria was not present because she could act as a deterrent but not always. On another occasion, when the Royal Family were not at Windsor, the Prince, Maria, the Cumberlands and Miss Pigott went to the castle. 'Going to see a cold Bath Miss P. expressed a great wish to bathe this hot weather. The D. of C. very imprudently pushed her in, and the Dut[chess]. of C. having the presence of mind to throw out the Rope saved her.' At this, 'Mrs. F. went into convulsion. Fitz. and the Dut. fainted away, and the scene proved ridiculous in the extreme, as Report [gossip] says the duke called out to Miss P. that he was instantly coming to her in the water, and continued undressing himself. Poor Miss P.'s clothes entirely laid upon the Water, and made her appear an awkward figure. They afterwards pushed in one of the Prince's attendants.'

There were still occasionally repercussions from Sheridan's statement in the Commons the previous year. That summer the Prince wanted to visit the Whig MP, Thomas William Coke, famous to later generations for his agricultural improvements. Coke's Norfolk home was Holkham Hall and by 1788 the Prince invariably paid a summer visit. However this summer another guest, Fox, a close friend of Coke, also paid Holkham a visit. During

207

their conversations Fox told his friend of his being duped by the Prince over the marriage. When, not long after, a letter arrived from the Prince regarding his visit, Coke supposedly replied, 'Holkham is open to Strangers on Tuesdays.' In the autumn the Prince saw an opportunity to repair two damaged friendships. He heard that Fox was to pay another visit to Holkham and raced there in order to join them at table. When the cloth had been removed he rose to propose a bumper toast, 'The health of the best man in England – Mr Fox!' This began a spate of drinking which went on until one the next morning.

Also that summer there was the excitement of a by-election in Westminster. At the time, when an MP accepted office, he had to stand for re-election. Lord Hood, who had been returned with Fox in 1784, accepted the appointment as a Lord of the Admiralty. He therefore had to stand again. This time Fox's supporters put up a rival candidate, Lord John Townshend, who won an election marked by vast expense, rioting and corruption. During the campaign the Prince gave Townshend his support and this led to a famous watercolour by Robert Dighton who in 1784 had painted a similar watercolour, *A View of Covent Garden during the Election 1784*. This had shown the Duchess of Devonshire's coach in the background, reflecting her role in the Foxite campaign. In the 1788 watercolour, *The Westminster Election of 1788* (now in the Museum of London) we see instead the Prince of Wales's phaeton going through a crowd of Townshend supporters. Beside the Prince and high above the crowd, is Maria: the replacement was significant. As *The Times* put it that August, 'The great object of The Party [the Prince's Whig friends] is to keep the Prince unmarried, well knowing that whilst he is fettered in the trammels of Mrs ——, they will do whatever they please with him.'

By the late autumn Maria was still waiting for the workmen to finish refurbishing yet another new London house at No. 105 Pall Mall, round the corner from Carlton House. Therefore the Prince and she stayed on in Brighton. Their circle of friends now included a disreputable but wealthy Irish family, the Barrys. Lord Barrymore was a few years younger than the Prince and 'alternated between a gentleman and a blackguard, the refined wit and the most vulgar bully . . . He could fence, dance, drive, or drink, box or bet, with any man in the kingdom.' He was not surprisingly known as 'Hellgate'. His brother, heir and co-rake was known as 'Cripplegate' because of his lameness. Another brother, a clergyman in the Church of Ireland, was known as 'Newgate' because of his frequent arrests for debt. A sister, famous for her vile language, was known as 'Billingsgate'. Lord Barrymore's most famous exploit came late in October when he rode his horse up the stairs of Maria's Brighton home. The difficulty was in getting the horse down again and to do this Maria had to send for two blacksmiths whose reward was a bowl of punch at the Castle Inn. A few days later Barrymore pretended to be Maria's postilion and, dressed in a jacket of pink silk, he added to 'the elegance of the equipage'. Her 'great good humour . . . seemed to give a zest to his capricious levities'.[20]

The couple's absence from London could not, of course, stop the talk about Maria. In September *The World* published what it called an 'epitaph' which probably was written by Sheridan:

MRS. F-TZHE-B--T.
To the Remembrance of one
Who was –, Wife and no Wife, Princess
and no Princess, sought, yet shunned,
courted, yet disclaimed: the Queen of all
parties, yet the Grace of none: the
Theme of Wonder, Curiosity, and
Submissive respect: yet
The constant Subject of Doubt, Reserve, and
Apprehension.
Mrs. F——
was fond of Sovereignty, and obtained it: fond
of the World's Friendship, and secured it:
fond of that best Courage, the Courage of being

unabash'd and contrived
To exercise it safely.

This may have been a ploy by Sheridan to get the Prince to buy *The World's* support. Whatever the reason, Carlton House silenced the criticism by agreeing to pay the editor an annual subsidy.

Not all comments were so mild. In October *The Times* stirred the water by publishing 'A Question'. This was really a lead article in the form of a news item and began: 'What is the reason that Mrs FITZHERBERT, who is a lady of fortune and fashion, never appears at Court? She is visited by *some* ladies of high rank – yet never goes to the Drawing Room at St James's.' The so-called 'person who pays no regard to the idle reports of the day' only wished 'to have this mystery cleared up'.

8

———◦———

HIS MAJESTY'S DISORDER

Throughout October 1788 rumours about the King's health began to circulate and they reached a crescendo following his trip to take the waters at Cheltenham. On 22 October the Prime Minister was told by one of the doctors that the King was 'nearly bordering on delusion' and that day the Prince put back his departure for Brighton. Maria, almost certainly, would have joined him there and of course knew the reason for the delay. Five days later he went to see his father and, once reassured that all was well, returned to Brighton. As what historians call the Regency crisis unfolded, even the Prince's critics admitted 'that his Royal highness has acted with the greatest attention to the King, and in all respects with the greatest propriety'. When the Prince went to Windsor early in November he was so alarmed that, as at any crisis in his life, he ordered himself bled and he repeated the futile exercise early in December.

The experience did not dampen all his spirits. In November Lord Abercorn, an elderly peer whose recollections went back to the reign of George II, claimed that 'Mrs. Fitzherbert's influence is rapidly on the wane, and the Prince is in full pursuit of a new Beauty, Mrs. Johnstone, Widow of the governor [of West Florida], who it is thought, will soon be what Mrs Fitzherbert has been.' The courtier, Mrs Harcourt, agreed that Maria 'has not the least remaining influence; that, he is quite tired of her, and in love elsewhere, therefore the public need have no further alarm on her account.' In the event Julia Johnstone proved to be just another diversion and both Lord Abercorn and Mrs Harcourt overestimated the strength of the Prince's infatuations.

On Monday, 10 November 1788 readers in London's coffee-houses were startled to learn that their King was now seriously ill. 'An express arrived from Windsor, late last night with the melancholy news that HIS MAJESTY'S disorder had returned with great violence and the consequences to be dreaded were very alarming.' The Prince once again returned to London and Maria followed him in a few days. On 12 November Dr Warren, one of the King's doctors, and Maria's own physician, told Lady Spencer that 'Rex noster insanit' but a week later the Duke of Gloucester told the Prince that 'the accounts from Windsor differ much.' It took some time for the news to get into the country as the few people who took papers tended to prefer the thrice weekly ones to the more expensive dailies. It wasn't until the 15th that the 'Ladies of Llangollen' noted: *'St James' Chronicle* accounts of his Majesty as bad as possible. They are received with universal Terror and Consternation.'

The day after Dr Warren wrote, Pitt realised he would have to bring in a Regency Bill. It appears that an anxious Maria spent most of November at Bagshot as the crisis deepened in London and Sheridan arranged for 'a person at Windsor to Night to learn whether was anything essential to the Prince's Service to be communicated' to her.[2] A parliamentary committee was set up to examine the doctors and on 20 November Parliament reassembled and, to give the government more time, it then adjourned for two weeks. The Prince was consulting his Opposition friends and by the end of the month newspapers were publishing the names of those who would make up the new government he would appoint as Regent. As John Wilkes, himself no stranger to political intrigue, put it, 'The political caballing is as great as I remember at any time.'[3]

For the next four months British political life would be turned upside down. For Maria these months would see the severest public upsets of her life, far worse even than those of 1787. Never before or after would she be exposed to so much public attention, speculation and ridicule. She would be attacked in newspapers and pamphlets, reviled in caricatures and would emerge as the main item of gossip, not only in London but throughout Britain, Ireland and much of Europe. Her character, her relationship with the Prince and her history would be debated in Parliament, while plans for her future would be a vital ingredient in the Regency crisis. This account of that crisis, therefore, will naturally be centred on Maria's role.

We are fortunate in having letters from one of Pitt's supporters, James Bland Burges, MP. He was particularly faithful in writing long letters, almost daily, to his wife in Montgomeryshire. As an MP he avoided paying postage by franking his letters, so he could easily afford daily missives. His give one of the best accounts of the ebb and flow of events during this period. Burges had little time for the Prince and his circle. To him the Opposition were 'desperate men', while the Prince was 'the mad and wicked youth under whose banners they are ranged'. Not surprisingly, he was interested in stories about Maria's future. While his views give an edge to his letters they do not lessen their value.[4]

By November it seemed likely that the twenty-eight-year reign of George III was coming to an end and that the Prince would become Regent. As such he would exercise royal power to construct governments, appoint and dismiss ministers, create peers and distribute patronage. It was assumed that within hours of taking over the Prince would dismiss Pitt and put the Opposition into power. The three great goals of eighteenth-century politics – the disposing of peerages, places and pensions – would be his at last. As for Maria, who could say what would happen to her?

Religion would play a crucial role in the following months. On the one hand magazines could comment on how Maria's co-religionists shared the concern for the King's health. The *Gentle-man's Magazine* noted in December that 'much to their honour' Catholics gave 'the strongest proofs of their zeal, loyalty, and affectionate wishes, for the recovery of their august Sovereign'. There were also newspaper reports of masses being said for the King's recovery in Britain and Europe. Anti-papists, such as Maria's enemy, Hester Thrale Piozzi, were not placated by this: 'an unlimited Regent:– how unconstitutional! how dreadful . . . The Prince's character makes his elevation to power extremely perilous . . . his Connection with a Catholic Lady increases our peril.' The timing of the crisis was, from Maria's point of view, unfortunate. Public concern really became acute just as Britain was commemorating the centenary of the Glorious Revolution. Indeed, the same newspapers that carried early news of the King's illness also carried reports of dinners with shoals of toasts to the 'blessed' memory of William of Orange and the 'Protestant Wind' which allowed him 'to deliver us and our posterity from POPERY and ARBITRARY POWER'. In addition, Catholic monarchies in France or in the Austrian-ruled southern Netherlands, seemed near virtual collapse. Even the Papacy seemed doomed: as *The Times* would pontificate in a few months, 'The present Pope will probably be the last.'

Party feeling rose to new levels and one backbench MP would later recall these months as having 'greater agitation, violence and mutual animosity than any other that I have witnessed in my time'. The Prince and his friends were playing for high stakes and their arrogance would startle the nation. Pitt's administration had succeeded in restoring not only Britain's prosperity, but her standing in Europe after the defeat in America. Pitt had the King's full confidence, a large majority and enormous popularity. As one paper asserted, with only mild exaggeration, he was 'the most popular man that the country has ever seen'.

The Opposition's only hope remained the Prince: as one pro-government paper had put it during the debates over his debts, he was 'the cock of their dunghill'. The Opposition was not helped by its divisions and rivalries. As one wag moaned: 'we have more Wit and Ingenuity on our side than sound Judgment in managing Parliamentary matters.'[5] 'The Party', as most newspapers sneeringly called the core of the Opposition, was led by the Duke of Portland. He was not the mere figurehead that some historians, with their all too predictable contempt for dukes, mistakenly think. The Duke and even more his Duchess, did not care for Maria. Fox's position remained difficult, in part due to Maria. Sheridan and Burke's rivalry for pre-eminence seemed at times to marginalise him and Burke resented Sheridan's increasing importance, much of it founded on his friendship with Maria and the Prince. Fox, for his part, felt challenged by all three: Burke, Sheridan and Maria. In addition, Fox's health had not been good and when the crisis began he was in Italy with his long time mistress, Mrs Armistead and did not return until 24 November. Mrs Armistead was a pleasant woman whose favours had been widely distributed throughout Society. In January this same Society would be shocked to hear that she and Fox had secretly married.

Finally, we should remember that it was not only the Opposition which would be divided during the coming months. The Royal Family would split into various factions and then re-group only to split along different lines. As with any large family, there was a constant shifting of alliances which loom large due to the survival of letters and diary entries: what is forgotten is the underpinning of love and affection. Much has been made of the King's fury at the Prince's behaviour, yet as the crisis developed the Duke of York told his older brother how the King had spoken with 'tears in his eyes and with the greatest affection concerning you'.

The Queen's position was an extremely difficult one. The poor woman was terrified at the collapse in her husband's health which she could only see as insanity. She sought to keep his frantic Household together and to protect him from his three eldest sons – the Prince, York and Prince William (who would not become Duke of Clarence until May 1789) – whom she saw as power-hungry and disobedient. The King's two brothers also fell apart during the crisis. The Duke and Duchess of Cumberland, still estranged from the King, enthusiastically backed their nephew and Maria, while the Duke of Gloucester tended to back the Queen. The King's daughters, as usual, obeyed their mother but the older ones longed to show their devotion to their beloved eldest brother. Whatever the Prince's faults, he was always exceptionally kind to his sisters.

Finally, even the doctors, ignorant as to the King's real illness, were split. They included outright quacks along with dedicated physicians but all subjected the poor King to a variety of insulting, horrifying and primitive treatments. They were divided not only on how to treat the King, whose condition varied from day to day, but along political lines. Pitt and the Opposition each had their own favourites, so that the prominent Whig doctor, Richard Warren, told his Opposition friends what they wanted to hear: there was no hope for the King. It is hardly surprising that this Society doctor was also Maria's and looked after her when she herself would fall ill in January.

By December 1788 the crisis was such that both the Cabinet and Parliament, let alone the Prince and his friends, were considering how to proceed. On the 3rd the King was taken from his beloved Windsor to Kew and on the 10th the Commons began debating proposals for a Regency. No one seriously believed that the Crown's powers should be vested other than with the Prince. The question was what his powers would be and when he should become Regent. Fox, anxious to force a decision on the Government and to grab the leadership of the Opposition, abandoned his traditional rhetoric about an over-mighty throne and pushed the Prince's claims.

Arguments raged over Maria's future. Early in December one rumour claimed that 'if the Prince of Wales is made Regent he will make the Fitzherbert a Duchess, and marry some princess for his consort,' but the Duchess of Devonshire noted that the Prince 'sd. Mrs. Fitz. shd. be as happy as he cd. make her, but shd. have no rank'. The Duchess knew the Prince's penchant for 'making himself agreeable to those with whom he happens to associate'. This accurate assessment makes one wonder what did he tell Maria and Sheridan? Three days later there was another version of Maria's future which was hinted at in newspapers and noted by Burges:

> The Party is so alarmed . . . that a grand caucus was yesterday held at Mrs. Fitzherbert's, when the following proposal was made to her. If she, on her part, would renounce all the pretensions and give up the proofs she has of the marriage, she should be allowed to keep her present settlement of £6,000 per Annum and her House and should have a further settlement of £3,000 per Annum and be made a Duchess. In answer to this she said, that her title was unquestionable, that she would never abandon it, that she possessed the most positive proofs which she would assuredly make public, should any further attempts be made to deprive her of her right.

The same day that James Burges noted the latest rumour, newspapers, such as the *Morning Post*, turned to poetry. After saying that some stories about Maria's royal ambitions were 'too severe' to be printed the paper published the following 'Impromptu':

> In vain my friends you cry, hold! hold!
> And think my satire much too bold;
> For what's the fear, a TRUTH to tell
> When all must own – it FITZ her well.

Two days later the same paper claimed that Fox would refuse office until 'the EXACT LIMITS of that connection are SATISFACTORILY DEFINED as he now has reason to believe that it is of a more COERCIVE and PERMANENT nature than he was once induced to *imagine* and ANNOUNCE'. They were speaking of 'a Lady well known in the higher circles' and 'a certain GREAT

CHARACTER' who had, it claimed, offered Maria the title of Duchess and an annual pension of £20,000 a year if she would live in Europe. Obviously the paper had heard a similar rumour to that reported by Burges. What the paper did get right was the observation, which would have pleased Maria, that 'character is to her of much more importance than affluence'. Indeed, rumours about her becoming a Duchess show how little people understood Maria. As she later told Lord Stourton, a title would have meant that she was nothing more than a mistress: such titles had been the rewards given by Charles II, George I and George II to their mistresses. Maria would never become another Duchess of Kendal, the mistress of George I.

Another story was circulating early in December which showed Maria in a much more humiliating light. It was noted by Burges and related, with some glee, to his wife:

> I have heard a good trait of Mrs F——. A week or two ago, there was a large dinner party at Carlton House. The Prince had arisen, and was standing with some people by the fire. The conversation at Table was on public matters; and someone observing that something or other went on badly, she exclaimed, when I am Queen of England things shan't go on in this way. The Prince, hearing this, turned round; and putting his hand on his heart, cried out, you ever will be Queen of my Affections, Madam, but as for Queen of England, never. This was the first intimation she had of the difficulties which now surround her.

This is a good tale, highly dramatic and an example of the way in which gossips embody perceived characteristics as stories. It was widely accepted that Maria was arrogant and it was known that the Prince had appeared to play a dubious game when it came to his relations with her. But she never would have said such a thing, even in jest. Other than with intimate friends, she always behaved in a most formal manner with the Prince in an age which valued formality in manners. Her 'arrogance' as well as her manners would never allow her to say or do anything that could call for a rebuke, let alone one that would show how tenuous was her hold on the Prince. As for the Prince, assuming he was sober, he would not have humiliated her in such a public manner.

As all these rumours were swirling about, the Commons had their most startling debate on the Regency. Fox, carried away by his own eloquence, said that in his view 'the Prince of Wales was Regent, invested with full regal authority immediately and *de jure* on the incapacity, however temporary, of the King, and that the two Houses of Parliament had no right to debate thereon even.' To this Pitt retorted that such a doctrine was 'TREASON against the Constitution'. Burges rejoiced that 'Fox has committed the greatest Error he was ever guilty of in his life . . . We are, at least I fear so, on the eve of dreadful things.' On a more practical level, Pitt laughingly said, regarding Fox's claims: 'I'll un-whig him.'[6] With such language in the air, no wonder opponents of the Prince concentrated on Maria's position.

The greatest source of difficulty was still the Devonshire MP, John Rolle. As another Member wrote to the Marquess of Buckingham: 'We are likely to have a conversation in Parliament, I am pretty authentically informed, of even a more delicate nature than the last; John Rolle intending to bring forward his old subject of Mrs. Fitzherbert. Rolle and Sheridan had a whispering conference under the gallery for some minutes.' Sheridan's pleas had little effect, however, according to the Solicitor-General, for 'he understood to be firmness on the part of Rolle, in his intention at a proper time to come forward'. Rolle knew his history: the Regency Act of 1765 had said that if the proposed Regent should at any time marry a Papist, he would be regarded as 'naturally dead'. This clause still applied in spirit: 'for if a Regent was disposable for marrying a Papist, a Person already married to a Papist cannot be chosen Regent.' As Burges told his wife, this 'will go near to shake the foundations of the projected Regency'.

A week later new rumours were circulating through London:

The Times claimed that Maria 'has renounced the ERRORS of Popery', although the paper added that this story 'may be attributed to the ERRORS of common report'. Three days later the paper had a new story. It was 'industriously circulated, that a certain Lady high in the estimation of a great Personage, is in secret cabal with some shrewd Members of the Romish Church'. The paper commented that it was 'cruel and ungenerous to trifle with the individual peace of any woman' and admitted 'the goodness of her disposition'. The difficulty for her, and for the paper, was 'her present *indefinite situation*'. Lest readers become too alarmed about a Papist takeover, it reassured them that 'a connection, which being unconstitutional and void, must be harmless'.

All this attention on Maria, especially the *Morning Post*'s story about her being sent to Europe with £20,000, upset the Prince. He got one of the few papers supporting him to dismiss the story as 'ridiculous nonsense' but the Duchess of Devonshire heard that her friend was 'very much out of spirits' when told that the *Post* 'mean to attack him about Mrs. Fitz. on the act preventing the Sovereign marrying a R C'. But Sheridan calmed him by saying that 'the Mg Post will be got over.' Poor Sheridan, caught between Maria and the Prince, was occasionally furious at the Prince's obsession that his 'marriage' would become established truth as opposed to established rumour: the Prince he said, had 'the most womanish mind' he had ever met. Sheridan also admitted to being 'sore on the subject [of] Mrs. Fitzherbert's difficulty in being reconcil'd to Fox', as it made his backstairs negotiations so much more difficult.

The *Morning Post*, the most notorious blackmailer among London newspapers, was under the control of a scoundrel called John Benjafield who was bought off with 1,000 guineas plus an annuity. In return he would stop the attacks on Maria and switch the paper's support from Pitt to the Prince and his Opposition friends. The control of the paper now rested in the equally scandalous hands of Louis Weltje, who was so instrumental in the Prince's various building projects in Brighton, and who was also trying to get into the Commons.

On 16 December the Commons accepted that the Prince would be Regent but not because he had a 'right' to be such, that such a Regency would have limits placed upon it, but that the control over the King's person would be placed in the Queen's hands, not in the Prince's. No wonder the Prince is reported as having shouted, 'God damn the old bitch. Why does she trouble her head about politics? What can a woman know about the matter.' As to his father, the Prince was said to have remarked, 'Damn him, he is as mad as Bedlam.' All this, however, only began the battle. The nature of the potential crisis facing the Prince and Maria was stated by Burges on 21 December when he told his wife that 'Rolle has opened his Battery on the Marriage business, by giving a hint, that he should not oppose the nomination of the Prince as Regent "provided he had done nothing to forfeit such a pretension."' (Unusually we also have a letter from Burges' wife, Ann. While she shared her husband's dislike of the Prince, and also his regard for Pitt, and while she was herself of Huguenot descent, she felt Rolle should not push forward his motion 'while the Prince is content to leave it in obscurity . . . What evils from a Catholic wife are equally to be apprehended, with those from a disputed Succession?')

Other problems plagued the Opposition. On 30 December, the Speaker suddenly died and a new battle began in which Pitt once again triumphed: the new Speaker was his cousin, William Grenville. Fox's health was still not good; the poor man was suffering from piles. Early in the new year there was a rumour that Fox 'certainly cannot live long' and that same day, 4 January, there was another story that he had died. To confound his enemies he turned up in the Commons on the following day very much alive even if he was, by his standards, 'very thin'. Burges noted gleefully that 'Sheridan, whose secret influence at Carlton House appears to disgust even his own party' will cause 'schism' among the Whigs. The reason was obvious as *The Times* noted on 24 January: it was 'the ingenuity with which he destroyed the effect of Mr. Fox's declaration' in the 1787 debates as well as his 'very handsome compliment to Mr. [sic] F——'s virtue'. As the paper concluded: 'What other inference could the public draw . . . than that she was actually the Princess of Wales? This matter will soon be ascertained.'

In January 1789 the Sheridans fled to Maria's house when the bailiffs took possession of their own home and carriage for non-payment of debt. Sheridan was now 'the prime favourite', even though the Duke of Portland told the Prince he would never serve in the same government with the playwright. To escape all this, and to regain his health, Fox now took off for Bath. Observers agreed that 'Mr. Fox seems to be offended at Sheridan's violent passion; his journey to Bath is not for health only.' Fox, however, was really ill, but he was also afraid of another debate on Maria: as the new Speaker told his brother, the Lord Lieutenant of Ireland, 'Fox is gone to Bath. Whether he is very ill, as some say, or wants to shirk the discussion about Mrs. Fitzherbert, as others assert, I know not.'[7]

The Opposition also began to abuse Queen Charlotte. Dr Warren spread the story that his medical rival, Dr Willis, 'slept every night with ye Queen'. No wonder Government supporters reported that the Opposition did everything it could 'to vilify and traduce' the Queen. 'This, added to the business of Mrs Fitz——t, which I believe will certainly be brought forward, affords us a pleasant prospect.' If all this were not bad enough the weather was atrocious: in London carriages and sedan chairs could not get through even major roads and shivering pedestrians were having a terrible time on the ice.

However the terrible weather did not stop the rumours. On 12 January Burges wondered if the Prince 'should refuse to declare whether he is married or not, or that the Marriage should be proved, I think it most likely that the Queen will be declared Regent. In this case, I look on a Civil War as an inevitable consequence.' Given all the tension, as well as the bad weather, it is not surprising to learn that Maria became ill. From Dr Warren she may well have heard many details about the King's illness and perhaps how the tortured monarch, who detested Warren, pushed the Whig doctor out of his room. Her illness may have been a collapse brought on by tension, for Mrs Harcourt noted that the 'report' that the Prince was tired of Maria was 'gaining ground'. The old Duchess of Bedford said that the Prince had written to her saying that 'he could not stand the unpopularity' of his 'connection with a Catholic' and had offered Maria £10,000 a year if she would go to France. Her reply, the only part of this that has a claim to truth, was that she 'would take her chance in England'. Maria's illness must not have been that severe for the following week she was giving a formal dinner party for the Prince.

Not long after this Maria joined the Prince, the Duke of York and Jack Payne at another dinner party, given by the married sister of the poor Miss Vanneck whom the Prince had chastised the year before. This occasion shows how heated arguments had become. The Prince and Duke were describing how they had gone through the King's jewels in the presence of the Queen who grew angry at their carrying on. (They were only trying to establish some order and protect their father's possessions.) York said he had told his mother, 'Madam, I believe you are as much deranged as the King', to which Payne added, 'Mr. Pitt's chastity will protect the Queen.' (This was a snide reference to gossip that Pitt's chastity was really a cover either for his impotence or for his homosexuality.) The only guest who was not an Opposition supporter was Pitt's devoted friend, the dowager Duchess of Gordon. She was a strong-willed woman, famous for riding through Edinburgh on the back of a pig. Gossips were divided between two rumours: that she wanted to marry Pitt herself or that she wanted Pitt to marry her daughter. Payne's prattle was too much and Her Grace turned on the Prince's secretary: 'You little insignificant, good-for-nothing, upstart, pert, chattering puppy, how dare you name your royal master's royal mother in that style.' The party was not a great success.[8]

Early in the New Year Maria also had to face a full attack from the pamphleteers. On 2 January Georgiana Devonshire noted that 'a hand bill was sent to Mrs Fitzherbert telling her yt. tomorrow 500 libels wd. be publishd.' This handbill came from the notorious publisher, James Ridgway, a radical bookseller and blackmailer. It was an invitation to buy silence and Sheridan was quickly sent to do the deed. Likewise when Lord George Gordon's Protestant Association, which had fomented the Gordon Riots, passed a resolution 'to remind and forewarn our Governors and fellow subjects' about the dangers of a Popish wife for the Prince, the *Morning Post*, now in the Prince's pay, refused to print it and even returned the fee. *The Times*, however, printed it and pocketed the money.

Far worse for Maria was the Rev. Philip Withers, a well established pamphleteer whose skill at digging dirt we inspected in Chapter 4. His works were advertised in and often alluded to by newspapers. Indeed, some of his invented stories about the King during his illness – such as the story that he went up to a tree in Windsor Great Park to shake its hand – still find their way into histories. The present crisis was too great an opportunity and Withers launched his first pamphlet, *History of the Royal Malady*, on 9 January. To get as wide an audience as possible he included in the long title the following explosive phrase: '"*Her Royal Highness the Princess of WALES." commonly called (The Hon) Mrs. Fitzherbert.*' To avoid lawsuits and libel trials Withers made part of his rambling pamphlet into a play about 'His Majesty of France', with the Prince as 'Prince Henry' and Maria as 'Lady Herbert'.

Withers continued his attacks on Maria throughout the first two months of 1789 with more pamphlets and with articles in *The World*, a government paper: Sheridan could not buy him off because, apparently, he couldn't find the wretch. To add a spurious credibility Withers occasionally claimed to be responding to that other rogue clergyman, Horne Tooke, who had 'defended' Maria the previous year. In *Alfred, or a Narrative* . . . Withers made another direct attack: 'Your Highness is married to a PAPIST . . . Your Highness cannot Legally be Regent or King . . . THE PEOPLE OF THESE REALMS ARE ABSOLVED OF THEIR ALLEGIANCE.'

Maria was 'a ***** [whore]'. However, the most damaging outburst, from Maria's point of view, was *Nemesis, or a Letter to Alfred . . .* published on 13 February. It was in this diatribe, discussed in Chapter 4, that Withers gave the world his concocted story of Maria and the French Marquis and her supposed illegitimate child. He also charged, with some truth, that vast sums of public money were being spent to pay newspapers not to criticise Maria, ignoring the fact that such bribes were the normal procedure, and he devised a secret Catholic cabal with Maria at its centre.

The unbalanced but energetic scribbler immediately began yet another pamphlet, *Alfred to the Bishop of London*, but before he could finish Maria filed an 'information for libel' suit against him, after which he was imprisoned until the end of February when someone – rumour claimed a government agent – paid his bail. He finished the pamphlet which declared that Maria was 'either a WIFE or a WHORE' and, worst of all, 'a CATHOLIC WHORE'. Maria realised she could lose more than she might gain because Withers, just like Lord George Gordon, could summon her as a witness. She now offered to withdraw the suit if he would back down by saying that he had no idea who had written the pamphlets: a lie but one that would do the trick. Withers, now once again riding high, published yet another pamphlet, *Alfred's Appeal: Containing an Address to the Country . . . on the Subject of the Marriage of Mary Anne Fitzherbert and Her Intrigue with Count Bellois*.

Withers continued with yet more pamphlets, including *Alfred's Apology, Second Part . . . with a Summary of the Trial of the Editor of Nemesis on the Prosecution of Mrs. Fitzherbert for a Libel*. When the Regency crisis had finally ended, *The World* threatened to publish various letters Withers claimed he possessed which would give all the details of the 1785 wedding, including the names of the witnesses and clergyman: they were never published and never existed. Finally, in July 1789, the wretched Withers was brought to trial for libelling Maria with respect to the 'Marquis de Bellois' story. *The Times* prudently proclaimed that 'we shall not shock the ears of our readers' by retelling the libel, especially because of the 'good opinion we entertain of the Lady in question'. It is interesting that the Bodleian Library's copy of *Nemesis, or a Letter to Alfred . . .* had once belonged to Lord Kenyon, the judge who presided at Withers' trial. The text is heavily scored beside those stories regarding the 'Marquis de Bellois' and the alleged birth of a child in Paris. Copies of Withers' pamphlets were also kept by Maria's Weld brother-in-law in distant Dorset.

One cannot of course survey all the surviving pamphlets and broadsheets brought out to attack Maria during this period. As most agreed in portraying her in a bad light it would be a repetitive exercise. There was, however, one exception, published in Dublin: *An Improved Edition of the Songs in the Burletta of Midas, Adapted to the Times.* Some of the scenes are set in Maria's house and the anonymous poet gives us a patter song of almost Gilbertian bounce when 'Mrs. Fitz' sings:

> Back to France they say he'll send me,
> But I vow I will not go
>
> . . .
>
> Ne'er will I be left in the lurch,
> For I am your honest rib,
> Altho' we were not wed in church:
> If this you deny, you fib.
> The apprehension of Rolle's intention
> hath made you mention
> To me a pension:
> But, Sir, I spurn it,
> And will return it
> Or else will burn it,
> And you may learn it
> In a newspaper squib.

Given all these attacks it is hardly surprising that Maria's brothers should feel inspired to defend her honour, especially against the attacks of *The Times*. At the start of February its proprietor, John Walter, received a visit in his new bookshop in Piccadilly from Maria's brother, Charles, accompanied by a friend. According to Walter's account, Charles, now twenty-nine, seemed 'to *command* rather than *solicit* an answer' as he 'declared in an AUTHORITATIVE tone that if the Paper should DARE in future, to mention one *disagreeable* or one disrespectful word of HIS SISTER, or even so much as her name, he would PUNISH him'. Walter replied in a manly fashion, at least according to his own record, that it was 'not the habit of the TIMES to treat any lady with *disrespect*' and that he was 'certain Mrs Fitzherbert's name had not been mentioned . . . with IMPROPRIETY. On the contrary, a great number of paragraphs had been rejected . . . out of respect to her.' Walter then opened his door so that two witnesses could hear him dismiss 'this kind of *bravado*'. The account in *The Times* proclaimed, 'we are not to be TERRIFIED.' The paper settled its score with Charles Smythe within a week with a poisoned compliment for Maria: 'Let us therefore do justice to the Lady's honour – let us defend her virtue from the tongue of scandal; and proclaim to the world, that the intercourse between her and the Heir Apparent is purely PLATONIC, – *love* without *desire*; – . . . Posterity shall read with admiration this wonderful story . . . [and] give credit to all that Plato has said on the powers of stern virtue over the strongest desires of human nature.' Walter's chance to suffer for the freedom of the press would come a few months later when the Prince and two of his brothers brought suits for criminal libel and won: Walter would spend over a year in gaol.

Society, which mirrored politics, was equally divided between King and Pitt on the one hand and the Prince of Wales and Fox on the other. Ladies favouring the Prince had begun sporting fashionable 'Regency Caps' and Mrs Harcourt was not amused to see them 'nodding at each other all over the room' when she went to the opera. Ladies could also wear ribbons which read '*Honi soit qui mal y pense, de la Regence.*' According to the pro-Pittite *Times*, 'the Milliners report that the Fitzherbert hat fits rather heavy on the CROWN.'

* * *

As February wore on it became only natural that foreign ministers resident in London became interested in the man who might become *de facto* King and his Catholic wife because the British monarch was also a player on the European stage as Elector of Hanover. One of the most perceptive foreign diplomats was Count Bruhl. Because James Bland Burges was an undersecretary at the Foreign Office, he had access to the intercepted and deciphered correspondence from Bruhl and dutifully copied out relevant passages. Not only had Bruhl represented Saxony for twenty years but he had married Lady Egremont, whose position in the Queen's Household gave him access to Court news. Writing in French, then the language of diplomacy, Count Bruhl sought to inform his sovereign, Frederick Augustus III, about the heir to the British and Hanoverian thrones. The Count, who also sent information to the King of Prussia, described the Prince as moving in a circle filled with 'la Dissipation et la Débauche', a man guided by scoundrels such as Hanger and the even more dangerous, Payne, who was an adventurer 'sans fortune'.

However Bruhl gave most of his attention to the ambiguous relationship – 'cette liaison ambigue' – with 'Madame Fitzherbert'. Like most who discussed the secret marriage, he reported that it had been conducted 'according to the rites of the Roman Church'. Bruhl rightly stressed that such a marriage was 'outside the laws of the Kingdom'. He added that the Prince's duplicitous action could not be justified by the 'passions of youth' even if it had been a practical necessity. He stressed that 'cette femme' herself believed that she was married in good faith and he stressed that she was recognised by many leading politicians and received by many of the first families of the nobility. No doubt similar reports, which Burges noted as 'the most accurate statement of the truth', were on their way to the courts of Vienna, Versailles and St Petersburg. It was rumoured that the rakish Duke of Queensberry had been sent to Paris to tell the Duc d'Orléans to stop talking about the Prince and Maria.

Insiders such as Bruhl also knew that behind the scenes some strange manoeuvrings had been taking place. In Hanover some prominent men were trying to arrange for the Prince to become Regent to prevent any attempt by the Holy Roman Emperor, Joseph II, to intervene. In the Minto Papers there is a letter from Hanover to Fox's friend, Sir Gilbert Elliot, urging that the Prince assert his rights, especially as the Hanoverian minister in London disliked him. There was a danger that the Holy Roman Emperor might intervene as a predecessor had done two centuries earlier when a member of the Brunswick family had an illness similar to George III's. The Minto Papers also contain a letter written by the Prince to the Hanoverian minister in London in which he announces 'my intention to take upon me immediately the Administration of Affairs in the electorate and to desire that you will without delay inform the Regency thereof'.[9]

In Parliament the Regency Bill was still slowly making its way through the Commons. On 7 February the lower house debated a clause in the bill to protect the Protestant religion in Scotland. After that the Commons moved on to the next clause which the clerk read out. If the Regent 'shall at any time marry a Papist, then and in every such case, all the powers and authorities vested in his Royal highness shall cease'. Here, again, was an invitation for Rolle to act. He now proposed his amendment: if 'it shall at any time be proved, that he [the Prince] has been married in fact, or in law, to a Papist or to a person of the Roman Catholic religion' he would cease to be Regent. Fox, this time in the Chamber, rose to defend Maria. 'There was,' he said, 'surely no foundation for supposing an indissoluble tie of marriage with a very amiable and respectable character, though she was deemed not to entertain those religious principles which were agreeable to the established system of this country.' If he meant to placate Maria by this lie he failed miserably.

Pitt followed Fox and claimed, with an equal disregard for truth, that when he considered 'all the circumstances of the case they were sufficient to satisfy his mind that such rumours [of a marriage] were groundless'. Lord North joined in to attack Rolle.

This should be, he said, 'the last time this unfounded, idle and pernicious question' should be discussed. Poor, honest Rolle claimed he spoke only 'in defence of the Protestant religion', to which Sheridan asked if Rolle would ever be satisfied: 'Why did he seek for more? Was not one declaration sufficient.' Grey also added his tuppence-worth and denounced Rolle's 'wicked and alarming calumny'. Never have so many famous MPs and Prime Ministers lied so well to the House of Commons. Henry Dundas, one of the most influential figures in Pitt's government, concluded the debate by saying that if such a marriage had occurred it should be investigated by the House of Lords but the allegation was 'so wild, so improbable, so contradictory to the sense and feelings of every man, that he could not believe . . . it could be true'. When Rolle attempted a few days later to re-open the debate the Speaker refused him time and the question went as unanswered as in 1787.

Impartial observers could, in response to Rolle, have recalled that there was only one way to prove the marriage: possession of Maria's wedding lines. Since under British law no one may be forced to incriminate himself, neither Maria nor the Prince, let alone the two witnesses or the clergyman, could be forced to say if he had been part of an illegal act – the marriage. Neither could Maria ever be forced to produce the lines. Had someone else found them, none of the five participants – the Prince, the Anglican clergyman, Maria or the witnesses – could be forced to say their signatures were valid, for this again would be self-incriminating.

Newspapers, inspired by the Commons debates, launched into a new campaign of scare stories. An old chestnut surfaced in the story that 'his Holiness the Pope' had not only sent a valuable diamond cross to a 'certain Lady who had more husbands than one', but, far more alarmingly for British freedom, he had thoughtfully included 'an absolution for all the sins she ever has, or ever may commit'. Unfortunately, for Maria, this was simply a regurgitation of the sixteenth-century charge that the Pope gave Catholics *carte blanche* to commit any sin against Protestants. A month later *The Times* was writing that 'during the life, and at the death of her late husband, a certain Lady in Pall Mall was remarkable for her strict adherence to the Catholic faith, abstinence from *flesh* – of all kinds.' (The *double entendre* would not have gone unnoticed.) Now, however, Maria had left the church: perhaps the Pope had given her permission to do so in order to mislead the British people? Poor Maria, she couldn't win.

On 12 February the Regency Bill passed the Commons. As had happened ever since October, events outside Westminster were already overtaking events inside. Two days earlier the news was that 'the King is in a state of Recovery' and on 16 February, that 'The King still better. The account to-day is that he is in a state of *convalescence.*' Political feeling was as high as ever and Sir Gilbert Elliot told his wife that 'the prevailing principle . . . is to consider the Prince of Wales, and everything that is suspected of the least attachment to him, as a prey to be hunted down . . . This . . . is the private conversation of the ministers and the Queen's whole set.' The day after Sir Gilbert's letter the Cabinet asked the House of Lords to delay discussing the Regency Bill to await events. This was the beginning of the end of the Regency crisis.

For the Prince, February must have been a terrible month. At last the see-saw nature of the King's illness had, it appeared, finally been resolved and the dream of power began to vanish. Not surprisingly he found consolation in drink and at one dinner party 'promised a regiment to Captain Macdonald, who has not the smallest pretension to one; but he keeps him to his promise.' On 23 February the Prince and his brother, York, were finally allowed by the Queen to have an audience of their father during which 'many tears were shed'. Later that same evening the King wrote to Pitt, praising his 'constant attachment to my interest and that of the public, which are inseparable'.

The Queen, unlike her consort, was unforgiving. During the audience on 23 February she had walked 'to and fro in the room with a countenance and manner of great dissatisfaction; and the King every now and then went to her in a submissive and soothing sort of tone.' She could not see her three eldest sons' machinations as anything other than disloyalty to their father. Early in April there was a dinner and concert at Windsor. At Pitt's place there was a device supporting his coat of arms 'and the number 268, the first majority in the House of Commons, written in sugar-plums or sweetmeats. At the concert the music had most of it some allusion to politics and Sir Gilbert Elliot also noted, 'All this is quite new at Court, and most excessively indecent, as the King is always expected to be of <u>no party</u> . . . it smells very strongly of the petticoat, or rather of <u>breeches</u> under petticoats.' In May, as a result of a dispute arising from the crisis, the Duke of York, whose popularity was falling as he followed his brother's profligate example, fought a duel with Colonel Lennox, heir to the Duke of Richmond, a member of the Government. The Queen went out of her way to express her relief that Lennox was not injured while showing no concern for her second son.

For her part Maria escaped from some of these tensions early in April by going to Newmarket with the Prince. But she was back in time for St George's Day, 23 April, when the King, the Queen and all the Royal Family, joined by both Houses of Parliament, attended a *Te Deum* and Eucharist in St Paul's Cathedral to give thanks for the King's recovery. The crowds cheered the King and Queen and Pitt and hissed Fox and the Prince. During the prayer for the Sovereign, the King was seen to cover his face with his handkerchief and even Sir Gilbert Elliot, a supporter of the Prince, admitted that he too had broken down. The King had lost three stone and wore a great coat, it was said, so that people could not see how thin his legs were. Because Maria had no invitation, she watched the procession from a vantage point in St Paul's churchyard. 'What,' wondered *The Times*, 'were her sensations on this joyful occasion?' These we do not know. We can assume they were a mixture of relief that the crisis was over and happiness that her King was restored to health as she was always intensely loyal to George III.

Two days earlier Maria had received an invitation from the exiled French minister, Charles de Calonne, asking her to come with the Prince to his house for dinner on the 23rd, 'at the return from the ceremony in St Paul's'. Whether the Frenchman acted from his own initiative or had had a nudge from the Prince, it was a soothing way in which to smooth any ruffled feathers. Six days after the great service, the final Regency crisis caricature featuring Maria appeared, the famous 'Funeral Procession of Miss Regency'. This was a strip cartoon and shows Maria as part of the party following the coffin of Miss Regency. Maria is wearing mourning and from her waist dangle a rosary and a crucifix. She clasps her hands in mock despair and says:

> Bane of my hopes! O Mock'ry of my fortune;
> They call me now, poor shadow, painted Queen,
> The flattering index of a direful Pageant,
> One heav'd on high, to be hurl'd down below;
> A dream of what I wish'd; a garish Flag
> New made the aim of every dangerous shot;
> A sign of Dignity, a breath, a Bubble;
> A Queen in Jest!!

If Maria's natural inclination was always to get on with life there were others who felt that the Prince's behaviour during the recent crisis needed to be explained. On the day of the Duke of York's duel with Colonel Lennox, Edmund Burke wrote to Maria: 'Thank God it has turned out, as every honest man must have wished, with an increase of honour to the duke of York in every point which can or ought to be honourable amongst men . . .' Burke then went to his second point: 'I cannot be persuaded, but that the present is a moment that absolutely demands that the Prince of Wales both for his own sake and that of the public, should lay before the King a fair and full state of what has been done during his first illness relative to the past (which may soon become the future) arrangements whether His Majesty be absolutely capable of attending to it or not.'

The Prince, who loved writing long and self-justifying works of prose, needed little urging. Helped not only by Burke but by Elliot and Sheridan, he set about drawing up a massive Memorial to the King concerning his and York's behaviour during the crisis. It began: 'Sir, I find myself at last not only at liberty but I think invited by Your Majesty to throw myself at Your feet and implore of Your Justice and Paternal Goodness at least an equitable if not a partial and indulgent hearing to the most solemn and anxious address that was ever made by a Son to a Father.' He went on for eighty-four folio pages to justify his behaviour and then attached to the Memorial a letter of forty-five folio pages, although there is some doubt that either was ever sent.

With the coming of summer Maria and the Prince plunged back into the whirl of social life. When she was not with him there were, as before, difficulties. On 4 June the capital celebrated the King's Birthday and Lady Eleanor Butler noted that: 'The Prince was drunk at the Birthday. He would not behave decently at either of the Ambassadors' galas because Mrs Fitzherbert was not invited.' On the 12th the Prince and Maria attended a fancy dress ball. Along with his two oldest brothers he came in Highland dress 'and looked very well'. When a female guest asked about his kilt he suggested she feel his legs, which she did. The three men 'had breeches, however, above, and only rolled up the breeches's knees'. Jack Payne came 'dressed as a young lady, and looked quite remarkably well, so well as hardly to be a joke, and infinitely better than in his own character. He was chaperoned by Mrs. Fitzherbert' who was in a white dress and black veil 'but unlike a Nun's dress'. The Prince had his own room for supper and he chose his own company 'so that neither Rank nor the Lady of the House decides that point'. (This was a custom that Maria would assume always applied. Years later, when it was laid aside, she would suffer immensely.) Other guests were 'Lady Jersey, dressed as a 'black-veil'd' nun. This 'nun', so unlike the nuns Maria had known in her youth, would also return to haunt her in a few years' time.

In July news started coming in of a major riot in Paris in which the mob had stormed the Bastille and butchered its hapless governor. This was same the man who had complained to Maria and Lady Anne about the 'false information' spread about the prison amongst the chattering classes of his day. Now he was paying the awful price for their chatter. As one Frenchman wrote to William Eden, 'My dear Sir, – I could a tale unfold, which would harrow up your soul, but that it is an undaunted <u>English</u> soul.' By August others were complaining that 'we have no news in England now, but from France . . . they send us more of that article than they do of their wine or their millinery.'[10] For Maria, as well as for most wealthy Catholics with their network of family connections, the developing story would have a particular poignancy.

The news from Paris did not, however, affect Maria's plans and by August she and the Prince were in Yorkshire where he did the rounds of the great Whig aristocrats. Naturally they attended York races, long a centre of Whig festivities, at the end of the month. In September Maria journeyed to the Isle of Wight to be entertained at Newport by the 'great Hampshire *Rats*' that is, two MPs who had come over from Pitt's side during the Regency crisis.

The autumn brought some good news when, on 26 November Withers, the mad pamphleteer, was found guilty 'of printing and publishing a very atrocious and scandalous libel on a Lady of Character and Station, Mary Ann Fitzherbert'. He was fined £50, sentenced to Newgate for one year and bound over to keep the peace for five years after that. Maria now probably felt that the £245. 5s. 4d. spent in legal costs in her failed prosecution against Withers had not been in vain. In December Maria had 'a great assemblage' at her house during which she wore a new gift from the Prince, a diamond which, it was said, had cost £22,000 [£1,247,180]. She still had her critics, as *The Times* complained inaccurately about the 'frugality of Mrs. Fitzherbert's table' – there were only five dishes and no second course, 'even when the highest personages dined with her'.[11] This was nothing to Maria: she had survived the Regency crisis; despite the gossips, she had kept the Prince and she remained one of the most important women in London Society.

9

—•◦•—

PASSIONS AND ERRORS

If Maria hoped that 1790 would inaugurate an era without more
upsets she was wrong. Even though the Regency crisis had passed,
her position and her religion meant that she would be seen as part
of the continuing movement, both inside and outside Parliament,
to allow Dissenters and Catholics to participate in public life. In
1787 a committee had been formed to 'watch over and promote
the public interest of the English roman catholics'. Maria's uncle,
William Fermor, was one of the first five elected, although Maria
herself played no active role. For Catholics it was a simple question of equal treatment as Lord Petre, one of the campaigners for
reform, wrote: 'We consider ourselves at least as good subjects as
the Protestant dissenters . . . with whom we have no intercourse
& whose Religious and political principles must for ever prevent
an union of any kind.'[1] Protestant Dissenters tended to be radical
in politics but Catholics, especially after the French Revolution,
were strongly royalist and conservative.

In June 1791 the campaign for further relief to Catholics culmi-
nated in a second reform act. Catholics could now build churches
and schools. They could legally live in the Cities of London and
Westminster. They no longer had to register or enrol their deeds

and wills and soon the double land tax was repealed. Catholics could now fully qualify as barristers, solicitors, clerks and notaries. The crime of 'recusancy' was abolished for those taking a new oath that was acceptable to Catholics. The laws which could put Maria in the dock or at the bar of the House of Commons for her involvement with the Prince were left untouched.

Officially the Prince stood aloof from the debate but not so in private. Years later a Mrs St John told the diarist Sylvester Douglas about a reception at Lady Salisbury's during this period. She heard the Prince say 'that he thought the Roman Catholic religion the only religion fit for a gentleman. Mrs. St. John expressed her surprise that he should think, and still more, that he should declare this opinion openly, in so large and mixed a company, when he replied, "My God, it is my opinion and I do not care who knows it."' Observers must have assumed that Maria's control of the Prince was now total but if she had overheard this rather silly remark she would have been utterly horrified. We can assume it was, as so often, an exuberance of spirits produced by wine.

Far more vicious than the parliamentary debates over Catholics were the continued attacks of Philip Withers. Confined in Newgate, Maria's old enemy fired off yet another pamphlet attacking the 'insolent exultation' among Catholics at Maria's position. He also, somewhat illogically, stated that she 'intends to qualify for the throne by a *public recantation*, and that a special licence will be granted for that end by the *Pope*.' Relief came on 24 July 1790 when Withers died in gaol. Five days later *The World* accused Maria of being both his murderer and his gaoler and insisted she look after his widow and children.

Behind everything that was done or said loomed the French Revolution. Maria had friends in Paris within that class whose lives were most at risk and we know that at least on one occasion she asked a friend, Sir Philip Francis, to take a 'pacquet' – probably of letters – with him on his trip to Paris. Her first husband's brother sent money to priests in France and the Smythes turned over part of Acton Burnell as a home for émigré Benedictine monks (who eventually established Downside Abbey) just as Thomas Weld would do for seven Trappist monks in Dorset. (In Weld's case his generosity would stir up local anti-Popery feelings.) Weld was also worried about his nieces who were in school in Bruges, while his bankers in London were worried about rumours that 'a Banditti of Frenchmen' had landed in Dorset and burnt Lulworth Castle. Had there been a French invasion Lulworth Cove could well have proved an inviting harbour.[2]

In 1793 Maria and the rest of the country heard of the judicial murders of Louis XVI on 21 January, of the Queen on 16 October and later, of Madame Elizabeth, the King's saintly sister, the three she and Lady Anne had observed at dinner in Versailles, when the Queen had taken up her glass to gaze back at the English visitor. The Princesse de Lamballe whom she had entertained to dinner at Brighton was butchered and Madame du Barry, whom she had bumped into accidentally at Marly, was dragged to the guillotine. In 1793 another of her acquaintances, the Duc d'Orléans, who had taken up the Revolution and had voted for the murder of the King, his own cousin, was himself guillotined. An *éminence grise* who had plagued her life was gone. When nuns and priests fled the developing Terror for the safety of English shores they included in their ranks those nuns Maria had known in her youth and her own sister-in-law, Mary Fitzherbert.

When, for example, the Benedictine nuns from Montargis reached Shoreham in total destitution Maria heard of their arrival, collected money and drove out to meet them. The Prince joined her in welcoming them, arranged for them to be lodged in the historic Ship Inn and visited them. When he entered the room they all stood up but he ordered them to sit down. When it was discovered there were not enough chairs he turned to Maria and said 'in that kind manner which is his characteristic, "See, we are keeping them standing; let us be off, I cannot suffer this any longer."' Throughout England individual acts of charity made the refugees welcome: in Dorchester Abbey there is a tombstone which honours the Archdeacon of Dol in Brittany who was buried there at the request of the Warden of New College, Oxford. His memorial recalls a man 'exiled since 1792 for his Religion and his King. Favourably received by the English Nation.' Christian charity had overcome religious prejudice.

When, in August 1792 another refugee, the beautiful Duchesse de Noailles arrived, disguised as a cabin boy, Maria befriended her as well. The liberal Duc de Noailles, whose family would suffer terribly during the Terror, had played an important part in the earlier stages of the Revolution and was a brother-in-law of Lafayette. He had arrived in England at least by the preceding July. In September Maria took the Duchesse to a cricket match, after which they dined in a marquee while the Prince's band played in the background. In the evening Maria, the Duchesse, Lady Clermont and Bell Pigot walked round the grounds to show the French exile to the spectators.

The changing political landscape would also affect Maria's future. By 1792, as war with France drew ever closer, Pitt sought to strengthen his government by bringing in some of the Opposition who had followed Burke in denouncing the French Revolution. British political life was about to undergo something of a sea-change. In May 1792 the Prince made his maiden speech in the Lords on a bill to suppress seditious publications. He praised the constitution and promised he would 'glory in professing' it until his dying day. This was a resounding success. However, the Prince's long association with radical Whigs such as Fox and Sheridan, combined with his well-publicised debaucheries and indebtedness, were still part of the political equation. The Duke of Portland told the Prince's friend, Harris: 'The circumstances of the times made a Coalition with Pitt a very necessary measure . . . Pitt was of such consequence in the country, and the Prince of Wales so little respected, that we considered it as impossible for him to form an Administration of which Pitt was not to be a part; that an attempt to the contrary . . . would produce the greatest confusion, and even go to endanger the succession.'

The Prince was not helped by the July publication of one of

Gillray's most remembered and vicious caricatures, 'A Voluptuary under the horrors of Digestion'. We see a grossly overweight Prince at table, having just finished a meal and picking his teeth with a fork. There are signs of drinking and medicines for venereal disease. An overflowing chamber-pot rests on (unpaid) bills and through the window we see the still unfinished Carlton House.

For his part the Prince was also changing. Even without Maria's hostility towards Fox, the Prince and his political mentor had been moving apart and with Fox's decline came a certain coolness with Georgiana Devonshire. When she asked the Prince's help in getting a place for a friend she wrote, that 'after all that's passed do not let my name appear, but tell Mrs Fitzherbert that you have thought of him at her recommendation and to oblige her.' Even before the murder of the French King and Queen and the onslaught of the Terror, grass root opinion wondered how Fox could praise the French 'in their present state of ferocity & pure republicanism'. His standing in the Commons was not what it had been, while up and down the country there were little groups of dissatisfied men, anxious to stir up trouble. As the writer, Hannah More, told her friend, Lady Amherst, regarding French republicanism: 'The principles of these people are more to be dreaded than their bayonets.'[3]

Fox was, in short, playing with fire and it was widely known that in January 1793 he had offered a toast to the 'Majesty of the People'. In the country, people were genuinely worried. Lord Wentworth spoke for most Englishmen when he wrote to Lord Denbigh: 'The French monsters have been guilty of greater bloodshed – Damn them all – I wish there were no traces left of their nation but the wines.' For both the Prince and Maria, a French-style revolution led by the London mob would not have been very pleasant.

The Prince was also sincerely distraught that the King would not allow him to play any role as the French threat grew larger. By now his closest friends, Jack Payne, Lord Moira and even Lord Barrymore, along with his four younger brothers were all actively serving in the army, militia or navy and his closest brother, York, would later command the British expeditionary force sent to Flanders, while Clarence and some of the youngest royal brothers saw service in other areas. When the Prince met Harris in the summer of 1792 he expressed his worry about the growing divisions among the Opposition with regard to the developing Revolution in France. 'He condemned Fox, and reprobated in the strongest terms, the conduct of . . . the Reformers.' The situation soon became even worse.

On 24 January 1793 at 1.30 news reached the King of the murder of Louis XVI. A scheduled Drawing Room was cancelled and a Privy Council meeting was held instead. Lord Amherst 'never saw the King more concerned than he appeared to be at the melancholy event'. The murder of the French King and the Reign of Terror shook the Prince as much as his father and he began giving audiences to MPs such as Burke regarding ways to strengthen the government. Two days after seeing Burke he summoned Pitt and Dundas. The Prime Minister wanted the Prince to move away from Fox and to get rid of his own Solicitor General, the radical MP and barrister, Thomas Erskine, in return for which Pitt would urge the King to help with debts and to give his heir the colonelcy he so much desired. On 28 January the papers announced Erskine's dismissal and three days later, the news that Lord Moira had left the Opposition.

The deal was struck and on 28 January 1793 newspapers also announced that the King had appointed the Prince as Colonel in command of the 10th (Prince of Wales's Own) Regiment of Light Dragoons. The Prince was ecstatic and wrote to the Queen in gratitude to his 'good and gracious father'. He was 'not equal to meeting you this evening overpowered with the shocking events of France and with the species of sentiment towards my father which surpasses all description.' The Prince then wrote to the Holy Roman Emperor offering his services in the Imperial Army in defence of '*la cause commune de tous les Princes et Souverains de l'Europe.*' On 30 January the *Oracle*, a newspaper in his pay, announced that the Prince had 'withdrawn himself from the

Political Discord' and had written to the Duke of Portland regarding 'his change of political sentiments' due, it claimed, to 'THE SACRED TIES OF FILIAL AFFECTION'. By October, however, the Prince, unhappy with his colonelcy, was sending for Lord Amherst, the Commander in Chief, because he wanted to have the rank of full general 'without going through the different Ranks'.[4]

As always when dealing with Maria's husband, we take one step forward and then two back. No sooner had the military appointment been announced than scandal arose. This time it was over a camp bed. On 25 July Maria closed her London home and the following day journeyed to Brighton where the Prince would join her after reviewing his troops at Waterdown. On 3 August papers told their readers about the Prince's new camp bed: 'The form of the Bed is square; the hangings of a very delicate chintz; a white ground, with a lilac and green cloud. The fringes, tassels and other ornaments are very rich and beautiful. The State Room in the tent has chairs which alone are said to cost £1000 [over £50,000]. The four corners are ornamented with the PRINCE'S Feathers and Motto.' By the summer of 1793 visiting the new army camps was all the rage. Maria therefore had her own tent 'for her occasional visits to the Camp, furnished . . . very little inferior, to the Prince's'.[5] A storm broke out over this wretched bed and within a fortnight a government-sponsored paper announced that when the Prince beheld his 'magnificent Camp Bed, his Royal Highness, so far from feeling any satisfaction at the splendour of it, ordered all the costly and elegant parts . . . to be taken away, as positively contrary to his orders . . . This is an absolute fact.'[6]

While the Prince was never allowed to take any real part in the fight against Republican France, Maria's own family was involved. In September 1793 her brother, Walter, toured the battle zone, visited the camp at Frichenfeld and was at some stage detained by French forces. Rather surprisingly he did not call on his and Maria's cousin, Lieutenant William Smythe who had followed the family tradition and was serving in the Austrian army.[7] Sadly

Maria's twenty-four-year-old kinsman was killed on 1 December 1794 when the Austrian forces were besieged by the French. A memorial to him as 'a victim to Valour in Defence of Religion and Humanity' survives in the north transept of Acton Burnell church.

As always, war or no war, there was the problem of debt. On 28 January 1790 the Prince had sent for his jeweller, Nathaniel Jefferys, and took him 'into an inner apartment, with very visible marks of agitation in his countenance and manner'. The Prince, according to Jefferys' account, 'said he had "a great favor to ask of me"'. A creditor had called on Maria and demanded payment of 'about Sixteen Hundred Pounds [£82,000]'. The Prince had immediately sent Weltje to ask that Maria's bill be added to the Prince's account but the tradesman refused because, he said, Maria 'was a woman of no rank or consideration in the eye of the law, as to personal privilege' and was therefore 'amenable to an immediate process, which was not the case with His Royal Highness'. The Prince asked his jeweller if he would 'interfere upon the occasion, and prevent if possible, any personal inconvenience to Mrs. Fitzherbert, which would be attended with extreme mortification to the feelings of His Royal Highness' or, in plain English, would he loan the Prince £1,600. Jefferys, a man anxious to climb the social ladder, paid the bill of £1,585. 11s. 7d. and brought the Prince the receipt the next morning. The Prince promised repayment within three months. That same afternoon the Prince and Maria called on Jefferys, apparently at Maria's instigation, 'for the express purpose, as his Royal Highness said, that she might herself thank me for the great and essential service I had that morning rendered her'. Jefferys, an embittered man when he described this meeting, remembered 'the mortified pride visible in the countenance of that lady'.[8]

Worse was to come. On 9 February *The World*, in the pay of the government, reported that an ultimatum had been given the Prince. 'The following *Plan* is talked of with much confidence in the higher circles of fashion: That a proposal has been made to a young *Personage* to marry. – The PRINCESS of PRUSSIA is the

Lady mentioned . . . in which case, the sum of 5,000*l.* a year is to be settled on *another Lady* – an addition is to be made to the income of the young PERSONAGE – and his Debts are immediately to be paid.' The paper added that the Prince was being given some time to consider this and on the following day added that the *'certain Lady*, besides a pension, is to be created a Peeress. MUNSTER is mentioned as the title.' In the event the title was kept for the eldest illegitimate son of the Duke of Clarence.

By December 1790 the Prince, joined by his brothers, York and Clarence, had secured another loan, this time helped by the Duke of Portland. Portland, who was himself so in debt that he could not pay his household bills, may well have had recourse to the same sources. The three Princes were said to have borrowed £300,000 [£15,400,000] at six per cent on post-obits. This was not all: there were also loans of £75,000 from the Duc d'Orléans and £30,000 from a Nathaniel Forth of Manchester Square. These debts, in modern terms, came to a staggering total of nearly £21 million. By May, 1791, the Prince would even be sending his 'diamond George', his 'diamond Garter' and personal jewels to secure another £25,000.

How money was spent is seen in March 1791 during what Horace Walpole called a 'literary saturnalia' at the home of Sir Joseph Bank, President of the Royal Society. Also present was the Prince of Wales who was fascinated by 'the smallest automaton that I suppose was ever created'. The watchmaker was one of the thousands of French émigrés flooding into England. 'It was,' Walpole continued, 'a snuff-box, not too large for a woman. On opening the lid, an enamelled bird started up, sat on the rim, turned round, fluttered its wings, and piped in a delightful tone the notes of different birds . . . It is the prettiest plaything you ever saw.' The price was 'tempting – only five hundred pds. [£26,000]. That economist the Prince of Wales could not resist it, and has bought one.'

By June 1792, however, the problem of the Prince's debts had grown even larger. When the Prince saw his old friend, James Harris, now Lord Malmesbury, he admitted that they totalled

£370,000 [just under £19 million]. Several 'executions' for debt had taken place in Carlton House and, just as he had saved Maria, so Lord Moira had saved him by a timely loan. In the preceding March he had once again given up the turf, thereby reducing expenditure by £30,000 per annum. The scandal-sheets commented that 'The Prince, out of all his sporting stud retains but ONE, which he has kept for his own riding.' He told his friend, who was back from war-torn Europe, that he wanted Parliament to raise his annual income to £100,000 a year, of which he would appropriate £35,000 a year to pay the interest on his debts and to establish a 'sinking fund'. If this could not be arranged – and it could not – then he would 'go abroad'. While the Prince 'did not stand so well with the King' he was 'better than ever with the Queen'.[9] She had advised him to ask the Lord Chancellor to press the King to press Pitt to press Parliament.

In October readers learnt that the Prince would devote five-sixths of his income to settle his debts and the rest to live in a small house 'served by half a dozen domestics in brown frocks' as a 'private gentleman'. He would devote what he had left to 'his most prevailing passion – benevolence to the wretched'. This obviously came from a friendly paper. Hostile editors reminded the Prince that his income came from taxpayers and was intended to 'support dignity, and not to feed dissipation'. Observers told friends outside London that the Prince would once again shut up Carlton House while 'the most strict economy is to be observed.' The Prince announced he would live in rural retirement at Kempshott Park in Hampshire, near to Uncle Errington and to the scenes of Maria's youth. His plate was removed from Brighton in November and it was said that Maria supervised the decoration of the drawing-room and the laying out of the gardens. Soon servants were being dismissed and Carlton House once again shut up although, as in 1786, the Prince did keep some rooms as a pied à terre.

Retrenchment was, as before, not enough and by the end of 1792 the Prince was approaching Thomas Coutts for yet another loan.

Coutts had earlier loaned the Prince £10,000 on Lord Moira's security: the Prince had used the money toward buying a house for Maria – presumably the one in Pall Mall – which he wanted her to have 'totally unencumbered'. Because the bank would not loan money on 'personal ornaments' Coutts agreed to a private loan secured by 'the personal bond and life income of his Royal Highness'. He urged the Prince to stick to the 'plan of reform'. Coutts would have been reassured by an advertisement that appeared in all the London papers on 7 January 1793 urging creditors to send their demands to Carlton House 'in order that the said Bills may as speedily as possible be arranged and put into a state of liquidation'.[10]

As an old woman Maria remembered fondly but not accurately 'that there was none of the Royal Family who had not acted with kindness to her. She particularly instanced the Queen.' The evidence does not bear this out and one of the Prince's earliest biographers recounted a notable scene in Westminster Hall on 13 February 1790. The Queen, along with three princesses, entered the Duke of Newcastle's box to watch another episode of the Hastings trial. Without warning, Maria then entered the box set aside for the Princes of the Blood and sat down between the Duchesses of Cumberland and Gloucester. According to Huish, 'The look of indignation which the Queen cast upon her, is represented to have been as deep and severe as it was possible for the human countenance to assume, and after addressing a few words to Lady Holdernesse, she rose with all the pride of offended majesty, and retired.' When the Prince arrived he tried to calm Maria and then left whilst she stayed in her place.

Huish then printed a series of letters, which are not in the Royal Archives, between mother and son. Queen Charlotte took the first shot and decried the presence of 'that lady' and added that she would never acknowledge her 'or any of her associates, at the court over which she presides'. The Prince is said to have torn up the letter and called for Sheridan who pieced it back together and suggested the Prince's reply. This was 'clever' and asked his mother to give the name of 'the individual who has given the offence'. Later that same day, when the Prince had gone to Brookes' Club, another messenger arrived with a note from the Queen's Lord Chamberlain, Lord Ailesbury. This denounced the Prince's letter as 'evasive' and said she would not see him 'until an assurance has been given that the insult shall not be repeated'. Now the Prince sent for reinforcements in the shape of Fox who, along with Sheridan, wrote another letter which the Prince sent the following day. He regretted that the Queen, by having 'recourse to the intercession of a third person, to whom his Royal Highness is a perfect stranger' had made this a public affair. The Prince would not discuss private matters with a third party, thereby calling his Mother's bluff. Thus out-manoeuvred the Queen left the field of battle. For his part the Prince left the next day for Brighton.

Despite the row over Maria's presence in Westminster Hall the Queen and her son were, by the spring of 1791, once again on speaking terms due to the intervention of Lord Thurlow, the Lord Chancellor. The Prince's relations with his father were also said to be improving and on 4 June, the King's birthday, the Prince once again appeared at Windsor. He wore a bottle green and claret-coloured striped silk coat and breeches and a silver tissue waistcoat embroidered in silver and stones and with coloured silk embroidered flowers. Everything was covered with spangles and there were diamond buttons on his coat and waistcoat. He also wore a 'diamond epaulette, star, George, sword and buckles'. (One wonders if these had been retrieved from Morland and Hammersley?) In the evening there was a ball which the Prince opened with his sister, the Princess Royal: minuets went on till 11.30 and then there were country dances.

From the Royal Family's point of view, as well as from Maria's, the two most important family developments in this period were the marriages of the Duke of York and of Prince Augustus. In the spring of 1791 the Duke, remembering the understanding with his brother that he would marry and eventually inherit the throne, set off for Berlin in search of a suitable bride, this time to be found in Protestant Prussia. Gossip sheets, remembering his penchant for tennis, hoped 'his Royal Highness's *balls* will be more effectual on the Continent'. The more circumspect Horace Walpole noted that 'The P. of W. is much out of order, spits blood, and fainted away after his levée on Monday', but did not say whether this had anything to do with York's departure for Berlin. Perhaps the attack indicated some deep-seated fears now that his 1785 plan was coming nearer to reality and he began to hedge his bets. Sir Gilbert Elliot was told by Lord Malmesbury that the Prince had 'behaved extremely well' regarding plans for his brother's marriage. He went on to record what Maria would not have been pleased to hear, that the Prince 'has put in a saving clause for himself in case he chooses to marry, which he thinks probable if he sees his brother happy with his wife'. The Prince also showed Malmesbury his ability to rewrite history when he recounted that he had told the King 'that had he permitted him to go abroad at the time he asked leave to do so, he meant to have looked out for a Princess who would have suited him, as he was too *domestic* to bear the thoughts of marrying a woman he did not like'.

By September the negotiations had been completed and the Duke married Princess Frederica on the 28th in Berlin. There was a second wedding at Buckingham House on 23 November when the Prince of Wales gave the bride away. Observers found the Princess to be 'a very short woman, with a plain face, but neat little figure, with a remarkably small foot'. Indeed, her small feet started a fashion and Mary Frampton recalled that 'it became the fashion for every one to squeeze their feet without mercy, in order to be like her Royal Highness, and as she wore heels to her shoes, so did the rest of the world.' While Maria had too much common sense to worry about her feet, she did worry about how she would be accepted by her first sister-in-law. Gossips enjoyed themselves, wondering how not only Maria but the Duke of Clarence's fecund mistress, Mrs Jordan, would cope with the new situation. *The Bon*

Ton Magazine asked, in terms equally applicable to Maria, if the marriage had not 'awakened all those injurious suspicions which had for some time slumbered in the lap of oblivion'. Maria might have taken some consolation in the magazine's reference to Mrs Jordan as the new possessor of the three F's: 'fat, fair and forty'.

The Duchess of York and Maria met for the first time at a ball given by the Duchess of Cumberland. Mary Noel wrote that 'the Dss of C. presented Mrs. Fitz to the Dss of Y at her Ball, who made her a very graceful courtesy, but said very little, did not speak to her again the whole night, & how the latter was rather at Coventry the whole time.' Cartoonists soon realised they had a new topic and in 'The Rival Dutchesses; or, The Royal Quartetto' they showed the Duchess dismissing Maria who is about to curtsey to her. Maria is shown saying that she is unable to endure 'the distinctions of honour and etiquette . . . daily heaped upon a younger sister-in-law.' In the background are two of the Duke of Clarence's mistresses, Mrs Jordan and the negress, Wouski, whom he was said to have kept busy when aboard ship.

For Maria all this must have been terribly galling. She usually had good relations with York who, like Uncle Errington, had apartments in Stable Yard, St James's from which he wrote on at least one occasion to Maria: 'Dear Madam, My box at Covent Garden Theatre will be very much at Your Ladyship's service next [?] Thursday evening.' The Prince and she had arranged their lives so that each could live separately. In January, 1792, for example, the Queen held her annual Birthday Drawing Room on 18 January. This was followed by a ball. For her part Maria gave a *petit souper* which was described 'in all respects a superb thing: the three Brothers Royal were of the party which did not break up until a late hour; a musical intermezzo of catches, glees, &c. by amateurs of distinction, added not a little to the hilarity of the evening.'[11] But this complementary way of life was being undermined by the new Duchess.

That April there was another cartoon, 'A Well Known Tea Table Altercation' which shows Maria and the Prince sitting at a tea table, with Maria throwing a cup of tea into his face and asking when she is to be introduced to the Duchess. He replies, 'Because I submitted to a few ceremonious matters in order to amuse you, and to gloss over your conduct to the censorious world, you begin *to be presumptuous.* An even more offensive caricature, *The Visit* to Piccadilly; –or– a Prussian Reception' appeared on 12 July 1792. Here we see the Prince leading a goat with Maria's head to a door of a large town house held open by the Duchess who says, 'Relation of mine, indeed? no, no! me know no Nanny-goat-Princess!' Such caricatures must have hurt Maria's pride, especially as the two ladies frequently came into one another's company, as in a 'grand field-day given in honour of the Duke and Duchess of York' by the Prince in Brighton. This contretemps also affected the relationship between the two brothers. In June 1792 Colonel St Leger called on Lord Malmesbury and told him all the latest gossip. Maria, he said, 'dislikes the Duchess of York, because the Duchess will not treat her "en belle soeur": it is that is the cause of the coolness between the two brothers.'[12]

Another brother who would upset Maria was Prince Augustus. Like the Prince's other brothers, Augustus was sent to Germany to be educated but, unlike them, he had bad health which made him unfit for the military. He was sent to Italy for his health and while in Rome in 1793 he found a Church of England priest who secretly married him to Lady Augusta Murray, a daughter of the Earl of Dunmore, the last Royal Governor of Virginia. Within weeks there was gossip in London about the marriage. By the autumn of 1793 the couple were back in England where they had a second ceremony in St George's, Hanover Square as 'Augusta Murray' and 'Augustus Frederick, bachelor'. They presumably thought that a second service could somehow square the circle. It did not and the King invoked the Royal Marriage Act.

In January 1794 Lady Augusta received a formal citation from the Court of Arches to answer a suit brought in under the Act. This church court, the Consistory Court of the Province of Canterbury, met in Bow Church and administered Church law which included annulments. On 27–28 January the Court examined the clergyman who married the couple as well as Lady Dunmore before eventually ruling that the Royal Marriage Act did not apply to marriages performed abroad. Whatever joy the Prince felt was quickly dissipated when the case went on appeal to the Court of Privileges which declared both weddings invalid. The point was clear: in the case of the Church of England, the validity of canon law was subject to statute law. In Maria's case this meant that her Church of England marriage might be valid in Roman Catholic eyes but not in Anglican, and this was without reference to the Act of Settlement. The fact that the Countess of Dunmore and the clergyman were hauled into court was not a very pleasant one to contemplate.

Amazingly, there is a letter from Maria to Lady Anne written within days of the Court of Arches' hearing but without reference to it. 'Town,' she wrote, 'is very dull.' She had been in London for two months and had only been out of her house six times in the evenings. 'I feel myself much more happy in living at Home with a friend or two than in rackitting about & by so doing I please another person . . . who you know is the most Domestick Creature in the world.' She told her friend, who had married Andrew Barnard the previous October, that the Prince 'holds himself in readiness to be call'd upon <u>for godfather</u> whenever you think proper. I told him I did not dare insert this but he is standing at my Elbow & insists upon my writing it & if he commands like a poor tame creature I am I <u>must obey</u>.'

On the surface, these years, 1790–4, appeared to be happy ones. During the London season there was the usual round of dinner parties, balls, routs, visits to be made and received, carriage outings to be taken and private moments together. Summers would find Maria and the Prince in Brighton where they enjoyed amateur dramatics, some organised by Maria to help impoverished actors, cricket matches, fencing competitions, dinner parties, concerts and dances. There were also the numerous race meetings where fashionable society gathered and where, in the

Prince's case, he actually won as well as lost money.

The couple were still surrounded, whether on the race course, in Town or elsewhere, by a rather motley circle of friends. There were some reputable people, such as Bell Pigot, or the Irishwoman, Lady Clare, who became Maria's friend but there were more who were not quite all they should have been. Among these was the young Duchess of Rutland: the death of her Duke in 1787 meant she could now join Maria and the Prince's circle without censure and could take a lover. There was also a couple which would help to discredit the Prince in the eyes of many, Sir John and Letitia, Lady Lade. While Sir John was a baronet his wife was far from lady-like. She had, it was said, served the Duke of York in a non-military capacity and, before him, Rann the highwayman. 'Some' said that Lady Lade acted as the Prince's procuress and, if 'some' are to be believed, sought out virgins from good families for his delight. She was famous for her foul language and for driving her own carriages at a furious pace.

In addition to Maria's brothers, Wat and Jack, there was the eleventh Duke of Norfolk, son of the tenth Duke, he who had thought of marrying the 'blowzy black', Miss Eld. There were also two elderly profligates, Lord Clermont and the Duke of Queensberry, known as 'Old Q'. The Prince eventually 'christened the facetious Duke of Q——y *Old Tick*. The cause was thus: The P—— observing the Duke gallanting at the Opera with Mrs. Harris the fruit-woman, pleasantly asked her, "if she was not afraid of the consequences?" "No, your Highness," said the fat handmaid of Pomona. "Alas! his Grace is like an old clock; he can *tick*, but he can't *strike*."'

The most disreputable friends were still Lord Barrymore and his brothers. The *Bon Ton Magazine* reported in September 1791 that one of the French émigrés living in Brighton, the Duchess de la Pienne, had recently invited the Prince and Maria to supper. 'Among the other persons invited was Lord Barrymore, without any notice taken of his two brothers' but the brothers 'accompanied him in Mrs F.'s landeau. Directly they made their appearance, the Dutchess was suddenly indisposed, and frequently left the company'. Her condition got worse after supper when 'the Hon. Mr B. began to sing abruptly, and to be merry: this made the Dutchess *very bad indeed*'. When the other guests inquired about her ill-health – she was pregnant – she replied that 'the presence of the two Mr B.'s was so very disagreeable, that she must insist on their leaving the house'. When Maria and the other ladies asked why, the poor woman said she 'was afraid that the presence of these gentlemen would make the coming offspring similar to one of them in presence and features – and, like the other, lame and disfigured'. To retaliate the two Barry brothers met outside the Duchess's window each morning 'and entertained her with making the most eccentric *grimaces*.' The poor woman fled to London.

Sometimes the antics and the drinking became too much for Maria and the Duke of York later told the diarist, Thomas Raikes, that she would sometimes hide under the sofa when the Prince and his drunken friends would return home. On finding the drawing-room deserted the Prince would 'draw his sword in joke, and, searching about the room, would at last draw forth the trembling victim from her place of concealment'. An anonymous pamphlet published in 1792, referred to the Prince's friends as 'the very lees of society', and by a judicious use of dashes singled out George Hanger, Sir John Lade and the Barry family. 'If a man of the most depraved, the vilest cast were, from a vicious sympathy, to choose his company, it were impossible for his choice to fix anywhere else'. As the Prince told his mother, this pamphlet was the 'most infamous and shocking libellous production that ever disgraced the pen of man', a product of the 'hell-begotten Jacobins' which should be prosecuted by the Government.

Maria's difficulties with her husband's friends was one of the forces that strained their relationship. A second difficulty was her temper and, according to the Prince, her jealousy. In a memorandum written sometime in 1791, Lady Anne noticed that the pair's 'domestic happiness was not so perfect, as it had been'. Occasionally the Prince complained to 'Sister Anne' about Maria's fierce temper and Anne herself felt that Maria was too domineering, 'drawing the cords of power too close'. The Prince moaned that 'if she loved and considered me as much as I love her, we should not quarrel as often as we do'.

A third difficulty, and a cause for Maria's jealousy was the Prince's way of life. By the summer of 1791 the Prince was once again on the sexual war-path. This time he was after the youngest daughter of Lady Archer, one of those 'ladies' who ran faro banks and befriended Maria's Uncle Errington. From Maria's point of view a more serious affair was with an actress and opera singer named Mrs Crouch who was also on the scene by the summer of 1791. Anna Maria Crouch lived in a 'triangle' with her husband, a naval officer, and the Irish actor and singer, Michael Kelly. The Prince's infatuation became the talk of the town, and to cope with this Maria 'piqued him by treating this with ridicule, and coquetted on her side. This hurt his vanity, and brought him back.' By June the affair was over and Colonel St Leger told Lord Malmesbury that 'the Prince was more attached to Mrs Fitzherbert than ever . . . he is now more under her influence than ever.' Gossips said that the Prince had to buy off Lieutenant Crouch with a pension of £400 per annum and a bond for £12,000 but having done so, only slept with the third angle in the triangle on one occasion. Contemporary diarists tell us that Mrs Crouch agreed to sell the bond back and the Prince's agents arrived with a bag containing 1,000 guineas. They came with two further bags, each with an additional 1,000 guineas, in case she raised her price but she was satisfied with what she was offered.

For her part Maria enjoyed flirting with young men and saw no need to avoid one of life's pleasures because of the Prince's obsessions. Letters in the Esher Collection show the degree of tension this caused. In one written to the Prince by Isabella Pigot in her usual gushing style she said she was 'happy to the greatest degree in seeing all so well between you, this new disquietude has so . . . destroy'd my hopes, & spirits, that I feel Myself the greatest Wretch on Earth.' She reassured the Prince that

> I thought it better we s'd try a few days quiet at home, as you seem so much to dislike assemblys & Certain Things that happen there, which I wish only to persuade you can not proceed from the degree of Obstinacy you suppose, & meant Merely to torment you, but from foolish habits which require a little time to conquer, & we are now always so much on our guard as to have recollection at the Moment, that we are doing what is forbid, & more particularly if it s'd Chance not to strike us with the same degree of impropriety it does you.

'All that,' she wrote, 'is to be attain'd by a little time. This I there-fore recommended but you seem'd not to wish it – and yet my Dr Sir, when she said she then w'd go out again, you replied that then all w'd End between you. In short your mind is so distracted, you are so miserable . . . I think I have still influence enough to persuade her to Consider her own interest and meet happiness where it is offer'd . . . for God sake point out to Me what you wish . . .'

It is hardly surprising that there were frequent rumours of a looming separation. Lady Jerningham's brother Edward, however, gave 'no credit to the separation, or at best think it an artificial one to deceive the K—— and Q——, whose pecuniary assistance he wants so much.' Six months later gossip-sheets wrote that 'Mrs. Fitzherbert is returned to town for the winter [of 1791–2], but she goes no where, and is only at home to a few of her most intimate friends. Her appearance is dejected, and her corpulency consider-ably diminished.'

Just as there had been a furious row in 1791 over Lady Archer's daughter, in 1792 there was one over a young friend of Maria, a Miss Paget to whom the Prince appeared to be laying siege. The Prince wrote to Miss Paget, who was living with Maria at the time. The young lady replied that she 'regrets that it is not in her power

256

to comply with the wishes of his Royal Highness . . . <u>to their full extent</u>: but in a matter of so much delicacy, and in which the character of his Royal Highness is at stake, there is not anything which Miss Paget would not undertake.' To keep things secret she arranged to meet at the Duchess of Cumberland's.

At the Duchess's establishment there were, it was said, certain rooms in which 'interruption was never feared' and Maria saw the Prince lead the young woman into one of these. She then ordered her carriage and stormed out, leaving Miss Paget to make her own way home. Gossips and the Prince's first biographer said that Maria was so furious that she threw a cup of coffee (or tea) into his face but they were probably making use of the caricature that had appeared earlier in 1792. When the Prince asked for proof of his guilt, Maria produced the letter. The truth was that he had asked Miss Paget for a loan of £10,000 and that the money had been handed over at the Duchess's. Because the story is only substantiated in Huish's book it should be treated with a grain of salt but there were numerous other incidents that brought the couple to the brink of a separation.

When recounting these years, one sometimes feels one is reading the plot of a melodrama in which over-wrought men and hysterical females storm round a stage with a quiet little peace-maker in the centre, all being performed for an audience that is never far away. On a more serious level we see two people, one strong-minded, the other impetuous and in love with love, each caught up in a relationship that was already fractured. It needed only a final crisis to pull it apart.

10

THE LATE PRINCESS FITZ

In the recollections Lord Stourton took down of Maria's conversations with him, she told him that:

> her first separation from the Prince was preceded by no quarrel or even coolness, and came upon her quite unexpectedly. She received when sitting down to dinner at the table of [the Duke of Clarence] . . . the first intimation of the loss of her ascendancy over the affections of the Prince; having only the preceding day received a note from His Royal Highness, written in his usual strain of friendship, and speaking of their appointed engagement to dine at the house of the Duke of Clarence. The Prince's letter was written from Brighton, where he had met Lady Jersey. From that time she never saw the Prince, and this interruption of their intimacy was followed by his marriage with Queen Caroline; brought about, as Mrs. Fitzherbert conceived, under the twofold influence of the pressure of his debts on the mind of the Prince, and a wish on the part of Lady Jersey to enlarge the Royal Establishment in which she was to have an important situation.

This 'authorised version' is how Maria wanted history to remember their separation in 1795 but this is not how things happened.

The Prince of Wales demanded tolerance but, like so many men, gave little in return. His and Maria's relationship should be, what a later age would call, an 'open marriage', but Maria, when not with him, should behave like the traditional wife. He himself observed no such restraint. Hitherto his occasional flings, while causing the explosions that were part of their relationship, posed no major threat. By 1793, however, a new affair had begun, one far more threatening to Maria. His latest companion was the Countess of Jersey whose husband was his Master of the Horse. She was friendly with the Queen through Lady Harcourt and often joined Queen Charlotte at cards or on outings. The Prince had known her since 1782 when she was one of the older women with whom he 'fell in love'. Lady Jersey, was said to be 'a clever, unprincipled, but beautiful and fascinating woman, though with scarcely any retrieving really good quality'. In society she was known as 'the Lucretia'. She was a manipulating woman who wanted power and who knew she would have to turn the Prince against Maria to get it. She was also a dominating woman whose husband 'almost trembled in her presence, and certainly never ventured to oppose her opinions, or wishes'.[1]

Lady Jersey's danger lay in the fact that she was, unlike the other women in the Prince's life, so similar to Maria. Like her she 'moved with a kind of regal dignity, as if she felt herself to be the queen of society'. She was a good conversationalist, knew famous people, was interested in public affairs and viewed them from an increasingly conservative point of view which tied in with the Prince's changing views. Like Maria, she also spoke French well. She was six years older than Maria and already a grandmother. She could therefore give the Prince those things he was looking for: graceful manners, a strong personality, charm, wit and a sympathetic ear but without what the Prince called Maria's 'obstinancy' and 'impropriety,' that is, her independent spirit.

Maria retaliated in the only way she could. By the spring of 1793 she either was, or was believed by Society to be, having an affair with a young French aristocrat whose relation she had befriended the previous summer. Charles de Noailles, who was twenty-two, was said to be 'as handsome as the day'. Evidence for the affair is meagre and comes from a biased source, a letter from the Prince written after he had learned of its existence.[2] According to the Prince, the Duke of Gloucester had said that the affair was 'the universal conversation of all the Women & their societies, who were all astonished & shock'd at her & not on <u>my</u> account, that they had said, that both Mrs Fitzherbert & Noailles were particularly careful of their conduct in not speaking to one another when I was in Society, & almost as much so of the Duke of Gloucester; but that whenever we were not present, he used to follow her about <u>every where</u>, that he never was absent from her elbow for a single moment.'

The couple were said to have met at Maria's house, when the Prince was out of town, or at Madame de Coigny's. The affair was supposed to have ended when Maria went to Brighton in the summer of 1793. Not surprisingly Bell Pigot was 'uneasy & unhappy at it'. As to the extent of the affair, there is conflicting evidence. The Duke was convinced that 'it had never gone beyond flirting'. The Prince, however, had overheard in the summer of 1794 statements about de Noailles, 'insinuating nearly that he had had a connexion.' When charged with this the Frenchman had replied, again according to the Prince's letter: 'No, I swear, not I! It just happened once. You don't believe that I could give any further thought to that fat old turkey. But, she was a Prince's mistress, and it's always nice to have the mistress of a Prince.' The 'fat old turkey' was thirty-seven. Thus the only evidence is the Prince's recollection of a third party's recollection of what a boastful twenty-two-year-old Frenchman claimed, knowing that no one could disprove his boast. It may have been true or it may have been nothing more than a consequence of Maria's flirting with a handsome young aristocrat. One suspects the latter but accepts that the jury will be forever out.

Even if the Prince had never heard of the Noailles affair he found plenty of other reasons to engage in one of his favourite pastimes, writing letters of enormous length, filled with self-pity and self-justification. Some of these letters survive in the Esher Papers and they make sad (and tedious) reading because syntax was never part of the Prince's prolixity. The handwriting races across the page and words are frequently underscored. Maria's replies have vanished so, at best, we have a one-sided view. Sometimes the Prince got friends to urge Maria to do what he wanted. Sometimes he poured out his numerous sorrows to Jack Payne or Isabella Pigot. Another letter, perhaps also written in 1793 after the couple had been apart for six weeks due to a row, shows that Maria must have fought back and probably treated the Prince's gush with a certain disdain. This led him to write bitterly about her previous letter which he felt had probably been written for her by someone else: 'I can not give her credit for so much feeling, for had she had the most trifling feeling, or idea of what is express'd in this Letter, she could not have helpt returning to me with open arms (who she well knew would have receiv'd her with open arms).' In this same letter the Prince told the ever-sympathetic Bell that 'all these fine sentiments and feelings of regard & interest which she has so often denied with her tongue tho' not with her Pen, & of which her conduct itself at the present moment is the strongest contradiction "<u>play round the head, but come not to the heart</u>".'

By the autumn of 1793 the Jersey affair had caused Maria's relationship with the Prince to deteriorate rapidly, as we see in a letter from Lady Anne to her friend. Lady Anne, who still saw Maria's as one of history's great love stories, was in Ireland, where she was visiting her fiancé's parents: 'If there is no final rupture have none for God's sake – if there is, remain where you are – no, nothing – nothing is final to those who have hearts & affections & who have loved totaly & sincerely – I add no more.' By the end of October things seem to have cooled down somewhat, for observers noted that 'The Prince of Wales always hands Mrs Fitzherbert to the top of the room whoever is there.' This may have been for public consumption because by the end of November newspapers announced that Maria's 'chief residence will continue to be in the neighbourhood of the *Pavillion*, Brighthelmstone' while the Prince spent the final months of 1793 in London where he was very in with the arch-Tory, the Duchess of Gordon, who gave dinners for him and his friends. During November the Prince sent someone to Brighton to see how Maria was doing and got a good report. While her health was 'less good than I had expected', the friend wrote, she did have 'the happiest disposition to conform to every wish of yours'. She agreed that if in the future she 'fails in obeying those wishes that it can only arise from not perfectly understanding them, and not from any other cause, as the principal object of her life is to study your happiness' and to forget 'former grievances and disagreements'.

While Lady Jersey had to a large degree replaced Maria, the old love was not thrown over for the new. In March 1794 he wrote to Henry Dundas, Pitt's right-hand man, regarding 'the small annuity of three thousand Pounds a Year which I pay to Mrs Fitzherbert'. Using standard court language he asked Dundas 'to lay me at His Majesty's feet & request that he would be graciously pleas'd to ensure in case of my death the continuation of this pension . . . in consideration of her good conduct towards me during the last ten Years'. If the King agreed, his heir was 'ready to relinquish every pretension to future favor of any kind on my own account'. Whether Dundas believed this last promise is not known. Eventually the request was granted and Maria's future financial position was secured, at least on paper for the Crown was not immune from late payment of monies owed.

By the summer of 1794, the Prince, at the height of his fury over the rumours about Maria and Noailles again poured out his feelings to Bell Pigot. The news 'has driven me, to become a Self Murderer & to win every peaceful moment of the short space I trust in God is allow'd for my destiny.' Maria 'has dishonor'd me in my own eyes & in the eyes of the World'. He felt as if someone 'had first open'd my breast & then pour'd boiling lead into it'. Where there was no proof there was 'the strongest air of probability'. In other words, he wanted to believe the rumours, though it is unclear whether it was her 'flirting' and alleged betrayal or his being cuckolded that was the major cause of his suffering. 'Let her but stay my friend & . . . I may still be in time to stop every thing . . . but it admits of no delay.'

After this, things seem to have calmed down and on 23 June Maria received the famous note from the Prince regarding their scheduled meeting on the following day at the Duke of Clarence's house at Bushey. The note began, 'My dearest Love' and said that he was unable to come to dinner because one of his sisters wanted him to go to Windsor. He signed his note: 'Adieu, my dear love, excuse haste. Ever thine, G.P.' The next day, as she was sitting down to dinner, a second note arrived, which, Maria later said, told her that their relationship was finished. Although Maria destroyed this second letter, she kept the first one and noted on it: 'This letter I received the morg of the day the Prince sent me word, he would never enter my house (Lady Jersey's influence).' Lady Jersey had destroyed her marriage.

The Prince's version was different. When writing to Jack Payne in July the Prince spoke of his most recent meeting with Maria: 'You know I love her too truly not to have felt more hurt than words can almost express, at leaving her in the temper wh. I saw she was determin'd not to get the better of.' As always the Prince saw himself as somehow detached from any dispute, which must have increased Maria's fury: 'God knows what I have done to merit it.' Payne could show Maria this letter but 'pray don't let me have any high flown letters from her upon this subject, for they really are too painful to me to be able to bear ym.' Whatever he had written on 24 June was not a dismissal because later he told Jack Payne of an enormous letter he was writing to Maria. What he wanted was a 'perfect understanding'. If it doesn't meet with 'the success which the good intentions with which it is written merit . . . I have nothing further to say or to reproach myself with.'

The letter on which the Prince's 'perfect understanding' was to be based was probably written on 7 July. In it he reads Maria a lecture about 'what my feelings & sentiments always had been respective to what the conduct of any woman I consider'd as attach'd to me, sh'd be in the World'. What he had already written would be approved by any 'liberal & justminded man, who from principles of finer interests in himself, & from the truest love & affection for the Woman, w'd not wish a Wife, a Mistress, a Sister, a Daughter, or any woman in whose conduct he might feel himself interested from ties of the purest & sincerest friendship, not to adhere & adopt most devoutly & strictly'. This line of conduct also applies to any 'Woman of Fashion'.

For his part the Prince was 'anxious to make her appear not only before his own eyes, but in those of the World in general, as the most amiable of her sex, & consequently as the most deserving of those sentiments which he was known to profess for her'. Maria must not criticise his choice of 'improper' friends. Nor must she allege that he talks about her to those friends. It is all Maria's fault for having listened to 'nonsensical or absurd stories or reports' which led to 'the unmerited treatment I had experienced at y'r hands'. From now he 'insists' (a word he underscored twice) that if Maria ever again hears gossip about the Prince she must tell him 'the name of the person who told it to you'. This will allow him to 'expose them & their damn'd schemes'. He had, he said, already explained all this when last in London but he supposed Maria 'did not sufficiently attend to me'. When next in Town he hopes the matter will not be mentioned: obviously he was dreading another scene. From Windsor Castle the Prince sent the letter to Payne who was to read it before delivering it to Maria. He told Payne that writing the letter had meant he had to 'rip up every & the most distressing feelings of my heart' and he added that this letter 'concludes everything on my part'. Lest we read this as a wish to end the marriage, he went on, 'whichever way this unpleasant affair ends I have nothing to reproach myself with'.

As always the Prince was totally innocent of wrong-doing. Rather surprisingly he also told Payne that there was no hurry 'in this business'.

For her part, 'The Fitz was in convulsions of rage and despair and astonishment' according to Lady Anne's sister, Lady Margaret Fordyce. When the Prince finally saw his parents and sisters and told them that all was over, the Royal Family, while hardly in a rage, was not enthusiastic either. 'The Prince came back with a *flea* in his royal ear.' According to this source it was Maria who 'determined to cut compleatly' and no longer to be subject to his 'ten thousand caprices which she says have made her life a burthen to her for years back'. She would still have her £3,000 plus her own £2,000 so she would not starve.[3] On 7 August, the day after this letter was written, *The Times* was already referring to the late separation and jointure settled on Maria. 'Unencumbered as she now is, the lady will probably be a happier woman than she ever has been.'

As an old woman Maria told Lord Stourton there were two causes for their separation: 'the pressure of his debts on the mind of the Prince' and 'a wish on the part of Lady Jersey to enlarge the Royal Establishment, in which she was to have an important situation'. In truth, it was the culmination of several years of quarrels and misunderstandings mixed with only partially successful reconciliations. In her recollections she also told Lord Stourton that 'she was deeply distressed and depressed in spirits at this formal abandonment, with all its consequences, <u>as it affected her reputation in the eyes of the world</u> [author's' emphasis].' She talked to her friend, Lady Clermont, who advised her to 'rise above her own feelings, and to open her house to the town of London'. She did so and 'all the fashionable world, including all the Royal Dukes, attended her parties.' This was not the behaviour of a heart-broken and abandoned woman. Her principal supporter, she later claimed, was the Duke of York, but he was the same man who would urge his brother to end the relationship because of her temper.

The news had quickly become public. As early as 15 July Lord

Mornington wrote to Lord Grenville, the Foreign Secretary: 'I heard last night from no less authority than Tom the Third [Thomas Coke] that a Treaty of separation and provision is on foot (if not already concluded) between His Royal Highness and the late Princess Fitz. I think you ought to marry His Royal Highness to some *frow* immediately.' Thomas Coke had also told Lord Mornington that the Prince 'is very well disposed to take such a wife, as it may be His Majesty's pleasure to provide for him'. On 30 July Lady Anne wrote to Maria to find out what was going on. All she knew was what she had read in the papers 'plainly put in by enemies of yours'. Her old friend referred to the Prince's 'love for you and your great influence over him, together with your sometimes taking up things so high as to have made me fearfull of your cracking the tyes which bind him to you'. Significantly Lady Anne assumes the latest row was caused by Maria's temper and went on: 'Dearest Fitz be not too violent for your own sake.' She had heard that Maria was thinking of a trip to Switzerland but urged her to stay calm and in Pall Mall 'and his natural choice directed to yourself, his long habits of confidence, and a thousand other motives connected with his heart and with the companionable turn for domestic life which as a Man he has, will bring him back to you as truly as ever'. As for Lady Jersey, 'it is not in her power, a married woman as she is, with other dutys to fulfill, to supply your place to him.'[4]

For her part Lady Anne was not prepared to see the relationship collapse. Early in August Lady Cork wrote to Lady Anne's future father-in-law, the Bishop of Killaloe, with the latest gossip: Maria was 'thought very unfeeling to the Prince who dotes upon her, wants still to be reconciled; so far as I can make out from the various stories told, I guess the truth to be that she always conquered him by violence of spirits.' Lady Anne saw this letter and then wrote to Maria who was annoyed that since June the Prince had complained to Lady Anne about her behaviour. Maria's old friend told her that 'I never heard a man express himself with more attachment to a woman than he did when talking of you and that the complaints he made of you and which I repeated (small ones they were), were the complaints of tenderness only, such as a private man might have made of his better half whose affection he doubted was inferior to his own for her. "Never" said he, "No, never have we been so comfortable together as we were before this!"'

Two days later Lady Anne's sister wrote that Lady Elizabeth Luttrell, sister of the Duchess of Cumberland and co-director of their faro bank, said that the Prince was now in Brighton, as was Lady Jersey, while Maria was in London. Lady Jersey's plan, she wrote, was for the Prince to drop Maria and marry so that the King would pay his debts. If Maria's later explanation was correct, it seems odd that the Prince sent Lord Hugh Seymour, Jack Payne, Bell Pigot and Lady Elizabeth Luttrell to see Maria. As Lady Margaret put it, the Prince is 'quite out of his wits, but the cruel nymph is actually gone to Margate where she has taken a house'. Lady Margaret, added, 'I think *we* are both well out of the scrape.' The whole thing would end in a reconciliation unless Maria loved someone else. For the Prince the situation is 'rascally . . . after all the pains he took to bring the Fitz into her present public point of situation!'

Throughout July and August the messengers referred to by Lady Margaret left London for Brighton and the various country houses and watering holes Maria was visiting. They carried notes and letters from intermediaries and the Prince who was, not surprisingly, once again ill. The tone of these letters was that, while the Prince wanted some sort of reconciliation, Maria was reluctant. In one letter Payne writes that she did not write herself 'more from the persuasion of the impossibility to your being happy in future, than any resentment of what is past, & the most violence you betray, will more strongly confirm this opinion'. Payne urged the Prince, in simple English, to keep his mouth shut: 'the anxiety you express'd perhaps to too many of those you thought your friends, but whose talkative dispositions, have spread thro every circle of a chattering world what it never could be your R H's's wish or interest should enter so widely into circulation.' All this 'town talk' horrified Maria. In particular, the Prince should avoid talking about Maria to 'a certain person' who was presumably Lady Jersey.

The Prince was now desperate for a letter from Maria whose nerves were obviously shattered by this emotional whirlwind and by the fear that any letter would be passed round his friends. At some stage there appears to have been a meeting between the two, as one undated letter from Jack Payne tells the Prince that Maria 'is compos'd and comfortable & will meet you with pleasure this evening at my house. She will be there a little after nine & wishes you would be there about a quarter of an hour after.' The Prince still wanted Maria on his terms but in addition he also wanted, it would appear, a second wife who would meet the criteria set by the King and Queen: a German Protestant Princess, 'some frow', as Lord Mornington put it. In the beginning of August the Church court finally declared Prince Augustus's marriage 'utterly null and void; and also declared that a former marriage pretended to have been had at Rome, was also, by a law of this country, invalid and illegal'. In addition, it now seemed obvious that the Duchess of York was not going to have a child. Instead she preferred her eighteen dogs. As the King observed, 'affection must rest on something'. The Prince's grand strategy of 1784, through which the Crown would pass to York's child, was now totally exploded. None of his other brothers was married. Clarence was busy settling down to life with Mrs Jordan. Prince Edward, Prince Ernest, Prince Adolphus and now Prince Augustus were all unmarried.

In politics there were growing fears about a revolution inspired by the example of French republicans and encouraged by French agents supposedly at work in London. Back in January a stone had been thrown at the King's coach as he went to Parliament; on 21 August troops were stationed in towns close to London; and in November a jury found Horne Tooke not guilty of treason. The government got ready for rioting but the worst that happened was that the mob forced MPs leaving Pitt's house to 'huzza' for Tooke. The month before, the Duke of Portland had obeyed the King's command 'to confer with Mr Pitt in order to form such an Arrangement as might enable me, and several other Lords & Gentlemen with whom I have long been connected in habits of political & private friendship, to serve His Majesty'. Eleven days later Portland became Home Secretary. Times were changing and the Prince, now a thirty-two-year-old man and not the twenty-one-year-old youth who had fallen in love with Maria, was changing as well. In an ideal world he could have made new arrangements and kept Maria but if she would not co-operate he had little choice. By 21 August he had taken his decision as he told Jack Payne:[5]

> It is now too late to think of any thing further respecting this very unpleasant Business. I have ~~already~~ at last taken my resolution, & ~~my plans are already in great forwardness~~ All I can say is that I shall ever be happy to contribute every thing that lays in my power to render Mrs Fitzherbert's situation as comfortable as possible, and to testify every sort of attention & kindness to her, & that too in the manner that can be most pleasing to her feelings, mais tout est fini. ~~So much has said, & so much has past since the recommencement of this very disagreeable & painful Business, & you are so thoroughly well acquainted with my feelings & sentiments in every point of view on this subject that~~ I think it perfectly needless to say any thing more upon it . . .

For his part, Payne 'felt happier than I have done my dear Prince, for some time past at the tranquility of your last letter'. He hoped that 'the unpleasant affair being now brought to a conclusion will leave no atom of dreg, to disturb either your Royal Highness's peace or that of Mrs Fitzherbert's hereafter, which I know is dear to you. I have written to her a letter today, expressing the terms of regard that you had us'd to me in your R. Hss's last letter.' When the Prince wrote to his brother, York, he referred to the 'very uncomfortable situation' he had experienced 'for some months: &

indeed for some years' but insisted that Maria and he were 'finally parted, but parted amicably'. Any faults were, naturally, not to be laid 'at my door'. 'However, tout est fini entre nous.' The Duke of York was delighted and had no doubts as to who was to blame: 'I have long been grieved to see how very miserable Mrs. Fitzherbert's unfortunate temper made you, and once, if you remember, some years ago, advised you not to bear with it any longer. I am rejoiced to hear that you are now out of her shackles.'

A few days before, the Prince had seen his father, then on holiday at Weymouth, who told Pitt that his son had 'broken off all connection with Mrs Fitzherbert and his desire to entering into a more creditable line of life by marrying: expressing at the same time the wish that my niece, the Princess of Brunswick, may be the person'. While the King was for delaying the wedding till the following spring, the Prince wanted to hurry. The die had now been cast.

By September Maria was at Margate and, in Miss Berry's famous phrase, was 'driving away sorrow in a phaeton and four'. The self-assurance that helped make her attractive to some men had obviously not deserted her. One undated letter from Maria, written from Margate, survived the burning of her correspondence. Because it was written from Margate we may date it from September 1794. It was in reply to a letter from the Prince that has disappeared but Maria's response shows that the contemporary gossips may have been more accurate than her later recollection. She could not doubt the importance of what was happening but it was not so much a total separation as a readjustment of relations:

> I received the honor of your Royal Highness's letter yesterday and cannot sufficiently express how sensibly I feel all your kindness towards me. Permit me to assure you, My Dear Sir, nothing can be more truly gratifying to me than the continuance of your Friendship & good opinion. It was a real mortification to me to hear of your sudden departure from hence as I had flattered myself with the hopes of seeing you again.

Prince Ernest was good as to give me his company at Dinner on Tuesday & yesterday he eat an early Dinner & embark'd immediately afterwards . . . My carriage is at the door and I am just going to step into it to begin my journey towards Town but I shall not arrive there till late on Saturday Night & I hope your Royal Highness will remember your kind promise as nothing will give me more pleasure than seeing you and of having an opportunity in person of expressing my gratitude for all your goodness to me and of assuring you, My Dear Sir, of the unalterable Regard and Respect with which I must ever remain Your Royal Highness's much Devoted and Much obliged Humble Servant.

Perhaps Maria's public confidence hid her more private feelings. When the Prince's brother, Ernest, visited her in October he found her 'to be very low spirited'. She never mentioned the Prince by name but 'was very low at anything mentioned that have any regard to you'.

Negotiations were hurriedly opened for the Prince's marriage and on 31 October Queen Charlotte noted in her diary that 'This Evening the Kg. brought upstairs The Treaty of Marriage between the P.W. & P. Caroline of Brunsvic which he signed. Lord Malmesbury who is abroad is to demand the Princess. The Copy of this Treaty with a letter was sent to the Dutchess of Brunsvic. As usual the Kg. came. Music began and played at Cards till 1/2 past 10. supped & retired at 11.' Five days earlier the Queen had made a special journey to London to see the Prince 'who desired me to buy the Cloath for the Princess of Wales' and to see jewellers, mercers, milliners and lace makers to 'chose Lace, Trimmings & Gowns for Princess of Brunsvic'. The Queen and the Prince also chose the 'robes' or wedding dress which was ready on 3 December. The Prince, who spent much more time with his mother this autumn, expected the Princess 'every other Hour' but 'neither the Duke nor Dutchess of Brunsvic would let their Daughter come away until She was demanded in Form' so the Prince had to be patient. Onlookers were fascinated with Lady Jersey's role and Lady Mount Edgcumbe asked her friend, Edward Jerningham, if 'your friend *the Lucretia*, [will] by her virtue, gain any situation in the new establishment'?

The Prince's anxiety about the Princess's arrival sprang from his heightened emotional state: as he told Lady Anne: 'You know me too well to doubt what I have gone thru . . . I have still to suffer before I can divest myself of habit, affections . . . that have now existed above 12 long years.' Maria had returned his letters unopened and the central problems remained, at least in his eyes: jealousy and her awful temper. Applying the 'double standard' he asked, 'is it for the Prince of Wales' supposed wife to lay herself out to catch the attention of a pack of boys? Is it for her to be running after every dissipation of this town.' This outburst did not reflect his settled view because on 1 November he let it be known that he wanted 'all his friends to shew the same attention as before to Mrs F.' This was a situation the Duchess of Devonshire found 'odd'.[6]

When Lord Malmesbury went to fetch the Princess he took his diary with him and noted that the Princess had a 'pretty face – not expressive of softness – her hair and eyebrows good, bust – short.' The unpublished parts of his diary would describe less flattering attributes of the Princess. The Royal Family was already divided as the Queen, who knew of the Princess's reputation, opposed the match. James Bland Burges noted: 'I do not believe there is a more unhappy family in the Kingdom than that of our good King.' Gossips were already exchanging rumours about the Princess, one of which claimed that she, too, was already married. Some would later put the choice down to the influence of Lady Jersey 'from the hope that disgust for the wife would secure constancy to the mistress. All well-informed persons agree that the preference of the Princess . . . was the choice of Lady Jersey and Lady Harcourt.'[7]

On 30 December the King announced the marriage to Parliament

in his Speech from the Throne. On a less happy subject, Pitt introduced what the *Annual Register* called 'the unpleasant topic of the
Prince's embarrassments'. The 'unpleasantness' came to a staggering £639,890 4s. 4d. (The war affected the purchasing power of
sterling. Using 1790 as our base the modern equivalent comes to
£32,807,160; using the value for 1800 makes the modern equivalent £18,454,427.) For her part Maria no longer lived in Pall Mall
and had already given up her house in St James's Square. She
eventually bought a house at No. 6 Tilney Street, near Park Lane,
which was to be her London home until her death.

Maria was always very good at looking after her financial affairs
and was annoyed, as she told her banker, that she had to buy the
lease and the furniture. 'Cash,' she told Thomas Coutts, 'is by no
means pleantyfull with me.' She was annoyed that 'no one step
has been taken to secure me even the very small allowance I am
now in possession of, nor does he I believe think it necessary I
should have an existence.' She had written to the Prince 'thinking
it would be proper to settle this matter before the Princess of
Brunswick came to England as after that period it might have
appeared indelicate my working [writing?] on any subject'. After
ten days she had nothing but an oral reply to say that 'he shall
not answer it.' Maria was furious and told Coutts:

> He must be very ill-advised to behave in this manner, consid-
> ering everything that has passed & instead of irritating me
> & adding insult to injury he ought even if it was only for his
> own credit endeavour to conduct himself better. I feel I am
> getting angry, & therefore I will drop this odious subject. It
> is only to you my good friend I speak so plainly, for I assure
> you however poignant my own feelings are upon this subject
> as well as every other that concerns him, I am perfectly silent,
> & tho it is a hard task I think I shall feel more comfortable
> hereafter. At least I shall have the approbation of my own
> conscience & heart in knowing however provoked I have
> never said or done anything to injure or hurt him . . . In my

next [letter] I will be more entertaining, but I am very nervous today & good for nothing.

Like people recovering from a divorce Maria developed a sense of injustice over money which would never really go away and in January she would complain to the architect, George Dance, 'That she has expended £8,000 in entertainments etc. provided for the Prince of Wales, and that if He wd. pay that sum, & trouble her no more she wd. be contented. She says she has lived the life of a Galley Slave for 4 years past.' This was of course a wild exaggeration but it revealed her growing sense of betrayal. (Ironically, on 19 December Lord Loughborough wrote that the King had agreed to continue the pension of £3,000 a year to 'a lady who had been distinguished by your regard' should the Prince die before her.) But this was only half the picture. Lord Hugh Seymour told Payne at the end of the year that a relation had just had a letter from Maria 'written in bad spirits but in a style that does her heart much honor, as the interest she still feels for the welfare of the Prince makes her dread his being without a friend to turn him from the mischief and numberless difficulties which his present connection exposes him to'. Lord Hugh, who was furious with the Prince, pitied Maria 'with all my soul'. As for the Prince: 'he is doom'd to be led by some bad character, male or female.'[8]

Gossips were busy planning Maria's future. Early in 1795 *The Bon Ton Magazine* wrote 'A marriage is confidently spoken of in fashionable circles, between an emigrant French nobleman [Noailles] and a certain celebrated widow, lately of Pall Mall.' While by June the new lover was Jack Payne: 'Commodore P——, lately wrecked on the rocks of Jersey, was fortunately picked up by the Fitzherbert jolly-boat, and safely carried into harbour.' Yet others, such as Mrs Piozzi, said that the Prince 'has paid 10 or 20 Thousand for quiet Possession of Lady Jersey . . . besides the immense expense of buying Mrs Fitzherbert's Consent to his Marriage – another Old Grimalkin of fifty year's standing at least'. (Maria was thirty-nine.) As for Lady Jersey, her pre-eminence was secure: 'The separation so anxiously and so long desired by certain august personages [the King and Queen], was effected solely by the management and address of an active countess. Hence the influence she possesses in all the royal circles, and hence the envy which attaches on her, as the natural consequence of female pre-eminence.' This has become the standard explanation for the separation and the one Lord Stourton perpetuated in his *Memoirs*. The reality, as *The Bon Ton Magazine* reported, was different. This was later recognised by one observer: 'The Wales marriage was not made by Lady Jersey' but 'in consequence of violent quarrels with Mrs Fitzherbert . . . He would have been glad to have been on terms again but she refused.' Her terms did not equal his demands.

The Prince's new bride finally arrived, after a tortuous journey through war-torn Europe, on 5 April 1795. Jack Payne commanded the ship which brought her across the Channel. The royal yacht docked at Greenwich but the bride had to wait an hour for her new lady-in-waiting, Lady Jersey. 'The acclamations of the people were unbounded.' When she arrived at St James's she was presented to the Prince by Lord Malmesbury. As the *London Chronicle* said, 'The meeting was very interesting.' That was an understatement. The Prince, having raised his fiancée from her kneeling position, turned away, walked to the other side of the room, and, approaching Malmesbury, announced: 'I am not very well; pray get me a glass of brandy', after which he went to the Queen. The Princess's view was equally unflattering, as she later told Lady Charlotte Bury, among many others: 'To tell you God's truth . . . I always hated it: but to oblige my father, any thing. But the first moment I saw my *future* and Lady J——y together I knew how it all was, and I said to myself, "Oh, very well! I took my partie."'

A few days before the wedding, Maria left London to stay at Marble Hill House, the exquisite mansion built for a former mistress of George II, although she left instructions that her London house was to be illuminated on the wedding night. Before the ceremony took place on 8 April Maria wrote to her closest friend a heart-breaking letter in which she referred to:

> this Crisis wh. one's Heart & mind is torn to pieces . . . indeed, Indeed, I have suffer'd & do Suffer a great deal & feel when everything is Concluded I shall be more tranquill perhaps it is all for the best . . . Still when I feel my <u>Situation</u> & the manner in which I have been so undeservedly ill treated I cannot bear my own thoughts I have no malice or revenge in my disposition & from my soul do I wish Him happiness . . . Wd you believe it possible . . . that the day after I got here purposely to get out of the way that taking a dismal airing in my carriage the first thing that presented itself to me close to my own house was the Prince riding furiously by my carriage so near that I could have touched him I really thought I should have died.

The couple had not spoken and later Maria learned that he had been riding opposite her house for some time. Maria now stayed in her garden and was comforted by the Duke of Gloucester. Interestingly, there was later gossip which blamed Maria for resisting 'the urgent application he [the Prince] made to her to come back to him, before his marriage'.

For his part the Prince suffered equal agonies. Before the wedding the King worried that his heir might 'bolt' and told the Duke of Clarence to look after him. The Duke later recalled: 'The only time the late King [George IV] had ever spoken to him on the Nature of his Union with Mrs. F. was on the Evening of his Marriage when George 3rd desired him not to quit the Prince & he drove with him to Carlton House to dress for the Ceremony after dinner & as he passed through the Garden the Prince said, "William tell Mrs. Fitzherbert she is the only woman I shall ever love."' On his way from Carlton House to the Chapel Royal the Prince was accompanied by Lord Moira to whom he said, 'It is no use, Moira. I shall never love any woman but Fitzherbert.'[9]

During the wedding ceremony which took place at night, as was the custom, the Prince was obviously drunk. He held onto the Queen's hand for as long as he could. As *The London Chronicle* said in its issue of 7–9 April, 'his attention was equally divided between his lovely bride and his amiable mother'. Another observer told the Duke of Leeds that he showed 'coolness and indifference' to his bride and kept looking at Lady Jersey, one of the four titled ladies attending the Princess; Lady Maria Stuart told Charlotte Jenningham that he was 'so agitated . . . it was expected he would have burst out in tears'. Afterwards the Prince 'looked like Death and full of confusion, as if he wished to hide himself from the looks of the whole world. I think he is much to be pitied . . . What an odd wedding!'

What most upset the Prince during the service was when the Archbishop of Canterbury read out the sentence, 'Therefore if any man can shew just cause why they may not lawfully be joined together, let him now speak, or else hereafter for ever hold his peace'. He looked hard at the Prince and then at the King. This was the same Archbishop who was at the 1785 dinner during which Maria's rumoured marriage was discussed. When he came to the words, 'forsaking all other, keep thee only unto her, so long as ye both shall live', he repeated the question. Mrs Harcourt noted that his 'manner of doing it shook the Prince and made me shudder'. Later the Archbishop described the scene to his brother-in-law:

> The crowd at St James' last night was immense and the heat intolerable. I felt my business a very solemn one indeed, and never said prayers in my life under more impression and fervency. The Prince's mind was certainly very seriously affected both in the service and after the service, but not in that part of the service from which one might be led to fear he had upon his mind a feeling that he had before bound himself by solemn engagements. There I saw no embarrassment.

On the Prince's way out of the Chapel Royal he saw Lady Anne and gave her a look that she remembered as 'miserable'.

After the wedding, and in the days to come, the Princess showed herself to be, in a phrase used by a modern courtier about another female member of the Royal Family, 'Vulgar, vulgar, vulgar.' Our knowledge of the marriage comes from both parties, but in recollections dated years after the event and after many bitter rows. The Princess later, and often, discussed her plight: the Prince was 'so drunk the night he married that, when he came into her room, he was obliged to leave it again; and he remained away all night and did not return again till the morning; that he then obliged her to remain in bed with him & that that is the *only time* they were together as husband & wife.'

The Prince had a different story. The Princess was apparently not a virgin, as he told Lord Malmesbury, 'for not only on the first night there was no appearance of blood, but her manners were not those of a novice. In taking those liberties natural on these occasions, she said, "<u>ah mon dieu qu'il est gros!</u>", and how should she know this without a previous means of comparison.' Secondly, the Prince had a love of cleanliness, unusual in the eighteenth century, which he discovered his new wife did not share: 'She the next night mixed up some tooth powder and water' and used it to cover up stains in her night-dress, 'both in the fore and *hind* part of her.' Not surprisingly, this made the Prince's stomach turn and he vowed '<u>never to touch her again</u>. I had known her three times – twice the first and once the second night.'[10] Somewhere between the two accounts lies the truth. For a man and a century which prized manners and deportment, and a man used to the dignified carriage of Mrs Fitzherbert and Lady Jersey, this was all a great shock. At first, however, the couple seemed happy enough but within weeks the Prince told the Queen that his wife was 'the vilest wretch this world ever was curs'd with . . . a very monster of iniquity'. Behind everything stood the evil genius of Lady Jersey.

For her part, Maria is reported always to have called 'the Princess of Wales only Princess Caroline'. The Princess, however, a good-hearted if coarse woman, 'speaks highly of Mrs Fitzherbert'. She is reported as 'always' saying 'that she is the Prince's true wife; she is an excellent woman; it is a great pity for him he ever broke vid her. Do you know I know de man who was present at his marriage, the late Lord B——d.' The Prince, now burdened with a wife he did not love and missing the wife he did love, as far as he could love, was at the centre of a growing political storm. The Stadholder of Holland and his family had fled to England in January. Fears of a French-inspired Irish uprising and of 'the imminent danger of the most formidable invasion of Great Britain', now haunted government. People were tired of the war and of the increased taxes. The King's coach was again attacked and in June, James Burges noted a mob assembled in St George's Fields, Southwark and also 'a party of near a dozen fellows in Mr Pitt's stable yard, who were telling each other to note the place, that they might have it on fire tonight'. The Guards, he also noted, were ready while the Prime Minister was told to leave London, which he did. The next month saw a mob taking possession of Whitehall while they ransacked houses and pelted the Horse Guards with 'several well dressed men harranguing the populace in the true Parisian stile, by the title of Citizens'. Two days later a mob attacked Pitt's house in Downing Street.[11]

The promise to settle the Prince's debts was proving a difficult task for the government. The King's message to the Commons regarding the debts in April 'excited a good deal of murmuring' and Pitt, who was not quite sure how to proceed, had no choice but to consult 'the sense of People in the House'. By June discussion on the debts produced confusion and laughter in the Commons. The young MP, George Canning, noted: 'We find ourselves reduced to the necessity of watching who goes out, & who stays in, & to vote most profligately & unconstitutionally rather by Example than from any studied consideration.'[12] The government's majority also shrank alarmingly. Eventually the government got its bill through and a commission was set up to sort out the mess and pay the bills. The Prince's annual income went up from £73,000 to £138,000, while £325,000 was set aside to pay for the wedding and £45,000 to finish Carlton House. Ironically, he actually had less spendable income than he had before.

For her part Maria seemed to disappear from the public gaze. There are few references to her in the newspapers and other than two caricatures in 1796 she did not feature in the shop windows until 1802. A dinner party she gave in the summer was reported by *The Times* on 29 July 1795, while *The London Chronicle*, in its issue of 10–12 September recorded that her grandmother, the Hon. Maria Molyneux, had died in August, reportedly in her nineties. In October *The Times* also noted that Maria, still living at Marble Hill, had bought Mr Beaufoy's 'Italian Villa' in Castle Bar Hill, Acton for 9,000 guineas. She may have been having some financial difficulties because her friend, Thomas Coutts, offered help. While Maria admitted that 'I have met wt. a thousand disappointments but I hope by the assistance of some friends to be able to succed as it would mortify me exceedingly to accept your friendly offer.'

Both parties to the 1785 marriage were miserable. There is a tradition that three days after his marriage the Prince called for his carriage to take him to see Maria and was dissuaded by an equerry from going: what he wanted was not necessarily a renewal of their marriage but a shoulder on which to weep. Lady Anne described Maria's plight: 'Mrs Fitz has purchased the country house of Beaufoy the late member & distiller . . . she got it [at] so great a bargain that she has been again into town, is much attended to, but is not happy – she feels herself nobodys object – & woud even be glad to be <u>tormented</u> – I believe rather than face the calm she does.'[13]

11

———————

LIKE BROTHER AND SISTER

Whatever feelings the Prince may have had for Maria by the beginning of 1796 she was adjusting to life without him and had taken a new house in Ealing. For his part, and despite the influence of Lady Jersey, the Prince could not adjust to life without Maria. On 7 January the nation rejoiced at the birth of Princess Charlotte – at long last the Prince had an heir and the succession was secured for another generation. However, Maria's husband brooded over his fate and, three days later he once again decided he was at death's door.

What more natural than to compose a Will in which to indulge his self-pity. When the Duke of Wellington saw it years later he pronounced it 'the most extraordinary Paper he had ever seen' and added, 'the late King was the most extraordinary man' and, he went on, 'little dependence [was] to be placed on his character'. The document, which fills seven and a half pages in the Prince's published correspondence, was eventually given to Maria. In Lady Anne's words, she 'attaches more consequence to a Will she possesses . . . than I do' and Maria kept it when she agreed to have her papers burned. It is now in the Royal Archives. Its appearance – the Prince's sprawling handwriting races across the pages with prodigious underscoring and a large amount of ink used – gives some indication of his mood.[1]

The document also gives us a fairly accurate insight into the Prince's peculiar character. Throughout he portrayed himself as above reproach and was more selective than most of us in what he remembered and in what he forgot. He began with an invocation: 'To thee, Oh! Almighty God do I in these my last moments with the truest fervour . . . unveil my whole soul.' He left all his property 'of every description' to 'my Maria Fitzherbert, my wife, the wife of my heart & soul'. Although 'by the laws of this Country she could not avail herself publicly of that name, still such she is in the eyes of Heaven, was, is, and ever will be such in mine, & for the truth of which assertion I appeal to to that Gracious God who I have here invoked'.

Obviously last year's separation plagued the Prince, as did the reasons for it and, turning from God, he now addressed the world in general. In light of what had been said 'relative to our separation she (my Maria Fitzherbert) has been most infamously traduced, that her person, her heart & her mind are, & ever have been from the first moment I knew her . . . as spotless, as unblemished, & as perfectly pure as anything can be that is human & mortal.' The Prince now turned to the stories about Maria and Noailles and almost admitted he was wrong in the conclusions to which he had so readily jumped: 'Had it not been for the most infamous & basest of calumnies, my too credulous & susceptible heart, and which knew no other feeling in life but for her, could never have been brought, even for a single instant to harbour a thought of separating from such worth, nor was such a separation, Oh my God, as thou well knowest, voluntarily sought by me.' (In essence he was half-correct: it had been Maria who had forced the issue and demanded a full separation.) The Prince now reminded God that his faults arose from no 'propensity to vice' but from 'those foibles which but too often fall to the lot of those who are born to fame, & no inconsiderable advantages in life'.

The Will left Maria Carlton House and all its contents – 'bronze

& ornamented chimney pieces, all the hangings, chairs, tables, ornaments & inlaid tables, bronzed tables, cabinets & consoles, girandoles, clocks whether of bronze or of other material, all my fine pier glasses . . . all my plate'. He also left her, in addition to any money in his various accounts, all his property, including the Pavilion and its contents. Not only that but he left her all the money which he and his supporters in Parliament claimed was owed him from his income as Duke of Cornwall before coming of age. As the Government had never accepted this claim this was of little real value. As to the Prince's private papers, Lord Moira, Jack Payne and Maria were to go through them; those not burnt were to become Maria's property. He demanded that those papers in a box labelled 'private' must be published 'without any mutilation or ejection of any paper'. These concerned the Princess and his aim was to ensure from beyond the grave that she would have no influence over their daughter.

As to the 'Mother of his child, call'd the Princess of Wales', she was to have no part in the education of Princess Charlotte because of her 'falsehood & treachery', which he now forgave. He left her one shilling. He asked 'my Maria' to provide an income for Bell Pigot on whom he had already settled £500 a year for life. '<u>My beloved & adored Maria Fitzherbert, my wife, in short my second self</u>, would, he was sure, honour his requests. He asked that he be buried with the small picture of '<u>my adored Maria Fitzherbert</u>' suspended round his neck, 'as I use to wear it when I lived' and placed '<u>right upon my heart</u>'. Furthermore, after Maria's death he wanted to be reburied next her so that their two coffins could be 'souder'd' together as George II and Queen Caroline's had been and as had recently been done in Vienna with Maria Theresa and her husband, Emperor Francis.

'Having thus closed the scene of a life <u>most full of trouble & misery</u>, I have only now to bid a last farewell to <u>her who whilst she and I were one did constitute the sole & only happiness of that life I am now going to resign; none have I enjoyed since we separated, & none could I ever expect under any circumstances</u>

whatever, unless we were once more to be united again . . . round thee shall my soul for ever hover as thy guardian angel . . . recollect that no woman ever yet was so loved or adored by man as as you were & are by him.' The Prince now read over the document which he appears to have enjoyed writing, made two copies and added two notes regarding those jewels used by the Princess and the annual pension of £3,000 which, he reminded his father, he had agreed to continue paying to Maria after the Prince's death. He only forgot one thing: to have the will witnessed, so that its legal value was highly dubious.

The Prince did not die and was soon recovered enough to return to his old way of life. Opposition politics still appealed and eight days after signing his will he was, according to Sylvester Douglas, 'generally understood to be as much in opposition as ever. I hear he speaks of that party as us and we.' Just over a month after writing the Will another MP, Charles Abbot, noted that the Prince was at a party at the Queen's House to which Lady Jersey had been invited. 'The Prince of Wales in the course of the evening repeatedly came up to her table, and publicly squeezed her hand. The King sees and disapproves of the Carlton House system. The Queen is won over to the Prince's wishes by his attention and presents in jewels, &c; the Princess [of Wales] says, her father . . . told her to observe everything, but say nothing.' As always life was a great romantic pageant in which the Prince had his role to play: the difficulty was in keeping all its supporting actresses in the company.

But neither politics nor Lady Jersey could banish Maria from the Prince's mind and by May he had found a new intermediary, his brother, Prince Ernest, to approach Maria with a letter asking for a reconciliation. Ernest reported that Maria 'is frightened to death, knows not what to say, as is natural to be assumed as you have come upon her so unexpectedly'. Maria admitted 'a very sincere regard for you, but I cannot get anything else out of her as yet'. She had agreed to meet Prince Ernest at Jack Payne's the following day, 18 May, and Ernest hoped he would 'be luckier'.

However he warned his brother: 'She always owns to this, that if she did make it up you would not agree a fortnight; <u>cela rest a voir</u>.' There the matter did rest because Maria could not be won over.

A far more pressing problem for the Prince was the increasingly public dispute with his official wife. On the same day that Maria was meeting Jack Payne, the Prince wrote to the Princess 'from sincere anxiety to prevent a rupture' and to propose a new modus vivendi. Once again the Prince wanted to keep the Princess, albeit at arm's length, and also have Maria. Within a few days these feelings disappeared when Caroline was given a rousing reception at the opera. 'Men stood on their seats waving their hats and shouting "huzza"' and the audience demanded the orchestra play 'God Save the King'. The Prince, smarting from Maria's aloofness, told his mother that 'the most active persons' behind the demonstration had been Lord Hugh Seymour, his wife, Lady Horatia, Jack Payne, Lady Stafford, the Lord Chancellor (Lord Thurlow), Lord Fitzgerald, 'the bosom friend of Mrs Fitzherbert' (and a man he once accused her of having as a lover), Lord Darnley and his brother, who 'ever since my separation from Mrs Fitzherbert have been constant inmates' of her houses, 'at all parties & on all occasions'. Their aim, he argued, was to punish him for his desertion of Maria by supporting his wife.

However, the Prince suppressed his anger and gave an audience to Lord Thurlow, during which he 'is said to have talked of a divorce, as having been married to Mrs Fitzherbert'. Someone 'leaked' the news to *The Times* which reported the meeting on 28 May. Within days the Prince asked the King to approve a 'final separation' which he refused. In the event it did not matter for the marriage was at an end. On 30 July the *Oracle* claimed that Maria was 'much indisposed at Brighton – the cause is supposed to be occasioned by that *green-eyed Monster – JEALOUSY*.' For her part, Maria was trying to avoid the Prince and the Royal Family. She wrote a chatty and affectionate letter to Thomas Coutts from 36 Pultney Street, Bath. She would have arrived 'some time ago but was prevented on account of company coming here, who as I was not particularly anxious to meet made me delay my journey, till I knew the coast was clear'. The only members of the Royal Family left were the Yorks who were leaving the next day: 'I am not sorry they are taking their departure for I never wish to meet or see any of the family & I shall feel much more at my ease when they are gone tho' they dont annoy me as I came here purposely to see my Mother who is in a very indifferent state of health, & I dedicated the whole of my time to her.' To add insult to injury, her allowance from the Prince was late for the first time and 'God knows when they will think proper to let me have my money.'[2]

For her part Lady Jersey, although regarded by the Prince's former friends, such as Lord Hugh Seymour, as 'that bitch', still held sway. In August the landscape artist, Joseph Farington, reported that the Margravine of Ansbach, who lived in London, said that when the Prince visits Lady Jersey 'she was accustomed to drop the linen blinds of the window', whether for privacy or as an advertisement is not known. In September her ladyship wrote to Edward Jerningham, one of the few people who liked her, that the Prince 'is in great beauty, spirits, and <u>pour amiable il est toujours</u> like himself, and not like any body else'. Three days later she reported that she was at Bognor with the Prince where he was delighted with the 'quiet life' he led there. As with all the other women in his life, Lady Jersey had her own fears and told Jerningham, 'I shall keep your letter and read it over whenever the devil of suspicion lays hold of me.'

The Prince's relationship with Lady Jersey was as confusing to onlookers as was his with Maria. In August 1798 Lady Stafford wrote: 'We are told that the Prince has discarded Lady Jersey, in Consequence of H.R.H. being *enamour'd* of a Miss Fox, who lived with Lord Egremont, and who has several Children.' Some reported she was young and pretty, while others wrote 'that she is oldish, fat, and looks like a good House-Keeper. Elderly Dames seem to be his Taste.' When that same month Colonel McMahon, part of the Prince's Household, visited Cheltenham he saw Maria and reported that she and her brother had heard gossip about the Prince's intrigues with an actress. Jack Smythe has '*not* been kind in speaking of it'. Maria, who thought, incorrectly, that McMahon was part of the Jersey set, would not confide in him but 'in look & manner she has been uniformly gracious & civil'. 'She goes everywhere & to everything & says that her spirits are better than for many years.' But, the Colonel added, 'I have reasons to think, by what has fallen from a lady of her acquaintance . . . that your R. Hss. occupies her thoughts a vast deal.'

By the end of the month Lord Moira was writing to McMahon about 'the new arrangement [a reunion]' which 'will be more for the comfort of the person we love than any in the former stile'. There should be no problem with the public if the Prince and Maria acted with discretion. Wisely Moira added: 'That which most offends great bodies of people is any appearance of braving their opinion.' The problem was the trouble-makers who would attack any reunion. But Maria still held aloof. The Prince's sisters, Mary and Augusta, wanted a reconciliation and Princess Mary, who wrote to Maria, also acted as a messenger for both of them. They liked Maria and valued the good effect she had on their brother. By December the Prince changed tack and considered a reconciliation with the Princess by inviting her back to Carlton House but she refused to come. For her part Maria was more concerned with a visit to Portsmouth that same month to discuss with Lord Hugh and Lady Horatia Seymour Maria's looking after their youngest daughter who had been born in November. The Seymours were going to Madeira to try to recover their shattered health.

In the following year, however, the Prince would have more luck. Early in February he thanked yet another female confidante, the dowager Duchess of Rutland, for her and for another unnamed person's help in getting Maria back. While 'there <u>never was an instant in which I did not feel for her,</u> as I am afraid she <u>never</u> felt for me', she was, even so, the only person 'who can <u>ever</u> give me <u>a taste again for life</u>'. He also approached Maria's mother, 'the old lady', who promised to help him when the time was right. As regards Lady Jersey, 'everything is finally at an end IN ANOTHER QUARTER.' By May Lord Wentworth could write that 'the Jersey reign is quite over'. It was the Prince and Lady Jersey's mutual friend, Edward Jerningham, who 'communicated to Lady Jersey the Prince's dissolution of the connexion with her'. When she got the news she told Jerningham, 'Damn you, I wish you joy of your new trade.' The Prince got a terrible shock on 22 February when newspapers reported that 'SHE *had died* at Bath'. 'There was,' he told the dowager Duchess of Rutland, 'almost an end to my existence.' Prince Ernest checked at the 'Paper Office' and then called on Maria's cousin, Elizabeth Butler. Eventually he got word from Maria's mother that she was 'quite out of danger & mending rapidly'. In the meantime the Prince had had himself bled several times and another terminal decline seemed in the offing.[3]

By the middle of March 1796 Maria was back in London and the Prince was in 'agitation & hurry'. However it does not appear that they met. Prince Ernest continued to be the latest intermediary, although in the summer the Prince asked Uncle Errington, who knew what was afoot, to deliver a message. If Maria and the Prince happened to meet he hoped 'she will not be surprised or offended with me, if . . . I bow to her and shake hands with her which will put an end to the difficulty we have both of us so long felt at meeting at a third house'. In the event Errington was at his Hampshire home and Payne acted as the postman. When the Prince eventually did write to Errington he was delighted to report that 'Mrs Fitzherbert has not the smallest objection to what I have propos'd.' This was another albeit small point scored on his behalf. Another point was scored when the Prince insisted that Errington should make no secret of his desire for a reconciliation 'either to Mrs Fitzherberts Family if question'd about it, or indeed to any other Individual of the Society in which You live'. Whether 'Society' meant fellow Catholics or Errington's London friends is not clear. What is clear is that gossip about a reconciliation might help bring one about.[4]

Charles James Fox, the Whig leader and opponent of Maria's marriage. He wanted her to be the Prince's mistress.

Richard Brinsley Sheridan MP, Maria's friend – some said Maria's lover. He was a rival to Fox as leader of the Whigs.

Carlton House, the Prince's London home in an 1809 drawing.
Maria reigned as hostess amid its extravagant splendour.

The great staircase of
Carlton House as of
1811, the year Maria
last saw it.

Frances, Lady Jerningham. A leading Catholic figure in society,
she called Maria's secret marriage 'a very hazardous undertaking...
God knows how it will turn out.'

This caricature, published on 26 February 1787, mocks the
Prince's attempt to reduce expenditure and shows Maria with a
baby by the Prince.

The Royal Pavilion as remodelled by John Nash after 1815. Maria only entered this building after George IV's death in 1830.

Above, this caricature, published on 21 May 1787 mocks Maria's alleged desire to become Queen. Her crown is blown away by Pitt while instruments of torture and execution refer to her Catholicism. *Below,* Gillray's caricature, published 28 February 1791, shows the Prince as an idle youth and Maria as a scheming older woman having an affair with Sheridan, whose hand is on her breast.

George Romney's portrait shows Maria in her thirties. The portrait gives some indication of the strength of her character.

This anti-Catholic caricature by Gillray, was published on 22 April 1805, during the legal wrangle over Minney Seymour. Based on a popular painting, it shows Maria capturing Minney for Catholicism. In the background is the Marine Pavilion in Brighton.

Maria Fitzherbert in 1836 aged eighty. Lady Holland noted,
'Mrs Fitz. is really in remarkable beauty, tho' her age is great.'

Now the Prince played his trump card in a letter which his brother delivered. It was, even by the Prince's standards, an extraordinary piece of writing with all the standard hallmarks: passion, self-justification and a threat of impending death unless his wishes were met. The outer wrapping had a note reading 'Private. Mrs Fitzherbert to be deliver'd to <u>her own hands only,</u> by the Duke of Cumberland.' He began in a scrawling hand with much double underlining and, as with his Will, covered many pages. 'Save me, save me, on my knees I conjure you from myself whet., after a SOLEMN PROMISE GIVEN, PLEDGED TO MY BROTHER TO BE MINE AGAIN, <u>is there honor in this world,</u> & YET NOT INHERENT IN YOU.' He asked God to 'TURN ONCE MORE I CONJURE THEE, THE HEART OF MY MARIA.' Maria knew that 'You are my wife' and if she does not agree he will announce their marriage publicly which will mean the loss of his 'RANK, SITUATION, BIRTH' and, to round things off, he will kill himself. The Prince put the letter aside and returned to it after two hours. If Maria would only agree, 'THERE IS NOTHING IN THIS WORLD I WILL NOT DO, & IN WHICH I WILL NOT BE GUIDED BY YOU . . . NOW AND FOREVER.' He repeated his death threat, referred to '<u>the wretched experiences of the last five years</u>' and added that he had written a letter to the King announcing their marriage which he would send if Maria said no. He reminded her that the witnesses were still alive and that others, such as Malmesbury, had been told: this was really turning the tables on Maria for the threat to reveal the marriage was supposed to be *her* trump card.[5]

Maria's reply, if she wrote one, has vanished but she was obviously weakening. Reinforcements were brought in and by the 12th Prince Edward reported that he had seen her. 'If I am any judge at all of the business, your wishes will ere long be accomplished, but it seems there are some points which she did not enter into . . . which she says you must give up to her.' He had no doubt that her attachment 'is worth any sacrifice'. Early in July Lady Jersey moved out of the house adjoining Carlton House. Two days after her move was made public, *The Times* announced that 'A gentleman of high rank and MRS FITZHERBERT are once more *inseparables*. Where one is invited a card to the other is a matter of course.' By early August the Princess of Wales was complaining that 'the real truth was . . . that Mrs Fitz. was extravagant & would ruin the Prince, who goes now twice a day to Gray's to buy diamonds for her.' The Prince began once again to look after Maria's interest in the public press and asked McMahon to contact James Christie, the auctioneer and newspaperman, 'to interpose your best offices' with the editor of *The True Briton* concerning 'offensive paragraphs' published on 22 August 'on the subject of Mrs F——t & which have given *him* & *her* the most poignant uneasiness. For God sake argue the cruelty of stabbing the happiness of those who never can have either injured or offended him.'[6] Despite the request, newspapers were soon talking about the expected reconciliation.

The couple met sometime in the autumn, although Maria was still holding back. In October Lord Minto heard that the Princess of Wales, hardly a reliable source, claimed 'there has been a sort of sounding', through Jack Payne, 'and a proposal from Mrs Fitzherbert, of seeing her [the Princess]'. According to Princess Caroline, Maria wanted to 'exert her influence with the husband on behalf of the wife [Caroline]'. Apparently, if the Princess is to be believed, Maria was trying to organise a rapprochement between the Prince and his official wife. As the Princess quotes Maria as saying that 'she [the Princess] had such power over the Prince she could do what she pleased with him' one wonders about Maria's sanity or, more likely, the Princess's honesty and accuracy.

In December the Prince, wishing to keep up the pressure, gave Maria his Will. She was wary of reading it but he urged her to do so, to know 'every feature of the heart & soul of your own, own, own George P'. 'Pray, dearest wife,' he wrote, 'let me see you soon again.' Far from being won over, Maria, now back in Bath, wrote to Lady Anne: 'I am persecuted from Morning till Night. What end it is to answer I know not for nothing can alter my present situation.' Her mother had been 'at death's door' and by the end of the year she would be back in London. 'Politicks I dont understand but we are all in greater Concern for defeat of the Neapolitans. I wish this odious Warr was an at end.' For his part the Prince was ecstatic and wrote 'a graceful letter' to Maria wishing her 'blissful enjoyment of Life' and asking the Almighty to witness 'the sincerity of his wishes'.

As 1800 progressed Maria was beginning to give in, to the horror of some, such as Lady Jerningham, who told her daughter in March that 'The affair of Mrs Fitzherbert and the Prince, becomes very incomprehensible, it is a fact that He meets her whenever he Can, and a conversation ensures that takes them both out of the Company. On Saturday . . . Mrs Fitzherbert, Mrs Butler, and the Prince were in a high Box all night in Conversation, the Princess at the opera and also Lady Jersey. I Comprehend it no longer, for I had thought Mrs Fitzherbert a woman of Principle.' For his part the Prince was convinced that a reconciliation was all but effected. That same month he told Lady Margaret Fordyce, 'You will be glad I am sure to hear that your friend has forgiven me . . . I have not been so happy for years by G—— I never did nor ever shall love any other woman.' He overlooked the fact that Maria would not see him unless Prince Ernest or Jack Payne was in attendance. For her part Lady Margaret felt, 'As to Fitz. she will have much still to suffer.' Hers would be 'a worried, akward, uncomfortable Life' and after four to five years the Prince would drop her yet again. Lady Margaret felt the Princess was satisfied: she will have got rid of Lady Jersey, whom she loathed, and she 'and the Fitz having had a sort of common cause for some years have carried on tacit courtesys to each other in a variety of ways.'

The difficulty, as Prince Edward had written, were those 'points . . . you must give up to her'. For Maria all this was not just a new understanding over those issues that had so often divided them but over her dignity. This ultimately rested not on the public belief that there may have been some sort of ceremony to still her 'tender conscience' but on the fact that there *had been* a marriage, in her eyes at least. This is one reason why she kept her marriage certificate. The Prince's second marriage in 1795 knocked all this on its head and should have showed her how much legality adhered to their 1785 marriage. For her to resume their pre-1795 relationship without a new understanding and without some new justification was to proclaim herself in her eyes as the mistress of a married man. She needed to re-establish her own standing.

To do this Maria needed some authority to confirm her view. Obviously she could turn neither to the courts nor to Parliament. As a Catholic, however, she did have a card up her sleeve. Like Catherine of Aragon she could appeal to the Vatican for a decision. While she later said she would have left England had the Pope declared her marriage void, she was in 1799 probably fairly sure the Pope would acknowledge the validity of her marriage from the Church's point of view. It was not so much that she was a devout Catholic – how does one separate out devotion from interest? – but that she had no other source available.

At some stage Maria asked her confessor, Father John Nassau, from the Warwick Street Chapel, to obtain a decision from the Pope. Indeed, it could have been Fr Nassau who suggested this somewhat bizarre, and still treasonous, expedition and the decision could have been taken in 1799. The difficulties facing Maria and the priest were sizable because the Catholic Church was in great disarray. The French Church had broken with Rome, while in Austria the Emperor had brought in reforms in the spirit of Henry VIII. The Papal States had lost many of their territories to the invading French and in February 1798 Pius VI had been expelled from Rome by invading French troops. He was exiled to Valence in 1799 and died there, a captive, in August. In Rome there were no cardinals and no Sacred Congregations (or church bureaucracy). Some wondered if the Catholic Church would continue at all. The Conclave to elect a successor to Pius VI did not meet until the spring of 1800 when, in Venice, it elected Pius VII on 14 March.

Now it made some sense for Maria's agents to set out and on 22 May Fr Nassau, along with another priest, left with introductions to the Pope and various cardinals. Only the Vicar Apostolic (in effect, bishop) of the London district, John Douglass, knew what was happening and fortunately he kept a diary.

Fr Nassau reached Rome on 4 July, the day after the Pope returned to Rome and had an audience, in Latin, four days later. The Pope asked Nassau to 'state the case in writing' for him to pass on to various counsellors who 'decided the case in favour of the [erasure]' that is in Maria's favour: she was indeed the Prince's wife in the eyes of the Church. The Pope approved the decision on 8 August. Fr Nassau stayed on in Rome for several weeks and did not land at Yarmouth until 10 October 1800. Because Bishop Douglass feared possible legal complications, he erased incriminating material. For her part Maria kept the judgement but later destroyed it when she feared it might be seized. Likewise the turbulent times means that there are no surviving records in the Vatican. Therefore we do not know the exact terms of the Church's decision. While it recognised the earlier marriage as valid and concluded that Maria could return to her husband, it had to refer to the 1795 marriage. It may well have insisted that the couple live 'as brother and sister'. Sometime after their reconciliation Maria told Lady Anne: 'I am now my dear the happiest of women. He is so much improved . . . all that was boyish and troublesome before is now become respectful and considerate . . . He is not so jealous of me with every foolish fellow that I speak to.' Maria went on, 'We live like brother and sister. I find no resentment tho' plenty of regret that I will have it on this footing and no other, but he must conform to my stipulations. I did not consent to make it up with the Prince to live [with] him either as his wife or his mistress.' The Prince would have to satisfy his sexual desires elsewhere.[7]

The living as 'brother and sister' could, of course, have been Maria's own demand as a means to lessen tensions. She had, after all, celebrated her forty-fourth birthday while waiting for the decision from Rome and may have decided she had had enough. By ending a sexual relationship she was, perhaps, conforming to Church advice. She might well have been establishing her control over their relationship or, most likely, doing both. Whatever was the case, outsiders were not to know and outsiders usually assume any relationship between a man and a woman, especially if the man be either a Prince or famous, must be sexual. This is why some may feel the Papacy had not acted with the greatest of discretion. Its decision was arrived at with little if any real evidence but on hearsay – Fr Nassau's statement that Maria had shown him her marriage lines. There was no one to oppose this or to question the evidence. No regard seems to have been taken as to the effect of this decision on the stability of the Royal Family and the monarchy in a country on whose navy the Papal States could ultimately depend for delivery from the French. Nor does there seem to have been any concern for public opinion in Britain which would know nothing of the decision and would only see a Catholic widow returning to a Prince of Wales who was now married.

In June Maria gave a 'public breakfast' for the Prince in her new London house which she had rented in Tilney Street. She invited 400 guests who filled three marquees in the garden, even though Fr Nassau still hadn't reached Rome. In her dictated memoirs she said that 'the day on which she joined him again at her own house, was the same on which she gave a public breakfast.' (Interestingly, she also remembered, falsely, that the Pope's decision had come *before* the breakfast.) The decorations chosen were white roses, the Prince's favourite flower. Later Maria told Lord Stourton that 'she hardly knew how she could summon up resolution to pass that severe ordeal, but she thanked God she had the courage to do so'. Lady Jerningham conveniently had 'a bad cold' and the Duchess of Devonshire told Maria's friend, Lady Melbourne, 'I cannot quite believe his entire reconciliation with Mrs F—— I think it certainly is in a way – but not complete, at least she certainly takes great pains to persuade the contrary. He certainly never appear'd more calm and contented.'[8]

In July, still with no word from Rome, Maria and the Prince

made another public appearance together at the Duchess of Devonshire's last great social event of the season. Among the invited guests was Lady Jerningham who found the Duchess 'setting with Mrs Fitzherbert by an urn. The Duchess and the 'fine People' gathered in a 'Temple' while 'we Goths took possession of the House'. Lady Jerningham, who left Chiswick between seven and eight, had been amused at how the Prince, dressed '*en Polisson*, a Brown Dress, round Hat and a Brown wig', stood for most of the afternoon beside his band with Dr Burney, 'ordering different pieces of Musick'. This kept him safely out of the clutches of Lady Jersey who 'was Coasting round the spot where he stood, with her daughters . . . The Prince was quite annoyed with her and eyed her askance; but she is resolved to plague Him; she professes it to be her Resolution.'

Lady Anne was now in Cape Town where her husband was secretary to the Governor and it took time for her to hear of the reunion. Maria's old friend thought her position 'equivocal & unsafe' and wished 'she had avoided what I fear will only lead to embarrassment & disgrace'. Sir George Seymour, Lord Hugh's son, noted in his copy of Langdale's *Memoirs* that Maria 'wished to God she had a friend on whose judgement she could rely [?] to advise her. Admiral Jack Payne encouraged his faithful Servant Jeftson to give his opinion: "If Mrs Fitzherbert expects to return she will rue it all her life". Mrs F told me this herself.'

Maria ignored Jeftson's warning and later remembered that 'the next eight years [after 1800] were the happiest of her connection with the Prince.' This was not just a fond memory because at the time she spoke of the Prince as a most alter'd person since they have last lived together & as more happy with him than She [word indecipherable] ever was before – when wicked people fill'd him with unjust Jealousy of her – & when he was in all ways a less rational companion.' She claimed 'they were extremely poor, but as merry as crickets' and recalled that once, on returning to London from Brighton, they found their joint purses would only yield £5 for a meal. Of course poverty is a relative term, especially when used by wealthy people with irregular incomes. Maria probably remembered that in 1805 she had to mortgage one of her houses 'to procure <u>absolute necessaries</u> both for yourself and me'. On the other hand, it was sometime in 1800 that Maria sold her Ealing house to Prince Edward, created Duke of Kent in 1799, and bought Lord Aberdeen's house in Tilney Street, at the corner of Park Lane, at a cost of £6,000 [£173,000]. Later the house next door was purchased, giving Maria twice as much room for entertaining. To help her maintain the new house the Prince increased her allowance to £4,000 [£116,000] a year. Poverty did not exclude expensive gifts and in 1810 the Prince gave her two Constable landscapes for which he had paid 2,000 guineas.[9]

In Brighton, where the reunited couple were cheered as they took their first drive along the Steine, the Prince carried on improving his Marine Pavilion. In 1801–2 he ordered the house enlarged and then had decorators redo the interior in a fanciful Chinese style. In 1803 builders began an impressive circular stable in an Indian style which almost dwarfed the house itself. Because the Prince had to pull down the house built next the Pavilion for Maria to allow the new wing, he now called in the Adam brothers to build a grander villa for her near by. In July papers were reporting on her new home: 'It is in the modern style, with a colon-nade, supported by six noble columns, 14 feet high, and orna-mented by a fanciful balcony, which runs the length of the building; the whole is painted a vivid green, which has a fine effect, when viewed from the promenade.' A wide flight of steps led up to the ground-floor verandah with the 'fanciful balcony' above that. Cast iron lattice work guaranteed privacy and still allowed Maria a splendid view of the sea-front. Three large windows, the height of two floors, made the front of the house airy and gave it a Mediterranean flavour. Inside, on an upper floor, was a small oratory with an altar set in an alcove. Maria claimed she paid for the house but there were letters later asking the Prince to stump up the cash and fend off her creditors.[10]

Brighton was witnessing an orgy of building which, by 1811, would include the Crescent. Its builder, eager to gain admission to the Pavilion, erected in front of the building a high pedestal on which he put an equestrian statue of the Prince made of artificial stone. It was painted buff and showed the Prince 'in the complete uniform of his Hussar regiment, with a round hat surcharged with feathers, and an enormous quantity of hair turned up under his hat'. The Prince did not like it – Lord Glenbervie found it 'frightful' – and then one of the arms was broken off so that people thought it was Lord Nelson.

For the Prince and Maria life had pretty much returned to what it had been before storm clouds had gathered in 1794–5. The couple appeared in public, visited country houses and were sometimes together at fashionable spas. They attended the races and spent time in Brighton where Maria was always popular. As before, Maria stayed in separate accommodation. Gossips declared that 'the Prince of Wales is going to declare his marriage with Mrs Fitzherbert' and bastardise his daughter. They wondered if 'we have the old case renewed of Henry VIII and the tables turned on the Protestants?' Later there was renewed talk among caricaturists about Maria's being made a duchess.

As before, the couple led separate social lives. When Maria was in Cheltenham in September 1810 the Duke of Clarence's mistress, Mrs Jordan, noted that she had rented a house and 'has taken a Box for every night' at the theatre. Three days later she wrote that Maria 'was looking quite handsome last night. I hope,' she went on, 'the Prince's bed will [be] well aired, for it has not been slept in for a long time.' She also reported that 'Lady Buckinghamshire & Mrs Fitsherbert quarrelled before the latter left this place, and that they call one another all sorts of names.' On one occasion, when Maria was in Bath, the newspapers carried stories of her bad health and, in some cases, of her death. As in 1799 this caused the Prince to panic. He wrote to Maria's mother, still living in Bath, to say he had heard that Maria 'lay under extreme danger from a pleuritic attack. God grant that the report may be false . . . I conjure of You either Yourself or any one in whom you can confide, to let me have <u>be it but a single line</u> by return of Post to say she is better . . . but for God's sake <u>tell me the truth</u>.'

When on his own, the Prince could return to his old habits. Dr Burney told the painter, Joseph Farington, that the Duke of Norfolk and Lord Guilford spent a week in Brighton with the Prince and drank so much that it took them days to sober up. On another occasion those invited to the Pavilion included Sir John Shelley, Bt. Although recently married, he was also the lover of Maria's sister, Lady Haggerston, 'a fascinating woman, moving in the best society'. Sir John often found the little suppers made up of the Prince, Maria, Lady Haggerston and himself, very dull. One evening he found the Prince kneeling in front of Maria 'in an attitude which suggested prayer, rather than devotion to a woman'. 'The broad expanse of the royal form' was too much, so he gave 'the royal posterior a vigorous push which sent his Royal Highness sprawling at his lady's feet.' (By December 1797 the Prince already weighed 17 stone 8 pounds. The scales used, in the Old Coffee Mill in St James's, may still be found in the same premises, now belonging to Messrs Berry Bros. & Rudd.) The Prince was in a fury at this act of lese majesty and 'with a terrible oath' advanced on Sir John who escaped just in time. Eventually the two sisters restored peace 'and things went on as before'.[11]

As always there were problems. 'The greatest interruptions to their happiness at that period', at least in Maria's later recollections, 'were his [the Prince's] bitter and passionate regrets, and self-accusations for his conduct.' True to her common-sense manner, Maria met these by saying, 'We must look to the present and the future, and not think of the past.' Equal to these were the never ending problems of money. In 1803 the King again asked Parliament to help his heir and it agreed £60,000 a year for three years when, it was fondly hoped, the debts would be liquidated. Lord Malmesbury was annoyed that the Prince was not required to use the money to 'restore his establishment' so that he could live as he ought. Instead Malmesbury assumed the money would 'be squandered away . . . without his assuming any one single <u>exterior</u> mark of royalty . . . to prove that he and his hangers-on do not consider it a farce.' These were strong words from a friend who had seen other monarchies undermined by a disregard for acceptable behaviour.

We are fortunate to have three first-hand views of Maria during these years. The first, by Mrs Calvert, a young Irish 'beauty', is a less favourable one that still gives us insights missing in the second, written by an enthusiastic Etonian. Mrs Calvert found Maria 'very fat but with a charming countenance, her features are beautiful, except her mouth, which is ugly, having a set of not good false teeth . . . she makes a great display of a very white but not prettily formed bosom, which I often long to throw a handkerchief over.' The Irishwoman found her 'good-humoured (though I think I can at times discern a look of ill-temper . . .) unaffected and pleasing but very absent and I have often thought she was not happy, for she heaves such deep sighs sometimes in one of those fits of absence . . . There does not seem to be any brilliancy about Mrs Fitzherbert . . . or powers of captivation.'

Our second source is an unnamed seventeen-year-old schoolboy who, whilst visiting Brighton, was invited to the Marine Pavilion. He immediately fell for Maria and, as an old man, remembered 'her exquisite blue eyes, her peach-like complexion, sunned by the most fascinating smile I had ever beheld'. On being introduced the boy bowed and Maria curtsied, as was the fashion. 'Her person might then be said to have arrived at womanly perfection.' She described a portrait of the Prince the boy had noticed and 'imperceptibly she glided from the painting to the original on whose excellencies she was even more eloquent'.

Our schoolboy then described an evening at Maria's house. The Duchess of Devonshire was there – whom Maria addressed as 'Duchess' and not 'Your Grace' – who asked the boy for his opinion of her book of verse, *The Passage of Mount St Gothard* . . . which had been printed privately. Verses were read aloud and then

Georgiana asked for some singing from her daughters and the visitor while she accompanied them on the piano. Some people were playing cards while others lounged on ottomans. Georgiana then suggested dancing and the boy accompanied the 'Beautiful Duchess' in a minuet de la cour followed by a gavotte which was interrupted by the arrival of the Prince. The Duchess then introduced the young man to the Prince whose hand he kissed. In this portrait we see Maria as the perfect hostess who allowed others, such as the Duchess, to shine. If the portrait is tinctured by the fond memories of an old man it balances Mrs Calvert's.

Our third visitor was the wife of the Whig MP, Thomas Creevey. Eleanor Creevey was in Brighton in the autumn of 1805 and her letters to her husband between October and December give us one of the best pictures of Maria's way of life, excelled only by the observations of Lady Anne.[12] On 29 October we have our first letter: 'Oh! this wicked Pavillion! we were there till 1/2 past one this Morning . . . the Invitation did not come to us till 9 O'Clock. We went in Lord Thurlow's Carriage & were in fear of being too late but the Prince did not come out of the dining room till 11 . . . I instantly saw He had got more wine than usual.' The Prince told Mrs Creevey that Mrs Fitzherbert wanted to see her but, Maria then added, 'not till *you* are gone & I can see Her *comfortably*.' After dinner the party went to see the Prince 'shoot with an Air Gun at a Target placed at the end of the room. He did it very skilfully & wanted all the Ladies to attempt to it. The Girls & I excused ourselves on account of our short sightedness but Ly Downshire hit a Fidler in the Dining Room.'

Four days later Mrs Creevey was again with Maria who did not feel like playing cards, something she loved doing. 'She seem'd to enjoy talking & I was constantly at her Elbow & she took me into her little Drawing room & said I must come some day & let her take me all over the House – What I have seen however gives me a notion that she is a good & perfect Catholic as to taste & knowledge of comfort – but she is much more fond of the economy of her [word indecipherable] than she could be of its beauty.' Maria loved to gossip about current scandals and 'laugh'd more last night than ever at the Johnstones – said he was a most vulgar man but seem'd to give him credit for his good nature to his sister & his generosity, – the Baron is preparing a Phantasmagoria at the Pavillion & she laughs at what he may do with Miss Johnstone in a dark room – I think I see that she has her Card playing friends.' When discussing Nelson's relationship with Lady Hamilton, Maria was 'all for Lady Nelson & against Lady Hamilton'.

Maria sensed she had a sympathetic ear and Eleanor Creevey's letters show us not only Maria and the Prince's private life together but Maria's life as she saw it. She was obviously proud of the Prince's 'unbounded confidence in her in a way that shew'd neither vanity nor the slightest anxiety for a moment <u>even with her</u> when she told him unpleasant truths but that it is now literally only for a moment & that he every day hears such things better & knows She is his truest friend & the most disinterestedly anxious for his credit – She says he hates to be away from her even for a day.' Maria was aware of her place in history and, as she had once talked to Lady Anne about her writing a biography so now she again mentioned it to her new friend. 'We talk'd of her Life being written – She said She supposed it some time or other would but with thousands of Lies, but She would be dead & it would not signify – I urged her to write it herself – but She said it would break her Heart – & if I may judge from some of the feelings she express'd I believe it would do so.'

Maria obviously trusted her new friend and talked about her own life, not without some exaggeration and discussed:

all her feelings & conduct towards the Prince – & if She is as <u>True</u> as I think her <u>wise</u> She is an extraordinary Person and most worthy to be beloved . . . I think of her having [word indecipherable] and constant attentions from the King & Queen – Letters of the former pledging himself to every thing for her Service even in the Event of the Princes death – even in this last illness two Letters from the Queen to enquire after her –

constant ones from all the Princesses – but above all think when she was last ill in London 15 special Messengers sent from the Princess of Wales to enquire after her – invitation to go to court – constantly refused

Maria went on to describe the Prince's altered relations with the Duchess of Devonshire: 'It was quite impossible to keep clear of Devonshire House . . . that he knows every thing – above all how promises (unauthorised) by him in the Event of his having power.' Georgiana Devonshire would have been furious to hear that, at least according to Maria, the Prince only entered Devonshire House 'from Motives of compassion & old friendship' and that 'he tells Mrs F. all he sees & hears there – shows her all the Duchess's Letters & Notes & she [Maria] says She knows the D[uchess] hates her.' For two years the Prince had known about 'that Child who lives with Lady Grey' (Georgiana's illegitimate daughter). In a fascinating insight Mrs Creevey added, at the end of Maria's discussion of the Duchess, 'I only slightly shew'd the acquiescence *She seem'd very naturally to expect* [author's italics].'

Like most visitors Eleanor Creevey was intrigued to know more about Maria's marital status vis à vis the Prince. She noted that the Prince said '"I went to Mrs Fitzherbert at one O'clock & stayed talking with her till past 6 – which was certainly very Unfashionable" – now was he not at that moment thinking of her as his lawful Wife? – for in no other sense could he call it unfashionable – I am pretty sure it struck him as it would have the moment he had said it – he stopt a moment & then added – "we had so much to say to each other after being separated 5 Days" – & then promptly turn'd the conversation.' Like other couples, Maria and the Prince had their disagreements and Mrs Creevey was there for one: 'I heard a very domestic kind of a dispute between her & her Husband about civilities to this Russian Woman & the Duchess de Renne [?] – & he said they were both d——d troublesome disagreeable Women & the less he saw of them the better.'

The atmosphere in the Pavilion was usually more sedate than it had been in the past. Occasionally 'Jockey' Norfolk appeared but Maria had learned a new trick: she would arrange for letters to be brought to the Prince which he had to retire to answer, thereby escaping from the drunken Duke. Sheridan's presence always guaranteed the unexpected and on one occasion he came disguised as a policeman to arrest Lady Sefton 'for playing at some unlawful game'. On another the Prince's German visitor entertained the guests by making 'Chinese faces' and the Prince took hold of the man 'by the Nose & the Chin to help put his features in their right places'.

During Mrs Creevey's stay news arrived of Nelson's death at Trafalgar. Maria immediately sent off a note to her new friend: 'The Prince has this moment rec'd an account from the Admiralty of the Death of poor Ld Nelson wh. has affected him most extremely. I think you may wish to know the news wh. upon any other occasion might be call'd a glorious victory . . . excuse this horrid scrawl. I am so nervous I scarce can hold my Pen. God bless you. Yrs. M. Fitzherbert.' Later Maria told Eleanor Creevey how they got the news and her story gives us a good insight into the Prince's behaviour, even in private: 'When he got the account of Lord Nelson's death he had been sitting with her a long time "talking of his mission" – & was so unable to bear the shock that he fell on the Sofa & was quite hysterical – in short, frighten'd her so much that She gave him such an immense Dose of Spirit of Lavender as he declares made him drunk – (what was equally natural) he soon fell asleep . . . & . . . was better when he wakened.'

The life the couple led during these years was conducted on rules laid down by Maria. Theirs was an unorthodox marriage but one that worked and the tensions of the past seem to have gone away. But these years also saw a new bond that would unite them and give the Prince a cause to fill his vacant hours. This came in the person of the baby daughter left behind by Lord Hugh Seymour and his wife when they left England to find health in Madeira.

12

THE FINAL BREAK

When the Prince was pursuing Maria in December 1798 she was in Portsmouth discussing the future of the baby daughter of Lord Hugh and Lady Horatia Seymour who had stood by her as loyal friends after the separation. In the event, Maria adopted little Mary Seymour and raised her as the child she had never had. In the end this child would mean far more to Maria than the Prince's fickle affections. To secure her possession she engaged in a nasty legal wrangle which divided Society and, for a while at least, strengthened her bond with the Prince. It became one of the eighteenth century's most famous legal cases and one ultimately played out on the floor of the House of Lords. In Lord Stourton's account Lady Horatia had 'entrusted her treasure to the care of her attached friend Mrs Fitzherbert, who, having no child of her own, soon became devotedly attached to the precious charge, and her affection for the child increased with the loss of the parents'. In time, 'one of the near relatives of the family . . . being jealous of the religion of its protectress, applied to the Chancellor to obtain possession of Miss Seymour. But Mrs Fitzherbert, now more than ever devoted to the child, and sharing in this affection with the Prince himself, exerted every means to retain custody of it, and, after all others had failed, had at last recourse to Lady Hertford, with whom she was formerly intimately acquainted.'

The Seymour family papers contain numerous letters and documents which shed a good deal of new light on a legal wrangle that fascinated the Establishment. At some stage Lord Hugh's son, Sir George Seymour, wrote a *Memoir* of his father and in this he gave a rather different history. Lady Horatia, he claimed, had a 'real reason of refusal' which was Maria's 'equivocal situation relative to the Prince with whom she had resumed her intimacy after his Marriage.' 'Poor dear Mrs Fitz.' she wrote to a sister, 'I had not the heart to tell her if I had a thousand daughters I could not let her educate one.'[1]

Surviving letters and newspaper accounts will help us to get some idea of what happened. The full story of all this will probably never be revealed because passions often overrode truth and recollections, at the best, are seldom fully accurate. We often remember what we wanted people to have said, not what they actually said, let alone meant. When the Seymours sailed to Madeira, the baby was left with its nurse. The understanding was that it was to go to Lady Horatia's sister-in-law, Lady George Seymour, and only to Maria if the former was unable to take care of it. After Maria had returned to London in February 1799 she got a message that measles had broken out in Lady George's house and that she must immediately collect little Mary, to be known as Minney. Later in 1799 Lord Hugh returned to England, apparently approved the new arrangement and left for Jamaica.

In June 1801 Lady Horatia returned to London and took a house in Charlotte Street but she was too ill and the accommodation was too small for her to have Minney. Lady Horatia then left for Bristol where she died on 12 July. Two months later her husband died in Jamaica. Lord Hugh's executors, his brother, Lord Henry, and his brother-in-law, the Earl of Euston, claimed to be guardians of Minney, as well as of the other children, although in the will Minney was not mentioned simply because she had not yet been born. In time the two men asked that Minney be handed over to

Lady Horatia's sister, Lady Waldegrave. When Maria and the Prince protested that Minney's delicate health would not allow this, the guardians agreed Maria could keep her until June 1803.

Before the deadline even approached, Maria and the Prince took action. The Prince had seen Lady Horatia during her return visit and, according to his account, had been told Maria should keep the little girl. To help Maria, he wrote to Lord Euston in February 1802 to say that he saw Minney as being a future companion for Princess Charlotte and he referred to 'my little favorite Minney'. By now Minney was the pseudo-daughter of the childless couple and they saw her as rounding out their new domestic bliss. The Prince also proposed to invest £10,000 [£289,000] on Minney's behalf and on 9 February 1803 a debenture for that amount was agreed. He suggested there be four 'guardians', in addition to himself, to look after Minney and to ensure that she was raised as a member of the Church of England. If the Seymours rejected this, he warned them he would 'resist their efforts to the utmost of his Power'.

In August 1802 Lady Waldegrave, Minney's aunt, wrote to Lord Euston rejecting his suggested compromise that Minney stay with Maria till she was eleven and then come to her. In her letter she gives the two underlying arguments levelled at Maria: her religion and her associates. Eleven would be too late because the girl's 'affection would be placed on those who have brought her up till then, who either would have no Religion at all or be a Roman Catholic, & whose Morals would be corrupted by the Society she had till then lived with'. 'The World' blamed the Seymours for leaving Minney with Maria: 'I know many of the most respectable men who consider it as a Circumstance disgraceful to us all.' Also, she wrote, Maria's possession of the little girl had distressed Lady Horatia who had written on 9 July 1800: 'No one names little Mary . . . It is so very distressing to have my child there – I did write by the Prince of Wales packet to beg she would give her up . . . every one tells me how fond Mrs FitzHerbert is of her, but there is an awkwardness in this – dear little Soul!' Lady Euston later told the Attorney General that in her recollection of the December 1799 meeting Lady Horatia had not wanted Minney to stay with Maria because she feared Maria might return to the Prince. No one could agree what Lady Horatia really wanted and everyone remembered differently.

In December 1802, Maria wrote directly to Lord Euston and added her own addendum to this confusing history. When Maria took Minney to see her mother after her return to England, she quoted Lady Horatia as saying, somewhat surprisingly for a woman who disapproved Maria's renewed involvement with the Prince, 'dont think I would be so unfeeling, as to take her from you you are now her Mother [more] than I am.' When Maria was taking her leave, Lady Horatia asked her to request the Prince to call 'as she wish'd to speak to him; I deliver'd her message &' – as we have already seen – 'the Prince accordingly went to her; the next day I saw her & she repeated to me the Conversation that pass'd between them', that is, his pledge to become Minney's 'friend & Protector thro' life', assuming of course that Maria kept her.

In Maria's letter to Lord Euston. in which she begged to be allowed to keep the little girl, now four years old, we see the love Maria now had for her adopted daughter. All that maternal feeling, dormant since her little Fitzherbert son died all those years ago, now blossomed. She wrote a five and a half page letter – long for someone who preferred short missives: 'The misery I have & do experience at the thoughts of having her taken away from me, is more than I can express.' She concluded her letter by promising that raising Minney 'ever will constitute the first, the happiest, & the most pleasing Occupation of my life.' 'The whole occupation of my life is center'd in her.' When Maria heard that one member of the Seymour family had gone over to Lord Euston's side, she wrote, 'Surely Lord Henry would condemn the unfeeling wretch who could by any Act or Neglect of hers throw up a Charge thus undertaken.' At some stage during the crisis she told Lord Thurlow, the former Lord Chancellor, 'that she had a mind to run away with the child. "If you do," he said, "It will be a felony, and by G——— you will be hanged for it."'

What neither Maria nor the Prince could accept was that the family wanted the child raised by one of its relations, someone who was of its own Church and someone who was not believed to be the mistress of a married man. The child had become one of the bonds that would unite Maria and the Prince into a family of sorts. Mrs Calvert, the Irish MP's wife, noted that Minney called Maria 'Mama' and the Prince, 'Prinny'. Mrs Calvert was told that when the child heard of her family's efforts to obtain possession 'she often clung with her little arms round the Prince, saying: "Prinny, wont you fight for me? You wont let them take me from you."'

By June 1803 Maria decided to bring matters to a head and filed a bill in the Court of Chancery in the name of Miss Mary Georgiana Emma Seymour to contest the claim of Lord Euston and Lord Henry Seymour to act as her guardians. The court, however, ruled on behalf of Lord Euston and Lord Henry. Maria appealed but the Lord Chancellor confirmed this arrangement, after which Maria appealed again to the House of Lords. She was not asking that she be made guardian but that the Marquess of Hertford, head of the Seymour family, along with his Marchioness, be appointed because they were nearest of kin and because she suspected they would be more amenable. There were affidavits submitted by the Prince, Maria, Lady Euston and the Bishop of Winchester.

In her affidavit, Maria described herself as 'Maria Fitzherbert, Widow'. She acknowledged that while she was 'bred in the Roman Catholic faith, she always entertained and expressed the opinion that a child ought to be educated in the religion professed by its parents; and that certainly the daughter of a great family, such as the Appellant, ought to be educated in the Established religion of her country.' Though a Catholic 'she did not consider it her duty either to make converts or to educate the children of Protestants in the Catholic religion.' Although the document was undoubtedly draughted by lawyers, this passage reflects Maria's religious views. Lady Euston, in her affidavit, stressed that Lady Horatia had only meant Maria's care of the lttle girl to be temporary.

Now the Prince again went into action and began shamelessly, and illegally, to canvass peers, illegal because the peers were assumed to be sitting as de facto jurors and not as legislators. In the event his work bore fruit and only eight peers stood out against him, including his cousin, the new Duke of Gloucester. For Maria it was a terrible time and friends noted that 'in consequence [she] is in such grief that she keeps Her bed and is in strong hystericks.' On 14 June 1806 the Lords 'upon appeal, reversed the order for appointing Lord Euston and Lord Henry Seymour' without actually taking a vote: they did so knowing that the Hertfords had agreed to become guardians and suspected that they had also agreed to leave their granddaughter with Maria, which they had. (Rumour had it that the Marquess had been won over by the Marchioness who had been won over by the Prince.) For once the Prince was true to his word and when Minney turned twenty-one he gave her the promised £10,000 plus the interest which had almost doubled the total.

Of course the case was not fought in a vacuum and behind the public debate was a mixture of vicious gossip, religious conviction and prejudice, politics and the feud between the Prince and Princess Caroline. Gossips claimed that little Minney was really the daughter of the Prince of Wales and not Lord Hugh and that Maria was about to become an Anglican. Religious conviction and prejudice met and mingled in the person of Spencer Perceval, MP, a foe of the Prince and a fervent anti-Catholic who acted for the Seymours. (He was also one of the barristers defending the Princess of Wales in the 'delicate investigation' into her private life which began in May 1806.) As Maria told Mrs Creevey, she dared not appoint a French governess for Minney for fear of stirring up anti-Catholic feeling. Likewise, political agitation for full Catholic 'emancipation' was increasing and in March 1807 the King would force the government to withdraw a bill opening all ranks in the Army to Catholics. When the Tory, Sir Walter Scott, was in

London he met Maria but did not know who she was and 'blundered out more of my joy at this political event than seemed to be agreeable to that great lady.'[2]

Not surprisingly, the whole Minney episode as well as these other passions were seen in the caricatures. Since Maria's return to the Prince she had figured little in cartoons and only eight between 1801 and 1804 included her. In 1805, however, she had once again emerged as a rival to the Princess of Wales for control of Princess Charlotte. In April there was a famous caricature based on Matthew Peters' 1782 painting, 'An Angel Carrying the Spirit of a Child to Paradise'. This shows Maria, bedecked with Catholic symbols, gathering up a reluctant Minney and carrying her towards a Marian altar. Beneath them is the outline of the Brighton Pavilion. As if all this were not enough, it was in 1806 that Jefferys published his pamphlet alleging that the haughty Maria did not pay her bills any more than did the Prince. Jefferys added that 'what I heard was not of a nature to increase the respect I had for the character of that lady.' All this would have been grist to the Seymour mills. As Edward Jerningham wrote, 'Mrs. Fitzherbert who is not well and who is made very unhappy with the Two Affairs of the Princess and of Jefferies [sic]. I really feel extremely for Her.'[3]

Maria's legal battles were of course only part of her life. Vital to her self-respect were her friendships within the Royal Family. She felt increasingly close to the Duke of Clarence, remained friendly with the Duke of York and became quite a confidante of the Duke of Kent. As she told Thomas Coutts, 'the three brothers [Wales, York and Clarence] are everything you could wish.' She would occasionally use her influence to pour some oil on troubled princely waters. Such efforts were of no use when it came to the Duchess of York, now rumoured to have been caught by the Duke *in flagrante delicto* with another man, for she had not changed. In 1803 the Duke asked Lord Malmesbury for help: the Duchess was uneasy lest she 'be forced to sup at the same table with Mrs.

Fitzherbert at the ball to be given by the Knights of the Bath . . . Says the King and Queen will not hear of it.' The Prince's friends were also caught up in the struggle between himself and his Princess over the education of their daughter. Again Malmesbury noted that: 'Ladies Moira, Hutchinson and Mrs. Fitzherbert were for his ceding the child to the King; the Duke of Clarence and Devonshire House most violent against it, and the Prince ever inclined to the faction he saw last. In the Devonshire House cabal, Lady Melbourne and Mrs. Fox [Mrs Armistead] act conspicuous parts; so that the alternative for our future Queen seems to be whether Mrs. Fox or Mrs. Fitzherbert shall have the ascendancy.'

At one stage it appears Maria tried once again to bring about some reconciliation between the Prince and his other wife. Lady Bessborough told her lover that 'the Prince's <u>fat friend</u> was all anxiety to send a message to the Princess, if she could find any body to take it.' Maria's object, that is the Prince's object, was to get the Princess to tell this third party what she had told the King during her audiences. Later that same month Lady Bessborough reported a dinner during which her brother had met the Prince and Maria. He was 'very unreasonable about his wife – Madame [Maria] very reasonable, and wishing to reconcile them, saying she only wishes to be his friend.'

It was all to no avail and by 1806 the rumours regarding the Princess's scandalous behaviour, especially with men, caused the King on 29 May 1806 to order Lords Erskine, Spencer, Grenville and Ellenborough to conduct what became known as the 'delicate investigation' into the allegations. The Prince hoped this might give him the excuse for a divorce but when the four commissioners finally presented their report to the King they refuted the specific charge that the Princess had had an illegitimate son. On the other hand they refused to clear her of other rumours of irregular behaviour with men. Public opinion was more divided than ever. A large number of people, especially radicals and the London mob, were more devoted to the 'injured' Protestant wife than before.

For Maria, the 'delicate investigation' caused a panic because the lawyer acting for the Princess was the same anti-Catholic, Spencer Perceval, who had recently acted for Lord Euston and Lord Henry Seymour and no one knew what might happen when the lawyers got to work. As the Earl of Carlisle would tell the Prince in 1807, Maria's situation was 'becoming most perilous' due to the feelings of 'the lower classes of people'. All one needed was someone with 'half the mischievous ability of a Lord George Gordon' and Maria 'might at any hour be liable to insult and danger not only in the streets, but also in her own home.' In the controversies which followed the investigation there was also something of a panic for Uncle Henry and her brother, Jack, and at their request she took a pair of scissors to her marriage lines and cut out their names 'to save them from the peril of the law.'

Lord Malmesbury had noted in 1801 that the Prince 'appears to side against the Crown and Pitt, and takes up and cherishes the avowed partisans of jacobinical opposition.' This return to Opposition politics only increased the hostility of Pitt's supporters without lessening the London mob's dislike. Things were made worse that same year when the King was once again ill and on the second day of his renewed attack the Prince met the former French minister, Calonne: '<u>Savez vous, Monsieur de Calonne, que mon Père est aussi fou que jamais?</u>' ('Do you know, Monsieur de Calonne, that my Father is as mad as ever?') There was again talk of a Regency but luckily by March the poor King had recovered his health. A new Regency crisis began in February 1804 and Pitt was now anxious to return to office to lead a broad-based ministry which included Fox. Once again rumours began flying round London. Lord Redesdale told the Speaker that the Royal Family was divided against itself. He had also heard 'strange rumours . . . that the marriage of the Princess of Wales is to be impeached. Surely this cannot be seriously thought of by any but the Roman Catholics: they talk pretty loudly that Mrs. Fitzherbert is the lawful wife . . . One's blood runs cold at such language.' No wonder during the previous year Lady Jersey spoke of 'a popish combination against her'.

In 1804, as in 1789, Maria had her role to play in plans for and talk of a Regency. Some aspirant office-holders, such as the Duke of Northumberland, looked to her 'to preserve me in his Royal Highness's esteem & regard'. 'Her interest,' he noted, 'is completely blended with his.' The Duke would later add that 'She can say many things to him which it would be impossible for anybody else to do, & can prevent him from heedlessly doing many things.' As the crisis worsened the Prince became agitated 'and talks all day without ceasing to Mrs Fitzherbert and McMahon'. He also fell ill and, contrary to her usual policy, Maria moved into the Pavilion to nurse him. She told her banker: 'The Prince, thank God, is well, he has had a very severe & dangerous illness . . . The present state of affairs are such as to distress him very much . . . He has not seen a creature . . . except the King's Ministers, who he is obliged to receive daily . . . as he belongs to no party & has never been consulted he feels he has nothing to do but remain passive & quiet. What is to become of both the King & Him time must determine.'

By the summer it seemed that the King was restored to health and in November the Prince was finally allowed to see him. A reconciliation of sorts was effected, although the Prince still felt aggrieved because of his father's support (or at least sympathy for) Princess Caroline and because he still refused to give his son an effective military command.

By 1807 Maria's world was changing once again. On 26 January her mother, to whom she had written so faithfully over the years and whom she nursed in Bath, died. As she told Lady Anne, the death 'quite knock'd me up'. The year before not only Fox and Pitt but the Duchess of Devonshire had died: when the Prince called to see his old friend a last time he found her delirious and 'when He approached the Bed-side He found her so disfigured that He threw himself back on a chair and appeared suffocating.'[4]

For Maria worse was to come. The controversy over Minney's adoption had thrown the Prince into the company of the Hertfords, especially Lady Hertford, who began to usurp Maria's place as Lady Jersey had done before. This time the estrangement would be gradual and, on the whole, free of the passions of 1794–5. Maria herself was caught in a bind. Lady Hertford was not Lady Jersey and seemed content to live in something of a *ménage à quatre*. Maria was not and later recalled:

> Lady Hertford, anxious for the preservation of her own reputation . . . even when she ruled the Prince with the most absolute sway, exposed Mrs. Fitzherbert at this time to very severe trials, which at last almost . . . ruined her health and destroyed her nerves. Attentions were required from her towards Lady Hertford herself, even when most aware of her superior influence over the Prince, and these attentions were extorted by the menace of taking away her child.

As early as April 1807 Maria told Lady Anne that she had 'nothing pleasant to say'. 'Everything goes on as usual, tho' I certainly have felt much happier by staying out of the way, & thereby preventing my enemies from personally tormenting me.' As late as June that year Maria gave an assembly at which were 'all the fine world', including the Prince and his brothers, York, Clarence, Cambridge and Kent, all in full dress uniform. By July however our Irish visitor, Mrs Calvert, was noting: 'I think poor Mrs Fitzherbert much deserted by him now. He has taken it into his head to fall desperately in love with Lady Hertford' who is still lovely but 'on a very large scale'. She was 'without exception the most forbidding, haughty, unpleasant-looking woman I ever saw'.

By October Lady Bessborough wrote that 'I really believe his Father's malady extends to him, and only takes another turn. He writes day and night almost, and frets himself into a fever, and all to persuade la sua bella <u>Donnone</u> [his beautiful old woman] <u>to live with him – publickly!!</u> A quoi bon, except to make, <u>if</u> possible, a greater cry against him.' The Prince was to be in London in a

317

few days and, Lady Bessborough added: 'I should not be surpriz'd if he and the ci devant were to quarrel quite during their meeting at Brighton. She has got irritated, and he bored; for this last there is, alas! no cure – the disease is fatal.' In November Mrs Calvert heard from Lady Winchester that she had heard 'from very good authority that the Prince don't mean to return any more to Brighton, that he is completely tired of Mrs Fitzherbert and means to spend his Christmas . . . with Lady Hertford'. Not surprisingly, by December gossips were noting that when in London the Prince was visiting Lady Hertford every morning and 'when they are both in town he often dines <u>en famille</u> with her and Lord Hertford'. Sometimes, when in Brighton, the Prince would spend his mornings with Maria at her house and then cut her in the evening lest Lady Hertford hear of it.

Occasionally Maria fought back, as in one very formal letter written sometime in 1808 asking for the Prince to sort out a bill for £300 from her builder. She reminded him that 'tho' we now have been married three-and-twenty years I never at any period solicited you for assistance'. She also ominously reminded him of the voluntary pledge he had made 'not only to Mr Errington but several others, from the beginning of my acquaintance with you, to give me an income of £10,000 per ann, instead of which till very lately I have subsisted upon . . . £3,000, now increased to £5,000.' She insisted that 'I would rather have lived in beggary than to have distressed you, or by any mean, dirty tricks have taken advantage of you.' In closing she once again said she wrote because 'as your wife I feel I have still a claim upon your protection, which I trust is not entirely alienated from me, as the whole of my conduct towards you is grounded on that foundation.'

In that same year, 1808, the Prince, especially when he could not sleep at night, wrote more of his impassioned letters, but this time to Lady Hertford. The reader will be spared the underscoring that marked every word. In the midst of all this verbiage, so similar to letters written earlier to Maria, or Lady Jersey, or Perdita, or Mary Hamilton are several lines about himself: 'Thou knowest most perfectly my own own own Isabella, that I am a different Animal, a different Being from any other in the whole Creation, that my feelings, my disposition, my nature, in short, all & every thing that is me, is in all respects different.' The Prince did not mean to boast or 'sett Myself above the rest . . . of Mankind, far, far, far, be this from Me, but I can not help seeing myself, & feeling myself, in my true colours, I am as an Animal, & such as it has pleas'd Providence & Nature to make me, & to form me.'[5] It may have been good therapy for a sleepless Prince but it makes tiresome reading.

By 1809 it was obvious that Lady Hertford would not answer the Prince's every need so he occasionally looked elsewhere. In December Lady Bessborough told her lover that the Prince 'has kill'd me – such a scene I never went thro'. He had first criticised her ladyship's lover, Granville Leveson Gower, because he was about to marry Harriet, the daughter of the Duchess of Devonshire, and because he had had affairs. He then:

> threw himself on his knees, and clasping me round, kiss'd my neck before I was aware of what he was doing. I screamed with vexation and fright; he continued sometimes struggling with me, sometimes sobbing and crying . . . Then mixing abuse of you, vows of eternal love, entreaties and promises of what he would do – he would break with Mrs. F. and Ly. H., I should <u>make my own terms!!</u> I should be his sole confidant, sole adviser – private or public – I should guide his politicks . . . then over and over and over again the same round of complaint, despair, entreaties, and promises . . . that really, G., had not my heart been breaking I must have laugh'd out at the comicality . . . and then that immense, grotesque figure flouncing about half on the couch, half on the ground.

Lady Bessborough felt 'revolted and indignant'. The Prince was forty-seven years old and should have remembered Neptune's 1784 warning that 'what are follies at TWENTY are vices at FORTY.'

In the event Lady Hertford did keep her new supremacy and at some period, probably in 1809, Maria wrote a heartbreaking letter to her husband: 'The constant state of anxiety I am perpetually kept in with respect to your proceedings, and the little satisfaction I experience when occasionally you make partial communications to me, have determined me to address you by letter.' She referred to 'the misery we have both suffered for the last three or four years on a subject most painful to me'. His infatuation with Lady Hertford 'has quite destroyed the entire comfort and happiness of both our lives; it has so completely destroyed mine, that neither my health nor my spirits can bear it any longer.' She reminded the Prince that 'scarcely three weeks ago, you voluntarily declared to me that *this sad affair* was quite at an end, and in less than a week afterwards the whole business was begun all over again'. She wrote 'to implore you to come to a resolution . . . You must decide, and that decision must be done immediately, that I may know what line to pursue.' She asked him to write 'to avoid all unpleasant conversations upon a subject so heart-rending to one whose whole life had been dedicated to you, and whose affection for you none can surpass'. As this letter was found, unsigned, among Maria's papers after her death it may have been a copy of a letter sent or it may be the draught of a letter never sent. There is no copy in the Royal Archives.

This 'sad affair' dragged on and in December 1809 Maria took another stand. This was not against Lady Hertford, nor against the Prince's affair with a young dancer, nor that with the courtesan, Harriet Wilson, nor that with the Frenchwoman he established in apartments near Manchester Square but against Benjamin Bloomfield. A former soldier, Bloomfield was one of the Prince's Gentlemen Attendants and his secretary, as Jack Payne had died in 1803. He was also the lover of Maria's friend, Lady Downshire. Maria now refused an invitation to the Pavilion because of Bloomfield's 'great incivilities' over the preceding two years to the lady whom the Prince 'four-and-twenty years ago placed . . . in a situation so nearly connected with your own'. The Prince had appeared to sanction Bloomfield's behaviour, yet 'something is due to my character and conduct.' The sting, however, was in the tail: she asked the Prince to show the letter to the Duke of Clarence and she would 'keep a copy to show to my friends . . . The disappointment to my dear little girl mortifies me very much.' In short, no Maria, no Minney. In his reply the Prince adopted his usual superior tone of the injured innocent: 'In whatever tone my dear Maria that You may be pleas'd to write to me, or in whatever way You may at any time think proper to act by me, deeply as I may feel & lament it, yet that never can nor shall make me deviate from, or forget those affectionate feelings I have ever entertain'd for you. I shall make no comment therefore upon Your letter, further than it relates to the dear Child & to my Brother William . . .' He was sorry that Minney should be unhappy and consoled himself that he could do her acts of kindness: 'she shall never under any circumstances experience any alteration from me.' When Maria asked the Duke of Kent for support, he got out by insisting that 'we never should touch upon that most delicate subject – the state of things between the Prince and yourself'. He was either a wise man or, like most men faced with emotional crises, simply a coward.

However, there was as yet no break and during 1810 the Prince was still said to be dividing his days between Lady Hertford and Maria. As in 1795 Maria showed that the innate robustness of her character, and her unfailing sense of humour (and of the ridiculous) had not deserted her. George Jackson, a young diplomat who was between postings, became a friend when in Brighton in March. Maria, he had been told, was seen 'at a grand musical party . . . besides two of her dinners, since I left, "<u>les diners exquis, les convives gaies et spirituelles</u>": so you see she is neither sad nor sorry, but enjoys herself in <u>her</u> way at Brighton, while her Prince and master amuses himself after <u>his</u> fashion in town.' After 'a good deal of confidential gossip, concerning you may guess whom', Maria amused her friends by showing them a letter from a man 'who had invented a powder for making excellent lemonade and which, by way of recommending more strongly to her, he assured her "was greatly approved of and constantly used by the Marchioness of Hertford!'"

Behind the humour and the badinage lay severely wounded feelings. Our young diplomat was invited to Maria's 'petites causeries' which were held in her 'little salon' with silhouettes of her favourite friends covering the walls. These occasions were only for people 'of much discretion': 'You get a cup of tea, and hear the scandal of the day. If you can contribute any piquant anecdote to the general stock, you are so much the more welcome a guest. It is permitted, or rather not forbidden . . . to discuss pretty freely the reported sayings and doings of a certain illustrious, but always nameless, personage. This is a pastime entered into with much gusto, and a good deal of mirth is the result.' But, the diplomat added, 'to my taste, it was mirth that left behind it a strong flavour of disgust.'

At about the same time Maria wrote to Lady Anne, that she was glad not to be in London: 'Bless my Stars I have nothing to do with anything.' However she found the Prince's situation 'very distressing' because of 'the set he has about him'. 'Notwithstand all the Miserys he has heap'd upon me I sincerely pity him tho' he has brought himself into all this trouble.' By June 1810 the relationship was nearing its end. Both Maria and the Prince attended an assembly at Mrs St John's. Mrs Calvert saw that 'He spoke but a word en passant to Mrs Fitzherbert, who looked much annoyed, and darted out of the room directly.' Lady Hertford had won but what is important is that Maria did not burst into tears or sink into a faint. Instead she grew angry and stormed out. She could be put aside but she could never be defeated.

In 1811 the modus vivendi arrived at by Maria and the Prince received a major shock from which it would not recover. In the preceding November the King's favourite daughter, Princess Amelia, died after a long and terrible illness. Her death proved too much for the aged King and his old problems returned, never to go away. The Prince would now have the Regency he had wanted in 1789 and set about putting a government together. Whether to bring in his old friends to form a new ministry or to keep the present administration headed by Maria's foe, Spencer Perceval, was the dilemma. He turned to various people for advice and on 3 February even sent for Maria to visit him at Carlton House and 'he was with her the greatest part of that day, and then returned again immediately to Brighthelmstone.'

Maria later recalled the meeting during which she urged 'in the most forcible manner she was able, his adherence to his former political friends . . . "Only retain them, Sir, six weeks in power. If you please, you may find some pretext to dismiss them at the end of that time; but do not break with them without some pretext or other."' It was good advice and had it been followed it might well have saved the Prince from much criticism but, as he told Maria, 'It was impossible, as he had promised.' One wonders therefore why he asked her opinion? Perhaps Maria, knowing that she might well never have another opportunity of talking privately with the Prince, recalled an occasion when his daughter had thrown her arms round Maria's neck and beseeched her 'to speak to her Father, that he would receive her with great marks of his affection'. Maria now asked if she might 'offer one suggestion, which she trusted he would not take amiss'. She 'urged' him 'as strongly as she was able' to treat his daughter with more kindness. '"You now, Sir," she said, "may mould her at your pleasure, but soon it will not be so; and she may become, from mismanagement, a thorn in your side for life." "That is your opinion, Madam," was his only reply.' Two days later the Regency began and Perceval's administration was retained.

In June the Prince planned a grand fête to celebrate the establishment of his Regency but it would be much more than this. The Prince and his government saw it as an important diplomatic occasion. By inviting Louis XVIII, the Bourbon King in exile, his consort, his heir, the Comte d'Artois, his heir's son, the Duc d'Angoulême and his duchess, the only surviving child of the murdered Louis XVI and Marie Antoinette, the Prince showed his regards for the Bourbons. This was in spite of Napoleon's numerous victories in creating a united Europe under French control and a widespread European acceptance of the new situation. As the Prince would say as the King walked into Carlton House, 'Ici Votre Majesté est Roi de France.'[6]

Maria assumed that she would be invited – as indeed she was – and, as she recalled in her conversations with Lord Stourton, she assumed seating at table would be 'without regard to rank', that is those at the Prince's table would be there because he had invited them. This would 'avoid etiquette in circumstances of such delicacy as regarded her own situation with reference to the Prince'. This had been the procedure in the past. However this occasion was different. The Prince was now *de facto* King and he had to remember the rigorous etiquette that surrounded the French monarchy. With thousands of guests there would have to be seating according to rank and Maria should have assumed this. With this in mind the Prince, as he told Lady Anne, called on Maria on 6 June to explain that she could not sit at the top table. He 'trusted she would forgive him if the places at his table were reserved for persons of a certain rank'. The Prince's table would include the French Royal Family, members of the British Royal Family and those duchesses and marchionesses, including the triumphant Lady Hertford, personally invited. The real insult probably lay in Lady Hertford's being invited. Maria exploded and asked the Prince where she was to sit. He replied, in her words, '"You know, Madam, you have no place [at the top table]." "None, Sir,"' she replied, "but such as you choose to give me."' Now it was Maria's turn to go to Lady Anne who advised her to go to the celebrations but to leave early, saying she was ill.

Instead Maria went back to Lady Anne and they worked on at least three draughts of a letter to the Prince. Lady Anne remembered that Maria's original version was 'cut down by me from vulgar violence to moderation'. Maria sent the revised version and said she could not come. She had never wished to embarrass the

Prince in thirty years but 'there are situations when one ought not entirely to forget what is due to oneself.' The Prince did not fully understand 'in your anxiety to fill your table with persons only of the highest rank, that, by excluding her who now addresses you merely for want of those titles that others possess, you are excluding the person who is not unjustly suspected by the world of possessing in silence unassumed and unsustained a Rank given her by yourself above that of any other person present'. Now Maria went on to define their 'marriage' in a way the Prince would have found startling: 'Having never forfeited my title to Your Royal Highness's public as well as private consideration by any act of my life, to what could this etiquette be for the first time imputed?' Maria could 'never submit to appear in your house in any place or situation but in that where you yourself first placed me many years ago'. The essential dilemma of her marriage now came to haunt her. She, however, saw it differently and docketed the letter: 'copy of letter to the Prince written June the 7, 1811, when persuaded by Lady Hertford not to admit me to his table'.

Insult was added to injury not just when the Hertfords sat at the top table but when Maria attended an assembly at Devonshire House. The new Duchess of Devonshire took her to meet the Duke and 'in passing through the rooms, she saw the Prince and Lady Hertford in a tête-à-tête conversation, and nearly fainted under all the impressions which then rushed upon her mind, but, taking a glass of water, she recovered and passed on.' Years later she told Lord Stourton that this was the last time she saw the Prince.

Maria also told Lord Stourton that this assembly in Devonshire House 'terminated this fatal, ill-starred connection, so unfortunate, probably, for both the parties concerned'. But this was an elderly Maria speaking with hindsight. At the time observers assumed that this was yet another low point in their relationship. Looking back at these events, Maria's oldest friend later noted that, as in 1795, the final quarrel and breakup were 'on her side' and this is confirmed by another observer, Lady Holland, who told a friend a month after the fête that 'Mrs. Fitzherbert has inflexibly resisted all his attempts to be admitted within her doors.'

Maria now set off on various visits round the country and by August 1811 she was revisiting, for the first time, her ancestral home at Acton Burnell: 'When I reflect on those happy days' she wrote to Lady Anne, 'many a pang crosses my mind & my heart grows sick at the reflection of the many miserys & persecutions I have suffered since that period all occasion'd by the man for whom I have sacrific'd everything & who never hesitates to sacrifice me to gratify every caprice that comes into his head & who is I fear a total stranger to principal or honor.' By the winter she was back in Brighton and Uncle Errington told McMahon that 'Mrs. F. has run it very near. Does her approach hasten his removal from Brighton or prevent him going to Ld. Egremont's. Entre nous, I wish she would commute her residence at Brighton for some other country house. The inhabitants will think she drives him [from] the place. There is no kicking against the pricks.' Maria was not kicking but she would not be moved: from now on the Prince could come to Brighton whenever he wanted but it would be a Brighton with Maria, not without.[7]

In 1812 Maria returned to the question of her allowance. This had been settled in 1808 when the Prince signed an indenture to Uncle Errington in the form of a mortgage on the Marine Pavilion: but this guaranteed Maria £6,000 a year, not the £10,000 promised to her parents and her Uncle. Once again Maria asked for Lady Anne's help as she wanted the difference between what had been agreed in 1808 and what had been promised in 1785. If she dated her demand from 1808 this would be £16,000 [about £400,000]. If she dated her claim from 1785 it would be an astronomical sum. Lady Anne's advice was that if she had no hope of getting the money, she should not demand it. Maria should stay in Brighton and if the Prince called round she should receive him with dignity: 'Make no scene – no flouncing – no reproaches.' Maria had obviously also asked for Errington's help and whenever she did this there was always, in the background, the implied threat of a public scandal or blackmail. This time there was more than a threat. As Lady Anne put it, her uncle is the only witness to 'the solemn promise the Prince bound himself by to yr. Father & Mother that ten thousand pr. an: shoud be yours from the day of your marriage.' (This dates the letter after 12 February 1812 because on that date Maria's closest brother, Jack, died.) The letter also shows that Maria had considered asking Uncle Errington to make a deposition before a magistrate. Lady Anne was not opposed to such an oath 'on every point & fact which he has to substantiate for the credit of yr. character shoud it ever be put in question hereafter'. Such a deposition would be a valuable negotiating tool, Lady Anne added. Later on Maria confessed how she now disliked going up to London and added that letters were no longer safe because they are opened at the Post Office: 'This I know to be a truth.'[8]

For his part the Prince wanted at least to keep open negotiations, to have, in short, a relationship on *his* terms and not on Maria's. The Prince needed constant companionship and Maria was his oldest female companion outside his family. Maria probably had this in mind when she later recalled that when in Brighton before June 1811 the Prince would spend 'part of his mornings with Mrs Fitzherbert on friendly terms at her own house' but, later in the evening at the Pavilion, 'did not even notice her in the slightest manner . . . she afterwards understood that such attentions would have been reported to her rival [Lady Hertford].' This is what he wanted now but Maria would have nothing of it.

However Maria's natural good sense and love of society marked her as much at fifty-five as they had done at twenty-five and she was hardly now going to retire into mournful solitude. Indeed, in February she gave a ball in Brighton at which the waltzing went on till five in the morning. 'I hear,' said her young diplomat friend, 'some of the ladies were very much fagged, and looked so.' In June 1811 she attended a public reception given by Catholics to honour Prince Augustus, now the Duke of Sussex, who was the chief promoter of their cause within the Royal Family and the

House of Lords. Lady Jerningham was intrigued to see Maria there because 'some say the Prince does not see Her any more; others that He divides His Hours equally'.

August and September of 1812 found Maria in Cheltenham where she took a house. She had come to take the waters and told Minney that the place was 'dull and stupid' – one of her favourite phrases – but she still filled her letter with society gossip even though 'there actually is not a human being I ever saw before . . . I am doing penance but I hope I shall hereafter feel the good effects.' Maria's friend, Mrs Creevey, told her husband in May: 'As for the Prince I expect to hear of his becoming quite mad and I think Hertford House has it all to answer for – his Love for that woman has been madness from the beginning & I have no doubt She and her son are now exerting a secret influence that will over power Moira & every one else if they cannot bring about an entire separation – he could not be so agitated by the mere contentions of politicians.'[9]

In December 1811 the Prince asked McMahon to write a New Year's letter – a precursor to the nineteenth-century Christmas card – to Maria to accompany a 'fine Necklace as a new year's gift'. Lady Bessborough, who heard the story from Maria's physician, Sir Henry Halford, added, 'Were I her, the beauty of the necklace would not make up to me for the letter from Col. McMahon.' In explanation she added that Lady Hertford was said to be particularly fond of diamonds, so much that 'the Prince's finances can hardly suffice'. Was not Maria's gift, she wondered, a means 'to be just in his dealings and make all even'? Sir Henry also hinted that the Prince would have written himself but for the fact that 'three of his fingers being compleatly numb'd and useless'. The Prince was 'much alarm'd, thinking it palsy, but Sir H. Halford says it is only owing to the quantity of rings and bracelets he wears, which stop the circulation'. It was a sad state of affairs and far removed from those heady days when Maria found in the young Prince the 'sweet clean handsome young fellow' of whom she had dreamed.

13

---·•·---

MRS FITZHERBERT WITHOUT A TITLE

Because Maria had always had her own social life her second separation from the Prince did not in many ways alter her life all that much. Her houses were seldom empty as there was a constant succession of visiting Smythes. Maria had her own resident chaplain in the tradition of the Catholic gentry into which she was born. She acted as patroness for various balls in Brighton. She went out to society events, often as the chaperone of Minney. She read her papers and kept up with the news: 'My Eyes are almost out of my head in reading all the Newspapers, some of the Speeches are very Entertaining but I am no politician, I have many friends I am anxious for on both sides.' Maria was not a reflective woman but from time to time she did turn her attention to her exotic past. Occasionally she would talk about the Prince or show her marriage lines to friends such as Humphrey Weld but as the years passed, her marriage became a thing of history. By 1833 she was telling Minney that 'I am not very well, and anything upon the subject always annoys me very much.'[1]

Of the four houses Maria had use of in the years immediately following her separation – Tilney Street, East End House in Parson's Green, Sherwood Lodge and Brighton, she spent a lot of time in Parson's Green with its sixteen acres of gardens. But by the 1820s Brighton had become her principal home and she, one of its greatest attractions. As she told Minney in 1827, 'there never were so many people of Fashion here before, and my house has been like a Fair all day yesterday and today.' When the German traveller, Prince Puckler-Muskau – known as 'Prince Pickle and Mustard' in London Society – appeared in Brighton during his wife-hunting expedition he was invited to Maria's. He found her 'very dignified and delightful *d'un excellent ton et sans prétention'*. At her house he could play whist with the men or loo with the young ladies: 'These small circles are much more agreeable,' he wrote back to his mistress in Germany, 'than the great parties of the metropolis.' All round were 'very pretty young women . . . loaded with jewels', and all anxious to try the new Austrian dance craze, 'the *waltz'*. Not all her receptions were so sedate and one diarist noted that 'some say Lady Harrowby was found at Mrs Fitzherbert's breakfast kissing Ed Montague in one of the alleys by Pss Esterhazy; it has produced a scene.' Maria also entertained when in London and her circle of friends still included various exiled Frenchmen. In December 1813, for example, diarists noted that 'she is going to get up a French play at her house here, at which the Baron and Baroness de Montalembert are to act the principal parts.[2]

During these years Maria became more religious and this development expressed itself in charity and good works. When friends were ill she would send her doctor to look after them or offer them accommodation in her house. 'The poor of Brighton, to whom Mrs Fitzherbert is endeared by her benevolences, will have reason to rejoice at her return, and we hope she will make a protracted stay' noted one newspaper at the beginning of one visit in 1823. Its rival agreed that 'in her the poor ever find a pitying and relieving friend.' After her death her parish priest praised her generosity to the charity school in donations for books and clothes: one forgets that there was considerable poverty in Brighton, especially among fishermen's families during bad weather. Maria was also a good

friend to those in need and scattered through her surviving correspondence are letters of sympathy and offers of help written with
great feeling to those whose loved ones were ill or who had died.[3]
Maria contributed £1,000 towards the cost of a new Catholic church
in Kemp Town, persuaded the Marquess of Bristol to donate the
land and suggested that Lord Egremont give the baptismal font.
(He had, after all, done a great deal towards providing candidates
for baptism during his own life.)

Maria knew that by making Brighton her home she was
bearding the lion in his own den. The gossipy Tory MP, J.W. Croker,
saw this in 1818: 'I cannot but wonder at her living here and
bearding the Prince in a way so indelicate . . . and I should have
thought so embarrassing to herself. To her presence is attributed
the Prince's never going abroad at Brighton.' To his own knowledge, Croker wrote, for seven or eight years the Prince did not
leave 'the limits of the Pavilion, and in general he avoids even
riding through the principal streets'. All this was doubly galling
because, starting in 1815 the Prince began transforming the Marine
Pavilion Maria had known into the many splendoured thing that
exists today with its oriental domes and towers. As Sydney Smith
said in his oft-quoted quip, it was as if 'the Dome of St Paul's had
gone down and pupped'. Maria admitted to being puzzled by the
appearance of the building 'which it is impossible for me, or indeed
any one else, to describe'. The building's costs were legendary:
£300 was spent each evening just to illuminate it. 'There is something effeminate about it,' noted the wife of the Russian
Ambassador, Princess Lieven. 'One spends the evening half lying
on cushions; the lights are dazzling; there are perfumes, music,
liqueurs.' It was all very un-English.

Far from being embarrassed, Maria enjoyed the Prince's
dilemma and, as she said to Thomas Creevey in 1818: 'The Regent
and all his household are here, but as he never stirs out of his
parlour and no one sees him, it makes no alteration in our proceedings.' On another occasion in 1829 she told Minney that Lady
Conyngham, then her husband's current favourite, 'is not well.

The thought of Brighton I believe has made her sick. You'll see by the Papers His Majesty does not intend honoring us with his presence.' One can feel the venom. When the Prince was in Brighton, he would invite Minney to balls for Princess Charlotte or receptions for Prince Esterhazy or Grand Duke Nicholas, later Tsar Nicholas I of Russia. Maria was not included.

There were two other reasons for choosing Brighton as Croker saw: 'She is treated as queen, at least of Brighton. They don't quite <u>Highness</u> her in her domestic circle, but they <u>Madam</u> her prodigiously, and stand up longer for her arrival than for ordinary folks, and in short go as near to acknowledging her for <u>Princess</u> as they can, without actually giving her the title. When she dines out she expects to be led out to dinner before princesses.' Also, by staying in Brighton Maria avoided London society and 'people's curiosity to find out what I think and what I do' which 'would annoy me so much, dull as it is here, I am spared many uncomfortable occurences that would annoy me.' The Duke of Kent 'applauded' her avoiding the Metropolis at present, which 'God knows is the focus of every thing that is odious.' However, when she was in Town, she did not hide her light under a bushel and in 1814 was seen 'driving herself in one of the fashionable carriages which resemble your old phaeton, only lighter. They . . . go at a great rate. One could not help moralizing, as the road she was on was the very one where the Princess of Wales is driven almost every day.' Finally, Brighton had become the most important resort for the titled, wealthy and fashionable. By having her main residence there Maria was at the hub of the social whirl which guaranteed a succession of visitors, conversation and company. When staying in London she complained about her plight, thereby giving us an insight into her life in Brighton: 'You have no Idea how dull & solitary is Tilney Street. I have the last two days din'd quite alone a thing very unusual to me but I prefer'd it to dining out as it gave me a great deal of time to myself.' Time to herself was not something Maria much enjoyed: she preferred company, cards and conversation. As Thomas Raikes remembered, her 'handsome dinners' gave her house 'at least a seigneurial, if not a royal appear-ance'.[4]

Try as Maria would, she could never rid herself of her connection to the Prince Regent. When in France in 1814 she asked Lady Anne, 'Why will he persist in dragging unpopularity on himself?' After her return from her French trip she had the ill luck to encounter him at a ball given by the Countess of Ailesbury. He looked at her but cut her completely, just as he had done with Lady Jersey after her fall. At this Maria was 'dreadfully overcome', but as the Duke of Wellington once said, the Regent 'was very brutal to those women whom he left. He was not at all a gentleman about that.' In time she learned that this was a game two could play. When at Devonshire House, Minney remembered meeting the Regent as they were going up the stairs. While he stopped to speak to her Maria simply swept past without regard. She cut him before he had the chance to cut her.

The caricaturists could not accept that the relationship was really dead after all these years. In 1812 there would be nine cartoons which included Maria, usually as a stage-papist associated in some way with the Prince or as the rejected mistress eying the victorious Lady Hertford. The most famous of this latter group was 'Worse and Worse or the sports of the 19th Century' which shows Maria playing battledore and shuttlecock with the Prince of Wales' feathers. The final caricature, 'Saluting the R——ts Bomb' groups Maria with Ladies Hertford and Jersey, all of whom unite to say 'We come – let who dare call us Hags . . .' But these were comments on the past, not on the present.

On 29 Jan 1820, when the poor, blind King finally died and the Prince Regent succeeded as King George IV, Maria was on one of her visits to Paris. We can only wonder at her thoughts: did she remember the promises made in 1785 as to her future status once the King died? All that was history and as far as Maria was concerned, the new reign meant that at last she might now get the £10,000 a year promised her back in 1785. For the new King, some of his past now came back to haunt him. His other wife, now Queen Caroline, returned from her amorous wanderings in Europe to claim her new position as what today would be called 'the people's queen'. Then as now, politicians on the make, backed by London's radicals and their mob, quickly took up her cause as a way to attack the monarchy and the King responded by demanding that Parliament give him a divorce. The case opened in the House of Lords on 5 July 1820 when Lord Liverpool introduced a Bill of Pains and Penalties to deprive Caroline of her title of Queen due to her adultery with an Italian servant: 'it would be the greatest state trial since Warren Hastings'.

The public's attention, now divided into two warring camps, largely ignored Maria, even though Gillray's 1786 cartoon, 'The Morning After', was republished. Maria's great fear, as in 1787 and 1788–9, was that she would be called as a witness before the House of Lords: were the truth of her marriage to come out her future could be very grim indeed. Such an event, she later said, 'would have broken her heart'. It was not a pleasant prospect for a sixty-four-year-old woman. The greatest threat came from Henry Brougham, one of that dreadful breed known as clever young barristers, who took up the Queen's cause. He was a man who thrived on controversy.

Brougham's first involvement with Maria had occurred in February 1813, in the warfare between Caroline and the Prince of Wales. A letter appeared in the *Morning Chronicle* in February, ostensibly written by Caroline, but really, most people believed, by Brougham in which the Princess defended herself. Georgiana Devonshire's successor as Duchess then expressed the view of many regarding Brougham: 'I believe him to be clever, but a cold-blooded, mischievous and malicious man.' Even then the Princess's advisers among the more radical Whigs were contemplating bringing forward the 1785 marriage to discredit the Prince.

In October 1820 Brougham was convinced that the Prince was guilty of 'seducing' Maria 'with a false and fictitious marriage'.

He had no doubt as to what his strongest weapon was and in his opening speech said, 'I dismiss for the present all other questions respecting the conduct or connexions of any parties previous to marriage.' Brougham had done his homework and the papers of the Queen's solicitor, now in the Royal Archives, contained information to prove the 1785 marriage. Brougham may not have known all the facts but he knew that Henry Errington had been a witness and he felt that if he were called and refused to incriminate himself, it would not matter. As he wrote years later to J.W. Croker: 'I could have proved it in 1820. I had as my witness H. Errington . . . who no doubt would have sheltered himself under the privilege of not committing himself . . . Mrs. F. herself, in like manner; and I had a communication from her in great alarm, and I rather think I quieted her with a promise not to call her; but of this I am not certain. H. Errington was enough for me, and his refusal would have been as good as his saying "yes."'

In a following letter Brougham recalled that Maria 'always had the greatest alarm about it, for fear of the penalties (praemunire, &c.), which she had not been aware of, any more than of the invalidity, at the time.' Brougham's claims, especially the claim that Maria wrote 'in great alarm' – an odd thing to do if she were concerned about self-incrimination – must be taken with a grain of salt for in most of Brougham's stories Brougham emerges as the hero. In later years Maria would refer to him as 'that odious Radical'. On 11 November the Government, knowing they could never get the bill through the Commons, dropped it after their majority in the Lords collapsed. The mob's rioting, the fear that there would be mutinies in the army and the knowledge that Brougham could at least attempt to prove the King's marriage to Maria, had left them no choice. For her part Maria waited in France with her wedding lines and the King's Will; the King stayed in Brighton to avoid the mobs.

Maria did not return to England until the new year by which time Queen Caroline's 'cause' had collapsed in Parliament. This extraordinary woman made one final bid when she tried to force her way into Westminster Abbey during the Coronation on 19 July. Having failed in this she did one last service to her husband by dying on 7 August. For his part, the King, now enjoying a triumphant tour of Ireland, was at last free – to a degree. As an old woman, Maria told Lord Stourton that 'after the death of Queen Caroline, upon the Prince [King] informing her that he was determined to marry again, she only replied, "Very well, Sir;" but upon his leaving her, she ordered horses with a resolution to abandon the country . . .' One wonders if her memory was playing tricks on her because she also claimed that she never met the Prince after 1811. Likewise, her recollection about leaving the country, though highly dramatic, is probably over-stated because she was constantly visiting Europe at this time. His announcement, if it really happened, remains as bizarre as most of his behaviour.

Rumour-mongers talked again of a possible reconciliation with Maria and in January Lady Anne told her that Mrs Davenport, once a celebrated beauty now reduced to gossip, claimed that the King had once again offered Maria the title of Duchess, to which Lady Anne replied, 'Mrs Fitzherbert without a title . . . is a greater woman than she could be with any the King could bestow on her.' A few months later, in the last letter in Lady Anne's papers, Maria wrote to deny the rumour and to comment that 'you have no idea what a set of I may call them Banditti he [the King] is surrounded with.' In the event the King did not remarry but sought consolation in the arms of the Marchioness of Conyngham, his last affair. The Marchioness was a fifty-one-year-old grandmother in 1821. She was a friend of the Hertfords, fat, greedy and politically conservative.

On 11 March the Duke of Wellington told his friend, Mrs Arbuthnot, of a meeting he had had with Madam de Lieven and of her encounter with the King and Lady Conyngham:

The King had made her [Madame de Lieven] sit by him in the eveg, Ly C being on the other side . . . & had told her that he had never known what it was to be in love before, that he was himself quite surprised at the degree to which he was in love, that he did nothing from morning till night but think what he could do to please Ly C & make her happy, that he wd do any thing upon earth for her for that he owed his life to her, that he shd certainly have died in his illness if it had not been for her, & that she was an angel sent from Heaven for him. He cried, Lady C cried & Madame de Lieven said that, being nervous & easily agitated, she had cried also; & all this passed in a crowded drawing room. One never did hear such folly!! from a man, too, of 58!!

In the Royal Pavilion, Brighton are some of the King's surviving love letters to 'Lady C' and in one from 1825 the sixty-three-year-old King writes that: 'Our Hearts . . . do, I think, understand one another, & beat so completely in unison . . . You are one of the brightest Ornaments, & to Me, one of the most indispensable ingredients, if every one is to be happy' and so on. Maria was, in modern parlance, well out of it. She had better luck with several of the King's brothers and they regretted her fall from grace. She had been not only a confidante but someone who could approach the Prince Regent for favours. In January 1812, when no one was quite sure what was happening, Kent had reminded Maria that she had twice been a witness to one of the Prince's promises and 'I am sure I should not want an advocate in you to urge him to fulfill them, but alas! I fear I dare not hope that you can now feel yourself warranted to interfere, and therefore I cannot think of being so indiscreet as to press you to write to him.' The Duke was right and Maria did not 'interfere'. She did however keep up her friendship, not only with Kent but with York and both princes were constant visitors. She also had good relations with the Duke of Cambridge (Prince Adolphus) and the Duke of Clarence who liked her for the interest she took in his various illegitimate offspring. Even the Duke of Cumberland, the most virulent of anti-papists, considered her a friend, as did the liberal Duke of Sussex, a supporter of Catholic emancipation.[5]

When, in 1817, the Prince Regent's daughter, Princess Charlotte, died in childbirth, the nation realised that there was now no direct heir and that the succession would pass from brother to brother to brother, none of whom had any legitimate children. Now began 'the race for brides' as the royal dukes headed for Germany. It was perfectly in keeping for the Duke of Kent, after he told his mother of his choice, to call next on Maria. The woman he selected was Princess Viktoria, the widowed sister of Princess Charlotte's husband, and in time the mother of Queen Victoria. When the Duke of Clarence, having dumped Mrs Jordan, married Princess Adelaide of Saxe-Meiningen, Maria was one of three ladies who welcomed her at the Royal York Hotel in Brighton, thereby beginning a close friendship with that kindliest of royal ladies. From time to time Maria would take advantage of her princely connections. In 1812 she asked for Kent's help in getting a chaplainship for an Anglican clergyman who was a friend and toward the end of the Napoleonic Wars she called on the Duke of York's friends at the War Office for help in getting commissions or promotions. Maria also had good relations with the surviving members of the 'sisterhood' living at Windsor Castle. Maria frequently wrote to Princess Elizabeth, who had married into a German princely family, and she was also a friend of Princess Sophia. Occasionally there were difficulties: in 1836 Maria was furious that the Duchess of Gloucester, George III's daughter, Princess Mary, had inherited a 'wicked prejudice' against Maria from her husband, the son of her old friend. Letters flew back and forth as Minney and Sir George Seymour, tried to placate Maria's feelings.[6]

Perhaps the most important part of Maria's life during her long retirement from centre stage was what she called 'her family'. In 1813 she inherited from her dead brother, Jack, his illegitimate daughter, Marianne. As Maria told Lady Anne: 'I have got an addition to my Family a dear lovely little Girl about six years old a Legacy of my poor Brother's I cherish it for his sake.' Therefore by 1813 Maria had a family of two 'daughters' – Minney, who was about to turn fifteen and now Marianne, a vivacious six-year-old presumably named after Maria's own mother.

Maria was devoted to Minney on whom she lavished affection and money. She would write to friends such as Thomas Coutts to arrange seats for Minney to see a procession pass through the City. When, in 1822, Minney went on a European tour, Maria told another friend; 'I cannot tell you how miserable I am at being separated from her & how much I have suffered this day in taking leave of her.' It was not long before Maria was faced with the awesome duty of arranging a 'good marriage' for Minney. The girl's social position and her good looks brought a variety of suitors including her cousin, Lord Beauchamp (later Marquess of Hertford) and George Fitzclarence (the Duke of Clarence's eldest illegitimate son, later created Earl of Munster). The £10,000 invested for her by the Prince had doubled in value and Maria was expected to provide a similar sum: whoever got Minney got a fortune. 'Mama' was furious to learn that Minney had fallen in love with a young officer, the Hon. George Dawson, a younger son of an Irish peer, Lord Portarlington. While he returned from Waterloo a hero, he had few 'prospects' a reputation as a rake, and, according to Maria he had been spoilt as a child.[7]

Maria, who also had the support of the Seymours, turned to the Duke of York for help and he arranged to have Dawson posted to the West Indies, while Minney was sent on a tour of France and Germany. Minney was forbidden to correspond with Dawson and told not to challenge Maria's view. When she did so the girl produced a sudden bout of illness: 'As to myself I am perfectly unequal either in mind or body to support the misery I have endured any longer and shall withdraw entirely from the world and everything in it as every prospect of happiness would be totally at an end for me.' Maria even asked her husband for help but Minney outflanked her and wrote to the King directly, asking him to 'recollect how much happiness or misery are in his hands'. He now accepted the proposed match if her dowry could be secured for her children. Maria admitted defeat and left London to take the waters in Buxton when the couple were married at St George's, Hanover Square in August 1825. A solution worthy of a Trollope novel now occurred when Lady Caroline Damer, George's aunt, announced her intention of leaving her Dorset estate, with an annual rent roll of £2,000, to her nephew provided he added Damer to his name. Minney now joined the ranks of the hyphenated classes. As Lady Holland wrote: 'The inheritance has been very considerable, a charming house ready . . . for immediate possession in Dorsetshire.'

Maria was fairly quickly reconciled to her honorary son-in-law and in 1829 bought a house in Upper Grosvenor Street as a present. (She also paid their pew rent in Grosvenor Chapel.) In addition Maria helped him to launch his parliamentary career as an Irish MP and to buy a commission in the Guards at £2,000. Maria's reconciliation gradually turned into friendship and by 1829 she was asking Minney to tell her husband 'not to call me Madame. It is so formal.' In time Maria relished the role of honorary grandmother and a touching letter survives in the Royal Archives to Minney's two children: 'I cannot tell you how much I am disappointed at not seeing you both as I fully expected you would have been here at this time. I have enclos'd you a little trifle to buy some *Bun Buns* with. Mama will be very angry with me if you shd. make yourselves sick wch. I hope you will not.' She signed her letter, 'Old Granny'. However, Minney's marriage would be disturbed by her husband's extramarital affairs, so perhaps Maria was right after all.[8]

There were fewer difficulties with Marianne who, like her aunt, was educated at a convent in France. She came out at a ball in Cheltenham in 1822 and the hunt for a husband began. She chose the Hon. Edward Jerningham, grandson of old Lady Jerningham. His father would succeed in reclaiming the Stafford barony and young Edward would be part of a newly ennobled family as well as an officer in the 6th Dragoon Guards. (Marianne had, unlike Minney, been raised a Catholic.) Maria found him 'very amiable, good-looking and gentleman-like'. The difficulty was 'ten younger children' which meant that Edward would only have £5,000, plus the £20,000 Maria could give Marianne: the Jerninghams must find more money. In the end the finances were sorted out and the couple were married.

Maria laid on the wedding breakfast in Tilney Street and in the evening gave a ball for the servants. For her part she went with her sister-in-law, Walter's wife, to drink tea at their niece's, Lady Stanley. Maria told Marianne, with obvious relish, the story of their return home:

> Mrs. Wat brought me home from Ld Stanley's & her new footman was so extremely in liquor that we were obliged to get one of Sir Tho's Servants to hold him behind the Carriage to keep him from breaking his neck. Her Carriage wheel broke down as she left this house in the morng . . . & now dearest God bless you. May every happiness attend you & yours is the most evident wish of my heart. I am looking forward wt. great delight to meeting you both again. Say a thousand kind things from me to my son in law & believe me ever most affectly. yrs., MF

Maria was also kind to her other Smythe nieces and nephews, legitimate and illegitimate. In the year before her death she asked Lord Melbourne, by now Prime Minister, to find a position worth £200 a year for a Smythe nephew. Her nephew seemed delighted with it as 'the fair Lady he wanted to marry has constantly refus'd his offers – he had been nearly four years lying about what his beautiful appearance would do & has unfortunately found no one so in love with him as he is with himself . . . I am miserable at writing on this horrid paper. I fear you will be scarce able to read this . . .' Maria was right: the paper is very thin and her hand-writing is extremely difficult to make out. Finally, Maria some-times used her influence to help Smythe relations get positions in the Austrian army and to procure a baronetcy for a favourite doctor. When Marianne began to have a family of her own Maria thoroughly enjoyed having the children stay with her. On one occasion, probably in 1834, Marianne and Edward Jerningham had come with their son, Augustus. After they had left Maria wrote to say that she had called on some old friends: 'They can talk of nothing but their admiration of your little Augustus and laughed very heartily at his telling them I had a <u>Roman Catholic nose</u>.' One can imagine Maria's robust laugh as she wrote this to Marianne and in years to come she would often refer to her 'Roman Catholic nose'.

Travel was part of an upper-class Englishman's way of life in the eighteenth century as he made his way from Bath to Cheltenham to Buxton to Tunbridge Wells to Brighton and from one country house to another. In Maria's case, travel had been part of her way of life from her childhood. In an age when such travel was not easy she had a resilience and enthusiasm which did not leave her in her old age any more than her looks. One observer commented during this period on her 'fresh, fair complexion and fine aquiline features'. Maria still had 'great remains of the beauty and charm which had captivated the fancy, although it could not ensure the constancy, of George IV'. She suffered from rheumatism and began to complain of 'asthma' which would explain her lament in 1831. 'I am such an object as I can scarcely see or breathe that I am fit for nothing but to go to my bed.' Complaints about her latest 'cold' were common in the 1830s as she sent her servants with little notes, neatly folded into triangles, as was the fashion. There was, also, her continuing problem about 'that Subject' – her over-eating. All this meant that finding a 'cure' remained essential to good health. As she once wrote to Minney, 'My mind is youthful but my body is very old.'[9] Her disposition kept her going but meant she was easily bored.

Maria recognised that Bath, this 'gay place', was no longer fashionable and while she derived 'great benefit' from its waters, she disliked it 'beyond anything'. She described her life there in October, 1826: 'Our evenings are always enjoyed in reading and working. I am down at the Pump every morning about nine o'clock. At three I take my bath and drink more water. At five we dine and at ten o'clock we go to bed, the pleasantest thing that happens to me during the four and twenty hours.' The worst part was that 'there is scarcely a creature I know here except some old *Fograms*, whose company I would rather be without.' When not visiting spas Maria joined the circuit of people paying lengthy visits to the great Whig country houses. Chatsworth was presided over by Georgiana's son, the 'bachelor duke'. Another favourite spot was Petworth in Sussex where she liked to spend time with her old friend, Lord Egremont. There she could, in the painter Benjamin Haydon's words, 'dine with the finest Van Dykes in the world' and enjoy the work of Lord Egremont's five chefs. In addition there were family connections: while she could not get on with her sister, Lady Haggerston, she did like her niece who married Sir Thomas Stanley, Bart and Maria visited her at her country house in Hotton, Cheshire, as she did Walter's daughter, Lady Bathurst, at Clarendon Park. Maria also sometimes visited her Fitzherbert connections at Swynnerton and was invited to stay with the Cholmondeleys and the Seftons.

Maria also made numerous trips to the Low Countries, Switzerland, Italy and Germany but her favourite destination remained Paris. During her first visit after Napoleon's defeat in 1814 she told Lady Anne: 'You would not know Paris it is so much alter'd and improv'd.' She was back in February 1815 when she was received by the restored Bourbon King, Louis XVIII, only weeks before he had to flee after Napoleon returned for his Hundred Days. During her 1817 visit Lord Glenbervie noted that Maria was one of the visiting English ladies 'most in fashion', a group that was known for 'more or less liberal conduct in their earlier days'. Maria, 'if not noble born, nor illustrious from any acknowledged marriage, her connection with British royalty makes her distinguished. She has indeed the universal reputation of many good qualities.' Maria was also friendly with the Duc de Morny, the scandalous brother of the Bonapartist pretender, Louis

Napoleon (later Napoleon III) and Louis XVIII's liberal cousin, Louis Philipe d'Orléans, son of George IV's old roué friend, Philippe-Égalité.

Maria's most important visit to France was that of 1820–1 as it kept her out of England during the trial of Queen Caroline. Although the visit gave Maria safety, it presented her with problems which show that her self-esteem had not diminished with the passing of the years. In the Stuart de Rothsay Papers are two letters from Maria to Sir Charles Stewart, H.M. Ambassador to France and later Lord Stuart de Rothsay. An obviously annoyed Maria wrote in the third person and mentioned 'not being invited to Lady Elizabeth Stewart's House fearing from it, that unintentionally, she [Maria] may have given her Ladyship offence, the more so as she had the Honor of leaving her card without its being returned – Mrs Fitzherbert again entreats Sir Charles Stewart's pardon for the intrusion which she hopes he will grant, as from the situation Lady Elizabeth Stewart holds . . . how important it is.' Obviously Maria got her invitation for later on she writes from Tilney Street regarding some of the '<u>eau Medicinal</u>' she had promised but had failed to get. Now she was 'fortunate enough to get a few bottles' which she sent.[10]

These trips to Europe were large undertakings which lasted sometimes for several months. In September 1833 Maria set out for Aix-la-Chapelle but did not return to England until August of 1834. During the stay she spent a considerable time in Paris. In theory the visits to Aix or Spa or Brussels were to 'regain' her health but in fact they often seemed to leave her bored when she was starved of interesting conversation and stimulating society. When she was back in Aix on her way home in 1834, for example, she wrote that 'I hate this place so much that nothing but absolute necessity should have brought me here again . . . I wish I could make myself some years younger and my health better . . . but alas! <u>mes beaux jours sont passés</u>, and I must make up my mind to my armchair and my fireside. I am not fit for anything else.' During this holiday she wrote to Minney on George IV's birthday.

In a postscript she noted: 'August 12. A melancholy and memorable recollection', as indeed it was.

While money meant a lot to Maria, the allowance promised her by the Prince was also the symbol of her injured dignity and rejected love. After 1811 she fought various battles over this and the fight would not be won in full until 1820. In 1812 she again asked Uncle Errington to help with her demand for all the money due her but then suddenly dropped that demand and insisted the Prince start paying her the £10,000 a year promised in 1785. But it was too late: the Prince now refused even to acknowledge her letters. At some stage she even considered raising the issue of the missing £4000 per annum in the Commons but Lady Anne warned her the Opposition will only make her 'their tool' to discredit the Prince Regent. When Maria was considering her visit to France in 1814 she would write, with Lady Anne's help, yet another letter demanding her money. Lady Anne's version ended as follows:

Adieu then, once Beloved as you were, & long so let the remembrance of former times act upon yr. feelings to shield my future years from poverty and disgrace – with me such recollections painfull as they are are unaccompanied with ill will; I have sacrificed too much for you, loved you too sincerely ever to be indifferent to yr. honor or your happiness & pray to God to give you that peace of mind in this world which may by degrees lead you on to a better.

This was too much for the more down-to-earth Maria who substituted: 'In whatever manner I may be regarded by you, I shall never be indifferent about what regards your honor, health and prosperity Sir.'

In the final version, preserved in the Royal Archives, Maria alternated between frustrated love and hints of blackmail. She insisted that the Prince 'do me the justice to acknowledge that I never was an interested person', that is, someone seeking favours. 'I have,' she went on with some exaggeration, 'no desire for riches; <u>comforts</u> at my time of life and <u>under my unfortunate circumstances</u>' had become necessary. (She was then fifty-eight.) Using her planned trip to best advantage, she wrote that this letter 'is most probably the last you will ever be troubled with from me, it being my intention to go very soon to the Continent'. She added ominously that she was not sure what her creditors would do without payment: 'that many distressing discussions may be stopped which <u>we</u> ought <u>both on every account</u> to prevent from becoming public.' While the Prince hears 'malignant insinuations against me' she has never 'uttered one syllable that could have affected your interests.' 'You ought to know me better, Sir, than to believe such representations.' The Prince knew she was telling the truth: 'Aware as you are of <u>how much</u> I have in my power, that power has remained <u>unused by me</u>. I have always acted from principles of honour and feeling towards you.' The hint was obvious: she could change if the £6,000 per annum were not increased to £10,000. Could not the Prince 'let me have a few lines <u>from yourself</u>, whom, Sir, notwithstanding all your prejudices against me and the misery and wretchedness you have entailed upon me, I shall ever rejoice to hear of your health, happiness and Prosperity'.

The perceptive Lady Anne gave several reasons for Maria's fight for the money: she 'wished to live more handsomely, to have more money to give away, to make more appearance, create more attention & pay off some little old scores [debts]'. Lady Anne was not happy with her friend's behaviour: 'Her reason had more of the waiting-maid than the lady in it. She then launched into much invective.' Lady Anne also observed a trait in Maria's character: 'The poor Fitz. is vainer & more triumphant when he behaves ill, than when he behaves well & to say the truth this is not unnatural.' The Prince, moved, or frightened, by Maria's latest letter, now sent McMahon to say that she could not have her £10,000 until the King died and would have to make do on £6,000 per annum, plus her own income. When Maria heard McMahon's offer she snapped. '"Dirty fellow," said she, "he pays none himself &

wishes to make a gain then of it on me by this trick: Oh how I hate his meanness."'

The fact is that after 1814 Maria was a wealthy woman. She had her £6,000 a year from the Prince and her own two jointures which altogether came to some £8,000 [£200,000] a year, plus her investments. We know that at the time of her death she had £28,726.18s.2d. in Three Percent Consols, Dutch guilders and Russian bonds. Although she had an interest in her childhood home, Brambridge, she had few if any obligations: for example, she had no estate or tenants' cottages to maintain. To put all this into some context we should remember that when Horace Walpole's friend, Mary Berry, drew up a budget in the 1790s for her intended marriage to a general, she calculated they would need £2,263 per annum to live in an upper-class manner of which £800 went to the general for his own pleasures.

Maria settled enormous sums on her two adopted daughters and helped various nieces. She also maintained sixteen servants in Brighton: three housemaids, a still-room maid, a kitchen maid, a scullery maid, a butler, underbutler, porter, coachman, two footmen, a housekeeper, a cook, a lady's maid, and 'Mrs Mills' who had joined her in 1799. There was also her chaplain, who was paid £50 a year, and two servants in Tilney Street. Maria also seemed to have a knack at buying and selling property. In 1824 she finally sold her Battersea home, Sherwood and she drove a hard bargain with the prospective buyer, Lord Darnley: 'Ld. D. has been with me every day since I saw you. I told him positively I could not think of parting with Sherwood for less than 12 [£12,000].' She also gave mortgages, a common practice for wealthy people who wished to get a higher return on their money and in 1830 she made over a £4,000 mortgage to her niece, Marianne. Her demand for her full annuity of £10,000 was finally realised in April 1820, some three months after George IV succeeded. Lady Anne described to her niece an incident when Maria called round in the wake of her triumph:[11]

I wish I had leisure to make you laugh at a visit I had from the Fitz. She affected not to care three straws about it. She said the Duke of Y. asked if she would not find it convenient now, 'I told him' said she 'that the only way the money could give me any pleasure would be to have it in guineas and throw it at the King's Head and knock him down with it' – 'If you did' said he, 'he would pick up the gold and pocket the affront' . . . she said that Miss Seymore was quite like a mad thing with joy to think there would be four horses now in both the carriages when they travelled, for the maids as well as for themselves . . . Fitz. can do nearly generous things, I doubt the young one a little . . . the Fitz. wished to suck my brains as to what she should do, or write without asking me to write it for her. She tried me in twenty ways.

Throughout his reign George IV was unpopular and increasingly he became a virtual prisoner of the Conyngham family and a man whose mind was constantly being poisoned against Maria by Sir William Knighton, his physician and, from 1822, private secretary. Knighton was as disliked as his master: Wellington called him 'the barber' and visitors to the King commented on the 'strange sort of power possessed by him' over George IV. If Knighton may be believed, during this period the King turned violently against Maria, as he did against so many former associates. Knighton claims the Prince 'had a horror of her' and never mentioned her name 'but with feelings of disgust and horror'. Regarding the marriage he claimed: 'it was an artificial marriage . . . just to satisfy her; that it was no marriage – for there could be none without a licence or some written document.' Maria's temper, he told Knighton, 'was violent in the extreme and there was no end to her jealousies'. During one 'fit of fury' she actually threw a slipper at him. According to the Prince's account, the 1794 separation resulted from 'an attempt, either real or artificial, to make the Prince jealous. The Prince thought it real but it was very possible

348

that he might have been mistaken.' Occasionally the King was capable of a more balanced view and in a postscript to Knighton in 1826 he wrote: 'Poor Mrs Fitz——t's suffering in spite of all, I can not help deeply participating in and commiserating.'[12]

While George IV's improvements to Windsor Castle gave us the splendid range of buildings we now have, he stayed within its walls, a virtual recluse. The Duke of Wellington believed that his ill health came from the 'effects of strong Liquors taken too frequently and in too large quantities. He drinks spirits morning, noon, & night; and he is obliged to take Laudanum to calm the Irritation.' This was in 1826 but twelve years earlier the Duke of Kent had told Maria that the King, then Prince Regent, was ill with snapped tendons and was consuming 'a most immoderate quantity of laudanum'. As the years wore on the poor man may well have been suffering from the same disease which had afflicted his father. Maria, who knew better than anyone the King's ability to sham illness and to make the most of real problems, did not take the stories of his situation seriously. In May 1830 she told Minney: 'The King is in the act of dying of a dropsy. I trust to his good constitution he will recover ... I remembered the King always liked to make himself out worse than he was to excite compassion, and he always wished everyone to think him dangerously ill, when little was the matter with him.' The reports from Windsor soon convinced her and the seventy-four-year-old lady travelled to her London home. There on a Sunday night she ignored the gout in her right hand that made writing so difficult and wrote her last letter to her 'secret husband' in a correspondence that stretched back at least forty-six years. In so doing she was opening herself to another rejection or at least, another unanswered letter. She sent it to the King's (and her) physician, Sir Henry Halford and it survives in the Royal Archives:[13]

Sir, After many repeated struggles with myself from the apprehension of appearing troublesome or intruding upon your Majesty after so many years of continual silence, my anxiety respecting your Majesty has got the better of my scruples & I trust your Majesty will believe me most sincere when I assure you how truly I have grieved to hear of your sufferings: from the late accounts I trust your Majesty's health is daily improving, and no one can feel more rejoiced to learn your Majesty is restor'd to complete convalescence, which I pray to God you may long enjoy, accompanied with every degree of happiness you can wish for or desire.

I have enclosed this letter to Sr H.H. as your Majesty must be aware there is no [other] person about him [the King] through whom I could make a communication of so private a nature attended with the perfect conviction of its never being divulged.

This is the letter of a proud woman who could not put aside her remembrance of past grievances. But it is also a generous letter of someone able to overcome her memories for the sake of a past love and because it was her duty as a Christian to forgive even if she could not forget. The letter was placed in the dying King's hands. The poor man was now so blind that it is highly unlikely he could have read it but he seized it with much emotion and placed it under his pillow. He was so ill that he could not even dictate a reply and Maria, not knowing this, later confessed to Lord Stourton that 'Nothing . . . had so 'cut her up,' to use her own expression, as not having received one word in reply to that last letter.' The King died on 26 June.

As he lay dying, however, the King made the Duke of Wellington promise that any ornaments he was wearing at the time of his death be buried with him and the Duke agreed. This later caused some confusion because the King's executors could not find Cosway's miniature of Maria which can only be opened by a secret spring. The Duke, who had also been asked by the King not to leave his body, explained: 'The Duke was quite alone with the body then lying in an open coffin and his curiosity being excited by seeing a small jewel hanging round the neck of the late King he was tempted to look at it, when he found it was the identical portrait of Mrs Fitzherbert covered with the diamond, for which the unsuccessful search had been made.' The Duke told the story to Minney who, when the time was right, told Maria. 'Mrs. Fitzherbert made no observation but soon large tears fell from her eyes.'[14] This story became public knowledge because Minney inherited Cosway's other locket-miniature, that of the Prince of Wales which she could not open. Once, when dining with the Duke she mentioned this and he showed her how to work the secret spring. The Duke then went on to tell his story.

The King, who died largely unmourned and unloved, was succeeded by his bluff brother, Clarence, who reigned as William IV. The new King commanded Maria to put her servants into royal livery and to go into mourning for her husband. He described his feelings for Maria later in a letter to the Duke of Wellington: 'The King has so long been upon terms of friendly intercourse with Mrs Fitzherbert and feels so great a regard for her', although privately, at least according to Sir George Seymour, he thought her marriage to his brother 'no Marriage whatever', a view also held by Wellington. William IV asked Maria to show him her marriage lines and afterwards commanded her to dine with him and the Queen at the Pavilion. The royal couple met Maria at the door thereby, in effect, paying her royal honours and afterwards the King took Maria into dinner on his arm. Most Sunday nights, when the King and Queen were in Brighton, Maria would dine with them. In exchange for the 1808 mortgage on the Pavilion, the King guaranteed her the same annual pension of £10,000 [£401,000] to be paid out of his Privy Purse and in this he was supported by his surviving brothers and sisters. The new King also ensured that the payment of this pension would continue after his death, and not be dependent on the will of his successor, Princess Victoria. Maria was, according to Marianne, delighted both at the honour and the money: 'Dear Mama is very much better & yesterday appeared in greater spirits than I have seen her in for some time past . . . Mama's despatch to the Bank concerning certain private

Papers proved extremely satisfactory . . . what she now enjoys is surely her right & as such who would attempt to deprive her of it?'

The King still wanted to give Maria a title and once, when Lord Egremont called and was shown into Maria's bedroom, she told him what had happened. The old roué drew his chair up to the bed and there followed a whispered conversation, out of hearing of Egremont's little granddaughter whom he had brought with him. 'The dear King came to me,' Maria told him with some exaggeration, 'and he went down on his knees to me, and begged me to be a Duchess.' The little girl overheard this part of their conversation and on their way home asked him, 'Grandpapa, why wouldn't that old lady be a Duchess?' 'Because she was an old fool, my dear.' Later William IV suggested making Minney a baroness in her own right with a remainder to her son. 'Mama, 'wrote Minney, 'is evidently tickled on the subject though she says Titles are nothing and money is what he ought to give.'[15] Nothing came of either proposal.

The King also ordered Sir George Seymour to deliver nine portraits of Maria, including two miniatures, which his brother had kept in the storeroom at Carlton House. Rather tactlessly, an unfinished portrait of Maria's predecessor, Perdita, came as well. The King and Queen's frequent visits to Brighton meant that Maria's declining years were filled with invitations, at last, to the exotic new Pavilion. When she visited in September 1830 it was the first time 'since I was drove away by Lady Hertford'. A typical evening was described by Lady Gower, later the Duchess of Sutherland. The party sat in one room whilst the Queen's Band played next door. The Queen sat with her ladies at a table where they worked at their sewing. The King fell asleep while the princesses played whist. The most explosive event of the evening was when the Queen pulled some detonating bonbons with Prince George of Cambridge. When Sir Francis Burdett, whose political career Maria and the Prince had helped decades earlier, was invited he found 'Mrs Fitzherbert looking handsomer than anyone. The

Queen was very particularly attentive to her. Indeed she merits it, in every point of view.'

These invitations by the King, combined with Maria's travels, her entertaining and her generally high spirits made these final years happy ones. Her passion for music and the theatre was as strong as ever and she raved about the playing of Paganini and the dancing of Taglioni. Her increasing Toryism meant that she was horrified by the 1830 revolution in France and by the Whig government of Lord Grey (the same man who had rushed to her rescue in 1787). By 1831 she was convinced that *'The People* are now our Sovereign, Ministers etc and their demands seem to be the order of the day.' Even in her eighties she was concerned that Minney, who was in Paris, send her a 'pot of rouge as I have not been able to get anything that is good for anything here'. 'I like it a dark colour and I put on very little but I must do something to make my pale face look its best.' Even Lady Holland, who seldom had a kind word for anyone, wrote that 'Mrs Fitz. is really in remarkable <u>beauty</u>, tho' her age is great.' For her part Maria regarded Lady Holland, who had a house opposite hers, as a 'dear friend', another example of Maria's fondness for ladies 'with a past'. Many would not receive Lady Holland who had been through a sordid divorce case.

But neither rouge nor high spirits could cure Maria of her increasing ailments. She was plagued by lumbago and rheumatism and she was beginning to lose strength in her legs but she remained undaunted: 'travelling and constant change of air does me always more good than all the medicines Halford or Jones can give me.' Even so, her declining health meant that on occasions her spirits were very low. On her seventy-fifth birthday in 1830 she told Minney, 'Dont wish me happy returns of this day. I do not desire them for myself. I often regret (though I am told it is wrong) that I ever was born' and she even returned Minney's gift which was 'much too fine to make use of'.

Like anyone who has a long life, Maria had to endure the deaths of those she loved and sometimes of those she did not: one suspects she shed few tears when Gillray died insane in 1815 and she must have inwardly rejoiced when informed of Knighton's death in 1836. Maria was never very close to any of her siblings other than Jack, who, as we have already noted, died suddenly in 1812. Walter had inherited Brambridge and died childless in 1822. When in 1831 Colonel John Gurwood, a retired officer who became a close friend in her declining years, passed on a plan for a family reunion from her brother, Charles, Maria showed no lessening of her old spirit and use of graphic language:

> Your account of Charles is really quite disgusting. He fancies himself the greatest lawyer and judicial man existing and he is so obstinate there is no doing anything for him. I cannot help laughing at his plan of reunion . . . I and Lady Haggerston have quarrelled more than twenty years ago about some trifling money concerns for she has always been, where money was the object, a counterpart of himself but now that she is in the possession of 8 or 9 thousand per annum she perhaps may alter her conduct. She has added so much to the miseries of my life that though I forgive I cannot forget and we have not seen each other for 17 or 18 years. It would be a comical assemblage were we all to meet in one of the Pig Styes. She might be tempted if she thought she could carry away two or three of his pigs. It can never take place but if it amuses him to think about it there is no harm done.

Charles, who had inherited Brambridge from Walter, died in 1832 and, as Princess Elizabeth noted, 'his two daughters come into a very large property.' Maria was left as executrix and had to arrange for the closing up of Brambridge and the rights of Charles's illegitimate daughter; she was left a 'fortune' but could not marry without Maria's permission. Four years later, in 1836, Lady Haggerston died, unreconciled to her more famous sister. The eldest child had survived the longest.

All those who had played important parts in Maria's early life went before her. Sheridan had died in 1816 and in the following year her Uncle Errington. John McMahon died that same year, 1817, and Lord Moira in 1826. Her closest female friend, and most acute critic, Lady Anne, died in 1825 and in 1836 Maria lost Lady Downshire, 'a constant & affectionate friend to me from our earliest youth'. Maria told Marianne, 'Alas almost all my old Friends are gone. It is melancholy to think of it.' In her 'other' family, that of George III, the Duchess of York, who never treated Maria as a sister-in-law, died in 1820, the same year as Maria's friend, the Duke of Kent. Seven years later the Duke of York died. With each death Maria was becoming a relic of the past.

Declining health, the conservatism that comes with increasing years and the death of George IV in 1830 naturally made Maria anxious regarding her 'papers', her marriage lines, the Will and letters from the Prince and other members of the Royal Family which she kept locked in a metal box that was always with her. The trouble first arose in 1817 when McMahon died and Sir William Knighton found letters from Maria on his desk. Knighton regarded Maria as an 'artful, cunning, designing woman, very selfish, with a temper of the worse description, and a mind entirely under the influence of Popish superstition'. The Prince Regent, increasingly afraid 'lest she should make use of some of the documents . . . to annoy or injure him' wanted Maria's letters and also those letters from himself in her possession. Perhaps he remembered what his Uncle Gloucester had told him years before: 'I must agree with you, Dear Sir, that letters are always dangerous things.' According to Knighton who tried to get them she was 'too artful to comply' and 'trumped up a story' that Knighton would not return her letters to McMahon in return for hers to him. In this she was backed by the Duke of York. Knighton had hurried to see Uncle Errington concerning a general exchange of letters between Maria and the Prince Regent but this came to nothing. According to the diarist, Charles Greville, this was not the whole story. Although Knighton was disliked by Maria he called at her house, 'when she was ill in bed, insisted upon seeing her, and forced his way into her bedroom. She contrived (I forget how) to get rid of him without his getting anything out of her, but this domiciliary visit determined her to make a final disposition of all the papers she possessed, that in the event of her death no advantage might be taken of them either against her own memory or the interests of any other person.'[16]

The next crisis came in 1826 with the declining health of her long-time friend and correspondent, the Duke of York. What would happen to her letters to him? She wrote in obvious relief that she was delighted 'to know that they are in such safe keeping, for I cannot tell you how much it annoy'd me the fear of their falling into improper Hands'. Maria and the Duke then agreed that 'all their correspondence should be destroyed' and after his death in 1827 she spent two years 'in the perusal and burning of these most interesting letters'. In her recollections the memory of her set-to with Knighton makes sense of an otherwise mysterious passage: 'When Sir Herbert Taylor [the late Duke of York's private secretary] surrendered them to her in person, she told him that she had been almost afraid that *they* [author's italics] would have got these papers from him. He replied, "Not all the kings upon earth should have obtained them."'[17] The letters were burnt and with them a remarkable insight into British history vanished.

George IV's death in 1830 brought affairs to a crisis because Maria was terrified at what Knighton, a co-executor with Wellington, might do. She must have brooded over this and once, when she was with William IV in Brighton in 1832 she told him of her fears. She was right to be terrified, as a letter from Knighton to the Iron Duke shows: 'Could His late Majesty have supposed it possible that Mrs. Fitzherbert would have been brought to the King's table immediately after his death, in widow's weeds, surrounded by the Royal Family?' Luckily for her it was the Duke of Wellington's duty (and not Knighton's) to sort out his dead sovereign's papers, including those relating to Maria. The Duke used Minney as a means to approach Maria, who wanted her letters returned. This the Duke rejected: he wanted everything burnt except her mortgage on the Royal Pavilion. This Maria rejected in a furious letter. She accepted that the Duke and Knighton had the power to dispose of papers relating to the late King but not those few documents that she felt secured her position as his wife:

> I cannot refrain from expressing my utmost surprise & I must add my Indignation that such a demand should be made to me. The papers & letters are too intimately connected with, & confined to my own private affairs, for me ever to listen to such a proposal as to one that would put them out of my own Keeping. I must be allowed to repeat that the more I reflect upon the subject the more surprised I am that such a request should ever have been intimated to me.

By March 1833 a compromise had been reached, although the subject 'makes me rather nervous': she and the Duke agreed for a mutual exchange and destruction. Maria insisted that Knighton have nothing to do with the matter and appointed Lord Albemarle, Master of the Horse to William IV, and her cousin, Lord Stourton, to represent her. Stourton was keen to have the marriage certificate retained or, if burnt, he wanted its destruction 'recorded'. The Duke rejected this 'as he conceived it would imply that he considered the document to a certain degree valid, and of some importance'. The obvious solution was to leave it with Maria. The one paper that could not be found was of course the letter from the Pope regarding Maria's return to the Prince which Maria had destroyed. She now asked that the papers be sent to her London home where she could look over them.[18]

On 24 August 1833 an Agreement was drawn up. The object was stated by Lord Albemarle in a letter to Maria: 'the destruction & the preventing of the unnecessary publication of the [word indecipherable] Papers and the preservation of the documents essential for us to keep'. The 'essential' documents were: the mortgage on the Pavilion; her marriage certificate; a letter from the Prince relating to the marriage; the Will of 10 January 1796; the letter of 25 February 1791 which Robert Burt had written regarding the prebend's stall at Rochester and on which Maria had written, 'The writer of this letter the Revd Mr Burt is the Clergyman that perform'd the Ceremony of the Marriage of H.R.H. the Prince & Mrs. Fitzherbert'; and, finally, the Prince's enormous letter of 3 November 1785 written to Maria just before she decided to return to England. The Duke's experience had given him a high view of Maria: she was 'the most honest woman he has met'.

Maria's 'essential' documents were then deposited in Coutts Bank where they stayed until the opening years of the twentieth century when King Edward VII gave W.H. Wilkins permission to publish selections in his biography of Maria. The King also ordered the papers removed to the Royal Archives. On 24 August 1833 the Duke of Wellington and Lord Albemarle met in Maria's drawing room in Tilney Street. She handed them a packet of letters and then left. The two men then began their task and after several hours the Duke commented, 'I think, my Lord, we had better hold our hand for a while, or we shall set the old woman's chimney on fire.' It is said the white mantel retained a smoke stain for years afterwards and Maria complained that the room 'smelt of burnt paper and sealing-wax for weeks.' The exercise left Maria emotionally drained and she soon left for the long visit to Aix-la-Chapelle mentioned earlier.

As late as July 1836 the Duke was still burning the Prince's love letters. In Maria's case the agreement only applied to correspondence with the Prince. That with other people, including other members of the Royal Family, was excluded. Shortly before her death she asked Minney to return to Princess Victoria, whom she regarded as her niece by marriage, those letters from her father, the Duke of Kent. In her note accompanying the letters Minney referred to 'my dear Mother (by adoption)'. In 1913 there was another proposed burning of letters when George V ordered Lord Esher, who detested George IV, to burn correspondence between

Maria and the Prince, what Esher called 'the rigmarole of Mrs Fitzherbert and "Bessie Pigott" her friend – masses of them'.[19] Given that the Esher Papers in the Royal Pavilion's Archives contain many letters from the Prince, as well as letters to and from Bell Pigot, one wonders if Lord Esher did as he was commanded.

If one of the reasons for burning her letters to and from the Prince was to keep them out of the hands of would-be hostile biographers, it was perfectly natural that Maria should wish to leave behind a history of her great romance as *she* wanted it remembered. She may have recently seen what writers could do. Within months of George IV's death two biographies appeared, both hostile to her. The first came out in 1830 and was written by the Rev. George Croly. A mixture of gossip and research, this book discussed the marriage in great detail but admitted that it 'has been neither proved nor disproved. It is rumoured that the lady's scruples were soothed by having the ceremony performed according to the rites of her own church.' Though it was no real marriage Maria 'still enjoys at least the gains of the connexion; and up to the hoary age of seventy-five, calmly draws her salary of ten thousands pounds a year! The theme is repulsive.' Croly had no doubt that this 'most unhappy intercourse' was the foundation for all the Prince's subsequent 'calamities'.

The following year Robert Huish, who was described by the *Quarterly Review* in 1836 as an 'obscure and unscrupulous scribbler', brought out his *Memoirs of George the Fourth* in two volumes. He savaged the dead King as a seducer of virgins and an accomplice in murder in his arrangements to borrow money from Holland. Like Croly, Huish paid a great deal of attention to Maria whom he described as vain and arrogant, as someone who demanded 'the sanction of some ceremony, whatever the nature of that ceremony may have been'. However his main desire was to discredit George IV and to play on traditional anti-popery feelings. In some passages he actually praised Maria for her moderate behaviour. Huish's book was followed in 1832 by a scurrilous work written by Lady Anne Hamilton, part of Queen Caroline's set. This actually had a good word to say for Maria and claimed that George III 'considered the Prince's marriage with Mrs Fitzherbert solemn and binding in the sight of heaven, though certainly in direct opposition to the law of the country'. With such support Maria had no need of enemies.

Maria, did need someone she could trust to write down the story of her great romance as *she* wanted it written. Lord Stourton, a fellow Catholic and her cousin by marriage, was one of the people – Mrs Creevey, Humphrey Weld, Sir George Seymour and George Dawson-Damer were others – to whom Maria confided her 'secret history' and showed various papers. Stourton admitted that 'from my earliest days I have been taught so highly to respect and regard' Maria. With this background it is not surprising that he engaged in those long talks which would later bear fruit as the first defence of her character. Lord Stourton was also something of a worrier: what use might people make of her surviving papers after her death? Of more importance to us, Stourton worried about the suggestion of any children from Maria's marriage: this was a question 'which may possibly be of value to more distant times, though of no apparent interest at the moment – namely, an acknowledgement in your own hand-writing of no issue under a marriage that the common Law of England or Roman Catholic law holds to be valid although the Parliamentary Law of England does not acknowledge its validity . . . History is full of claimants of a doubtful origin.' Stourton said Maria might 'confirm or laugh at my over-scrupulous care of the interests of future generations'. Maria chose to laugh and with a gentle smile refused to write out such a statement, thereby perversely giving apparent support to those who over the years have claimed the very thing Lord Stourton was trying to avoid.[20]

1837 saw Maria's health start to decline but even so her spirits were good and she was beginning to make plans for another visit to Paris in May 1838. For the time being she kept up her routine and, despite her tendency to colds and the bad weather, she insisted on her carriage rides. One such ride, on 21 March, brought on another cold and produced a high fever. When this did not go down, Minney and Marianne, along with their children, were sent for. They found Fr Lopez at her bedside, having administered the Last Rites. On 27 March, a rough and windy day with the odd burst of sunshine, Maria grew weaker and quietly, and without effort, yielded up her soul. She had told her solicitor that 'the Cemetery on the Harrow Road [Kensal Green] wd. be the best place, but that she understood there wd. be some objection on acct. of her religion – she added, with one of her sweet smiles, "it is a matter of not the slightest importance where I am placed."' There must also have been some talk that Maria's nephew by marriage, Thomas Weld, who had become a priest and then a cardinal after his wife died, might take the service but this proved impossible.

Father Lopez converted Maria's bedroom into a *chapelle ardente* where her body lay in state for several days. When someone went to remove her wedding rings only two were found: the third, that given her by the Prince of Wales, had already been removed by Minney. When Maria's coffin was closed it was covered with a crimson pall on which were placed a few white roses, George IV's favourite flower, the same flower that had decorated her house at the grand reunion breakfast which marked their reconciliation in 1800. Nuns watched over the body until the funeral on 4 April. It was arranged for someone to paint a last picture of Maria on the day she died. A friend of Minney, Lady Morgan, saw the portrait, the last in that long line that included works by Gainsborough, Romney, Rowlandson, Cosway, Reynolds and Hoppner: 'It was curious (but not an unusual thing) that her face had fallen into its original form; its fine osteology was perfect; the few furrows that time had traced upon its round muscles had disappeared – it presented a fine and firm oval face – the beautiful mouth – a high and rather Roman nose. The simple dress of death (not the most unbecoming she ever wore) added to the solemn beauty of her appearance.'

Maria's funeral procession wound its way from the Steine to the new Catholic church of St John the Baptist in the Bristol Road. The funeral was an impressive sight: it began with two mutes followed by the undertaker and his assistant, after whom came a page and the 'state line of feathers' supported by a 'featherman' and five more mutes. Then came four more pages, a hearse drawn by six horses decorated with feathers and velvets, and then five mourning coaches, each drawn by four horses – each with feathers and velvets – and accompanied by a page. The final vehicle was Maria's private coach. The principal mourners, who would have been men, were the Earl of Munster, the King's eldest illegitimate son, representing William IV, Colonel Dawson-Damer, the Hon. Edward Jerningham and Colonel Gurwood. Sixteen of her servants were in attendance and Minney and Marianne waited in the black-draped church.

Maria was buried in a vault under the church. The entrance is in the floor of the central aisle, almost directly opposite the memorial her two honorary daughters would later erect. On the stone covering the entrance is written, simply:

Maria Fitzherbert

1756–1837

R.I.P.

Perhaps appropriately, the window to the left shows St Elizabeth of Hungary, a much-wronged Queen who suffered at the hands of her husband. The monument which was put up later, shows Maria kneeling at a *prie-dieu* on which rests an open book. On one page is a cross and on the other, a quote from Acts XX. 35: 'It is a more blessed thing to give than to receive.' On top of the book is a lamp. On the third finger of her left hand there are three wedding rings for Edward Weld, Thomas Fitzherbert, and the Prince of Wales.

Maria died a wealthy woman. Her estate was valued at £36,859.1s.6d. [£1,443,000], although there were debts for

£2,791.18s.9d. She left £1,000 to her sometimes tiresome sister-in-law, 'Mrs Wat', and the same amount to each of her nieces. A trust fund had already been set up for Minney's children. Her cherished possessions were divided between her two 'daughters'. As she had written in a codicil: 'I pray to God they may both live long with sincere affection and attachment to each other . . . I have loved them both with the tenderest affection any mother could do, and I have done the utmost in my power for their interests and comfort.'

Maria left the two large portraits of her by Gainsborough to George Dawson-Damer – these had hung in her dining room. Minney received the portrait of George IV by Vigée Le Brun and a round Sèvres table, and Marianne, a small commode inlaid with Sèvres china. Maria's plate, valued at £1559.12s.0d. [£61,000], and 'her personal trinkets' or jewellery, valued only at £950 [£38,000], were divided between Minney and Marianne. (This implies that she had already given away most of the jewels she had bought or been given over the years.) The mourning for her twenty-two servants was paid for by her estate and, while her servants received £30 per annum annuities, some of her oldest and most trusted also got legacies ranging from £25.12s.0d, to £400.

One rather thinks Maria, with her capacity for frank language and her robust sense of the ridiculous, would have enjoyed over-hearing a conversation between Lord Hatherton, a Staffordshire landholder, and a member of the Fitzherbert family a few days after her death. Richard Fitzherbert 'told me', noted Lord Hatherton, 'that his Brother would get £1000 a year by her death – she having received that amount of jointure from the estate of Swinerton for 59 years.'[21]

One of the last views we have of Maria comes from an upholsterer named William Saunders who came to do some work for her in the late 1830s. In 1903 he told W.H. Wilkins how he helped Maria rearrange the hundreds of silhouettes of her friends that lined the walls of her little salon where select friends came for her *petites causeries.* She asked the young man about himself and about how he liked his work and spoke in 'a low, sweet voice, and every word was very distinctly uttered'. Her complexion was pale, indeed 'her face was as colourless as wax, which made her bright, dark eyes seem all the brighter by contrast.' The young workman could still see 'the remains of a beautiful woman. She seemed happy, even cheerful, but except when her face was lit up with her sweet smile, she wore a look of settled sadness . . . I venerated her for the kind, though dignified, manner in which she could speak to a young working-man as well as to a prince.'

The old woman, as this biography has tried to show, was not the same as the young woman. Time and disappointment take the edges off our faults and sometimes expose our virtues. Maria's last years, in which her hitherto frustrated maternal instincts could flourish, did this. The fires that had roared in earlier years were largely dampened. After 1830 the great passion that had so altered her life – perverted, Lady Anne might have said – was over. The fire was put out and only the embers survived. Some of her less attractive passions, her arrogance and pride, were lessened, while her best traits, her frankness, her robust sense of humour, her honesty and her independent spirit – which had won and helped to lose the Prince – survived, as did her capacity for kindness.

Among Lord Esher's papers in Brighton's Royal Pavilion is a poem written by the Prince of Wales. Although it is not specifically addressed to Maria, we may assume it was composed for her. It is not great verse but it helps to explain the love that inspired this extraordinary romance:

> For such as these, my Torch burns bright & pure
> And shall to Life's last moments so endure.
> Yes cried the God, each Year shall in its wing
> Unfading & substantial pleasures bring.
> And when at length, age sheds his silv'ry snows
> Upon their Head, & when no longer glows
> Their frame with smiling Youth's ethereal fire,

Still in their Hearts *my* flame shall not expire.
Blest in each others' Hearts, these *well tried*
Each other's dearest Blessing, comfort, pride
They shall remain – & when his course is run
And set in death is Life's glorious Sun
Hand link'd in hand, they both Shall wing their way
To blissful regions of eternal Day.

The last words on Maria's great love should come from two people who knew most about it, the Duke of Wellington and the Duchess of Devonshire. The Duke reflected in 1835 that: 'No woman was ever really attached to him – Mrs. F. perhaps the most. He was too selfish.' The Duchess of Devonshire, writing during the Regency crisis, admitted that the Prince usually told people what he thought they wanted to hear. But, she insisted: 'his talents are good, and his manner and deportment superior in grace to any thing I ever saw. And however he may have appear'd to deviate from strict honor, or to be capricious and unsteady, I cannot believe his heart to be bad – but he has obey'd the Star of the moment which has unfortunately been in general Malignant.' On Maria, however, the last word must come from her friend and close observer, Lady Anne: 'In spite of much nonsense, some haughtiness, some duplicity, I like her. She is . . . lovely and lovable amidst her circle of foibles and follies . . . whose inconsistencies will deserve a long chapter from some historian who will attempt to draw her character.' Elsewhere Lady Anne wrote: 'There is no evil in her beyond the infirmities of Human Nature.' She may be defined as an ordinary woman who found herself in a most extraordinary situation and therein lay her appeal, then as now.

EPILOGUE

---◆---

MRS FITZHERBERT'S HONOUR

Within days of Maria's death *The Times*, on 5 April, was pronouncing on 'the marriage'. The paper declared it, 'invalid'. It was 'either a cruel imposition to silence the scruples of a virtuous though weak minded woman, or an hypocritical pretext adopted by the lady herself to cover her shame'. It accepted, however, that some constitutional lawyers, including the late Sir Arthur Pigott, regarded it as 'valid' but it warned Maria's 'friends' not to talk about the marriage – 'observe strict silence' – for everyone's good. In part the paper had in mind a meeting, four days earlier, of the South London Protestant Association. Amongst those giving addresses was a Captain Gordon who talked about a 'confederacy of Popery and infidelity'. He reported that in 1796 there were no more than twenty Catholic chapels but now there were more than five hundred; in 1796 there was not one Catholic college, whereas in 1837 there were eleven, plus several monasteries and convents, Catholics were now ready for the 'enslavement of the people'. Instead *The Times* said, Maria's friends should talk about, 'her unaffected and never-failing courtesies, her unpretending and amiable demeanour, her constant and active benevolence'. If her friends do not stop talking about the marriage, the paper warned, 'we must reluctantly go more fully into the subject'.

Chief among these 'friends' were John Gurwood and, more especially, Lord Stourton who came forward as Maria's knight in shining armour. In 1837 he approached the Duke of Wellington for permission to publish the papers in Coutts Bank 'as justification of Mrs Fitzherbert's honor'. The Duke almost agreed but then changed his mind and told Stourton he would get a court injunction if necessary to stop them. Stourton gave up for the time being but in 1838 defended Maria's behaviour in the *Edinburgh Review*. After his death his brother, the Hon. Charles Langdale, tried to get hold of the papers at Coutts, saying he had been given 'control of the above packet' by his brother. He was anxious to publish both his brother's 'memoirs' and the supporting evidence 'as justification of Mrs Fitzherbert's honor' but the Duke of Wellington remained opposed and told him to ask Lord Melbourne, the Prime Minister, for a decision. There the matter dropped. Then, in 1854, Lord Holland's *Memoirs of the Whig Party* were published. In which he praised Maria's character but argued that she knew her marriage 'to be invalid in law; she thought it nonsense, and told the Prince so.' This so annoyed the Langdale family that in 1856 Charles Langdale once again approached those now in charge of the box at Coutts. The bank refused to co-operate and Langdale then published Lord Stourton's *Memoirs of Mrs. Fitzherbert* which gave the world the story of Maria's great romance as she wished it told.[1]

It was not until 1905, when W.H. Wilkins brought out *Mrs. Fitzherbert and George IV*, that proof of the marriage was published. In 1936 Maria's story once again gained the Royal Family's attention during a dinner party given by Edward VIII. In addition to Mrs Simpson, his guests included the Duke and Duchess of York (later King George VI and Queen Elizabeth) and Winston Churchill. Churchill, a cousin of Shane Leslie, introduced the topic of Maria's 1785 marriage, perhaps as a half-serious solution to the King's marital dilemma. The Duchess of York replied. 'That was a very long time ago!' After this the future Prime Minister turned the conversation to the Wars of the Roses to which the Duchess replied even more firmly, '*That* was a very, *very* long time ago!'[2]

Three years later, in 1939, Shane Leslie's biography was published by the Catholic firm, Burns Oates. In 1940 he published a collection of most, but by no means all, of her letters. Largely because of his work, Maria Fitzherbert's great romance has been kept alive in the British imagination. (Leslie was the great-grandson of Maria's adopted daughter, Minney.) In 1947 Maria gained even wider fame when the film, *Mrs. Fitzherbert*, was released and years later she was represented in two stage plays, *The Madness of King George III* and *Battle Royal*. She has featured in numerous television programmes and romantic novels whilst a mid-twentieth century Staffordshire figurine now sells for over £1000. Meanwhile the number of her and the Prince's alleged 'descendants' grows by leaps and bounds.

The buildings associated with Maria's life have not survived as well as her memory. The Acton Burnell Hall that she had known as a child was rebuilt in the classical style in 1811. The family later abandoned the house, after which it became the Convent of Our Lady of Sion and the Smythe baronetcy died out in 1942. The building now houses Concord College, an international school. Maria's childhood home at Tong Castle fared much worse. The village and its church became famous after Dickens used them in *The Old Curiosity Shop* – Tong was the place where Little Nell and her grandfather found a home. The Castle was eventually abandoned and by 1913 it was unoccupied. The buildings gradually became ruins and in the 1950s a child was killed while climbing on the walls. On 18 July 1954 the ruins were blown up by the Territorial Army. Insult was added to injury when the M54 motorway was built over the site.

Brambridge, where Maria spent most of her childhood, suffered a similar fate: the building was destroyed by fire in February 1872 and a new house, now divided into flats, was put up on its site.

However, the fast-running Itchen still flows nearby and a famous avenue of limes, planted on the suggestion of Charles I, has survived. The land once owned by Maria's father and brothers has given way to a nature reserve and the Brambridge Park Garden Centre which does boast that it is 'the childhood home of Maria Smythe'.

Lulworth Castle, Maria's first home as a wedded bride, almost shared the fate of Tong Castle. During the Great War the Welds allowed the army to use the outer parts of the estate, especially Bindon Hill, for gunnery practice and after the war the War Office compulsorily purchased the land for nearby Bovington Camp (itself made famous by its association with Lawrence of Arabia). For the family the thud of cannon fire and the roar of tanks were not as bad as a lawsuit which meant that the then owner had to sell about one-third of the estate, and also lost so many of the objects associated with Maria. The painting of Edward Weld with his two wives, the earliest painting of Maria Fitzherbert, had already disappeared.

As if this were not bad enough fire broke out in the Castle in August 1929 and, although much furniture was rescued, the building was gutted and by the 1980s looked set to follow Tong's history. Luckily the Weld family, working with English Heritage, were able to rescue the building, rebuild the walls and install a new roof. This means that the famous Castle is now once again usable for various functions. The family, which has done so much to preserve its famous home, lives nearby. The wonderful views from its four towers remain remarkably similar to what Maria would have seen 226 years ago.

Swynnerton, still the home of the Fitzherbert family, is the only one of Maria's homes to have survived as it was in her time. Its grandeur is intact, its views remain splendid and it resonates with the sounds of a new generation of Fitzherberts. But the Fitzherberts are now the Staffords. Marianne's daughter married a Fitzherbert and in 1913 their son inherited the barony, which the son of the Lady Jerningham of our story fought so hard to regain.

Of Maria's own homes, only Marble Hill survives largely as she would have known it. Her houses in Tilney Street and Park Street were both pulled down in the twentieth century, while those she occupied in Parson's Green and Sherwood Lodge are also gone. Sadly her splendid house in Brighton still stands but in a form she could hardly recognise. In 1884 it passed into the hands of the YMCA which, in 1924, added an extra floor and altered the front. It is now a centre for homeless people with drink or drug-related problems. While the great staircase, up which Lord Barrymore rode the horse that could not be got down, survives, the building has been divided into scores of tiny rooms, each occupied by someone for whom life has become a tragedy. Maria's great drawing-room, where the Duchess of Devonshire once danced with the young Etonian and where Maria told her secrets to Mrs Creevey, is now a recreation room but one hardly used in this saddest of buildings. One can still see, just, faint memories of Maria's ownership. One staircase leads to the oratory with a door entering through an alcove in which the altar must have stood. In a large cupboard one may still see the marvellous Delft tiles, with their scenes of military horsemanship, that would have been on either side of her Adam fireplaces: nothing else survives.

Yet all is not gloom. In 1999 Russell's pastel portrait of Maria, some of her jewellery, her work-box in the shape of a spinet and her circular silver enamelled box were on display in the Northern Treasures Exhibition. The Catholic church of St John the Baptist is still there and is well looked after and round the corner is the parish's Fitzherbert Centre which is used for day care and other activities for the local community. On the church's outside wall there is a small round plaque which reads: 'Herein Lies the Tomb of Maria Fitzherbert 1756–1837.'

Even greater fame has been given to Maria's 'Roman Catholic nose'. On the Internet a plastic surgeon, Dr Michael Bermant of Chester, Virginia has created a web-site (www.plasticsurgery4u.com) in which he uses the Gainsborough portrait of Maria as an example of those in need of a 'nasal dorsal hump reduction'. The website also displays a 'corrected' version of the portrait to show what the surgeon's knife can do. One can almost hear Maria's rich laughter echoing down the years.

Notes

---•◦•---

Abbreviations

H.R.O.	Hampshire Record Office
H.M.C.	Historical Manuscripts Commission
J.B.B.	James Bland Burges
M.F.	Maria Fitzherbert
P. of W.	Prince of Wales
R.A.	Royal Archives

Full information for shortened entries of sources frequently cited will be found in the Bibliography.

Chapter 1 A Recusant Childhood

1. *London Chronicle*, 7–10 Sept. 1771.
2. *Advice to Protestants . . .*, Stafford MS, D641/3/X/2/2.
3. Register of Papists' Estates. Smythe MS, QE 3/3/1 (1717–1788).
4. Anon [The Rev Joseph Berington], *The State and Behaviour of English Catholics . . .* (1780), p. 115. John Bossy, *The English Catholic Community 1570–1850* (1975), pp. 329, 150.
5. Anon., [Richard Challoner], *The Garden of the Soul . . .* (1755), p.155. S.B. [Simon Berington], *A Modest Enquiry . . .* (1749), pp. 1–2, 143.
6. [Joseph Berington], *State and Behaviour of English Catholics*, p. 95.
7. [Simon Berington], *A Modest Enquiry*, pp.1–2. [Challoner], *The Garden of the Soul*, pp. 141–2.
8. Charles Butler, *Reminiscences* (1824, 4th edn.), pp.4–5, 8. Butler, who would become the first Catholic barrister to plead since the reign of James II, was at Douai from 1759–66. He would later be involved in

arranging Maria's second marriage settlement. [Joseph Berington], *State and Behaviour of English Catholics*, p. 128.

9. Dr Peter Broucek, Direktor des Österreichisches Staatsarchiv: Kriegsarchivs to the author, 30 July 1997. We do know that Walter's son visited a cousin in Waldeeks Dragoons in 1793 and families often favoured one particular regiment. See William Smythe to Hugh Smythe, 30 Sept. 1793 in Hugo Smythe MS., 1655/7.

10. M.F. to Lady Anne Barnard, 28 Aug. 1811, Crawford-Balcarres MS., II and M.F. q. by Lady Anne Barnard, Crawford-Balcarres MS., I. Miles Langdale to Sir Edward Smythe, 23 Nov. 1758, Smythe MS., 1514/1/124. Paul Stamper, *A Survey of Historic Parks and Gardens in Shropshire* (The Archaeology Unit, Shropshire County Council, 1993), Report No. 41. 1993, p.291.

11. Henry Moody, *Antiquities and Topographical Sketches of Hampshire* (1846), q. in R.C. Baigent [ed], *The Catholic Registers of the Brambridge . . .* (1927), *Catholic Record Society Miscellanea*, Vol. XXVII.5. In 1717 the 'Roll of Particulars of Papists' Estates' for Hampshire show two 'Wells,' Thomas and Henry. Between them they owned two 'mansion houses', manors, woods, seven houses, ten farms, a mill, and several cottages. Quarter Session Records, H.R.O., Q25/3/7. Charles Wells, his wife, two daughters and a son are the second entry, in 'A Lyst of the names of the Popist Recusants within the county of Southton.', H.R.O., Top Hants. 3/1/2.

12. Langdale, pp. 113–4.

Chapter 2 Twice Wed, Twice Widowed

1. Wilkins, p. 9. Leslie, *Mrs Fitzherbert*, p. 8.

2. Lady Anne Lindsay, Preface to a Tour to Spa, Brussels, Holland & Paris 1784 & 1785, Crawford-Balcarres MS, Vol. I. This information could only have come from M.F. Edward Weld, *Engagement Book [for 1773]*, Weld MS., D/WLC/F/42.

3. *Deo Opt. Maximo Conclusiones Phylosophicae. Ex Physica.* in Weld MS., D/WLC/C/22. Edward Weld Jnr to Edward Weld Snr. 2 March 1761, Weld MS., D/WLC/C/22. Edward Weld Jnr to Edward Weld Snr. 2 Aug. 1761 in Weld MS., D/WLC/C/22.

4. J. Jones to Edward Weld, 23 June 1774 in Weld MS., D/WLC/C/80.

5. J. Jones to Edward Weld, 23 June 1774 in Weld MS., D/WLC/C/80. Thomas and Mary Weld to Edward Weld, 16 Dec 1774 in Weld MS.,

D/WLC/C/52. Mary Weld to Edward Weld, 18 Dec. 1774 in Weld MS., D/WLC/C/69.

6. John Wall to Edward Weld, 22 Febr. 1775 in Weld MS., D/WLC/C/85.
7. The Rev. Henry Bate q. in W.T. Whitley, *Thomas Gainsborough* (1915), pp. 355–6.
8. Joan Berkeley, *Lulworth and the Welds* (Gillingham, Dorset, 1971), p.56.
9. Thomas Weld to Edward Weld, 8 Jan. 1774 in Weld MS., D/WLC/C/52.
10. Joseph Weld q. by Charles Weld Blundell to W.H. Wilkins in *Wilkins*, p. 10. H.G. Belsey, Curator, Gainsborough's House, Sundbury to the author, 7 Aug. 1998. For the portrait seeCh. VI.
11. Tobias Smollet, *The Expedition of Humphry Clinker* (1771),p. 103–5.
12. Richard Trappes-Lomax, 'Boys at Liège Academy 1773–1791' in *Catholic Record Miscellany* VIII (1913), p.210.
13. Lord Glenbervie, 16 June 1812 in Walter Sichel [ed], *The Glenbervie Journals* (1910, two vols.). II.157. Mary, Lady Jerningham to her daughter, Lady Bedingfeld, 12 Jan. 1819, *Jerningham Letters*, II. 127–8. Amanda Foreman, *Georgiana Duchess of Devonshire* (1998), p. 123.
14. Charlotte Papendiek [Mrs Vernon Delves Broughton, ed], *Court and Private Life in the Time of Queen Charlotte* . . . (1887, two vols.), I.230. Katherine C. Balderston [ed], *Thraliana: The Diary of Mrs Hester Lynch Thrale* . . . (Oxford, 1951 2nd ed., two vols.), II.918. Mrs Thrale ties the presentation with carrying her daughter, Susan, who was actually born on 23 May 1770. Mrs Thrale must have meant her daughter, Cecilia, born on 8 February 1777. This would put the presentation, if it occurred, sometime between July 1776 and February 1777. Confusion was probably a by-product of twelve pregnancies. Lady Anne Lindsay, Crawford-Balcarres MS., Vol. I.
15. Lady Anne Lindsay, Crawford-Balcarres MS., Vol. I.
16. Charles Butler, *Historical Memoirs* . . . (1819–1821, four vols.), II.83. *Gentleman's Magazine* (June 1778), p. 282.
17. William Archer, 'Goods and Effects of Thomas Fitzherbert the Father', Stafford MS, D641/5/T(S)/4/13iii.
18. Lady Anne Lindsay to M.F., 20 April 1813, Crawford-Balcarres MS., Vol. II. M.F. to Lady Anne Lindsay, n.d. [June or July 1785], Crawford-Balcarres MS., Vol. II.
19. Sylvester Douglas, diary entry for 27 Mar. 1796, Francis Bickley [ed], *The Diaries of Sylvester Douglas (Lord Glenbervie)* (1928, two vols.), I.69. Judith Milbanke to Mary Noel, 11 July 1784, Malcolm Elwin [ed], *The Noels and the Milbankes* . . . (1967), p. 238.
20. M. F. to Mrs Fermor, [1 April 1780], Fermor MS., Letter No. 1. The six

letters to the Fermors were published in L.G. Wickham Legg [ed], *Tusmore Papers* (Oxfordshire Record Society, 1939), vol. XX, Section xxii, pp. 52–60. Both Maria and her husband often disregarded giving dates and in only one case can we be positive.

21. G.L. Dawson Damer, Memorandum of 14 Nov. 1836, q. in Anita Leslie, *Mrs Fitzherbert* (1960), p. 21. A somewhat jumbled version of the same story, brought forward to 1784, was recorded by J.W. Croker, journal entry for 7 Dec. 1818 in Louis J. Jennings, *The Croker Papers . . .* (1884, three vols.),I. 122–3.

22. *Wraxall: Memoirs*, I.233. Richard Dyot to his Father, n.d. [? June 1780, Staffordshire Record Office, D3388/16/1. ? to ?, n.d. Weld MS., D/WLC/C/103.

23. Christopher Hibbert, *George III: A Personal History* (1998), p.225. *Wraxall: Memoirs*, I.255.

24. The Rev. John Kirk [J.H. Pollen, S.J. and Edwin Burton, eds.], *Biographies of English Catholics in the Eighteenth Century* (1909), pp. 85–86.

25. MS Book of Deeds, Stafford MS., q. in Leslie, *Mrs Fitzherbert*, p. 12.

26. D.M. Stuart, *Dearest Bess . . .* (1955), p. 13. Smollett, *Travels Through France and Italy*, p. 196. The author is grateful to Fr Jerome Bertram for his assistance.

Chapter 3 The Most Accomplished Prince of His Age

1. M.F. to William Fermor, 5 Aug. [1783?], Fermor MS., Letter No. 4. Anon., *A Description of Brighthelmstone . . .* (Brighthelmstone and London, n.d. [1781?]), p. 29.

2. Isabelle Pigot to P. of W., n.d., Esher MS., Nos. 12–13.

3. Horace Walpole to Sir Horace Mann, 17 May 1781 in *Yale Walpole*, 25.153–4.

4. Lady Campbell to Emily Eden, n.d. [1822] in Violet Dickinson [ed], *Miss Eden's Letters* (1919), p. 79. Lord Wentworth to Judith Milbanke 15 Nov. 1783, Lovelace Byron MS., 1 ff 155–6. R. Arnott to Earl of Denbigh, 5 July 1785, Feilding MS., CR 2017 pp. 329–30. Christina and David Bewley, *Gentleman Radical: A Life of John Horne Tooke 1736–1812* (1998), p. 52.

5. *The Bon Ton Magazine*, (April 1791), p. 49. *Ibid*, (May 1791),p. 97. *Ibid*, (June 1791), p. 138.

6. P. of W. to Capt. Hugh Conway, 18 Apr. 1785, Seymour MS., CR 713/2, no fol. Huish, I.25.

7.   Elizabeth and Florence Anson [eds.], *Mary Hamilton . . . at Court and at Home . . . 1756–1816* (1925), 83–4.

8.   P. of W. to the Earl of Hertford, 8 Febr. 1785, Seymour MS., CR 713/2, no fol. P. of W. to Isabella [Lady Hertford], 19 Sept. 1808, Esher MS., Nos. 39–40.

9.   Papendiek, *Court and Private Life . . .*, I.91. George III q. in J.B.B. to his wife, 18 Dec. 1797, Bland Burges MS. 11/3–5. Horace Walpole to Lady Ossory, 17 May 1778, *Yale: Walpole*, 33.7–11.

10. In September 2000 the British Association for Romantic Studies held a day conference at the University of Warwick to commemorate Perdita as a 'poet, novelist, philosopher, feminist, actress, celebrity.' So far M.F. has been spared this fate.

11. Horace Walpole to the Hon Thomas Walpole, 14 May 1781. *Yale: Walpole*, 36.193–5.

12. M.F. to Minney Dawson-Damer, 4 May 1830 in Leslie, *Letters*, II.223–4 and Duke of Wellington q. in Sir George Seymour, *Conversation with Duke of Wellington, 26 April 1837*, Seymour MS. CR 730/13/5. Huish, I.138.

13. Second Earl of Minto, 'Draught of a Biography of Charles James Fox', Minto MS., Literary Papers, 12851, ff. 22,47. Huish, I. 89.

14. *Gentleman's Magazine*, (January 1784), p. 69.

15. Lord Wentworth to Judith Milbanke, 20 Apr. 1784, Lovelace Byron MS, Dep. 1 f 186. *Morning Post*, 31 March 1784. Duchess of Devonshire to her Mother, 20 [Mar. 1784], Bessborough, *Georgiana*, pp. 78–9.

16. Thomas Orde to Duke of Rutland, 3 June 1784, Rutland MS. III.101.

17. Lord Wentworth to Judith Milbanke, 11 Mar. 1784 in *The Noels and the Milbankes*, p.233. Bessborough, *Georgiana*, p. 76. *Morning Herald*, 20 March 1784.

18. Langdale, pp. 117–8. Huish, I.124–5.

19. q. in Lady Charlotte Bury, diary entry for 12 Dec. 1818, Anon. [Lady Charlotte Bury], *Diary Illustrative of the Times of George the Fourth . . .* (1838–39, four vols.), III.274–5.

20. [George Hanger (4th Baron Coleraine)], 'A Prince's Opinions of Female Virtue' q. in Huish, I.257.

21. Duchess of Devonshire to her mother, 5 July 1784, Devonshire MS., 628. P. of W. to Prince Frederick, 6 July 1784, Aspinall,*P. of W.*, I.148–9.

22. Duchess of Devonshire to her mother, 8 July 1784, Devonshire MS., 629. Bessborough, *Georgiana*, p. 86.

23. Duchess of Devonshire to her mother, 8 July 1784, Devonshire MS., 629.

Chapter 4 Miladies Abroad

1. Lady Anne Lindsay, Crawford-Balcarres MS., Vol. I. Lady Anne's journal provides the basis for the discussion of MF's time in Europe.
2. P. of W. to M.F., 17 July 1784 q. by Sir George Seymour in 'Papers Relating to the Disposal of Mrs Fitzherbert's Papers,' Seymour MS., CR730/13/6.
3. Sir George Seymour, 'Memorandum of Sealed Packets in Executor's Mahogany Box, 17 April 1837, Seymour MS., CR 730/13/1. Foreman, *Georgiana Duchess of Devonshire*, p.164, n.1. M.F. q. in Langdale, pp. 120–1.
4. q. in Henry Richard, Lord Holland [Henry Edward, Lord Holland (ed)], *Memoirs of the Whig Party . . .* (two vols., 1854), II.126.
5. 'Philo-Veritas', 'Diamond Cut Diamond . . .' (1806, 2nd ed.),p. 8.
6. Sir Joshua Reynolds to Edmund Burke, 14 Aug. 1781 q. in Palmer, *The Age of the Democratic Revolution*, I.325. Langdale, p. 120. Neither the Court Archives in the Koninklijk Huisarchief nor the Stadholder's *Audiëntieregisters* in the Koninklikse Bibliotheek, Department of Special Collections, The Hague [MSS 78 G 1–68] contain any reference to M.F. but the records are incomplete while only the names of politicians and military men were usually entered.
7. [Lady Anne Lindsay], *Memoirs of Lady Anne Barnard – Parisian Anecdotes . . . 1784–5*, Crawford Muniments. Acc. 9769.27/4/10/1 & 2. All quotations relating to M.F.'s visits to Paris are based on these.
8. French authorities do not include the aristocrat Withers named, first, as Bellevoye and then as Bellois. (F. Aubert de la Chenaye des Bois et Badier [ed], *Dictionnaire de la noblesse* (Paris, 1863–77, 19 vols. 3rd ed.), II.882–885. Ludovic Lalanne, *Dictionnaire historique de la France* (Paris, 1777, 2nd ed.), p. 249 and J. Balteau et al., *Dictionnaire de biographie française* (Paris, 1929–, 18 vols. to date).) They do list a Provençal family named Marin or Marini.
9. Lord Southampton to George III, 29 Mar. 1785 and George III to P. of W., 29 Mar. 1785 in Aspinall, *George III*, I.147–8, 149–151.
10. Sir James Harris (First Earl of Malmesbury), 'Conference with the Prince of Wales at Carlton House, Monday, May 23rd 1785', Malmesbury MS, 9M73/G2324. See *The Daily Universal Register*, 9 May 1785.

Chapter 5 A Dangerous Greatness

1. Crawford-Balcarres MS., Vol. I. Mrs Creevey to her husband, 10 Nov. 1805, Creevey MS., NRO 324/L8/35.

2. *The Daily Universal Register*, 27 May 1785. Lord Sheffield to William Eden, 15 July 1785, *Auckland Journal*, I.347.
3. Mary Noel to Judith Milbanke, 9 July 1785, *The Noels and the Milbankes*, pp. 272–3.
4. *Wraxall: Memoirs*, V.370. q.in Philip Ziegler, *Melbourne: A Biography . . .* (1976), p. 14–15.
5. Sylas Neville, diary entry for 3 May 1785, Basil Cozens-Hardy [ed], *The Diary of Sylas Neville . . .* (1950), p. 326.
6. *The Daily Universal Register*, 9 August 1785. Duke of Gloucester to P. of W., 18 Sept. 1785, RA GEO/54371. Duke of Gloucester to P. of W., 13 Feb. 1786, RA GEO/54372. Lord Wentworth to Judith Milbanke, 19 Aug. 1785, Lovelace-Byron MS., Dep. 2 f 18. M.F. to Lady Anne Lindsay, 19 Sept. 1785, Crawford-Balcarres MS., Vol. II.
7. P. of W. to M.F., 3 Nov. 1785, RA GEO/50236–7. The letter is printed in Aspinall, *P. of W.*, I.189–201.
8. Mary, Lady Soames, *The Profligate Duke . . .* (1987), p. 153. Lady Anne Lindsay to Lord Mansfield, 12 Dec. 1785, Crawford-Balcarres MS. Vol. II.
9. The Rev. S. Johnes Knight to his daughter, Louisa, Lady Shelley, 28 Sept. 1830 q. in Wilkins, pp. 61–65. Sir William Augustus Fraser, *Hic et Ubique* (1893), pp. 259–262.
10. Simpson, *Maria Fiztherbert and Robert Burt . . .* pp. 3–11. The legend of the £500 may be traced to Charles Abbot who heard the story from Francis Burton, MP in 1796. Charles, Lord Colchester [ed]. *The Diary and Correspondence of Charles Abbot . . .* (1861, three vols.), I.68. Robert Burt to P. of W., 25 Feb. 1791, RA GEO/50211–2.
11. R.A. GEO/50210. Langdale, p. 121.
12. Aspinall, *P. of W.*, I.211.

Chapter 6 The Buzz of the Day

1. Queen Charlotte to Herzog Karl von Mecklenburg-Strelitz, 28 Nov. & 28 Dec. 1785, RA GEO/Microfilm. Prince William to the P. of W., 30 Jan. 1786 in Aspinall, *P. of W.*, 1.216. Duke of Gloucester to the P. of W., 19 Mar. 1786, RA GEO/54374–5.
2. Mrs Creevey to her husband, 12 Nov. 1805, Creevey MS., NRO 324/L8/43. Henry Swinburne to Sir Edward Swinburne, Feb. 1785 [sic 1786] in Henry Swinburne [Charles White, ed.], *The Courts of Europe at the Close of the Last Century* (1841, two vols.), I.390.
3. Earl of Denbigh to Maj. Bulkeley, 4 Mar. 1786 and Lord Wentworth to

Earl of Denbigh, 4 Mar. 1786, Feilding MS., CR 2017/C244, pp.340, 341.
Maj. Bulkeley to the Earl of Denbigh, 7 Mar. 1786 & the Earl of Denbigh
to Hugh Carleton, 7 Mar. 1786, Feilding MS., CR 2017/C244, p. 342.

4. *The Daily Universal Register*, 31 Mar. 1786. Lord Wentworth to ?, 17 Mar.
    1786, Feilding MS., Warwicks. R.O., CR 2017/C340–44. Mrs Talbot to
    Francis Fortescue Turvile, 17 Mar. 1786, q. in Leslie, *Mrs Fitzherbert*, p.64.

5. Duke of Gloucester to P. of W., 10 Nov. 1787, RA GEO/54389. M.F. to
    Lady Anne Lindsay, n.d. [1786], Crawford-Balcarres MS., Vol. II.

6. The indispensable sources for caricatures are the four volumes by M.
    Dorothy George in the eleven volume series, *Catalogue of Political and
    Personal Satires Preserved in the Department of Prints and Drawings in the
    British Museum*. These were published by the British Museum as follows:
    Vol. VI, 1784–1792 (1938); Vol VII, 1793–1800 (1942); Vol VIII, 1801–1810
    (1947); and Vol IX, 1811–1819 (1952).

7. Diana Donald, *The Age of Caricature: Satirical Prints in the Reign of George
    III* (1996), p. 20. George IV. Private Papers: *Lists of Suppressed Caricatures
    with Receipts for Sums Paid 1819–1822*. RA GEO/51382(a). Several drawers
    of prints and drawings were burnt on the orders of Sir William Knighton
    after George IV's death. Joshua Calkin to J.H. Glover, esq., 24 Mar. 1845
    [copy], RA VIC/Add T/73.

8. R. Arnott to the Earl of Denbigh, 14 Mar. 1786, Feilding MS., CR
    2017/C244, p.343.

9. Lord Wentworth to Earl of Denbigh, 7 Apr. 1786, Feilding MS., CR
    2017/C244, p. 349. George, *Satires*, VI. No. 6953. 'The Pot Calling the
    Kettle Black . . .' was not included in George, *Satires*. It was seen in
    Harvard University's Houghton Library in a five volume, grangerized
    edition of James Boaden's *The Life of Mrs Dorothy Jordan*, first published
    in two volumes in 1831.

10. Francis Rawdon-Hastings (1754–1826) was also a veteran of the American
    war. He was created Baron Rawdon in 1783 and succeeded as second
    Earl of Moira in 1793. In 1817 he was created Marquis of Hastings. In
    this book he will be referred to throughout as Lord Moira.

11. George Hanger [William Combe, editor], *The Life, Adventures, and
    Opinions of Col George Hanger . . .* (1801, two vols.), I.11,44,61; II.411, 415,
    448. Huish, I.164–6. *The Bon Ton Magazine* (Mar. 1792), pp. 26–7.

12. P. of W. to George III, 15 June 1786, Aspinall, *P. of W.*, I.228–9. The 'enclo-
    sure' which breaks down the debts obviously contains no reference to
    M.F. It does list £8000 as 'private debts' and £30,000 as 'incidental
    charges', i.e. an approximation for unknown bills yet to be presented.
    [Aspinall, *P. of W.*, I.229.] Papendiek, *Court and Private . . .*, I.257.

13. Lord Wentworth to the Earl of Denbigh, 10 July 1786, Feilding MS., CR 2017/C244, p. 349. Thomas Ord to Duke of Rutland, 17 July 1786, Rutland MS., III.324. A.M. Storer to William Eden, 30 June 1786, *Auckland Journal*, I.384. Duke of Dorset to William Eden, 13 July 1786. *Auckland Journal*, I.142.
14. Ord's story is based on two items in the Georgetown University Archives Alumni Files, Washington, D.C. *History of James Ord as Related by Himself* . . . and Mary Ord Preston, *Memoranda concerning James Ord . . . by his Granddaughter*. University Library, Special Collections, 90A469. Saul David, *Prince of Pleasure: The Prince of Wales and the Making of the Regency* (1998), pp. 75–80.
15. Information from the 29th Earl of Crawford and Balcarrres.

Chapter 7 Questions in the House

1. John A. Graham, L.L.D., *Memoirs of John Horne Tooke* . . . (New York, 1828), p. 111.
2. *The Daily Universal Register*, 30 Apr. 1785.
3. *The Daily Universal Register*, 28 Apr. 1787.
4. Gen Cuninghame to William Eden, 25 May 1787, *Auckland Journal*, I.426. Lord Sheffield to William Eden, 10 May 1787, *Auckland Journal*, I.418.
5. P. of W. q. in J.W. Croker's Note Book for 25 Nov. 1825 in *The Croker Papers*, I.292. Second Earl of Minto, 'Draught Biography of Charles James Fox', Minto MS., 12851. ff. 22, 46.
6. *Wraxall: Memoirs*, IV.454.
7. *The Daily Universal Register*, 1 May 1787.
8. Horne Tooke, *A Letter to a Friend* . . . (1786), pp. 40–41.
9. *Morning Chronicle*, 5 May 1787. Sir Gilbert Elliot to his wife, 5 May 1787 in Minto, *Life and Letters*, I.159–60. Earl Stanhope, *Life of the Right Honourable William Pitt* (1867, four vols.. 3rd ed.), I.335–6.
10. R.B. Sheridan to William Pitt, [3 May 1787], R.B. Sheridan to William Pitt, [3 May 1787] and R.B. Sheridan to William Pitt [4 May 1787] in Cecil Price [ed], *The Letters of Richard Brinsley Sheridan* (Oxford, 1966, three vols.), I.176–78. A.M. Storer to William Eden, 11 May 1787, *Auckland Journal*, I.421.
11. Charles Grey q. in Holland, *Memoirs of the Whig Party*, II.138–40. Charles Grey q. in Russell, *Memorials . . . Charles James Fox*, II.288.n.1 & II.289.n1. Thomas Moore, *Memoirs of the Life of the Rt. Hon. Richard Brinsley Sheridan* (1825, two vols.), I.306–7.

12. Moore, *Memoirs of . . . Sheridan*, I.306. Holland, *Memoirs of the Whig Party*, II.140. *The Daily Universal Register*, 5 May 1787.

13. *The Daily Universal Register*, 7 May 1787.

14. Lord Ailesbury, diary entry for 25 May 1787, H.M.C., *Ailesbury Manuscripts*, (1898), 15th Report, Appendix VII, II.314. Gen Cuninghame to William Eden, 25 May 1787, *Auckland Journal*, I.426.

15. *The Daily Universal Register*, 14 July 1786. M.F. to William Fermor, n.d. [25 or 26 June 1787], Fermor MS., Letter No. 6. *Gentleman's Magazine* (July 1787), p. 550.

16. John Doran, *Lives of the Queens of England . . .* (1855, two vols.), II.162. Thomas Campbell, 1 Aug. 1787 q. Leslie, *Mrs Fitzherbert*, p. 89. Anon. q. in Wilkins, p. 153.

17. *The Times*, 24 Jan. 1788. On 1 Jan. 1788 *The Daily Universal Register* changed its name to *The Times*.

18. A.M. Storer to William Eden, 18 Jan. 1788 in *Auckland Journal*, I.462–3.

19. J.B.B. to his wife, 25 May 1788, Bland Burges MS, 8 f 73.

20. Henry Angelo, *Reminiscences . . .* (1828–30, two vols.) I.117. *The Times*, 6 Nov. 1788.

Chapter 8 His Majesty's Disorder

1. For Julia Johnstone see Harriette Wilson, *Memoirs of Harriette Wilson written by Herself* (1825, four vols.) and *Confessions of Julia Johnstone . . .* (1825).

2. *Morning Post*, 10 Nov. 1788. R. Warren to Lady Spencer, 12 Nov. 1788, H.M.C., *The Manuscripts of Lord Spencer*, (1871), p. 14. Duke of Gloucester to P. of W., 19 Nov. 1788, RA GEO/54393. Lady Eleanor Butler, diary entry for 15 Nov. 1788, Mrs G.H. Bell [ed], *The Hamwood Papers of the Ladies of Llangollen . . .* (1930), p. 148.

3. Sheridan to J.W. Payne, n.d. [8 Nov. 1788?], *Letters of . . . Sheridan*, I.190. Sir Gilbert Elliot to his wife, 26 Nov. 1788, Countess of Minto, *Life and Letters of Sir Gilbert Elliot . . .* (1874, three vols.), I.240. John Wilkes to his daughter, 28 Nov. 1788, [Sir W. Rough, ed], *Letters . . . to His Daughter* (1804, 4 vols.), [Rough], IV.245. Letter LXVII.

4. J.B.B. to his wife, 12 Jan. 1789, Bland Burges MS., 8 f 152. Burges's early frustrated love for Lady Margaret Fordyce had inspired her sister, Lady Anne, to write *Auld Robin Gray*. Decades later, Burges, by now an elderly widower, finally took the widowed Lady Margaret as his third wife.

5. *Daily Universal Register*, 2 May 1787. Lord Palmerston q. in L.G. Mitchell,

Charles James Fox (1997 edn.), p. 84.

6. Lord Radnor q. by Sir William Young to the Marquess of Buckingham, 11 Dec. 1788, The Duke of Buckingham and Chandos, *Memoirs of the Court and Cabinets of George the Third* . . . (1853, two vols., 2nd ed.), II.49. J.B.B. to his wife, 10 Dec. 1788, Bland Burges MS., 98 f 105.

7. The Archbishop of Canterbury to William Eden, 16 Jan. 1789, *Auckland Journal*, II.267. Madame Huber to William Eden, 3 Feb. 1789, *Auckland Journal*, II.393. W.W. Grenville to the Marquis of Buckingham, n.d. [Jan. 1789] q. in Buckingham, *Court and Cabinets*, II.97.

8. Miss Sayer to Madame Huber, 27 Jan. 1789, *Auckland Journal*, II.179–80. Lady Harcourt's *Diary* and Locker MS. q. in W.M. Massey, *A History of England during the Reign of George the Third* (1855–1863, four vols), III.389.n.s.

9. E. Brander to Sir Gilbert Elliot, 20 Jan. 1789, Minto MS., 11193 f 62–65. 'Papers Referred to in the Memorial from the Prince of Wales to the King' in Letter from the Prince of Wales to the King, accompanying the Prince's Memorial [June 1789.]. Third Set.' Minto MS., 11204.

10. M. Huber to William Eden, 14 July 1789 & A.M. Storer to William Eden, 21 Aug. 1789, *Auckland Journal*, II.328 & II.349.

11. *The Times*, 12 Sept. 1789. *The Times*, 23 & 26 Nov. 1789. The King ag. Withers, RA GEO/31099–31104. George, *Satires* . . ., VI. No. 7965. *The Times*, 22 & 25 Dec. 1789.

Chapter 9 Passions and Errors

1. Butler, *Historical Memoirs*, II.102–142. Lord Petre to John Mitford, 8 Mar. 1790, Redesdale MS., Gloucestershire Record Office, D 2002 c 4.

2. See W.H. Chamberlaine, *A Tale of Lulworth* (Bath, 1888); Anon., *On the Building of a Monastery in Dorset* (Oxford, 1795); and Anon, *The Canonization of Thomas . . . [Weld] Esq. who has Lately Erected at East L——h Dorset a Monastery and there Established a Body of Monks* (London, 1801). Sir Philip Francis to M.F., 7 Nov. 1791, Sir Philip Francis MS., British Library, BL Add Ms. 40763 f 216. Weld MS., D/LWC/117 and D/LWC/c/124.

3. Duchess of Devonshire to P. of W., 19 Oct. [1791], Aspinall,*P of W.*, II.212. E.W. Bootle to George Canning, 20 Mar. 1791, Canning MS, Envelope 65, no fol. Hannah More to Lady Amherst, 25 Apr. 1793, Amherst MS., U1350 c 76/1.

4. P. of W. to Queen Charlotte, [?24 Jan. 1793], Aspinall, *P. of W.*, II.334–5.

P. of W. to Emperor Francis II, undated draft letter, RA GEO/42375–6. Lord Amherst, diary entry for 16 Oct. 1793, Amherst MS., U1350 Vol. II.

5. *Gazetteer*, 27 July 1793. *The World*, 3 Aug. 1793. *Lloyd's Evening Post*, 5 Aug. 1793.

6. *Public Advertiser*, 15 Aug. 1793.

7. William Smythe to Hugh Smythe, 30 Sept. 1793, Hugo Smythe Letters, Hugo Smythe MS., Royal Pavilion Archive, Brighton, 1655/7. There are six letters, written between 3 July 1793 and 20 Oct. 1795, in the collection.

8. Anon. [Nathaniel Jefferys], *A Review of the Conduct of His Royal Highness the Prince of Wales . . .* (n.d. [1806]), pp. 10–15. Claudio, *An Antidote to Poison . . .* (1806, 2nd ed.), p. 29.

9. *The Bon Ton Magazine* (Mar. 1792), p. 36. Malmesbury, diary entry for 4 June 1792, *Malmesbury: Diaries*, II.450–2.

10. Edna, Lady Healey, *Coutts & Co 1692–1992: The Portrait of a Private Bank* (1992), pp. 157–9. *The Times*, 7 Jan. 1793.

11. Duke of York to M.F., n.d. [22 Feb.], Autograph File/Letter, Houghton Library, Harvard University. *The Bon Ton Magazine* (Jan. 1792), p. 449.

12. Lord Malmesbury, diary entry for 8 June 1792, Diary of Home Transactions, June 1792 to January 1793, Malmesbury MS., HRO 9M73/G2005–1–6. The printed version, which differs somewhat, is in *Malmesbury: Diaries*, II.452.

13. Isabella Pigot to P. of W., n.d. [July 1792?], Esher Collection, No. 17.

Chapter 10 The Late Princess Fitz

1. Christopher Hibbert, *George IV, Prince of Wales: 1762–1811* (1972), p.131 n l. Mary Frampton, diary entry for 1795, Harriet Georgiana Mundy [ed], *The Journal of Mary Frampton . . .* (1886, third edn.), p. 84. Countess of Mount Edgcumbe to Edward Jerningham, 20 Sept. 1794, Lewis Bettany [ed], *Edward Jerningham and His Friends . . .* (1919), pp. 218–22. Frances, Lady Shelley, diary entry for 1807, Richard Edgcumbe [ed], *The Diary of Frances Lady Shelley 1787–1817* (1912), p. 37.

2. Mme. de La Tour du Pin q. in Lucy Ellis and Joseph Turquan, *La Belle Pamela (Lady Edward Fitzgerald)* (1924), p. 363 n 1. P. of W. to Isabella Pigot, n.d. [summer 1794], Esher MS., Nos. 47–50.

3. Lady Margaret Fordyce to Lady Anne Lindsay, 6 Aug. 1794, Crawford-Balcarres MS., Vol. II. M.F. q. in Langdale, p. 125, 127. Duke of York to P. of W., 2 Sept. 1794, Aspinall, *P. of W.*, II.454.

4. Lord Wentworth to the Earl of Denbigh, 10 July 1794, Feilding MS., CR 2017 c 244, p. 448. Lord Mornington to Lord Grenville, 15 July 1794, *Fortescue MS.*, II.599. Lady Anne Lindsay to M.F., 30 July 1794, Crawford-Balcarres MS., Vol. I.

5. Lord Amherst, diary entries for 21 Jan. & 21 Aug. 1794, Amherst MS., U 1350 Vol. III (1794). Lord Amherst, diary entry for 22 Nov. 1794, Amherst MS., U 1350 Vol. IV, (1794). George Canning, diary entry for 22 Nov. 1794, Canning MS., 29 d ii. Duke of Portland to P. of W., 4 July 1794, Portland MS., PwV 107, pp. 172, 173, 176. P. of W. to John Payne, 21 Aug. 1794, Esher MS., No. 22.

6. Queen Charlotte, diary entries for 31 Oct., 26 Oct., 29 Oct., 22 Nov., 5 Dec., RA GEO/Add 43/3. Countess of Mount Edgcumbe to Edward Jerningham, [20 Sept. 1794], *Edward Jerningham and His Friends*, pp. 218–22. Mrs Harcourt, 6 Mar 1795 [?], Edward William Harcourt [ed], *The Harcourt Papers* (1880–1905, fourteen vols.), IV. Part II. 635. P. of W. to Lady Anne Lindsay, 1 Oct. 1794, Crawford-Balcarres MS., Vol. I. Duchess of Devonshire to Thomas Coutts, 1 Nov. 1794, Bessborough, *Georgiana*, p. 209.

7. Malmesbury MS., 9M73/G2008. This has the unedited record of Malmesbury's involvement in the wedding preparations. J.B.B. to his wife, 1 Dec. 1794, Bland Burges MS., 10/132–7. M.F. q. by George Dawson-Damer in Leslie, *Mrs Fitzherbert*, I.119. Lord Holland, *Memoirs of the Whig Party*, II.143–4.

8. George Dance q. by Joseph Farington, diary entry for 18 Jan. 1795, *Farington Diary*, II.293. Lord Loughborough to the P. of W., 19 Dec. 1794, RA GEO/50213. Lord Hugh Seymour to John Payne, 31 Dec. 1794, Aspinall, *P. of W.*, II.532.

9. Duke of Clarence and Lord Moira q. in Sir George Seymour, Papers Relative to Mrs Fitzherbert in Connection with Mr Langdale's Book Principaly [*sic*] & Memo of the Duke of Wellington. Seymour MS, CR 114A/536/6.

10. P. of W. q. in Lord Malmesbury, *Detailed Account by Malmesbury of what he was told by the Prince of Wales about the Princess's character and behaviour, their wedding night, etc* (1796), Malmesbury MS., 9M73/G2031.

11. Finch Diary, 19 Dec. 1813, f.61ʳ. Princess of Wales q. by Lady Charlotte Bury in late 1810 or early 1811, *Diary*, I.29. Lord Fitzwilliam to the Duke of Portland, 23 Jan. 1795, Fitzwilliam MS., Sheffield Central Reference Library, WWM/F5/23–27. J.B.B. to his wife, 29 June 1795, Bland Burges MS., 10/152. J.B.B. to his wife, 12 July 1795 & 14 July 1795, Bland Burges MS., 10/159 and 10/165.

12. George Canning, diary entries for 27 Apr., 8 May, 1 June 1795, Canning MS., 29.d.ii.
13. M.F. to Thomas Coutts, 6 Oct. 1795, RA GEO/Add 16. Duke of Clarence to P. of W., n.d. [Dec. 1795], Aspinall, *P. of W.*, III.120–1. Lady Anne Barnard to Judith, Lady Milbanke, 4 Jan. 1796, Lovelace-Byron MS., Dep. 12 ff 13–22.

Chapter 11 Like Brother and Sister

1. P. of W., Last Will and Testament, 10 Jan. 1796, RA GEO/50214–50222 and Aspinall, *P. of W.*, III. 132–139. Duke of Wellington q. by Sir George Seymour, Papers Relating to . . . Mrs Fitzherbert's Papers, Seymour MS., CR 730/13. Lady Anne Barnard, 'The Lion & the Lamb', Crawford-Balcarres MS., Vol. II. This is an allegorical tale based on the Prince and M.F.
2. M.F. to Thomas Coutts, n.d. [1796 or 1797], Burdett Coutts MS., ff 53–54.
3. P. of W. to Duchess of Rutland, 12 Feb.1799, Aspinall, *P. of W.*, IV.12–13. Lord Wentworth to the Earl of Denbigh, 9 May 1799, Feilding MS., CR 2017 c 244, p. 573. Finch Diary, 10 Dec. 1813, f 50^v. P. of W. to Duchess of Rutland, [?] 23 Feb. 1799, Aspinall. *P. of W.*, IV.16–17. Lady Anne Barnard, diary entry for 1 Apr. 1800, Crawford-Balcarres MS., Vol. I.
4. P. of W. to Henry Errington, 21 June 1799, Esher MS., Nos. 2 (& 3).
5. P. of W. to M. F., 11–12 June 1799, RA GEO/50205–6 & Aspinall, *P. of W.*, IV.48–50.
6. Princess of Wales to John Payne, 4 Aug. 1799, Aspinall, *P. of W.*, IV.61–2. John McMahon to James Christie, 23 Aug. 1799, Morgan Library, New York, R-V. Rulers of England. George IV. Misc. Nr. 3.
7. Bishop Douglass' diary is used extensively in Bernard Ward, *Dawn of the Catholic Revival* (1905, two vols.), II.226–28. Mgr Gerard McKay of the Roman Rota to the author, 3 Oct. 2000. M.F. q. by Lady Anne Barnard, Crawford-Balcarres MS.,Vol. I.
8. Sir George Seymour's MS. annotations on Langdale's *Memoirs of Mrs Fitzherbert*, p. 149, Seymour MS., CR 114A/536/7.
9. Mrs Creevey to her husband, n.d. [Nov. 1805], Creevey MS., NRO 324/L8/42. Langdale, pp. 126–129. M.F. to P. of W., 14 Aug. 1814, Aspinall, *P. of W.*, VIII.317–8. Sylvester Douglas, diary entry for 14 Oct. 1801, Bickley, *Diaries of Sylvester Douglas*, I.258. *The Times*, 3 Jan. 1801. Annuity Receipt, 22 July 1808, Fitzherbert MS. G.W. Fulcher [E.S. Fulcher, ed], *Life of Thomas Gainsborough, R.A.* (1856, 2nd ed.), p. 193.

10. *The Times*, 26 July 1804. Fitzherbert MS., Nos. 10–12.
11. Joseph Farington, diary entry for 16 Feb. 1804, *Farington Diary*, VI.2245–6. Frances, Lady Shelley, diary entry for 1805 in Edgcumbe, *The Diary of Frances Lady Shelley*, I.34–5.
12. Unless noted otherwise, the following section is based on fourteen letters written by Mrs Creevey to her husband between 29 Oct. and 5 Dec. 1805. Creevey MS., NRO 324/L8/25, 29, 30, 32, 34–36, 39, 42, 43, 47, 50, 51, 55.

Chapter 12 The Final Break

1. Sir George Seymour, *Memoir of Vice Admiral Lord Hugh Seymour . . .*, Seymour MS., CR 114A/392. Papers relating to the case are in CR 114A/392 & CR 114A/536.
2. Mrs Creevey to her husband, 10 Nov 1805. Creevey MS., NRO 324/L8/39. Sir Walter Scott to his wife, 20 [?] March 1807, Sir Herbert Grierson [ed], *The Letters of Sir Walter Scott* (1937, 12 vols.), XII.95.
3. [Jeffreys], *A Review of the Conduct . . .* (1806, 2nd ed.), pp 18–19, 59. Edward Jerningham to Mrs Jerningham, Stafford MS., D641/3/P/ 3/14/1–2, 20–97.
4. M.F. to Lady Anne Barnard, n.d. [Jan. or Feb. 1807], Crawford-Balcarres MS., Vol.II. Edward Jerningham to Mrs Jerningham, 2 Apr. 1806, Stafford MS., D 641/3/P/3/14/75b.
5. P. of W. to Isabella [Lady Hertford], 19 Sept. 1808, Esher MS., Nos. 39–40.
6. P. of W. q. in Philip Mansel, *Louis XVIII* (1999 ed), pp. 154–6.
7. Henry Errington to John McMahon, 5 Nov. 1811, RA GEO/18805–6.
8. Indenture by P. of W. to Henry Errington, Esq., 16 Mar. 1808, RA GEO/50239. Lady Anne Barnard to M.F., n.d. [1811?], Crawford-Balcarres MS., Vol. II. M.F. to Lady Anne Barnard,5 May 1812, Crawford-Balcarres MS., Vol. II.
9. M.F. to Minney Seymour, 25 Aug. 1822, Leslie, *Letters*, II.169. Mrs Creevey to her husband, Friday [May 1812], Creevey MS., NRO 324/L 15/28.

Chapter 13 Mrs Fitzherbert Without a Title

1. Smythe MS., Brighton, Letters 1,5,6. M.F. to George Dawson-Damer, 11 May [1827], Dawson MS., Brighton. M.F. to Minney Dawson-Damer, [3 Mar. 1833], Leslie, *Letters*, II.270.

2. M.F. to Minney Dawson-Damer, [29 Nov. 1827], Leslie, *Letters*, II.199. Lady Emmeline Stuart Wortley, *Etc* (1853), p. 110. Prince Pückler-Muskau to his mistress, 24 Feb. & 20 Apr. 1827, E.M. Butler [ed], *A Regency Visitor* . . . (1957), pp. 173, 194. Henry Edward Fox, diary entry for 22 June 1822, Earl of Ilchester [ed], *The Journal of the Hon. Henry Edward Fox* . . . (1923), p. 127. Finch Diary, 19 Dec. 1813 f61^r.

3. M.F. to ?, n.d., Morgan Library, New York. V-2/G/M1755. *The Brighton Gazette*, 18 Dec. 1823. *Brighton Herald*, 24 Jan. 1824. Fr Cullin to Minney Dawson-Damer [14 Mar. 1844], Leslie, *Letters*, xxviii. M.F. to ? Bruce. n.d. [1 Oct. 1814], Bodleian Library, Oxford, MS Eng c 5753 ff 5–6. See M.F. to George Dawson-Damer, 28 Apr. 1837, Dawson-Damer MS., Brighton, 5 & 6.

4. M.F. to Minney Dawson-Damer, [4 May 1830], Leslie, *Letters*, II.223. Duke of Kent to M.F., 23 Jan. 1812, RA GEO/45288–9. Dowager Lady Vernon to Mary Frampton, 2 July 1814, *Journal of Mary Frampton*, p. 234. M.F. to Marianne Jerningham, [June 1828], Stafford MS., D/641/e/P/3/29/9. Thomas Raikes, diary entry for 31 Mar. 1837, *A Portion of the Journal Kept by Thomas Raikes* . . . (1856–57, four vols.), III.146–8.

5. George IV to Marchioness of Conyngham, 22 Feb. 1825, Conyngham MS., Letter No. 4. Duke of Kent to M.F., 23 Jan. 1812, RA GEO/45288–9. Anthony Bird, *The Damnable Duke of Cumberland* (1966), p. 57.

6. Duke of Kent to M.F., 5 May 1818, RA VIC/Letters of H.R.H. the Duke of Kent. Confidential Family Papers/M.1. Lord Mulgrave to M.F., 16 July 1813, M.F. to Lt Frank Dawson, 27 Sept. [1814] and M.F. to Frank Dawson, 30 Feb. 1816, Frank Dawson MS., Nos. 1–3. M.F. to [Macleod], draft & 23 Dec. 1811, Fitzherbert MS., Letters 3 & 4. *Memo: HRH the Duchess of Gloucester & Mrs Fitzherbert, 1836.* Seymour MS., CR 730/13/item 11.

7. M.F. to Thomas Coutts, n.d., Burdett Coutts MS., ff 56–57. M.F. to Lady Guilford, n.d. [ca 24 July 1822], North Family MS., d 31 f 41.

8. George Dawson-Damer to M.F., 20 [June], 26 July 1826, Dawson Damer MS., Kent, EK/U924/C2/2; EK/U924/C2/4. M.F. to Minney Dawson-Damer, 19 Oct. 1829, Leslie, *Letters*, II.211. M.F. to Minney and Blanche Dawson-Damer, n.d., RA GEO/41715. Richard Buckle [ed], *The Prettiest Girl in England* . . . (1958), p. 9.

9. Sir Courtenay Boyle [ed], *Mary Boyle: Her Book* (1901), p. 83. M.F. to Lady Guilford, 8 May 1831, North Family MS, d 30 f 181. M.F. to George Dawson-Damer, [11 May 1827], Dawson MS., No. 5. M.F. to Minney Dawson-Damer, [21 Dec. 1827], Leslie, *Letters*, II.200.

10. M.F. to Sir Charles Stewart, 5 Dec. [1820], M.F. to Sir Charles Stewart,

9 June [1820s], Stuart de Rothsay MS., National Library of Scotland, 21288 f 49 & 21321 f 59.

11. M.F. to ?, n.d. [1824], Morgan Library, New York, R-V. Rulers of England. George IV. Misc. Nr. 4. *Mrs Fitzherbert's Affairs: Trust & Executorship No. 1.'*, Seymour MS., CR 114A/536/4. Note, Sir Benjamin Bloomfield, 10 Apr. 1820, RA GEO/29894. Lady Anne Barnard to her niece, Mrs Isabella Hayes, n.d. [1820], Anthony Powell [ed], *The Barnard Letters 1778–1824* (1928), pp. 276–7.

12. Sir William Knighton, diary memorandum regarding George IV, 5 Nov. 1830, Aspinall, *George IV*, III.477–83. George IV to Knighton, 1 Feb. 1826. RA GEO/51295.

13. Duke of Wellington to Mrs Arbuthnot, 28 Sept. 1826, Duke of Wellington [ed], *Wellington and His Friends* (1965), p. 70. Duke of Kent to M.F., 23 Jan. 1812, RA GEO/45288–9. M.F. to Minney Dawson-Damer [4 May 1830], Leslie, *Letters*, II.223. M.F. to George IV, 23 May 1830, RA GEO/24823.

14. William IV to Duke of Wellington, 4 Mar. 1832, RA GEO/51376. William IV q. by Sir George Seymour, diary entry for 24 Apr. 1837, Seymour MS., CR 114A/536/6. Draught of M.F.'s Release and Discharge, RA GEO/24862–3 and Copy signed by M.F., RA GEO/24864. Warrant of William IV, RA GEO/50229. John Forster to M.F., 24 Aug. 1830, RA GEO/50228. Thomas Creevey to his daughter, 23 Sept. 1830, John Gore [ed], *Creevey's Life and Times . . .* (1934), pp. 324–5.

15. M.F. q. in Anna Maria Wilhemina Pickering, *Memoirs . . .* (1903), p. 136. Minney Dawson-Damer to Sir George Seymour, 13 Dec. 1833, Leslie, *Mrs Fitzherbert*, 314–5.

16. Charles Greville, diary entry for 31 Mar. 1837, Henry Reeve [ed], *The Greville Memoirs . . .* (1888, new ed., eight vols.), III.404. Duke of Gloucester to P. of W., 19 Mar. 1786, RA GEO/54374–5. Knighton, Diary Memorandum regarding George IV, 5 Nov. 1830, Aspinall, *George IV*, III.477–83. Charles Greville, diary entry for 31 Mar. 1837. *The Greville Memoirs*, III.404.

17. M.F. to Charles Greenwood, 17 Sept. 1826, RA GEO/Add 38. M.F. q. in Langdale, pp. 142–3.

18. William IV to the Duke of Wellington, 4 Mar. 1832, RA GEO/51376. Sir William Knighton to Duke of Wellington, 9 Mar. 1832, RA GEO/51378. Frances Mary Gascoyne-Cecil, diary entry for 30 Oct. 1833, Carola Oman, *The Gascoyne Heiress . . .* (1968), pp. 92–3. M.F. to Duke of Wellington, 5 Apr. 1832 [copy], RA GEO/24890–1.

19. Frances Mary Gascoyne-Cecil, diary entry for 10 July 1836, Oman, *The*

Gascoyne Heiress, 207. Burt's letter is RA GEO/50211–2. The P. of W.'s letter of 3 Nov. 1785 is RA GEO/50236–7. *Copy of Agreement between the Executives of George the Fourth and Mrs Fitzherbert about Letters*, 24 Aug. 1833, Seymour MS., CR 730/13/item two; Seymour MS., CR 730/13/6 & 12. Minney Dawson-Damer to the Duchess of Sutherland, 13 Mar. 1838. RA VIC/Confidential Family Papers/M.1. Six letters from the Duke of Kent were given to Queen Victoria that same year.

20. Lord Stourton to M.F., 29 Nov. 1836, Hugo Smythe MS.
21. Lord Hatherton, diary entry for 30 Mar. 1837, Hatherton MS., D/260/M/F/26/14. Information regarding M.F.'s estate may be found in the Seymour MS., CR 730/13/8–9 and CR 114A/536/4–5 and in a collection of 202 documents in the Brighton Library's Fitzherbert Papers.

Epilogue

1. Duke of Wellington, Memorandum by Sir George Seymour, 11 June 1838, Papers Relative to Mrs Fitzherbert . . ., Seymour MS., CR 114A/536/6. See letter from Lord Stourton in [Henry Brougham], 'George the Fourth and Queen Caroline – Abuses of the Press', *Edinburgh Review*, LXVII (April 1838), pp. 1–80. See [W.N. Massey], 'The Life and Times of Henry Lord Brougham', *Edinburgh Review*, CXXXV (April 1872). Coutts Bank to Earl of Albemarle, 18 Dec. 1846 and Coutts Bank to Hon Charles Langdale, 18 Dec. 1846 [copy], RA GEO/50231 & 50232. Sir George Seymour, Papers Relative to Mrs Fitzherbert. . ., Seymour MS., CR 114A/536/6. Lord Holland, *Memoirs of the Whig Party . . .*, II.141.
2. J. Bryan III and Charles J.V. Murphy, *The Windsor Story* (1979), p. 190.

BIBLIOGRAPHY

Manuscripts

Amherst MS: Centre for Kentish Studies, Maidstone.

Autograph File: Houghton Library, Harvard University.

Bland Burges MS: Bland Burges Deposit., Bodleian Library, Oxford.

Burdett Coutts MS: Correspondence of Thomas Burdett-Coutts, Bodleian Library, Oxford, MS Eng lett d 92.

Canning MS: Harewood Deposit, City of Leeds, Archives Office.

Conyngham MS: Royal Pavilion and Museums Department, Brighton.

Crawford-Balcarres MS: Balcarres, Colinsburgh, Leven, Fife. Material relating to Maria Fitzherbert was gathered into two volumes by the twenty-seventh Earl of Crawford and Balcarres. Volume I contains extracts from Lady Anne's Journal (unless noted otherwise); Volume II contains letters to Maria Fitzherbert and Lady Margaret Fordyce and copies of Lady Anne's letters.

Crawford Muniments: National Library of Scotland.

Creevey MS: Northumberland Record Office, Newcastle-upon-Tyne.

Dawson MS., Brighton: Royal Pavilion and Museums Department, Brighton.

Dawson-Damer MS., Brighton: Royal Pavilion and Museums Department, Brighton. Letters from M.F. to George Dawson-Damer.

Dawson-Damer MS., Kent: Stebbing Bequest: Dawson Damer Correspondence, East Kent Archives Centre, Maidstone.

Denbigh MS: Warwickshire Record Office, Warwick.

Devonshire MS: Calendar of the 5th Duke of Devonshire, Devonshire Collections, Chatsworth.

Esher MS: Royal Pavilion and Museums Department, Brighton.

Feilding MS: Feilding of Newham Paddox MS., Warwickshire Record Office, Warwick.

Fermor MS: Royal Pavilion and Museums Department, Brighton.

Finch MS: Diary of R. Finch from 29 Oct. 1813 to 2 Feb. 1814. Bodleian Library, Oxford, MS Finch e 6.

Fitzherbert MS: Royal Pavilion and Museums Department, Brighton.

Fitzwilliam MS: Sheffield Central Reference Library.

Frank Dawson MS: Royal Pavilion and Museums Department, Brighton.

Hatherton MS: Staffordshire Record Office, Stafford.

Hugo Smythe MS: Royal Pavilion Library and Museums Department, Brighton.

Lovelace Byron MS: Lovelace-Byron Deposit, Bodleian Library, Oxford.

Malmesbury MS: Papers of Sir James Harris, first Earl of Malmesbury, Hampshire Record Office, Winchester.

Minto MS: Papers of the first and second Earls of Minto, National Library of Scotland, Edinburgh.

North Family MS: MSS North d 30 & 31, Bodleian Library, Oxford.

Portland MS: University of Nottingham Library.

Quarter Session Records, Hampshire Record Office.

Redesdale MS: Gloucestershire Record Office.

Royal Archives, Windsor.

Rulers of England MS: Morgan Library, New York City.

Salt MS: Shropshire Records and Research Centre.

Seymour MS: Seymour of Ragley MS., Warwickshire Record Office, Warwick.

Smythe MS: Smythe Family Papers, Shropshire Records and Research Centre, Shrewsbury.

Smythe MS, Brighton: Letters from M.F. to her nephew, Henry Smythe, Royal Pavilion Library and Museums Department, Brighton.

Stafford MS: Stafford Family Papers, Staffordshire Record Office, Stafford.

Stuart de Rothsay MS: National Library of Scotland

Weld MS: Weld Family Papers, Dorset Record Office, Dorchester.

Printed Sources

All titles were published in London unless noted otherwise. Short titles are given for those sources cited frequently in the notes.

Allison, A.F. and Rogers, D.M. [eds.]. *Biographical Studies, 1534–1829* (Bognor Regis, 1951, two vols.)

Andrews, C. Bruyn [ed]. *The Torrington Diaries Containing the Tours through England and Wales of the Hon. John Byng (Later Fifth Viscount Torrington) between the Years 1781 and 1794* (1934–1938).

Angelo, Henry. *Reminiscences of Henry Angelo* . . . (1828–30, two vols.).

Annual Register.

Anon. *Advice to Protestants of All Capacities, how to behave themselves when they are tampered with to change their Religion.*

Anon. *The Canonization of Thomas* . . . *[Weld] Esq. who has Lately Erected at East L——h Dorset a Monastery and there Established a Body of Monks* (London, 1801).

Anon. *A Description of Brighthelmstone and the Adjacent Country, or, The New Guide for Ladies and Gentlemen resorting to that Place of Health and Amusement* (Brighthelmstone and London, n.d. [1781?]).

Anon. 'An Evening at Mrs Fitzherbert's' in *The St James's Magazine* (Oct. 1862).

Anon. *A Guide to the Collegiate Church of St Bartholomew, Tong.* (1993, 5th edn. revised).

Anon. *An Improved Edition of the Songs in the Burletta of Midas, Adapted to the Times* (Dublin, 1789).

Anon. *Lulworth Castle* (n.d.).

Anon. *The New Weymouth Guide* (1785).

Anon. *On the Building of a Monastery in Dorset* (Oxford, 1795).

Anon. *The Genuine Book. An Inquiry, or Delicate Investigation into the Conduct of Her Royal Highness The Princess of Wales* . . . (1813).

Anon. *Shropshire: Historical Descriptive Biographical in Mate's County Series* (Bournemouth, 1906, two vols.).

Anon. *The Standard Library Cyclopaedia* . . . (1849, four vols.).

Anson, Elizabeth and Florence [eds.]. *Mary Hamilton . . . at Court and at Home . . . 1756–1816* (1925).

Aspinall, A. [ed]. *The Correspondence of George, Prince of Wales 1770–1812* (1963–1971, 8 vols.). [Aspinall, *P. of W.*].

Aspinall, A. [ed]. *The Later Correspondence of George III, 1783–1810* (Cambridge, five vols., 1962–70). [Aspinall, *George III*].

Aspinall, A. [ed], *The Letters of King George IV 1812–1830* (1938, three vols.) [Aspinall, *George IV*].

Aspinall, A. *Politics and the Press, c. 1780–1850* (1949).

Auden, J.E. 'The Minister's Library in Tong Church' in *Transactions of the Shropshire Archaeological Society* (4th ser., 1929–30).

Baigent, F.J. [ed]. *The Catholic Registers of the Brambridge (afterwards Highbridge) Mission in Hampshire 1766–1869* in *Catholic Record Society Miscellanea*, Vol. XXVII.5.

Baigent, F.J. [ed]. *Notes on Some Entries Relating to Recusants in the Registers of the Parish Church of Twyford (Hampshire)* (1927).

Bibliography

Baily's Racing Register from the Earliest Records to the Close of the Year 1842 (1845, three vols.).

Balderston, Katherine C. [ed]. *Thraliana: The Diary of Mrs Hester Lynch Thrale (later Mrs Piozzi) 1776–1809* (Oxford, 1951 2nd ed., two vols.).

Balteau, J. et al. *Dictionnaire de biographie française* (Paris, 1929–, 18 vols to date).

Banerji, Christiane and Donald, Diana [trans. & eds.]. *Gillray Observed: The Earliest Account of his Caricatures in London und Paris* (Cambridge, 1999).

Bateson, Edward. *A History of Northumberland* (Newcastle-upon-Tyne & London, 1893–1940, 15 vols.).

Bell, Mrs G.H. [ed]. *The Hamwood Papers of the Ladies of Llangollen and Caroline Hamilton* (1930).

Bence-Jones, Mark. *The Catholic Families* (1992).

Benjafield, John. *Statement of Facts* (Bury St Edmunds, 1813).

Berkeley, Joan. *Lulworth and the Welds* (Gillingham, Dorset, 1971).

[Berrington, The Rev Joseph], *The State and Behaviour of English Catholics from the Reformation to the Year 1780 with a View of their present Number, Wealth, Character, &c* (1780).

Bessborough, The Earl of [ed]. *Georgiana: Extracts from the Correspondence of Georgiana, Duchess of Devonshire* (1955). [Bessborough, Georgiana].

Bettany, Lewis [ed]. *Edward Jerningham and His Friends: A Series of Eighteenth Century Letters* (1919).

Bewley, Christina and David. *Gentleman Radical: A Life of John Horne Tooke 1736–1812* (1998).

Bickley, Francis [ed]. *The Diaries of Sylvester Douglas (Lord Glenbervie)* (1928, two vols.).

Bird, Anthony. *The Damnable Duke of Cumberland* (1966).

Birt, Henry Norbert. *Obit Book of the English Benedictines 1600–1812* (Edinburgh, 1970 reprint).

Bissell, Willard [ed]. *The Diary of Benjamin Robert Haydon* (Cambridge, Mass., U.S.A., 1960–63, five vols.).

Blake, Mrs Warrenne [ed]. *An Irish Beauty of the Regency compiled from 'Mes Souvenirs' – the Unpublished Journals of the Hon Mrs Calvert 1789–1822* (1911).

Bossy, John. *The English Catholic Community 1570–1850* (1975).

Boyle, Sir Courtenay [ed]. *Mary Boyle: Her Book* (1901).

Brooke, John. *King George III* (1972).

Brooke, John and Gandy, Julia [eds.]. *The Prime Ministers' Papers: Wellington. Political Correspondence I: 1833 – November 1834* (1975).

[Brougham, Henry]. 'George the Fourth and Queen Caroline – Abuses of the Press', *Edinburgh Review*, LXVII.

Brougham, Henry, Lord. *Historical Sketches of Statesmen who Flourished in the Time of George III: Second Series* (1839).

Bryan III, J. and Murphy, Charles J.V. *The Windsor Story* (1979).

Buck, Samuel and Nathaniel. 'The East View of Tong Castle, in the County of Salop' (1731).

Buck, Samuel and Nathaniel. 'The South View of Acton Burnell Castle, in the County of Salop' (1731).

Buckingham and Chandos, The Duke of. *Memoirs of the Court and Cabinets of George the Third from Original Family Documents* (1853, two vols, 2nd ed.).

Buckle, Richard [ed]. *The Prettiest Girl in England: The Love Story of Mrs Fitzherbert's Niece from Journals* (1958).

Burke, Sir Bernard. *Reminiscences Ancestral, Anecdotal and Historic* (n.d.).

Burke, John. *A Genealogical and Heraldic History of the Commoners of Great Britain and Ireland* (1836–38, four vols.).

Burton, Edwin H. *The Life and Times of Bishop Challoner, 1691–1781* (1909, two vols.).

Burton, Elizabeth. *The Pageant of Georgian England* (1967).

[Bury, Lady Charlotte]. *Diary Illustrative of the Times of George the Fourth, interspersed with Original Letters from the Late Queen Caroline, and from Various Other Distinguished Persons.* (1838–39, four vols. Vols. 3 & 4 were edited by John Galt and published in 1839).

Butler, Charles. *Historical Memoirs Respecting the English, Irish, and Scottish Catholics, from the Reformation, to the Present Time.* (1819–1821, four vols.).

Butler, Charles. *Reminiscences* (1824, 4th edn.).

Butler, E.M. [ed]. *A Regency Visitor: The English Tour of Prince Pückler-Muskau Described in his Letters 1826–1828* (1957).

Carder, Timothy. *The Encyclopaedia of Brighton* (Brighton, 1990).

Castle, Egerton [ed]. *The Jerningham Letters (1780–1843) being Excerpts from the Correspondence and Diaries of the Honourable Lady Jerningham and of her Daughter Lady Bedingfeld* (1896, two vols.).

[Challoner, Richard]. *The Garden of the Soul . . .* (1755).

Chamberlaine, W.H. *A Tale of Lulworth* (Bath, 1888).

Chapman, John H. [ed]. *The Register Book of Marriages belonging to the Parish of St George, Hanover Square . . . 1725–1787* (1886).

Chenaye des Bois et Badier, F. Aubert de la [eds.]. *Dictionnaire de la noblesse* (Paris, 1863–77, 19 vols. 3rd ed.).

Claudio. *An Antidote to Poison; or, a Full Reply to Mr Jefferys's Attack upon the Character and Conduct of His Royal Highness The Prince of Wales . . .* (1806, 2nd edn.).

Clifford, Sir Thomas, Bart. and Clifford, Arthur. *A Topographical and Historical*

Description of the Parish of Tixall, in the County of Stafford. (Paris, 1817).

Colchester, Charles, Lord [ed]. *The Diary and Correspondence of Charles Abbot, Lord Colchester Speaker of the House of Commons 1801–1817* (1861, three vols.).

[Combe, William]. *The Royal Dream; or the P—— in a Panic. An Eclogue, with Annotations* (1785).

Copeland, Thomas W. et al [eds.]. *The Correspondence of Edmund Burke* (Cambridge, 1958–1978, ten vols.).

Cozens-Hardy, Basil [ed]. *The Diary of Sylas Neville 1767–1788* (1950).

Croly, The Rev George. *The Life and Times of . . . George the Fourth . . .* (1830).

Daniell, Frederick B. *A Catalogue Raisonné of the Engraved Works of Richard Cosway, R.A.* (1890).

Dickinson, Violet [ed]. *Miss Eden's Letters* (1919).

Dillon, Henriette-Lucy (Marquise de La Tour du Pin) [Harcourt, Felice, ed & trans]. *Memoirs of Madame de La Tour du Pin* (New York, 1971).

Dixon, W. Hepworth [ed]. *Lady Morgan's Memoirs: Autobiography, Diaries and Correspondence* (1862, 2 vols.).

Donald, Diana. *The Age of Caricature: Satirical Prints in the Reign of George III* (1996).

Doran, John. *Lives of the Queens of England of the House of Hanover* (1855, two vols.).

Edgcumbe, Richard [ed]. *The Diary of Frances Lady Shelley 1787–1817* (1912).

Egremont, Lord. *Wyndham and Children First* (1968).

Ehrman, John. *The Younger Pitt: The Years of Acclaim* (1969).

Ellis, Lucy and Turquan, Joseph. *La Belle Pamela (Lady Edward Fitzgerald)* (1924).

Elwin, Malcolm [ed]. *The Noels and the Milbankes: their Letters for Twenty-Five Years 1767–1792* (1967).

English Heritage. *Register of Parks and Gardens of Special Historic Interest in England: Shropshire: Shrewsbury and Atcham: Acton Burnell.*

Environment, Department of. *Listed Building Schedule: Acton Burnell Hall* (1952).

Erdeswicke, Sampson. *A Survey of Staffordshire . . .* (1717).

Fairbridge, Dorothy. *Lady Anne Barnard at the Cape of Good Hope 1797–1802* (Oxford, 1924).

Farrant, Sue. *Georgian Brighton, 1740–1820* (Brighton, 1980).

Fitzherbert, Nicholas. *The Fitzherbert Family 1125–1988,* (unpublished T.S.)

Fletcher, The Rev W.G.D., 'Notes on Some Shropshire Royal Descents' in *Transactions of the Shropshire Archaeological and Natural History Society* (1908).

Foreman, Amanda. *Georgiana Duchess of Devonshire* (1998).

Francis, Lady. *Memoirs of Sir Philip Francis, K.C.B., with Correspondence and Journals* (1867, two vols.).

Fraser, Flora. *The Unruly Queen: The Life of Queen Caroline* (1996).

Fraser, Sir William Augustus. *Hic et Ubique* (1893).

Fulcher, G.W. [Fulcher, E.S., ed]. *Life of Thomas Gainsborough, R.A.* (1856, 2nd edn.).

Garlick, Kenneth and Cave, Kathryn [eds.]. *The Diary of Joseph Farington* (New Haven, 18 vols., 1978–1998). [*Farington Diary*].

G.E.C. [White, G.H., ed.] *The Complete Peerage: Vol XII Part I* (1953).

George, M. Dorothy. *Catalogue of Political and Personal Satires Preserved in the Department of Prints and Drawings in the British Museum: Vols. VI – IX* (1938–1952).

Gillow, Joseph and Trappes-Lomax, Richard [eds.]. *The Diary of the 'Blue Nuns' or Order of the Immaculate Conception of Our Lady, at Paris. 1658–1810* (1910). Catholic Record Society, Vol. VIII.

Gillow, Joseph. *A Literary and Biographical History, or Bibliographical Dictionary of the English Catholics from the Breach with Rome, in 1534, to the Present Time.* (n.d. [1855], five vols).

Gore, John [ed]. *Creevey's Life and Times: A Further Selection from the Correspondence of Thomas Creevey Born 1768 – Died 1838* (1934).

Graham, John A. *Memoirs of John Horne Tooke . . .* (New York, 1828).

Granville, Castalia, Countess [ed]. *Lord Granville Leveson Gower (First Earl Granville) Private Correspondence 1781 to 1821.* (1916, two vols.).

Gray, Denis. *Spencer Perceval: The Evangelical Prime Minister 1762–1812* (Manchester, 1963).

Grierson, Sir Herbert [ed]. *The Letters of Sir Walter Scott* (1937, twelve vols.).

Griffiths, George. *A History of Tong, Shropshire, Its Church, Manor, Parish College, Early Owners, and Clergy, with Notes on Boscobel* (1894, 2nd edn.).

Haile, Martin and Bonney, Edwin. *Life and Letters of John Lingard 1771–1851* (n.d. [1911]).

[Hamilton, Lady Anne]. *The Authentic Records of the Court of England, for the Last Seventy Years* (1832).

Hanger, George [Combe, William, editor]. *The Life, Adventures, and Opinions of Col George Hanger. Written by Himself.* (1801, two vols.).

Harcourt, Edward William [ed]. *The Harcourt Papers* (1880–1905, fourteen vols., privately printed).

Harcourt, The Rev Leveson Vernon [ed]. *The Diaries and Correspondence of the Right Hon. George Rose: Containing Original Letters of the Most Distinguished Statesmen of His Day* (1860, two vols.).

Healey, Edna, Lady. *Coutts & Co 1692–1992: The Portrait of a Private Bank* (1992).

Herbert, Lord [ed]. *Pembroke Papers (1780–1794) Letters and Diaries of Henry, Tenth Earl of Pembroke and his Circle* (1950).

Hibbert, Christopher. *George III: A Personal History* (1998).

Historical Manuscripts Commission. *Ailesbury Manuscripts* (1898).

Historical Manuscripts Commission. *The Manuscripts and Correspondence of James, First Earl of Charlemont* (1891–1894, two vols.).

Historical Manuscripts Commission, *The Manuscripts of His Grace the Duke of Rutland* . . . (1888–1905, four vols.) [*Rutland MS*].

Historical Manuscripts Commission. *The Manuscripts of J.B. Fortesque, Esq., Preserved at Dropmore* (1892–1927, ten vols.). [*Fortesque MS*].

Historical Manuscripts Commission. *The Manuscripts of Lord Spencer* (1871).

Hodgson, The Rev. John et al. *A Topographical and Historical Description of the County of Northumberland* . . . (n.d. [1810]).

Hogge, G.[ed]. *The Journal and Correspondence of William [Eden], Lord Auckland* . . . (1861, four vols.) [*Auckland Journal*].

Holland, Henry Richard, Lord [Holland, Henry Edward, Lord, ed]. *Memoirs of the Whig Party During my Time* (two vols., 1854).

Home, J.A. [ed]. *The Letters and Journals of Lady Mary Coke* (1970 edn., four vols.).

Howell-Thomas, Dorothy. *Lord Melbourne's Susan* (1978).

Huish, Robert. *Memoirs of George the Fourth* . . . (1830, two vols.). [*Huish*].

Hutchins, John [Shipp, William and Hodson, J.W., eds.], *The History and Antiquities of Dorset* (1861–70, four vols., third edn.).

Ilchester, The Countess of and Stavordale, Lord [eds.]. *The Life and Letters of Lady Sarah Lennox 1745–1826* . . . (1901, two vols.).

Ilchester, Earl of. *Elizabeth, Lady Holland to her Son 1821–1845* (1946).

Ilchester, Earl of. *The Home of the Hollands 1605–1820* (1937).

Ilchester, Earl of [ed]. *The Journal of the Hon. Henry Edward Fox (afterwards fourth and last Lord Holland) 1818–1830* (1923).

Jackson, Lady [ed]. *The Bath Archives. A Further Selection from the Diaries and Letters of Sir George Jackson* . . . (1873, two vols.).

Jacob, W.H. *Hampshire at the Opening of the Twentieth Century* (Brighton, 1905).

[Jefferys, Nathaniel]. *A Review of the Conduct of His Royal Highness the Prince of Wales in his Various Transactions with Mr Jefferys* . . . (n.d. [1806]).

Jennings, Louis J. [ed]. *The Croker Papers. The Correspondence and Diaries of . . . John Wilson Croker* . . . (1884, three vols.).

Johnson, R. Brimley [ed]. *The Letters of Lady Louisa Stuart* (1926).

Johnstone, Julia. *Confessions of Julia Johnstone, written by Herself, in Contradiction to the Fables of Harriette Wilson* (1825).

Jupp, Peter. *Lord Grenville, 1759–1834* (Oxford, 1985).

Kirk, The Rev John [Pollen, J.H. and Burton, Edwin, eds.], *Biographies of English Catholics in the Eighteenth Century* (1909).

Lamington, Lord. *In the Days of the Dandies* (1890).

Langdale, Charles [ed]. *Memoirs of Mrs Fitzherbert; with an Account of Her Marriage with H.R.H. the Prince of Wales, afterwards King George the Fourth* (1856). Langdale edited Lord Stourton's notes of his conversations with M.F. [Langdale].

Lansdown, The Marquis of [ed]. *The Queeney Letters being Letters Addressed to Hester Maria Thrale . . .* (1934).

Latouche, Robert. *Histoire de Nice* (Nice, 1951, two vols.).

Leconfield, Maud, Lady and Gore, John [eds.]. *Three Howard Sisters: Selections from the Writings of Lady Caroline Lascelles, Lady Dover and Countess Gower 1825–1833* (1955).

Lees-Milne, James. *The Enigmatic Edwardian: The Life of Reginald, 2nd Viscount Esher* (1988 edn.).

LeFanu, William [ed]. *Betsy Sheridan's Journal: Letters from Sheridan's Sister 1784–1786 and 1788–1790* (1960).

Lelanne, Ludovic. *Dictionnaire historique de la France* (Paris, 1777, 2nd edn.).

Leslie, Anita. *Mrs Fitzherbert* (1960).

Leslie, Shane. *Mrs Fitzherbert: A Life Chiefly from Unpublished Sources* (1939). [Leslie, *Mrs Fitzherbert*].

Leslie, Shane. *The Letters of Mrs Fitzherbert and Connected Papers being the second volume of the life of Mrs Fitzherbert.* (1940). [Leslie, *Letters*].

Lewis, Lady Theresa [ed]. *Extracts of the Journals and Correspondence of Miss Berry from the Year 1783 to 1852* (1865, three vols.).

Lewis, W.S. et al. *The Yale Edition of Horace Walpole's Correspondence* (1937–1999, 55 vols.). [*Yale: Walpole*].

Lindsay, Lord. *Lives of the Lindsays; or A Memoir of the House of Crawford and Balcarres.* (1840. 3 vols. privately printed).

Lloyd, Stephen. *Richard & Maria Cosway: Regency Artists of Taste and Fashion* (Edinburgh, 1995).

Lock, F.P. *Edmund Burke: Volume I, 1730–1784* (Oxford, 1998).

[Lockhart, J.G.]. 'Chapters of Contemporary History,' *Quarterly Review*, LV.

Macalpine, Ida and Hunter, Richard. *George III and the Mad Business* (1969).

Macdonald, John. *Travels, in Various Parts of Europe, Asia, and Africa . . .* (1st publ. 1790, 1927 reprint).

Madden, R.R. *The History of the Penal Laws Enacted against Roman Catholics . . .* (1847).

Malmesbury, Earl of [ed]. *The Diaries and Correspondence of James Harris First Earl of Malmesbury* (1844, four vols.). [*Malmesbury: Diaries*].

Manners, Lady Victoria. *Matthew William Peters, R.A. His Life and Work* (1913).

Mansel, Philip. *Louis XVIII* (1999 edn.).

Marshall, Dorothy. *English People in the Eighteenth Century* (1956).

Mason, Margaret J. 'Nuns and Vocations of the Unpublished Jerningham Letters . . .' in *Recusant History*, XXI.

Massey, W.N. *A History of England during the Reign of George the Third* (1855–1863, four vols.).

[Massey, W.N.]. 'The Life and Times of Henry Lord Brougham', *Edinburgh Review*, CXXXV.

Mathew, David. *Catholicism in England. The Portrait of a Minority: Its Culture and Tradition*. (1948, 2nd. edn.).

Maxwell, Sir Herbert [ed]. *The Creevey Papers: A Selection from the Correspondence & Diaries of the Late Thomas Creevey, M.P* . . . (1923).

McGurk, John. 'Wild Geese: The Irish in European Armies (Sixteenth to Eighteenth Centuries)' in Patrick O'Sullivan [ed], *The Irish World Wide History, Heritage, Identity. Vol. I. Patterns of Migration*. (Leicester, 1992).

McManners, John. *Church and Society in Eighteenth Century France. Vol I. The Clerical Establishment and Its Social Ramifications* (Oxford, 1998).

Millar, Oliver. *The Later Georgian Pictures in the Collection of Her Majesty the Queen* (1969, two vols.).

Mingay, G.E. *English Landed Society in the Eighteenth Century* (1963).

Minto, Countess of [ed]. *Life and Letters of Sir Gilbert Elliot First Earl of Minto from 1751 to 1806* (1874, three vols.).

Mitchell, B.R. & Deane, Phyllis. *Abstract of British Historical Statistics* (Cambridge, 1971).

Mitchell, L.G. *Charles James Fox* (1997 edn.).

Mitchell, L.G. *Charles James Fox and the Disintegration of the Whig Party 1782–1794* (Oxford, 1971).

Moore, Thomas. *Memoirs of the Life of the Rt. Hon. Richard Brinsley Sheridan* (1825, two vols.).

[Mount Edgcumbe, Richard, Earl of]. *Musical Reminiscences of an Old Amateur* . . . (1827, 2nd edn.).

Mundy, Harriet Georgiana [ed]. *The Journal of Mary Frampton, from the Year 1779, until the Year 1846* . . . (1886, 3rd edn.).

Murray, Venetia. *High Society: A Social History of the Regency Period, 1788–1830* (1998).

Namier, W. and Brooke, John. *The History of Parliament: The House of Commons 1754–1790* (1964, three vols.).

Neptune [Miles, William Augustus]. *A Letter to the Prince of Wales* (1784).

Oman, Carola. *The Gascoyne Heiress: the Life and Diaries of Frances Mary Gascoyne-Cecil 1802–1839* (1968).

Page, William et al [eds.]. *Victoria County History of Dorset* (1908–1968, three vols.).

Bibliography

Page, William et al [eds.]. *The Victoria County History of Hampshire and the Isle of Wight* (1900–1912, five vols.).

Page, William et al [eds.]. *The Victoria County History of Shropshire* (1908–1989, eight vols.).

Page, William [ed] *The Victoria County History of Staffordshire* (1908–1984, twenty vols. to date).

Palmer R.R. *The Age of the Democratic Revolution* (Princeton, N.J., 1959, two vols.).

Papendiek, Charlotte [Delves Broughton, Mrs Vernon, ed]. *Court and Private Life in the Time of Queen Charlotte* . . . (1887, two vols.).

Parker, George. *A View of Society and Manners in High and Low Life* . . . (1782, two vols.).

Parkes, Joseph and Merivale, Herman. *Memoirs of Sir Philip Francis, K.C.B. with Correspondence and Journals* (1867, two vols.).

Parliamentary History.

Parliamentary Papers: House of Commons Sessional Papers of the Eighteenth Century, XXIX George III. Bills 1778–79 and 1779–80. (Wilmington, Delaware), 1975.

Parliamentary Papers, House of Lords. 1806. 'Between Mary Georgiana Emma Seymour, an Infant, by William Bentinck, Esquire, her next friend, *Appellant*. The Right Honourable George Fitzroy, commonly called the Earl of Euston, and the Honourable Henry Seymour, commonly called Lord Henry Seymour, Respondents.'

Paterson, Daniel. *A New and Accurate Description of all the Direct and Principal Cross Roads in Great Britain* ([1772], 2nd edn.).

Patterson, M.W. *Sir Francis Burdett and His Times (1770–1844)* . . . (1931, two vols.).

Petre, The Late Hon Edward [Husenbeth, the Rev D.C., ed]. *Notices of the English Colleges & Convents Established on the Continent after the Dissolution of Religious Houses in England* (n.d.).

Pevsner, Nikolaus. *The Buildings of England: Staffordshire* (1974).

Phillips, The Rev Peter. 'A Catholic Community: Shrewsbury.Part I: 1750–1850' in *Recusant History*, XX.

Philo-Veritas. 'Diamond Cut Diamond; or . . . a Free and Impartial View of Mr. Jefferys, as a Tradesman, Politician, and Courtier, during a Period of Twenty Years.' (1806, 2nd edn.).

Pickering, Anna Maria Wilhemina. *Memoirs* . . . (1903).

Pigott, Charles. *The Jockey Club* (1792).

Powell, Anthony [ed]. *The Barnard Letters 1778–1824* (1928).

Price, Cecil [ed]. *The Letters of Richard Brinsley Sheridan* (Oxford, 1966, three vols.).

Bibliography

Quennell, Peter [ed]. *The Private Letters of Princess Lieven to Prince Metternich 1820–1826* (1937).

Raikes, Thomas. *A Portion of the Journal Kept by Thomas Raikes, Esq. from 1831 to 1847* . . . (1856–57, four vols.).

Reeve, Henry [ed]. *The Greville Memoirs: A Journal of the Reigns of King George IV. King William IV. and Queen Victoria* (1888, new ed., eight vols.).

Reynolds, E.E. [ed]. *The Mawhood Diary: Selections from the Diary Note-Books of William Mawhood, Woollen-Draper of London, for the Years 1764–1790* (1956).

[Rough, Sir W., ed]. *Letters of John Wilkes . . . to His Daughter* (1804, four vols.).

Russell, Earl. *Life and Times of Charles James Fox* (1859–66, two vols.).

Russell, Lord John. *Memorials and Correspondence of Charles James Fox* (1853, four vols.).

Rutherford, Jessica M.F. *The Royal Pavilion: The Palace of George IV* (Brighton, n.d.).

Saul, David. *Prince of Pleasure: The Prince of Wales and the Making of the Regency* (1998).

S.B. [Berrington, Simon]. *A Modest Enquiry How Far Catholicks Are Guilty of the Horrid Tenets laid to their Charge . . .* (1749).

Scantlebury, Canon Robert E. *Hampshire Registers. I. The Registers and Records of Winchester* (1948).

[Seymour, Lord Robert]. *Collections & Recollections by One Who has Kept a Diary* (1898).

Shaw, Stebbing. *The History and Antiquities of Staffordshire* (1798–1801, two vols., 1976 one volume reprint).

Sheppard, Edgar. *Memorials of St James's Palace* (1894, two vols.).

Shropshire County Council Local Studies Library, Shrewsbury. *Documents concerning the Parish of Tong* (1988).

Sichel, Walter [ed]. *The Glenbervie Journals* (1910, two vols.).

Sichel, Walter [ed]. *Sheridan from New and Original Material: Including a Manuscript Diary by Georgiana Duchess of Devonshire* (1909, two vols.).

Simpson, D.H. *Maria Fitzherbert and Robert Burt, Vicar of Twickenham* (n.d.).

Smith, Barbara M. *A History of the Fitzherbert Family* (1995).

Smollet, Tobias. *The Expedition of Humphry Clinker* (1771).

Smollet, Tobias (Felsenstein, Frank, ed]. *Travels Through France and Italy* (Oxford, 1979).

Soames, Mary, Lady. *The Profligate Duke: George Spencer Churchill, fifth Duke of Marlborough, and his Duchess* (1987).

Stamper, Paul. *A Survey of Historic Parks and Gardens in Shropshire* The Archaeology Unit, Shropshire County Council. Report No. 41. 1993.

Stanhope, Earl. *Life of the Right Honourable William Pitt* (1867, four vols. 3rd edn.).

Bibliography

Sterne, Lawrence [Petrie, Graham, ed]. *A Sentimental Journey through France and Italy* (1967 edn.).

Stewart, Robert. *Henry Brougham 1778–1868: His Public Career* (1985).

Stirling, A.M.W. *Coke of Norfolk and His Friends* (1912, new edn.).

Stuart, D.M. *Dearest Bess: The Life and Times of Lady Elizabeth Foster afterwards Duchess of Devonshire from Her Unpublished Journals and Correspondence* (1955).

Surtees, Robert. *The History and Antiquities of the County Palatine of Durham* (1816–40, four vols.)

Swinburne, Henry [White, Charles, ed.]. *The Courts of Europe at the Close of the Last Century* (1841, two vols.).

Tooke, Horne. *A Letter to a Friend . . .* (1786).

Tooley, Sarah A. *Royal Palaces and Their Memories* (1902).

Turner, Michael and Mills, Dennis [eds.]. *Land and Property: The English Land Tax, 1692–1832* (Gloucester, 1986).

Vickery, Amanda. *The Gentleman's Daughter: Women's Lives in Georgian England* (1998).

Walpole, Horace [Russell Barker, G.F., ed]. *Memoirs of the Reign of King George the Third First Published by Sir Denis Le Marchant Bart . . .* (1894, four vols.).

Ward, Bernard. *Dawn of the Catholic Revival* (1905, two vols.).

Weinreb, Ben and Hibbert, Christopher. *The London Encyclopaedia* (1993).

Weld Blundell, Mr. 'Lulworth Castle' in *Proceedings of The Dorset Natural History and Antiquarian Field Club* (1892), XIII.

Wellington, Duke of [ed], *Wellington and His Friends* (1965).

Werkmeister, Lucyle. *The London Daily Press 1772–1792* (Lincoln, Nebraska, U.S.A., 1963).

Werkmeister, Lucyle. *A Newspaper History of England 1792–3* (Lincoln, Nebraska, U.S.A., 1967).

Wheatley, Henry B. [ed]. *The Historical and Posthumous Memoirs of Sir Nathaniel William Wraxall 1772–1784* (1884, five vols.) [*Wraxall: Memoirs.*]

Whitley, W.T. *Thomas Gainsborough* (1915).

Wickham Legg, L.G. [ed]. *Tusmore Papers*. Oxfordshire Record Society, Vol. XX, Section xxii.

Wilkins, W.H. *Mrs Fitzherbert and George IV* (1914, one vol. edn.) [Wilkins].

Williams, C. [ed & trans]. *Sophie in London* (1933).

Williamson, George C. *Richard Cosway, R.A. and His Wife and Pupils: Miniaturists of the Eighteenth Century* (1897).

Williams, J.A. *Bath and Rome: the Living Link* (Bath, 1963).

Wilson, Harriette. *Memoirs of Harriette Wilson written by Herself* (1825, four vols.).

[Withers, the Rev. Philip]. *Alfred, or a Narrative of the Daring and Illegal Measures to Suppress a Pamphlet . . . respecting 'Her Royal Highness the Princess of Wales,' commonly called Mrs Fitzherbert* (1789, 2nd edn.).

[Withers, the Rev. Philip]. *History of the Royal Malady . . .* (1789).

[Withers, the Rev. Philip]. *Nemesis or a Letter to Alfred. From* ****** (n.d. [1789]).

[Withers, the Rev Philip]. *Theodosius: or a Solemn Admonition to Protestant Dissenters, on the Proposed Repeal of the Test and Corporation Acts in which are considered the political and religious Characters of . . . Mr Sheridan . . . Mrs F*********** (1790).

Worrall, E.S. [ed]. *Returns of Papists 1767: Vol I. Diocese of Chester; Vol II. Dioceses of England and Wales except Chester.* Catholic Record Society. (1980, 1989).

Wright, Patrick. *The Village that Died for England: The Strange Story of Tyneham* (1995).

Wrigley, A. and Schofield, R. *The Population History of England* (Cambridge, Mass., U.S.A., 1981).

Yale: Walpole. see Lewis, W.S. et al.

Yorke, P.C. [ed]. *Letters of Princess Elizabeth of England Daughter of King George III., and Landgravine of Hesse-Homburg* (1898).

Ziegler, Philip. *Melbourne: A Biography of William Lamb 2nd Viscount Melbourne* (1976).

Newspapers

The Bon Ton Magazine.

Brighton Herald.

Gazetteer.

Gentleman's Magazine.

London Chronicle.

Morning Chronicle.

Morning Post.

Public Advertiser.

Salopian Journal.

Telegraph.

The World.

Brighton Gazette.

The Daily Universal Register.

General Advertiser.

Lloyd's Evening Post.

London Packet.

Morning Herald.

Oracle.

St. James's Chronicle.

Sussex Weekly Advertiser.

The Times.

INDEX

Acton Burnell 5–8, 12, 17, 238–9, 244, 326, 369
Adelaide, Queen 351–3
Adolphus, Prince (Duke of Cambridge; P's brother) 269, 337
Albemarle, 4th Earl of 357–8
Amelia, Princess (P's sister) 322
Amherst, 1st Baron 242, 243
Archer, Lady 62, 255
Armistead, Mrs (later Mrs Fox) 67, 95, 102, 142, 215, 314
Augusta, Princess (P's sister) 289
Augustus, Prince (Duke of Sussex; P's brother) 248, 251–2, 269, 327–8, 337

Barnard, Andrew 175
Barry Family 208–9, 253–4,
Barry, Madame du 110–11, 239
Barrymore, 7th Earl of 208–9, 241, 253–4, 371
Bath 203, 342
'Bellois, Marquis de' 115–6, 225
Berlin Gazette 160
Bessborough, Countess of 314, 317–9, 328
Bloomfield, Benjamin 320–1
Bond Street 25, 31
Bon Ton Magazine, The 249–50, 253, 275–6,

Bouverie, Edward 87–90, 94, 130,
Brambridge 17, 18, 369–70
Bridgeman, Orlando 99, 147, 191
Brighton 55–7, 130, 173–4, 200–1, 252–3, 298–9, 330–2, 371
Brougham, Henry 334–5
Broughton, Lady (M's aunt) 18, 58, 154, 155, 163
Brummel, George Bryan ('Beau') 170
Burdett, Sir Francis 352–3
Burges, James Bland 213, 221–2, 228, 273, 385n
Burke, Edmund 169, 170, 173, 181, 196, 197, 204, 215, 233, 242,
Burt, the Rev Robert 145, 147
Bury, Lady Charlotte 77–8
Butler, Elizabeth (M's cousin) 192, 290, 293
Byng, John (later 5th Viscount Torrington) 200–1

Calvert, Mrs 301, 311, 317–8, 322
Cambridge, Duke of: see Adolphus, Prince
Canterbury, Archbishop of: see Moore, John
caricatures 166–9, 174, 191, 205, 233, 241, 250–1, 281, 313, 333
Carlton House 73, 88, 103, 106,

153, 170, 173, 179, 194, 198, 218, 246–7, 281, 284–6, 323–4

Caroline, Princess (P's wife) 259, 272–82, 286–7, 292, 286, 293, 304, 312–4, 316, 332, 334–6

Carpenter, Lady Almeria 60, 155, 203

Catholics: 'Anti-Popery' 5–15, 16, 154, 164, 196, 200, 224–5, 214, 220, 230, 239–40, 296, 312, 315, 359, 367; Catholic bias of previous biographers 2–3, 124; Catholic Relief Act (1778), 40–1; Catholic Relief Act (1791) 237–8; Catholicism, attraction when in Europe, 92; collapse of church in France & Netherlands 214; distribution of, 11–12; 'emancipation', campaign for 312, 327–8, 337; English history and society, place in 5–15, 16; Fox on prejudice against 143; French emigres 239–40; 'gentlemen, religion fit for' 238; gentry 26; Gordon Riots (1780) 48–50; growing tolerance of 14–15; growth of, 1796–1837 367; laws against 6, 8–11, 164–5; M's appeal to Pope (1799) 293–5; M's marriage, Catholic view of 83; M's marriage, people assume by Catholic priest 169, 156, 228; numbers of 13; Regency Crisis of 1788–9 213–234

Challoner, Bishop Richard 13–15,

Charlotte, Queen (P's mother) 80, 85, 120–1, 154, 215–6, 221–2, 231–2, 246–8, 260, 272, 276, 286, 303, 314

Charlotte, Princess (P's daughter) 283, 309, 313, 323, 332, 338

Charlotte, Princess (Princess Royal; P's sister) 248

Chartres, Duc de (after 1785, Duc d'Orléans) 95, 98, 109–11, 114, 171, 202, 207, 228, 239, 245

Churchill, Sir Winston 368–9

Clarence, Duke of: *see* William, Prince

Clermont, Earl and Countess of 155, 253, 266

Coke, Thomas William 207–8, 267

Combe, William 120

Conway, Capt the Hon Hugh: *see* Seymour, Lord Hugh

Conway, the Hon Robert (Lord Robert Seymour) 206

Conyngham, Marchioness of 336, 348

Cosway, Richard 66, 140, 350–1

Coutts Bank 358, 368

Coutts, Thomas 246–7, 274, 281, 287, 313, 316, 339

Creevey, Eleanor 4, 302–5, 328

Croker, J.W. 331, 376–7n

Croly, the Rev George 359

Cruickshank, Isaac 167

Cumberland, Ernest, Duke of: *see* Ernest, Prince

Cumberland, Henry, Duke of (P's uncle) 56, 59, 71–2, 134, 139, 154, 160, 164, 201, 207

Cumberland, Duchess of (P's aunt), 62, 134, 139, 143, 180, 207, 216, 250, 247, 257, 268

Daily Universal Register, The: *see The Times*

Darnley, 4th Earl of 287, 347

Dawson-Damer, George 339–40, 362–3

Denbigh, 6th Earl of 159, 165, 173, 241

Dessein or Dessin (Pierre Quillac) 92

Devonshire, Elizabeth, Duchess of: *see* Foster, Lady Elizabeth

Devonshire, Georgiana, Duchess of 38, 47–8, 68–9, 75–6, 80, 86, 88–90, 95–6, 98, 116–7, 129, 139, 144, 147, 155–6, 158, 170, 176, 216–7, 220, 223–4, 241, 273, 296–7, 301–2, 304, 314, 316, 365

Devonshire, 5th Duke of 70, 139, 144, 147

Dighton, Robert 208

Dorset, 3rd Duke of 111–2, 113, 129, 174

Douglas, Sylvester, (1st Baron Glenbervie) 44, 69, 238, 286, 299, 343

Douglass, John 295

Downshire, Marchioness of 302, 320, 355

Dundas, Henry 230, 242, 263

Edward VIII 368

Edward, Prince (Duke of Kent; P's brother) 269, 291, 298, 321, 313, 332, 337–8, 349, 355, 358, 395n

Egremont, 3rd Earl of 61, 70, 288, 343, 331, 352

Elizabeth, Princess (P's sister) 338, 354

Elizabeth, Queen (the Queen Mother) 368–9

Elliot, Sir Gilbert: *see* Minto, 1st Earl of

Elliott, Hugh 134, 138–9

Ernest, Prince (Duke of Cumberland; P's brother) 269, 272, 291, 293, 286–7, 290, 337

Errington, Henry (M's uncle) 18, 36, 59, 62, 75, 135, 145, 147, 154, 163, 191, 250, 290, 315, 318, 326–7, 335, 345, 355

Erskine, Thomas 170, 242

Esher, 2nd Viscount 3, 358–9

Esher Collection 255, 262, 359, 364

Euston, Countess of 309–12

Euston, Earl of 308, 310–11

eyes, fashion for miniatures of 140

Farington, Joseph 288, 300,

faro 62, 120

'fat, fair and forty': *see* under M

Fermor, Frances (M's aunt) 200

Fermor, William (M's uncle) 45–6, 53, 163, 200, 237

Fitzherbert, Basil (M's brother-in-law) 46, 99, 100, 105, 113

Fitzherbert, Family 18, 42, 370

Fitzherbert, Maria: age, exaggerated by critics 166, 168, 169, 275; allowance from P, 172, 298, 326, 333, 345–8; appearance, 30, 48, 58, 114, 179, 301, 353, 361, 364; Barry family, relations with 209–21; biographer, choosing 2–3, 86, 303, 359–60; blackmail of P. 291, 318, 326–7, 345–6; birth and childhood 16–18; bosom 78, 179; Brougham 334–5; buildings associated with 369–71; cards 302; Caroline, Princess 279, 314,334–6; Catholicism 5–16, 125, 127, 148, 311–2; character 20, 57–9, 97, 124–8, 151; Charlotte, Princess 313, 323; children ability to have, 44–5; children by P 174–8, 360, 369; Commonplace

Book, 125–7, 151; Commons' debate (1787) over P's debts 182–98; Court, presentation at 38–9, 376n; dancing, fondness for, 97; death & funeral 360–2; 'Delicate Investigation', 314–5, 334–5; dignity 293–6; dilemma as P's wife 170, 325; education 18–20; estate of 362–3; Europe, 1784–5, trip to 84–122, 131–3; family background 5–8; 'Fat, fair and forty', first used for her 168; films about 369; Fitzherbert, Thomas 39–40, 41–2, 45–7, 50–54, 149, 203; 'Fitzherbert hats' 227; flirting, enjoyment of 124, 255–6, 261–2, 295; Fox, hatred for 190, 220; France, 1785 visit to 105–114, 129; frankness, 142, 188, 193, 345, 352, 354; French Revolution 235, 238–40; friends, difficulties with P's 253– 4; gambling 97, 302; Gloucester, Duke & Duchess of 132– 3; Gordon, Lord George 198–200; Gordon Riots 48–50, 164; gossip, love of 303, 322, 328; 'grandmother' 340–2; Hertford, Marchioness of 316–322, 324–5, 327–8; Holland, 1784 visit to 128–9; 'Holland Plan', 101–2; honeymoon 148; humour, sense of 59, 95, 209, 321, 372; intellectual outlook, 127; jealousy 254–5, 273–4; Jefferys, Nathaniel 244; jewels 235, 363; kindness 330–1, 363–4; Lady Anne Lindsay's analysis of 128, 141, 151, 365; Jersey, Countess of 259–60, 262–4, 266–7, 269; Marin, Comte

de 114–6, 380; marriage to P, validity of 81–4, 137, 149, 150, 252; money 274–5, 288, 298, 318, 333, 345–8, 352, 362–3; music 97, 353; newspapers, pays for 'puffs' in 165; Noailles, affair with 261–3, 284; obese, caricatured as 168, 169; obesity, problem of 342–4; ocean travel, hatred of 91; old age & death 329–55, 360–365; Paris, 1785 visit 105–11; Paris, 1814 visit 343–4; peerage 153, 216–8, 245, 299, 336, 352; plays about 369; Pope, 1799 appeal to 293–6, 357; pregnancy by P, rumours of 161, 168, 174; pride 113, 137, 148–9, 218–9, 304, 324–5, 344, 346, 364; P, last letter to 349–50; P, reasons for marrying 136–7, 148–51; private papers, disposal of 355–9; pronunciation of maiden name 7; prude, M. no, 95, 124; Regency 323; regency crisis of 1788–9 211–234; regency crisis of 1804 315–6; religious views of, 104, 125, 127, 311, 330–1; 'Roman Catholic nose' 342, 371–2; Royal Family, relations with 247–8, 313; St James's Sq., house in 163, 172, 173 179, 274; separation, talk of 256; separation (1794) 259–72, 348–9; separation (1811) 322–8, 333; Seymour, Minney, wrangle over 307–12; son, 44–5; Steine, house in 298; temper 127–8, 254–5, 264, 267, 271, 273–4, 348, 357; theatre 353; Tilney Street home 274, 332, 371, 358; Versailles, M's 1785 visit to

111–13; wedding rings 361; Weld, Edward 24–36; widowhood after Edward Weld's death 36–37; widowhood after Thomas Fitzherbert's death, 52–54; Will of 1796, P's 283–6, 292–3 *see*: Brighton; caricatures; Charlotte, Queen. feet, small 249

Fitzherbert, Sister Mary (M's sister-in-law) 108

Fitzherbert, Thomas (M's 2nd husband) 39–42, 44, 46–7, 50–1, 52–4, 149, 203

Fordyce, Lady Margaret 43, 44, 59, 93, 105, 134, 177, 266, 268, 293, 385n

foreheads 22, 64

Foster, Lady Elizabeth (2nd wife of 5th Duke of Devonshire), 129,176, 325, 334

Fox, Charles James 70–1, 88, 95, 117–20, 142–3, 170, 172–3, 181, 183, 187–90, 191–7, 207–8, 215–7, 219–222, 229, 232, 240–2, 248, 316

Frampton family 24, 30, 34, 50, 73–4, 249

Francis, Sir Philip 170, 193, 238

Frederick, Prince (later Duke of York; P's brother) 79, 87, 102, 120,121, 138–9, 143, 165, 190, 202, 215, 223, 231–3, 241–2, 245, 248–51, 253–4, 266, 270–1, 288, 313–4, 337–9, 348, 355, 355–6

French Revolution 234–5, 238–40, 269, 280

Gainsborough, Thomas 27, 30–1, 84, 90, 179, 363, 371–2

gambling 62, 97

Geneva 131, 132

Genlis, Comtesse de 109–10

George III (P's father) 62–5, 70, 74, 80, 85, 103–4, 117–21, 138, 146, 149–50, 154, 172, 178, 181,183, 193, 202, 203, 211–234, 241–2, 246, 248–9, 251, 269, 271, 273, 276–7, 280, 286–7, 291, 303, 314–6, 322–3, 333

George IV *see* Wales, Prince of

Gillray, James 166, 169, 195–6, 241, 334, 354

Gloucester, Duchess of (P's aunt) 132–3, 154–5, 157,

Gloucester, William Henry, Duke of (P's uncle) 56, 60–1, 71–2, 82, 132–3, 149, 154–5, 157, 162, 178, 203, 212, 216, 247, 261, 355

Gloucester, William, Duke of (P's cousin) 312, 338

Gordon, dowager Duchess of 197, 223, 263

Gordon, Lord George 48, 50, 170, 198–200, 224, 315

Gordon Riots (1780) 48–50, 164

Grey, Charles (2nd Earl Grey) 170, 188, 230, 353

Gurwood, John 354, 362, 368

Haggerston, Sir Carnaby (M's brother-in-law) 153, 199

Haggerston, Frances, Lady (M's sister) 17, 36, 43, 132, 300, 343, 354

Halford, Sir Henry 328, 349

Hamilton, Lady Anne 177, 360

Hanger, George 62, 78, 87, 139, 168, 169, 171, 194, 254

Hanover 229

Hardenburg, Countess von 67–8

Harris, James   See Malmesbury, 1st
    Earl of
Hastings, Warren   181, 203–4
Hertford, 1st Marquess of   161,
    311–12, 316–7
Hertford, Marchioness of   308,
    311–12, 316–22, 324–5, 327–8, 333
Hervey, Henry Augustus Frederick
    175–6
Holland, 3rd Baron   150, 194, 195,
    368
Holland, Lady   325–6, 340, 353
Huish, Robert   149, 176–7, 247, 257,
    359

Invalides, Les   108–9

Jackson, George   321–2, 327
Jefferys, Nathaniel   244, 313
Jerningham, Edward   256, 273, 288,
    313
Jerningham, Hon Edward   340–1,
    362
Jerningham, Frances, Lady   20, 37,
    38, 158, 165, 293, 296–7, 328
Jersey, Frances, Countess of   234,
    259–60, 262–4, 266–7, 269, 273,
    275–6, 278, 283, 286, 288, 290–3,
    297, 315, 333
Johnstone, Julia   211–2
Jordan, Mrs Dorothy   169, 249–50,
    269, 299, 338

Keate, Thomas   87–90
Kempshott Park   246
Kent, Duke of: *see* Edward, Prince
Kenyon, Lloyd 1st Baron   226
Knight, the Rev Johnes   144
Knighton, Sir William   178, 348,
    355–7

Lade, Sir John & Lady   253–4
Lamballe, Princess de   201, 239
Langdale, Charles   368
Langdale, Lady (M's aunt)   179
Langdale, 5th Baron (M's uncle)   8,
Langdale, Thomas   49
'Lass of Richmond Hill, The'
    79–80
Leslie, Sir Shane   3, 21, 30, 368–9
Lindsay, Lady Anne (later Lady
    Anne Barnard)   43–4, 58–60, 76,
    80, 84–6, 91–130, 133–7, 141–2,
    146–7, 151,156, 162–3, 168–9, 170,
    175, 177, 193, 262, 267–8, 279,
    281, 283, 297, 325–7, 336, 345–7,
    355, 365
'Llangollen, Ladies of'   212
London Chronicle   276, 278, 281
London und Paris   166
loo   24, 330
Lord Hardwicke's marriage Act
    (1753)   10–11, 82, 83–4
Lothian, 5th Marquess of   165, 161
Louis XV   19
Louis XVI   112–3, 239
Louis XVIII   323–4, 343
Louise, Princess, of Orange   100,
    104, 129–30, 141
Lulworth Castle   21, 26–28, 29–30,
    32, 50, 239, 370

McMahon, John   288–9, 292, 316,
    326, 328, 346, 355
magnetism   172
Malmesbury, 1st Earl of   101,
    119–22, 240, 242, 249, 251, 245–6,
    255, 273, 276, 279, 291, 300–1,
    313–5
Mansfield, Lord (Lord Chief Justice)
    146

Marie Antoinette 111, 112–4, 199–200, 239

Marin (Marini), Comte de 52, 114–6, 129

Marine Villa (Brighton) 130,179, 201, 298, 301, 326, 351–2 *see* Royal Pavilion

Mary, Princess (P's sister) 289

Melbourne, Viscountess 97, 131, 296

Melbourne, 2nd Viscount 61, 341, 368

Minney (M's adopted daughter) *see* Seymour, Mary

Minto, 1st Earl of 153, 182, 190–1, 204–5, 229, 231, 232, 249, 292

Minto, 2nd Earl of 187

Moira, 2nd Earl of 170, 241, 246, 285, 289, 328, 355, 382–3n

Molyneux, the Hon Maria (M's grandmother) 55

Molyneux, Viscountess (M's cousin) 179

Moore, Rt Rev John 146, 197, 278

Morning Chronicle 334

Morning Herald 79, 201,

Morning Post 156, 201, 205, 217, 220, 224

Mornington, Earl of 174, 267

mouths, fashion for miniatures of 140

Murray, Lady Augusta 251

Nassau, Fr John 294–5

necklace, affair of the 113–4, 200

Nelson, Horatio 299, 303,305

'nemesis': *see* Withers, Philip

'Neptune' 73, 319

Newnham, Nathaniel 181–3, 184, 185, 193

newspapers 165

Nice 51–2

Noel, the Hon Thomas: *see* Wentworth, 2nd Viscount

Noailles, Charles de 261–3, 275, 284

Noailles, Duc de 240

Norfolk, 10th Duke of 131

Norfolk, 11th Duke of 253, 300, 305

North, Lord (later 2nd Earl of Guilford) 40, 169, 170, 178, 229, 300

Northumberland, 2nd Duke of 316

Onslow, Lord 87–90

opera, importance of 153, 155, 157–8, 197, 204, 227, 287, 293

Oracle 242–3, 287

Ord, James 175–6

Palais Royal 114, 109

Papendiek, Charlotte 63, 65, 146

Paris 19, 53, 93, 100, 105–111, 134, 343, 360

Payne, John Willett 170–1, 173, 223, 228, 234, 241, 262, 264–6, 268–70, 275–6, 285–7, 290, 292–3, 297, 320

Perceval, Spencer 312, 315, 323

'Perdita' (Mary Robinson) 66–7, 151, 165, 171, 352, 378n

Peters, Matthew William 198, 313

Petre, Hon Juliana 23

Petre, 9th Baron 159, 163, 237

phaetons, 46, 205–6, 208

Pienne, Duchess de la 253

pig, learned 131

Pigot, Isabella (Bell) 163–4, 166,

Index

207, 253, 255–6, 261–4, 268

Piozzi, Mrs Hester (Thrale) 38–9, 114, 178, 214, 275, 376n

Pitt, William 134, 138, 149, 165, 173, 181–3, 186–7, 189, 193, 195–6, 199, 203, 211–4, 216, 220–1, 223, 229, 231–2, 240, 242, 269–71, 274, 280–1, 315

Portland, 3rd Duke of 119, 173, 181, 197, 202, 215, 222, 240, 243, 245, 269–71

Portland, Duchess of 155

Princess Royal: *see* Charlotte, Princess

Puckler-Muskau, Prince 330

Queensberry, 4th Duke of 253

Raikes, Thomas 254, 332–3

Rambler's Magazine 205–6

Ranelagh 31, 45, 130, 172

Regency Act (1765) 219

Regency (1811) 323

Regency Crisis of 1788–9 211–234

Regency Crisis of 1804 315–6

Reynolds, Sir Joshua 31, 104, 172, 1798

Richmond Hill (M's home at) 55

Ridgway, James 224

Robinson, Mary: See 'Perdita'

Rolle, John 184–90, 195, 219, 221, 226, 229–30

Rosenhagen, the Rev Philip 143–4

Royal Archives xi, xiii, 89, 147, 167, 247, 283, 320, 335, 340, 345, 358

Royal Marriage Act (1772) 70, 80–4, 118, 144, 149, 183, 191, 251–2

Royal Pavilion 331, 337, 352

Russell, Lord John 192, 194

Rutland, Duchess of 48, 74, 201, 253, 289–90

Rutland, Duke of 153, 165, 174

Scott, Sir Walter 312–3

Sefton, Charles William Molyneux, 1st Earl of (M's uncle) 37, 75,

Sefton, Isabella, Countess of (M's aunt) 37–8, 55, 59, 74, 76,155, 305

Settlement, Act of (1701) 81, 83–4, 118, 143, 252

Seymour, Lady George 308

Seymour, Lady Horatia 287, 289, 307–8,

Seymour, Lord Henry 308, 310–11

Seymour, Lord Hugh 99, 172–3, 173, 206, 268, 275, 287–9, 307–8

Seymour, Mary (Minney) 307–12, 321, 328, 338–40, 351–2, 356– 8, 361–3

Seymour, Sir George 297, 308, 338–40, 351–2

Sheridan, Elizabeth 192, 204, 222

Sheridan, R.B. 60, 78, 119, 170, 172, 174, 181, 185–9, 191–2, 194–6, 198, 202, 207, 209–10, 212, 215, 217, 219– 22, 224, 240, 247–8, 305,355

skin 48

Smythe, Barbara (M's sister) 17, 36

Smythe, Charles (M's brother) 17, 36, 43, 145, 227, 354

Smythe, Edward (M's brother) 17

Smythe Family, background to 5–8

Smythe, Frances: *see* aggerston, Frances, Lady

Smythe, Henry (M's brother) 17, 36, 43, 46, 145

Smythe, John (Jack) (M's brother) 16, 36, 43, 52, 123, 128, 145, 147, 158, 253, 289, 315, 327, 338

Smythe, Marianne (M's niece) 338–41, 351–2, 361–3,

Smythe, Mary Ann (M's mother) 16–19, 135, 145, 163, 289–90, 299–300, 316

Smythe, Walter (M's brother) 16, 36, 42–3, 145, 153–4, 199, 243, 253, 354, 374n

Smythe, Walter (M's father) 15–19, 25, 58, 135, 145, 179, 203

Smythe, Mrs Walter (M's sister-in-law) 341, 363

Smythe, Lieut William (M's cousin) 243–4

Sophia, Princess (P's sister) 338

Southampton, 1st Baron 87–90, 103, 117–8, 173,

Spa 93, 96–100

Spencer, Countess 155, 158, 212

Stafford, Marchioness of 287–8

Stewart, Sir Charles (1st Baron Stuart de Rothsay) 344

Stourton, William, 17th Lord (M's cousin) 2–3, 8, 87, 89, 147–8, 176, 307–8, 357, 360, 368,

Sussex, Duke of: *see* Augustus, Prince

Swinburne, Henry 159, 162

Swynnerton Hall 41–2, 343, 370

Tarleton, Banastre 67, 171

Theatre Royal 157

Thrale, Hester: *see* Piozzi, Hester

Thurlow, 1st Baron 248, 287, 310–11

Times, The 118, 120, 157, 160–1, 166, 198, 205, 208, 210, 214, 220–2, 224–7, 230–2, 235, 266, 281, 287, 292, 367–8

ton, the 61, 62, 73, 76, 170, 185

Tong Castle 16, 369

Tooke, Horne 60, 183–4, 191, 224, 269

True Briton, The 292

United States 102, 167

Versailles 19, 111–3

Victoria, Princess 358, 395n

View of Covent Garden during the Election 1784, A 208

waists 48

Waldegrave, Countess of 309

Waldegrave, Lady Horatia 162

Wales, George Augustus Frederick, Prince of (George IV): affairs after 1785 255; affairs before 1785, 64–9; Bessborough, Lady 319; bleeding 211; bosoms 78; caricatures, buys up 167; Caroline, Princess 272–82, 312, 333–4; Catholism 238; character 64, 69, 318–9; Charlotte, Princess 283, 309, 323, 332; childhood & education, 62–3,64; cleanliness 279; Conyngham, Marchioness of 336; debts 102–4, 117–9, 120, 172–3, 179, 181–98, 202, 240, 244–6, 257, 266, 274, 280–1, 300, 383; deceitfulness 118, 249; drunkenness 75, 86, 231; Europe, idea of escape to, 68, 87; Fox 70–71, 74–5; friends, lack of, in youth, 69; Hertford, Marchioness of 316–22, 324–5, 327–8; Holland Plan, 101–2, 135; honeymoon 148;

honour, sense of 141; horseplay
206–7; illegitimate children 175,
177; illness, use of 68, 69, 86–7
249, 268, 305, 349; Jersey, Lady
286, 288, 290–2, 297; Knighton,
Sir Wm. 348; letters, love of
writing long 233–4, 262; love
letters 97–8, 137–40, 291, 318–9;
manners, 78, 162, 239; M's appeal
77–9; M, love for 96, 364–5;
marriage to M, on legality of 84,
252; marriage to M, denies
publicly 161–2; marry, plan not
to, officially 121; military ambitions 242–3; newspapers, pays for
'puffs' in 165; persuasion,
powers of 144; public attacks on,
73, 120; Regency Crisis of 1788–9
211–234; Regency Crisis of 1804
315–6; Regency, 323; separation
(1794) 259–72, 348–9; separation
(1811) 322–8; Seymour, Minney,
battle over 309–12; suicide,
threats of & attempts at 80, 87–9,
95–6, 140, 97, 291; unique, sees
himself as 64, 318–9; USA,
threatens to fly to 102; weight in
1797 300; will of 1796 283–6,
292–3; work, lack of 69, 178. *see*:
Brighton; caricatures; Charlotte,
Queen; George III
Walpole, Horace 60, 61, 65, 71–3,
140, 156–9, 161, 178–9, 245, 249
Walter, John 60–1, 226–7
Warren, Richard 212, 216, 222
Weld, Edward (M's 1st husband)
21–26, 29–36, 29–30, 32–33, 370

Weld family 26–9, 49, 370
Weld, Thomas (M's brother-in-law)
30, 50, 226, 238–9
Wellington, 1st Duke of 69, 97,
176, 283, 333, 336, 348–51, 356–8,
365, 368
Wells Family 17, 374n
Weltje, Louis 168–9, 174, 201, 220,
244
Wentworth, 2nd Viscount 44, 159,
161, 169, 173, 241, 290
Westminster by-elections: (1784)
74–5; (1788) 208
Westminster Election of 1788, The
208
whist 24, 168
Wilkes, John 61, 161, 165, 212–3
Wilkins, W.H. 3, 33, 358, 363, 368
Willem V 100–1, 102, 104, 280
William, Prince (later Duke of
Clarence & William IV; P's
younger brother) 154, 169, 176,
202, 215–6, 242, 245, 259, 264,
269, 277, 313–4, 321, 337–8,
351–2, 356, 362
Withers, the Rev Philip 115–6,
224–6, 235, 238
World, The 209–10, 224 225, 238,
244–5
Wraxall, Sir Nathaniel William 72,
171–2, 185,

York, Duchess of (P's sister-in-law)
249–51, 269, 288, 313, 355
York, Duke of (P's uncle), 56
York, Duke of (P's brother) *see*
Frederick, Prince